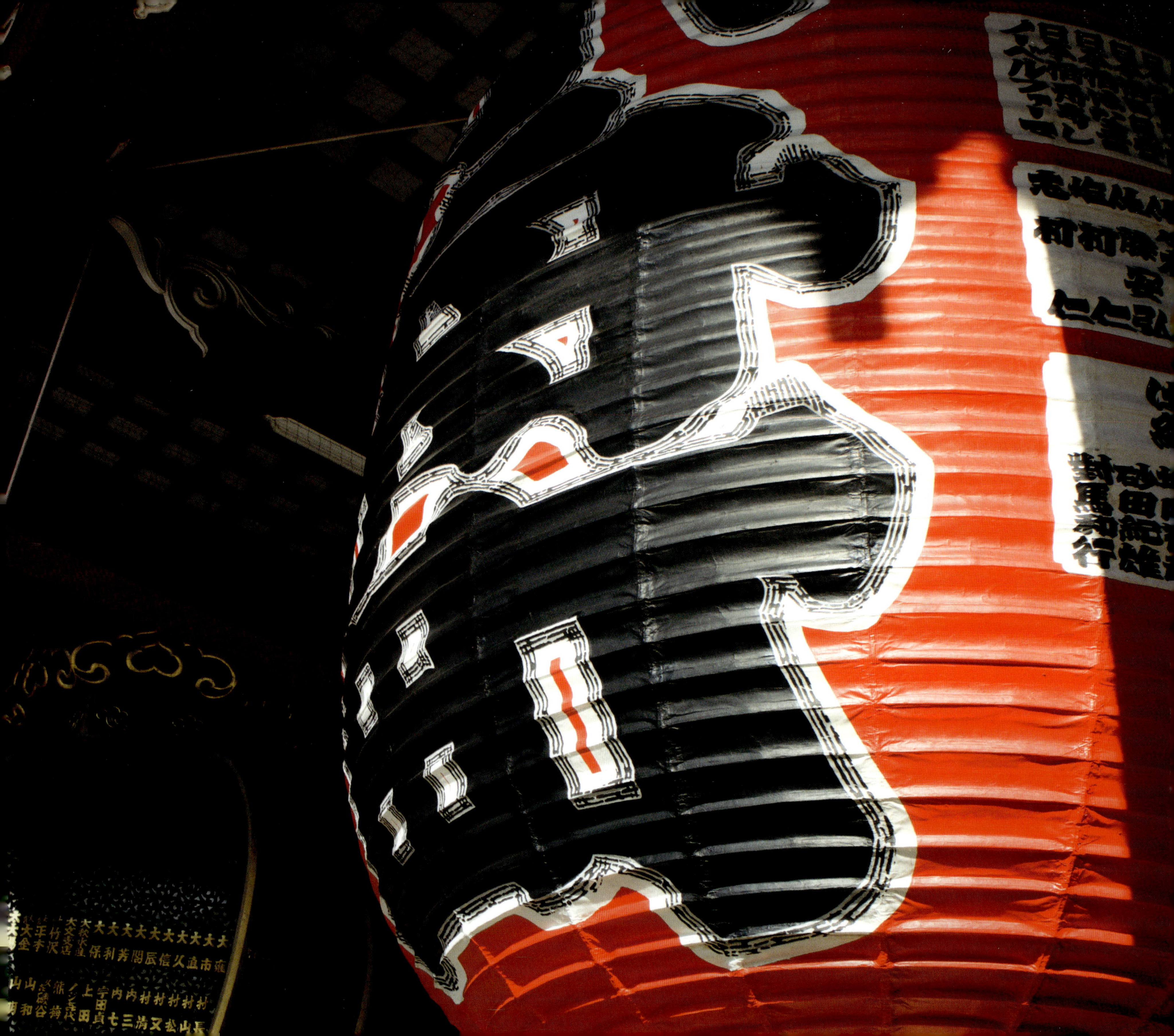

# SIGHTS and SCENES of JAPAN

Marc Popelier

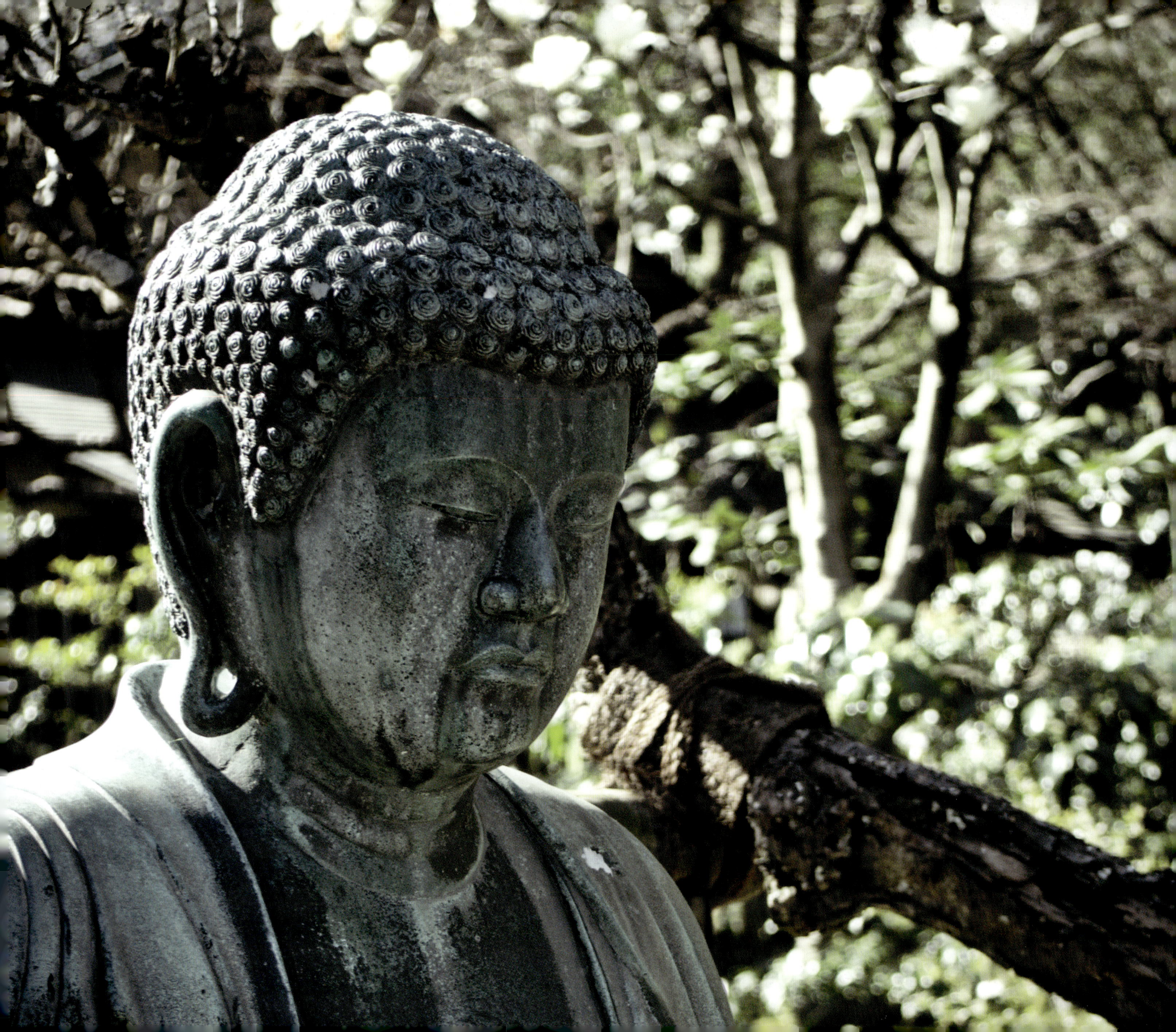

# Preface

Forty years of experience and over hundred visits to Japan have given me a better insight in Eastern mysticism, the rich culture of the country, but also the secrets behind the economic success of Japan, their power to work, the often misunderstood reserve of the Japanese, the long road to winning their trust and last but not least the loyalty of the people.
This book can help the occasional traveler as well as the professional visitor to learn more about this fascinating country and to be even more impressed with one's trip to Japan, or can simply be a tool to give the first impulse for a fruitful business relation.

*Frans Hoorelbeke*
*Chairman, Member of the Board*
*of Directors of Daikin Europe*

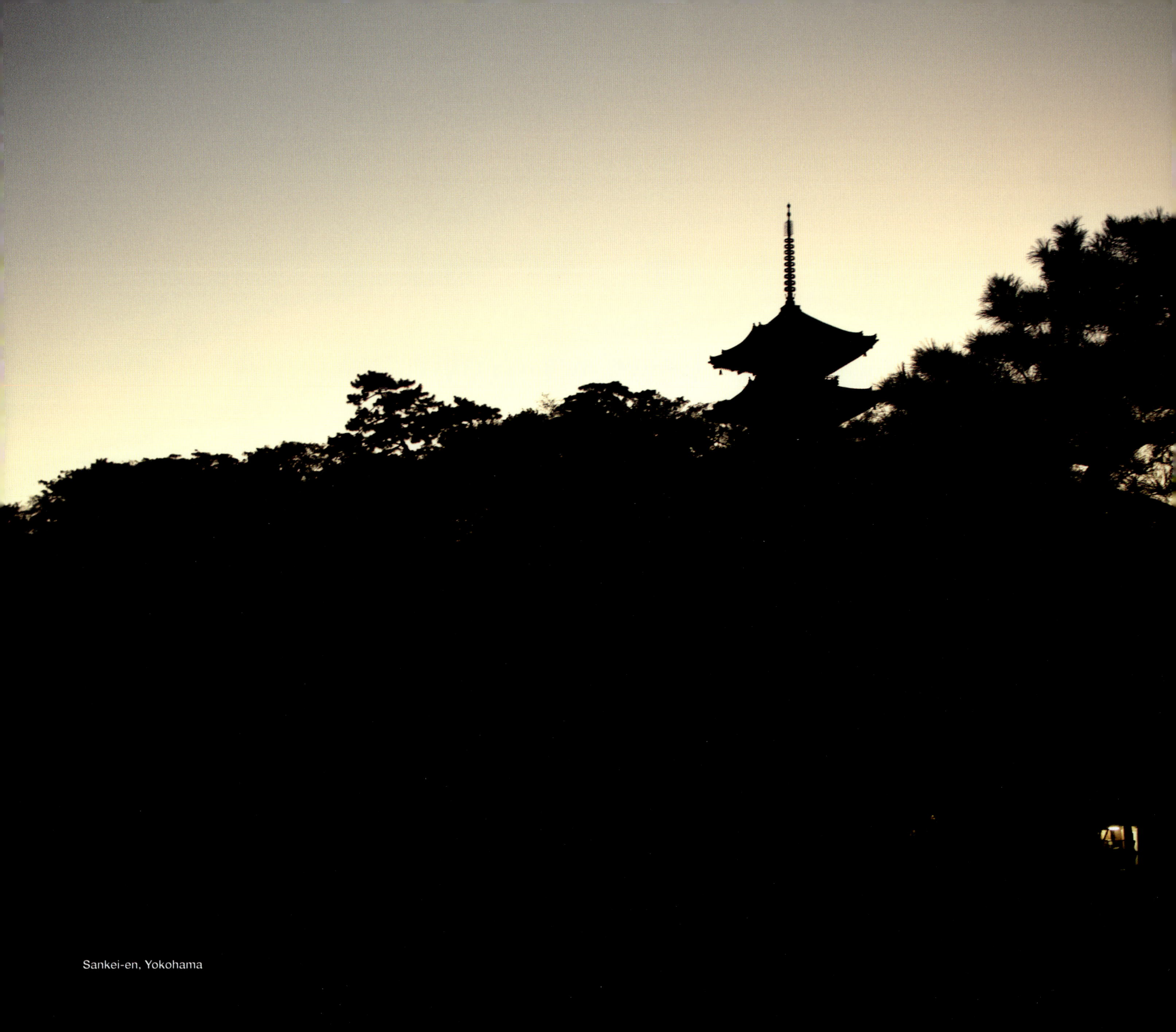

Sankei-en, Yokohama

To most first-time travelers Japan is a country with a rather unique and somewhat mysterious culture. It made the same impression on me. Since my first trip in the summer of 2002 I have always wondered why I immediately felt at home in Japan: a far away country, different in many aspects and sometimes the opposite of what I learned in my childhood and as a student. Maybe it was the warm relationship with its people, the food, the respect for their cultural heritage, their work and business attitude or simply the reward of enjoying splendid scenery after a long hike.
Even after many visits for both work and leisure, I still feel privileged every time I have a chance to visit this fascinating country. It is truly a land of diversity and contradictions that keeps surprising me and that I will never fully understand.

Being a mountainous country, the majority of the population of Japan lives in vast coastal cities such as Tokyo, Yokohama, Osaka and Fukuoka. Once you leave these urban agglomerations you will soon discover that the Japanese archipelago is actually made up of thousands of islands with abundant nature and stunning landscapes. When traveling in Japan, especially when staying in a ryokan, a Japanese inn, you will be amazed about the courteous way visitors are treated and the delicacy of the Japanese cuisine. It is also a country where you will find ancient customs, cherished and unchanged for over thousands of years, as well as cutting edge technology and the latest gadgets.

Since decennia recognized as a world economic power, Japan has had to overcome many problems in its long history. Due to its geographical location on the Pacific Ring of Fire, Japan, more than any country is faced with the constant threat of natural disasters. Over the past millennium Japan's population was not spared of the consequences of domestic conflicts and political choices or decisions of its leaders. Yet defeat has always been overcome, respecting the spirit of 'wa' social harmony. Resilience and an exceptional flexibility to adapt to a new situation are embedded within the Japanese culture and spirit.

'Sights and Scenes of Japan' is built around a collection of photos I took during my journeys in Japan. It covers places and scenes that caught my attention when I was passing by at a particular moment in time. When making a portrait every photographer will emphasize the light, ambiance, setting and general atmosphere in a different way. The same goes for this book. It is a small personal selection of photos which I hope will shape a portrait that captures the beauty and essence of Japan and will tempt anyone to make a first time visit or to rediscover this fascinating country.

*Marc Popelier*

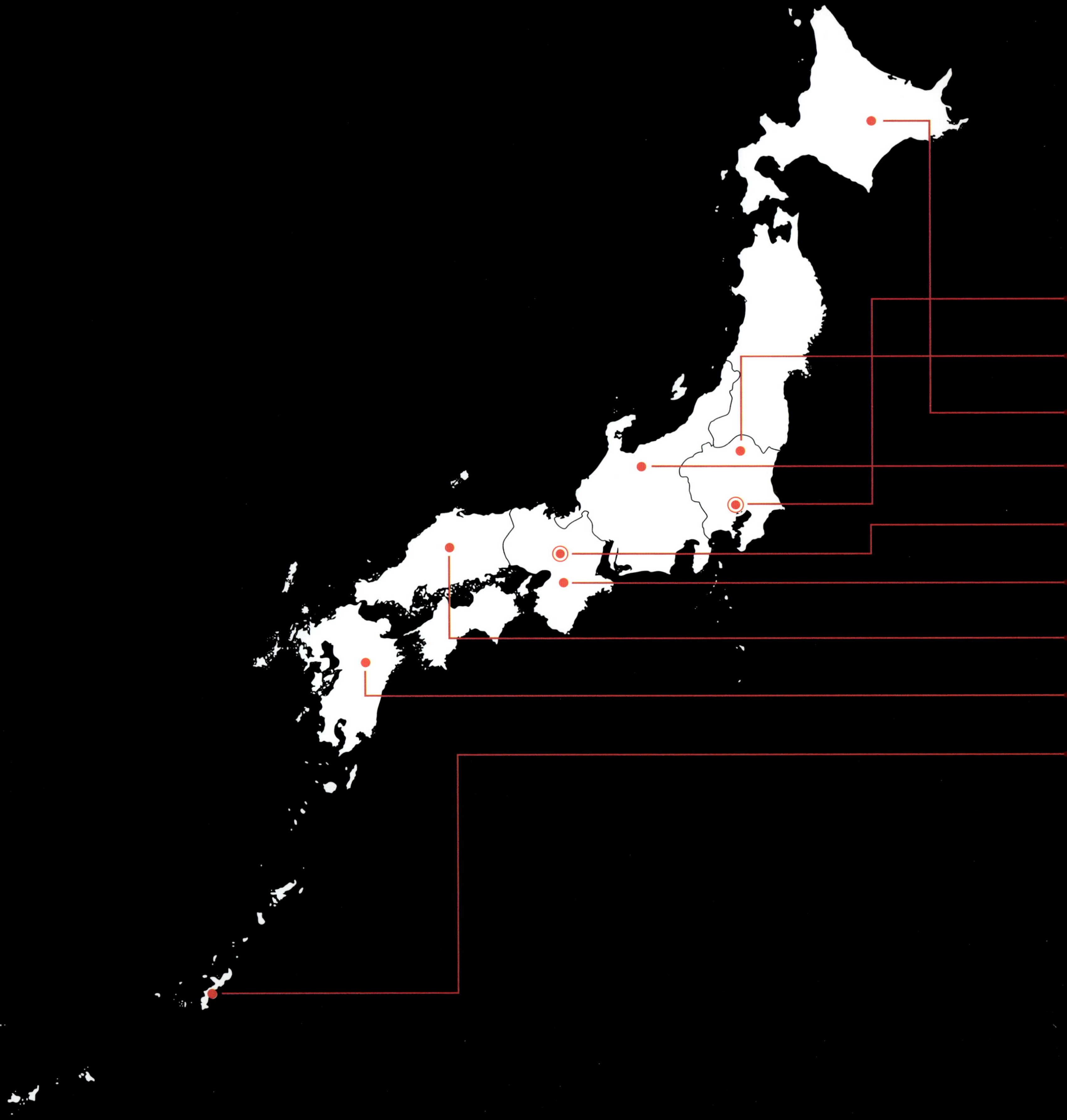

# Table of contents

TOKYO 11

KANTŌ 43

HOKKAIDŌ 81

CHŪBU 87

KYOTO 117

KANSAI 135

CHŪGOKU 163

KYŪSHŪ 173

OKINAWA 181

SEASONS 198

TIMELINE 206

東京

Tokyo, the capital of Japan, is one of the largest and most densely populated cities in the world. This complex and fascinating metropolis keeps reinventing itself and adjectives fall short to describe the speed at which this is happening. In 2016 the population was ca 13.5 million, roughly eleven percent of the population of Japan.

In the 16th century Tokyo, at that time named Edo, was a small town in a bay of the Pacific Ocean. It started to prosper when the powerful Tokugawa shogunate made of Edo its stronghold in the early 17th century. Roughly 150 years later the population reached more than one million.

In 1868, after the fall of the Tokugawa shogunate, Emperor Meiji moved the imperial seat from Kyoto to Tokyo, the 'eastern capital' as was Edo renamed. It was the start of a period wherein large public works were undertaken and elements of the western lifestyle were adapted. In September 1923 fires caused by the Great Kantō earthquake burned down almost the entire city center. Yet Tokyo kept developing quickly and by the mid-thirties had well over 6 million inhabitants.

World War II halted the prosperity of the city and, even worse, by the end of the war most of the city center was devastated by the allied bombings. In the fifties Tokyo rose from its ashes in record breaking time. In this period Japan laid the foundation for its economic success in the decades to come. When in 1964 the Olympics were held the city had over 10 million inhabitants.

Although entire books have been written about Tokyo the cliché 'seeing is believing' is well placed. Tokyo is a city that never sleeps and where many modern subcultures have emerged and co-exist next to traditional rituals maintained in the temples and shrines that still can be found across the city. You will be amazed to see the latest technological gadgets in Akihabara electric town. Then again, it is possible to learn old dyeing and weaving techniques from the Edo period nearby. One is never more than a block away from a crowded Starbucks that can be neighbors with a Japanese pub that serves traditional food and drinks in a setting as if it was 100 years ago.

Tokyo will embrace everyone, from foodies over Manga lovers to addicts of modern art. If it is your first visit do not hesitate and book one of the well-organized guided day tours. Otherwise use the excellent train and subway network to move around in this huge city and walk within the area you want to explore. The best advice I can give is to be very selective in what you want to see and have eye for detail. This is also how the locals discover their city on a free day.

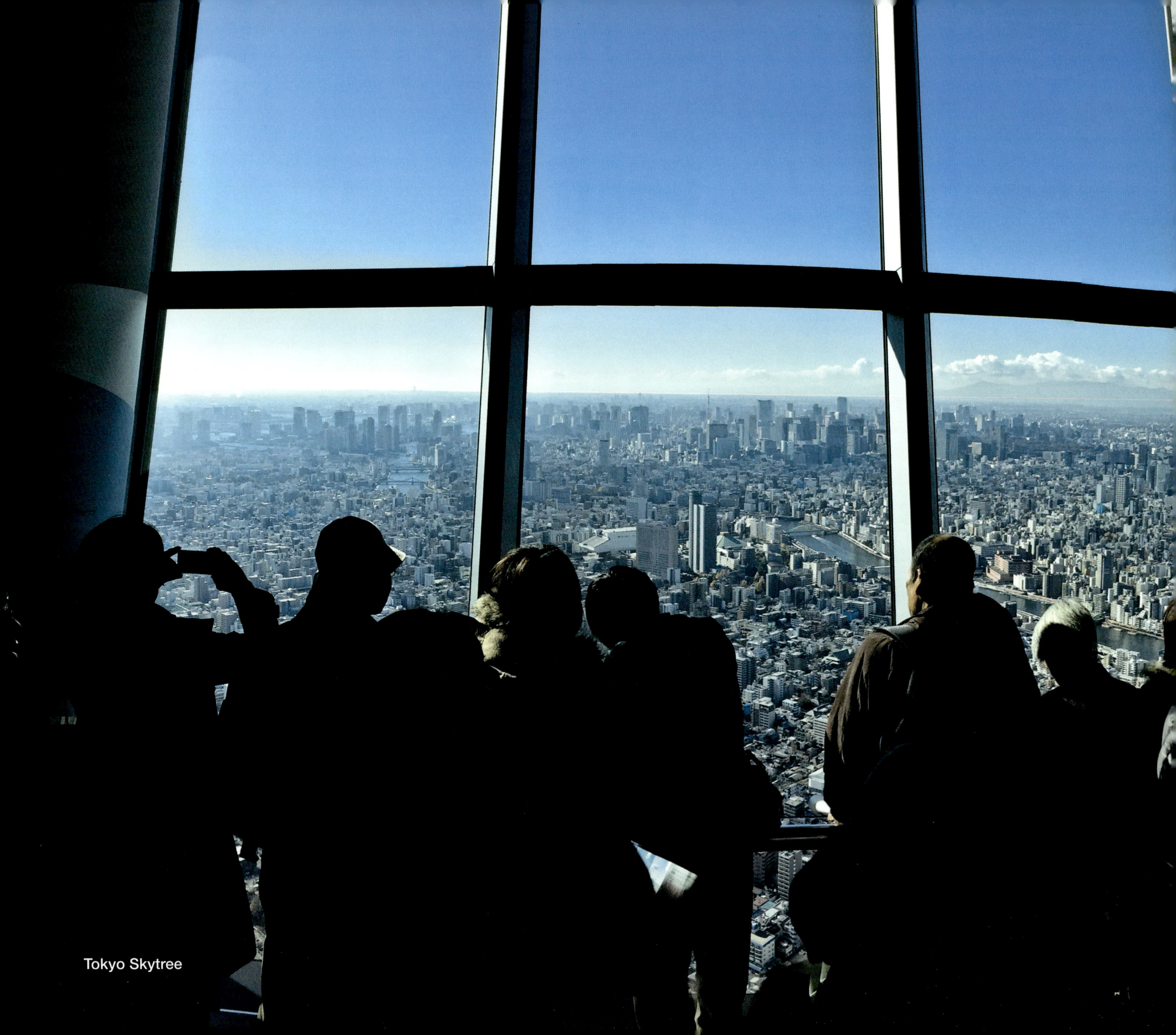

Tokyo Skytree

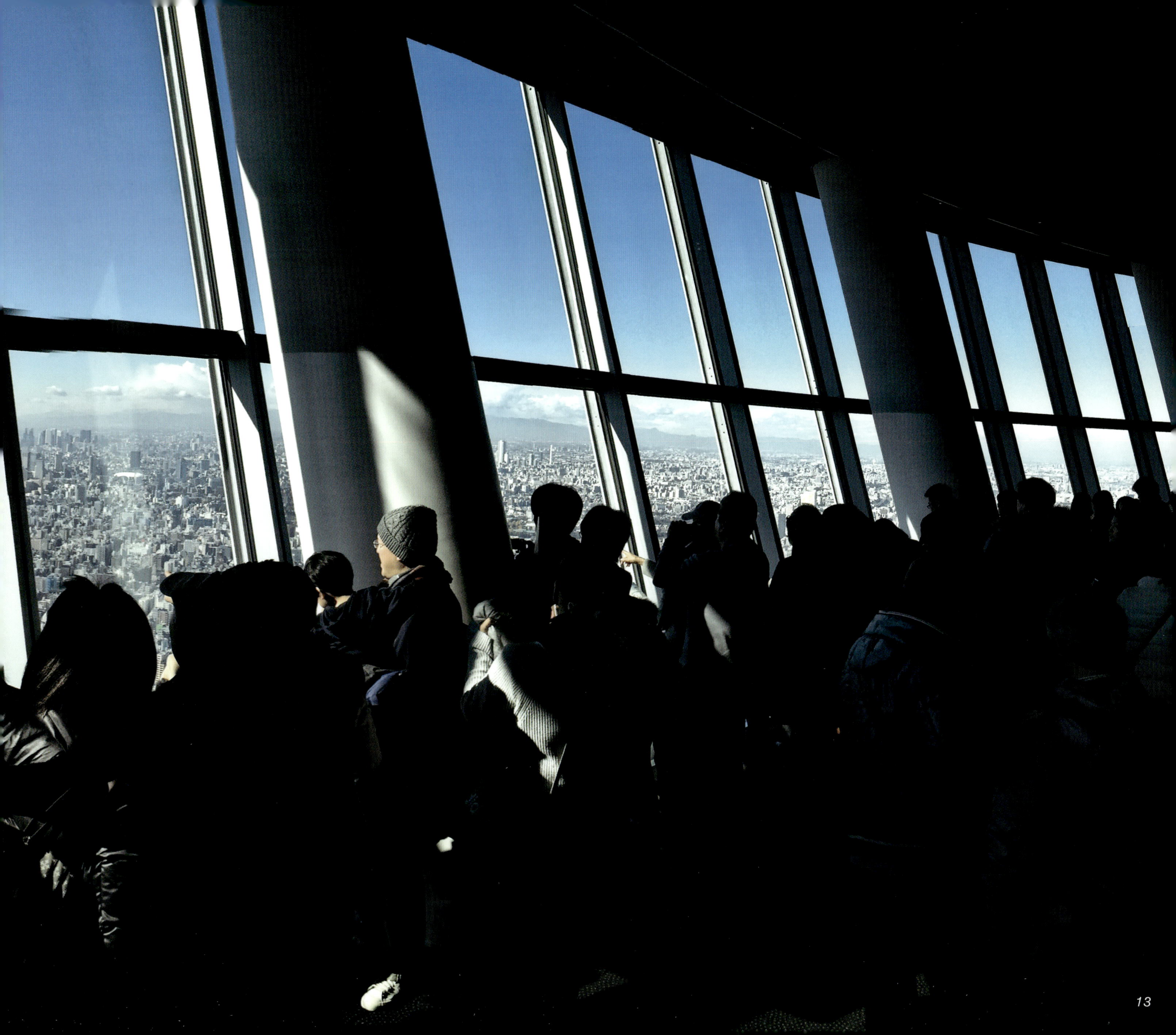

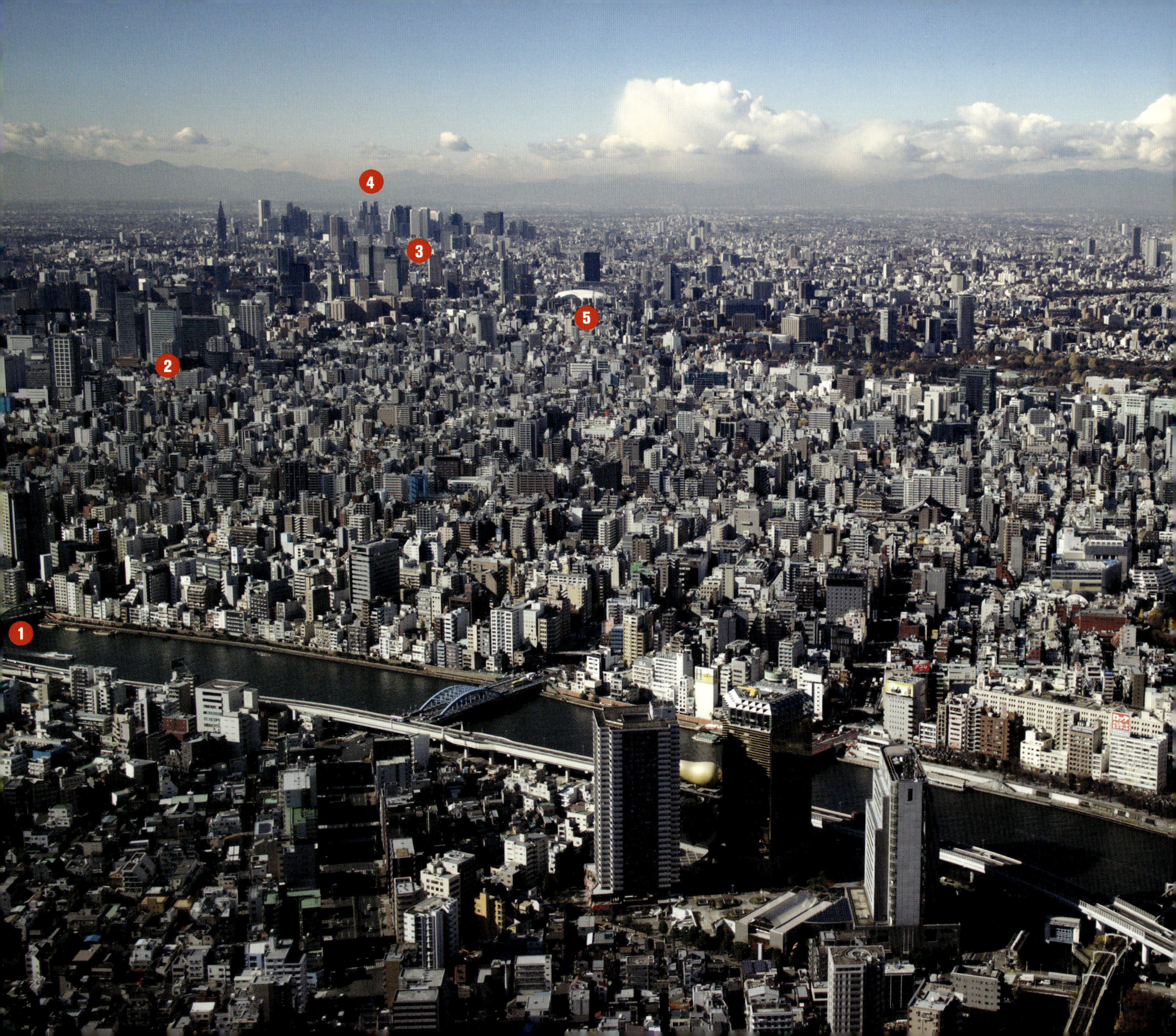
4
3
5
2
1

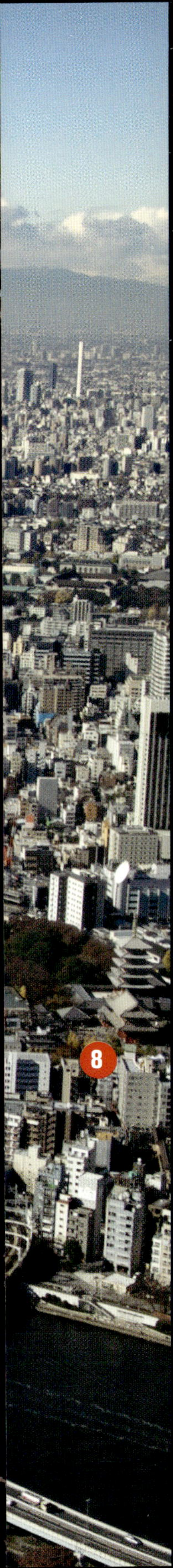


## Tokyo Skytree

1 Umaya Bridge
2 Akihabara (Electric Town)
3 Shinjuku
4 Mount Takao and the Southern Alps
5 Tokyo Dome
6 Ikebukoro
7 Ueno Park
8 Sensō-ji (Asakusa Kannon)

The Tokyo Skytree Tower, became in no time one of the most popular attractions of Tokyo. The tower is 634 meter high and Japan's tallest structure. On a clear day the observation decks unfold a 360° panoramic view that covers almost the entire Kantō region.

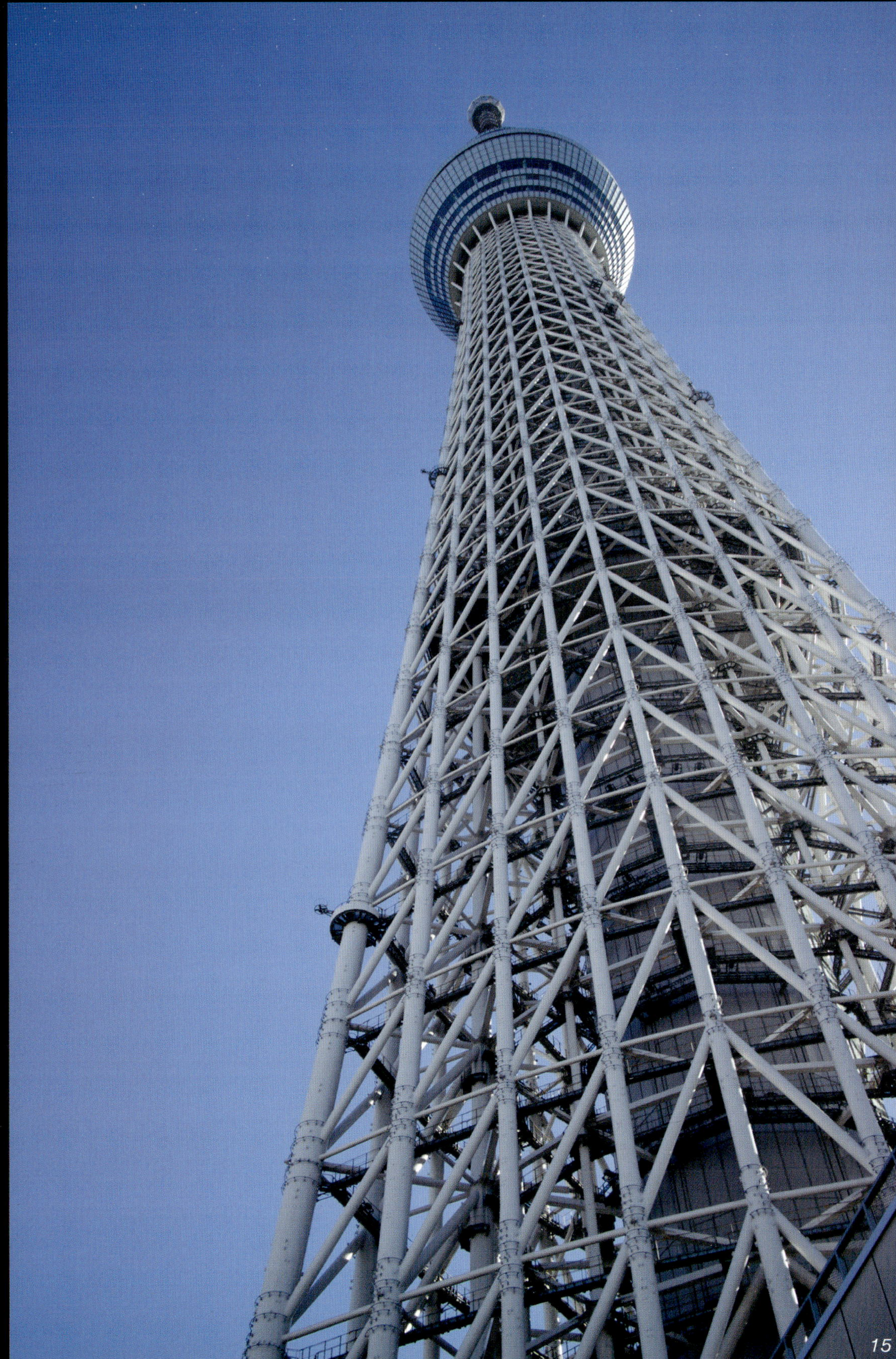

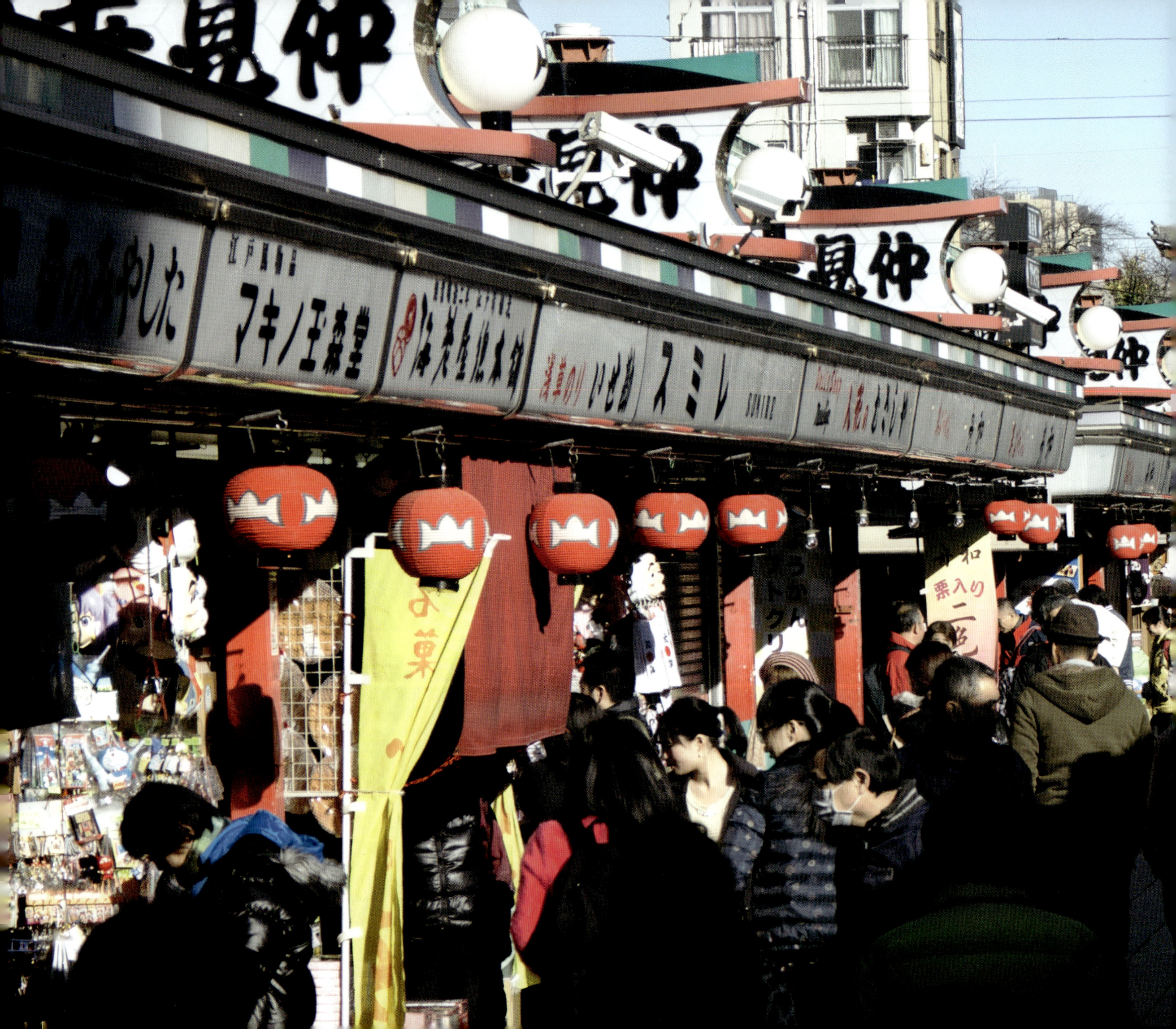
スミレ
SUMIRE

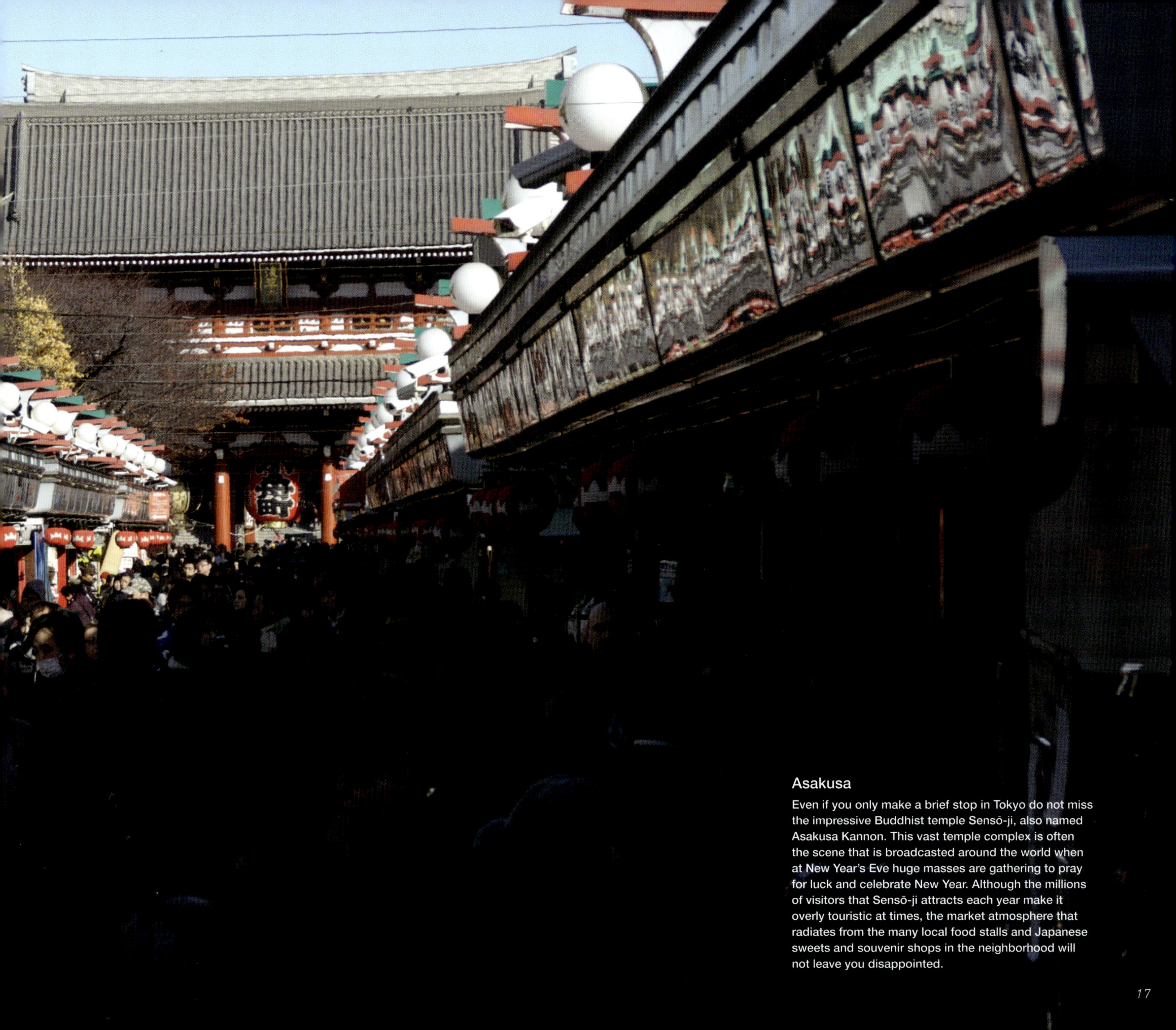

## Asakusa

Even if you only make a brief stop in Tokyo do not miss the impressive Buddhist temple Sensō-ji, also named Asakusa Kannon. This vast temple complex is often the scene that is broadcasted around the world when at New Year's Eve huge masses are gathering to pray for luck and celebrate New Year. Although the millions of visitors that Sensō-ji attracts each year make it overly touristic at times, the market atmosphere that radiates from the many local food stalls and Japanese sweets and souvenir shops in the neighborhood will not leave you disappointed.

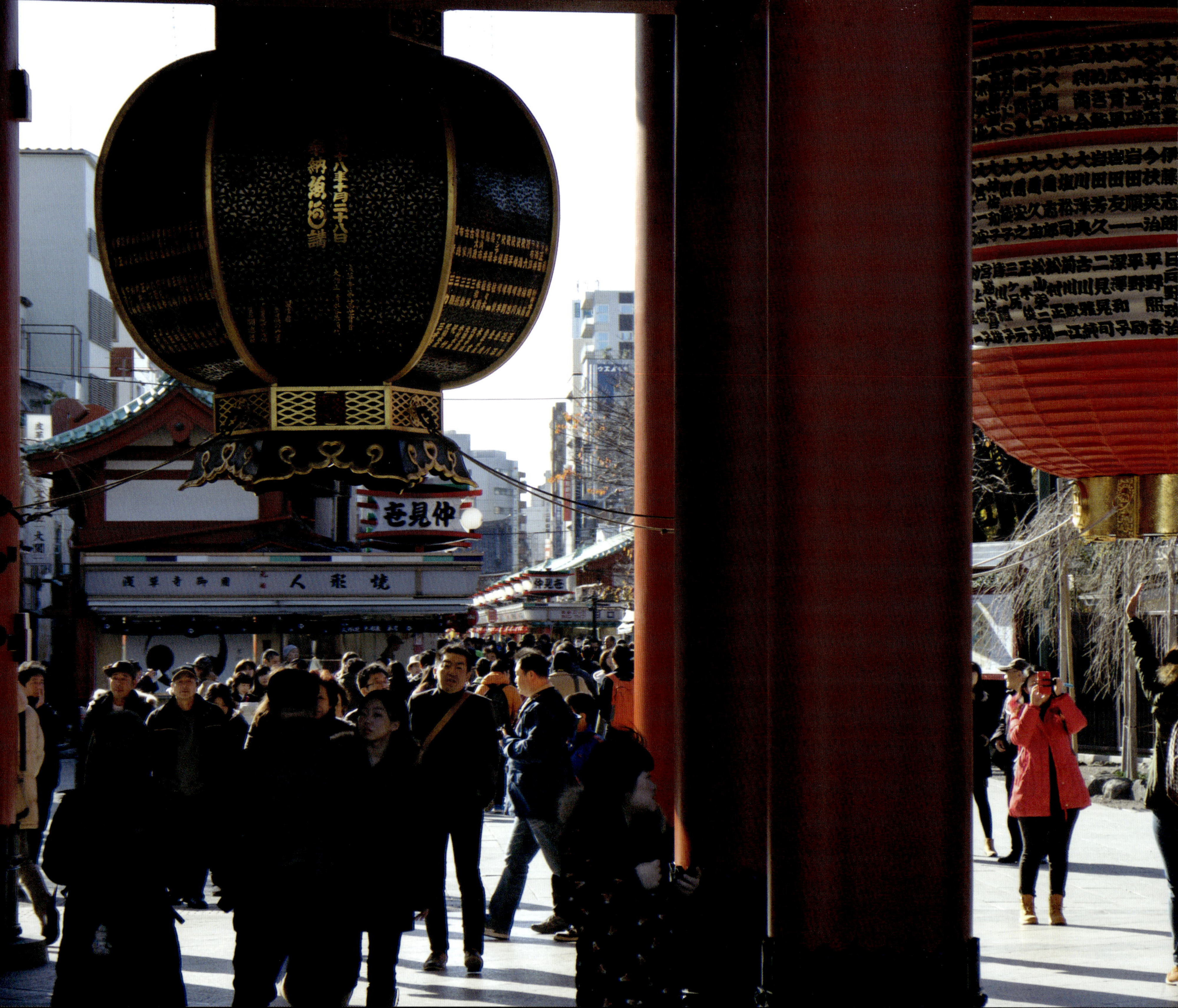

仲見世
浅草寺御用 人形焼

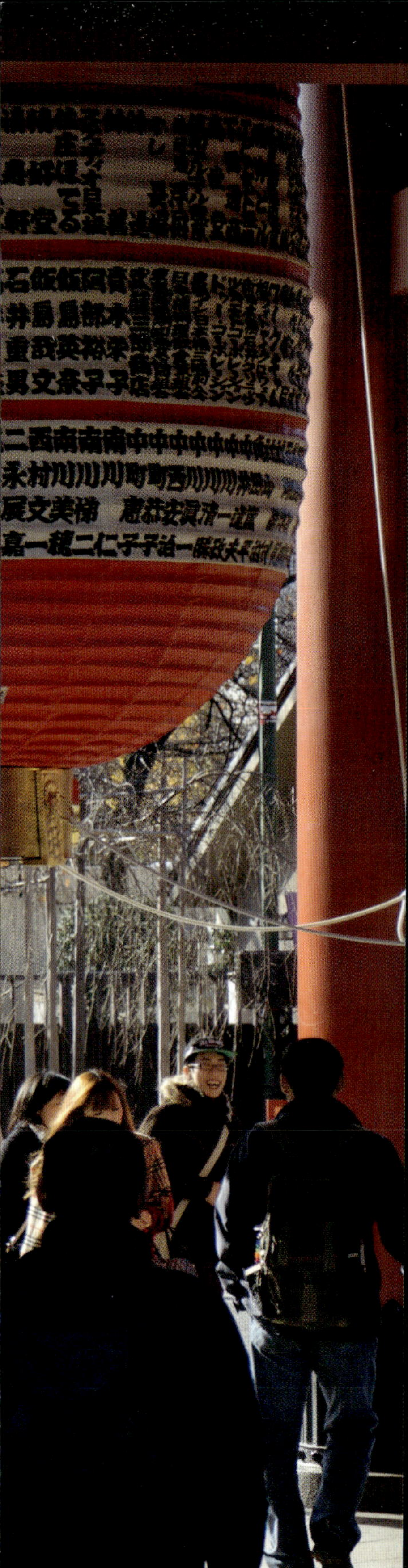

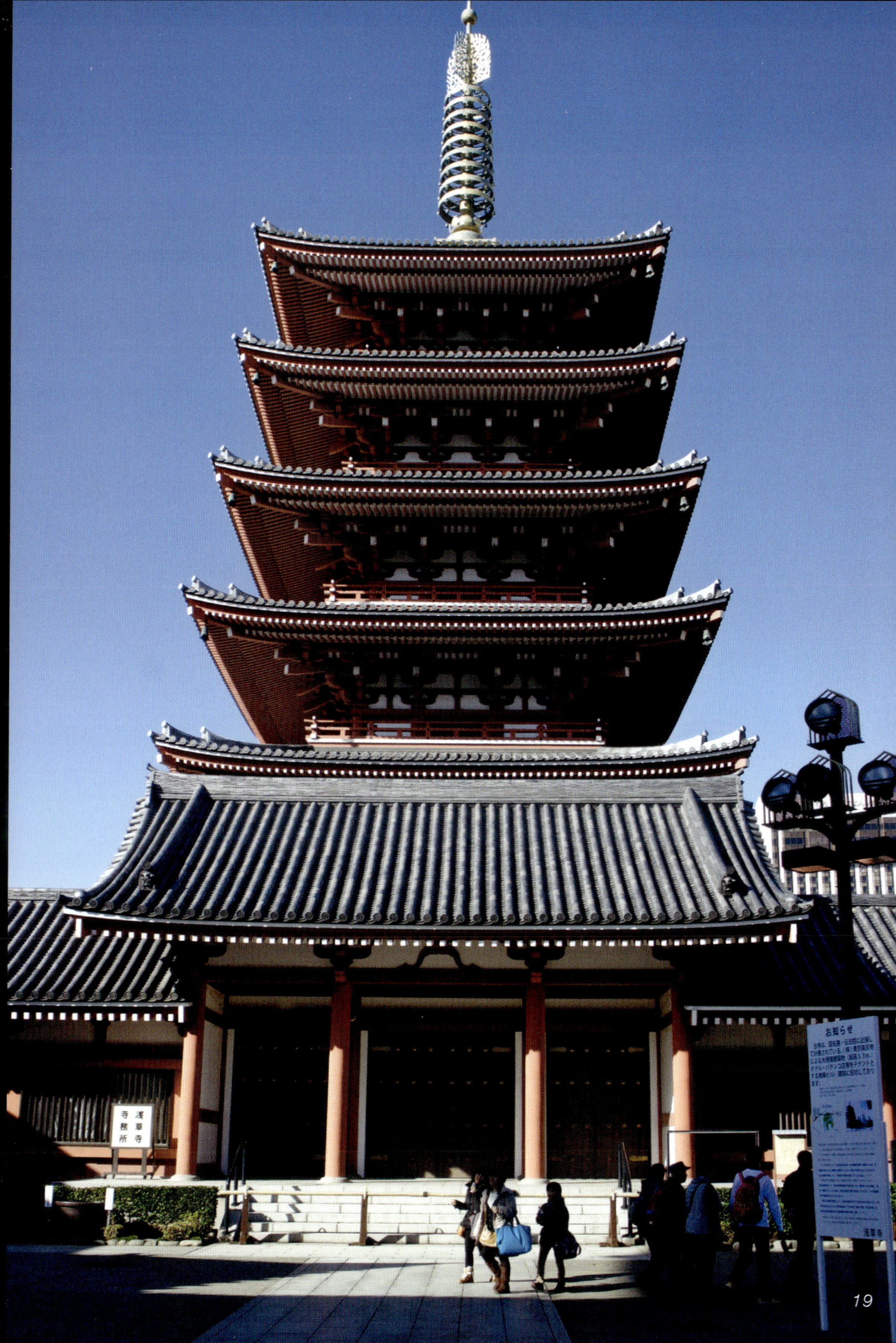
浅草寺
寺務所
お知らせ

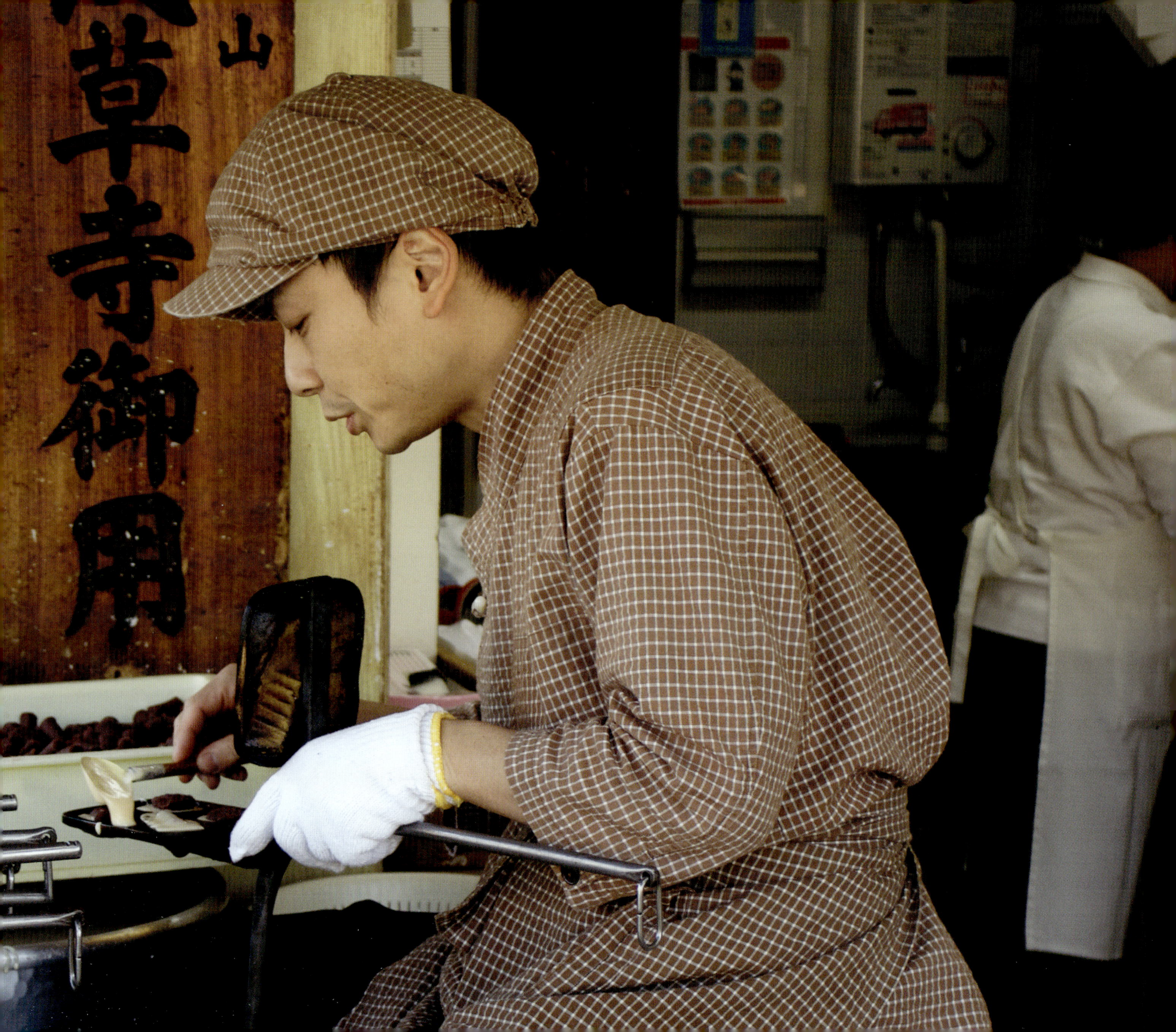
山
草寺御用

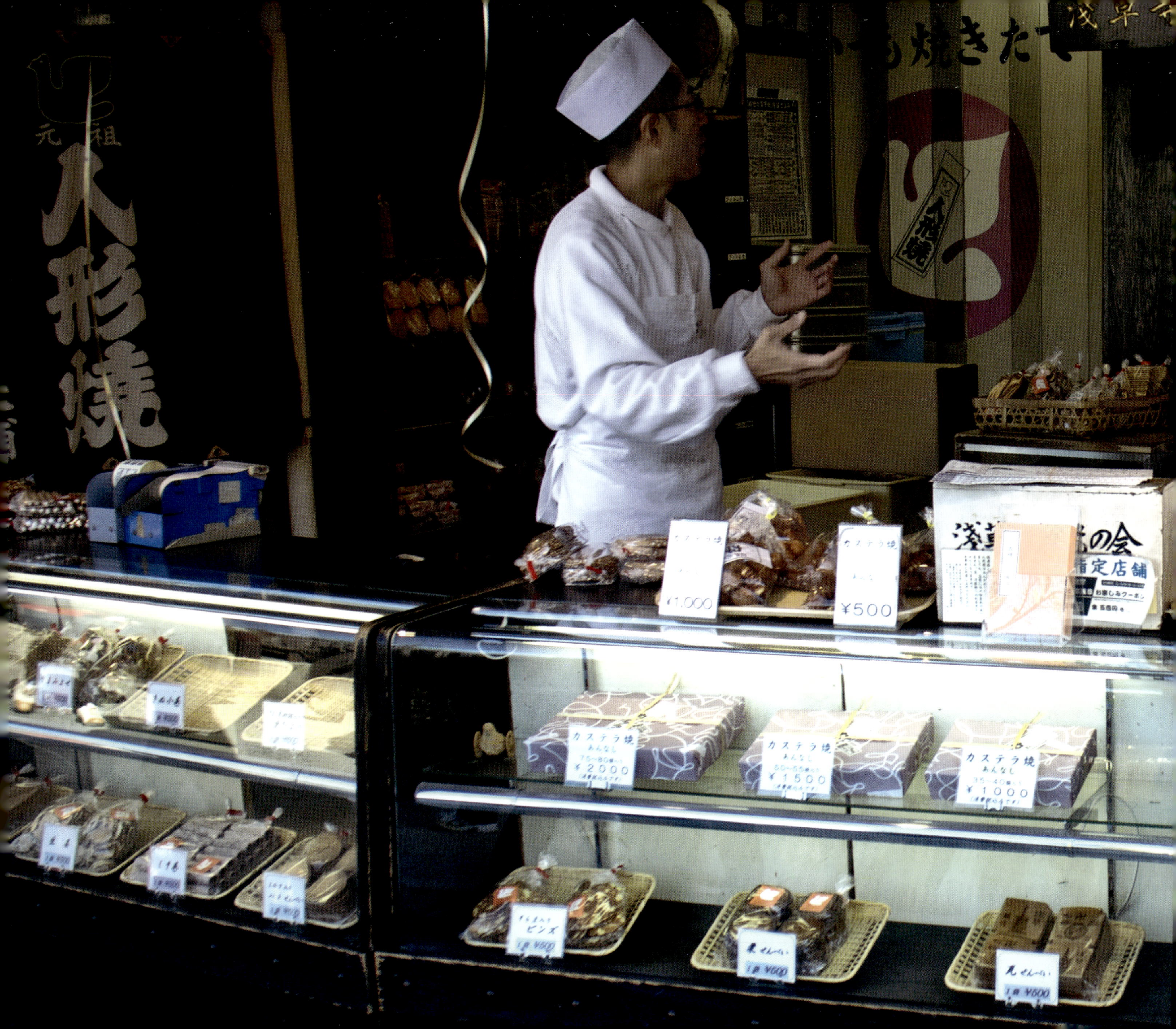
元祖
人形焼
人形焼
カステラ焼
¥1,000
カステラ焼
¥500
指定店舗
カステラ焼
あんなし
¥2000
カステラ焼
あんなし
¥1500
カステラ焼
あんなし
¥1000
ピンズ

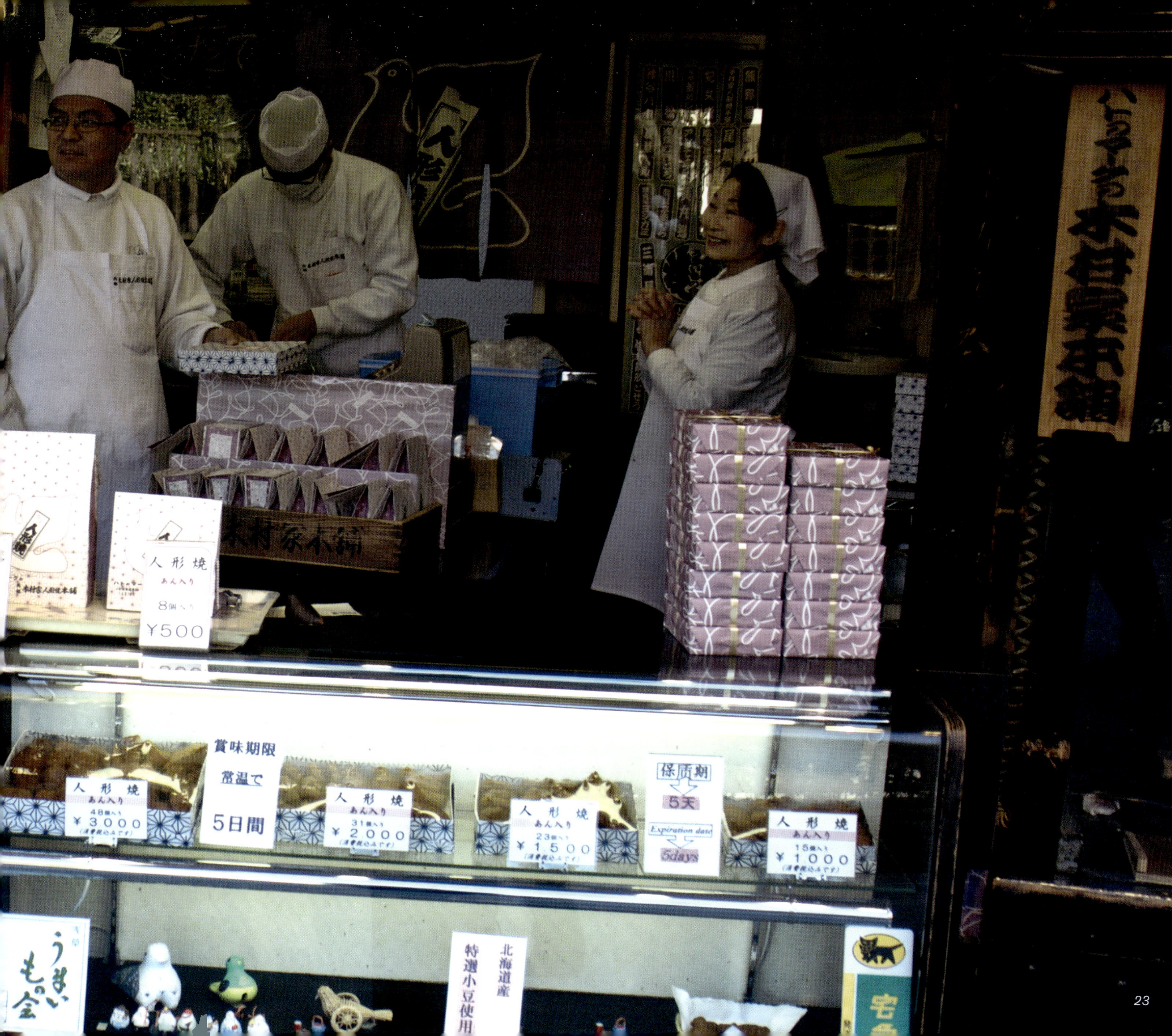

木村家本舗
人形焼
あん入り
8個入り
¥500
賞味期限
常温で
5日間
人形焼
あん入り
¥3,000
人形焼
あん入り
¥2,000
人形焼
あん入り
¥1,500
保质期
5天
Expiration date
5days
人形焼
あん入り
¥1,000
うまいもの会
北海道産
特選小豆使用

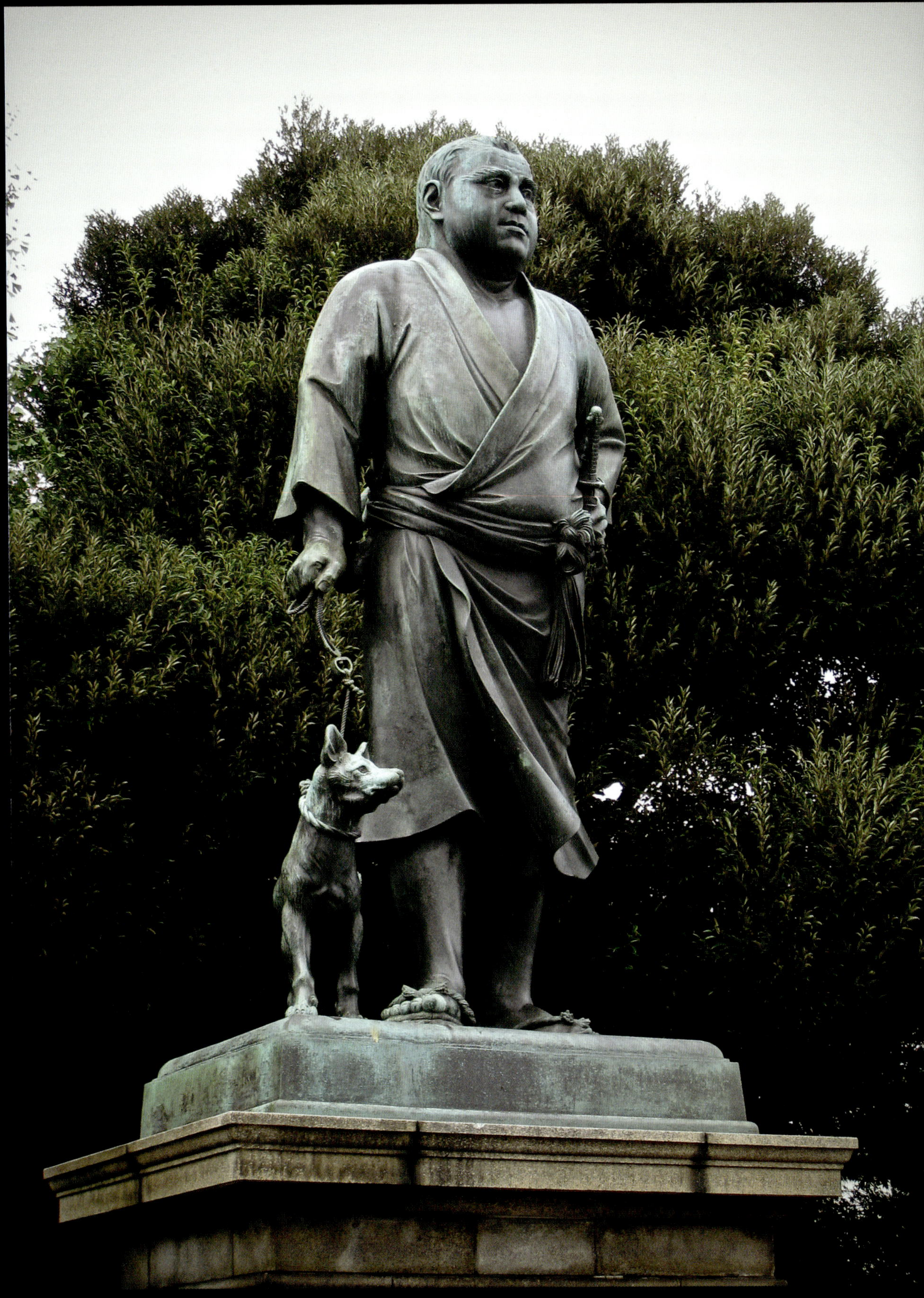

## Ueno Park

Takamori Saigō's statue can be found at the south entrance of Ueno Park. He was a great samurai and statesman who played an important role in the restoration of the imperial rule in the mid 19th century. Dissatisfied with the way the Meiji government progressed he quit from his official functions. Growing discontent and student uprise in his home province Satsuma, part of present day Kagoshima prefecture, made Saigō to lead an armed rebellion against the Meiji government in 1877. After months of fierce fighting his army was defeated and Saigō, 'the last samurai', committed suicide in what was basically the end of the samurai era. Later Emperor Meiji pardoned him. Saigō remained a kind of national hero and in 1898 this statue commemorating his dramatic life was unveiled.

Ueno Park is most famous for being the home of some of the city's largest museums such as The National Museum of Western Art and especially the very impressive Tokyo National Museum. The latter has magnificent antiquities from the ancient Silk Road era and not surprisingly the world's largest collection of Japanese art.

If due to lack of time you can only visit one part of the museum, I recommend a visit to The Gallery of Hōryū-ji Treasures. Taniguchi Yoshio designed this delicate and beautiful modern building in 1999. It is furnished with best in class conservation technology for the invaluable collection of Buddha statues from the 7th and 8th century coming from Hōryū-ji in Nara.

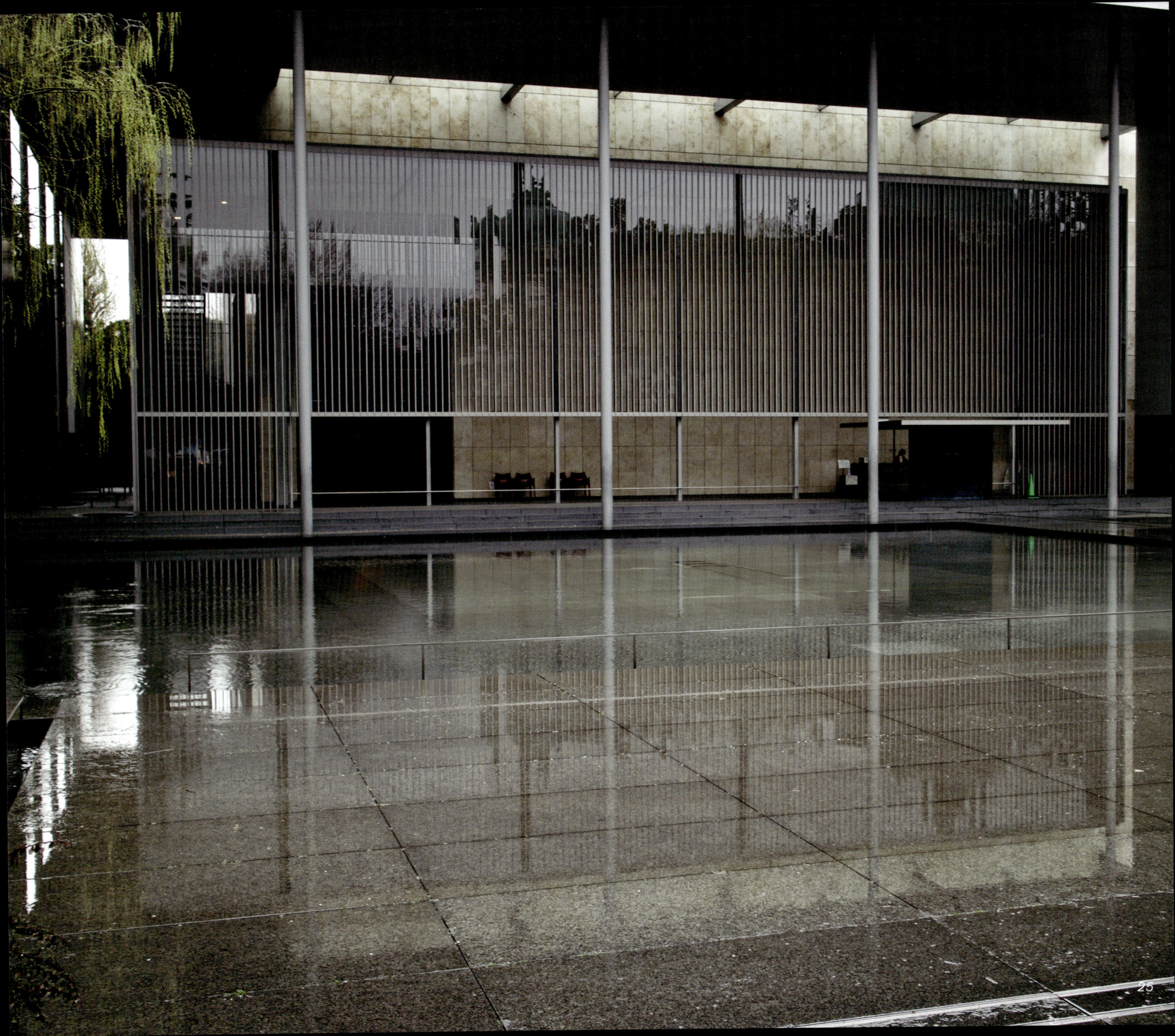

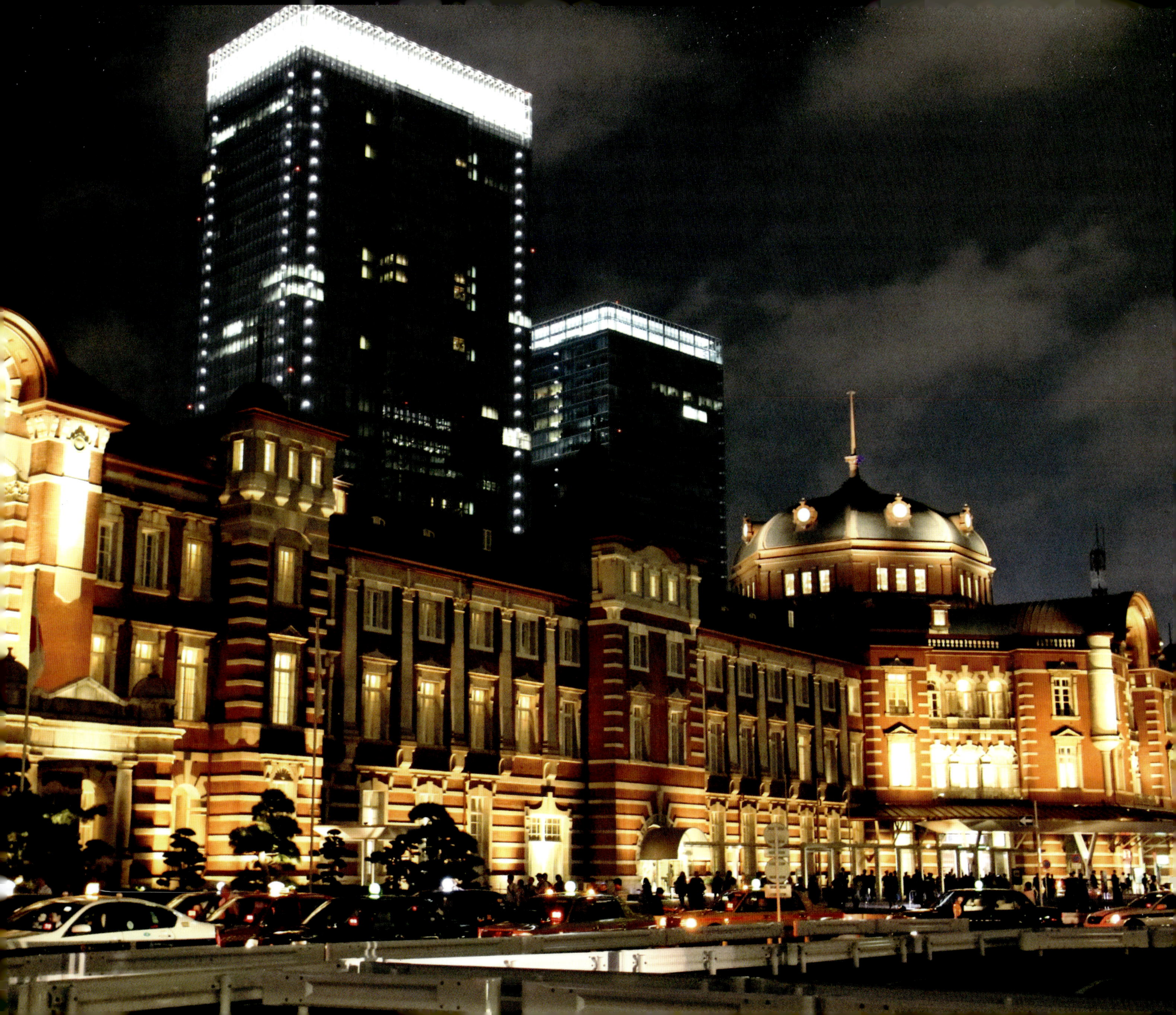

## Tokyo Station

Tokyo station, the magnificent red brick building in the prestigious Marunouchi area close to the Imperial Palace is one of the landmarks of Tokyo. Lying on the circular Yamanote line and directly connecting the city center with Narita airport it receives more than 500,000 travelers per day. There is a fair chance you will be one of them when arriving for the first time in Tokyo.

The station and adjacent hotel are more than 100 years old and were reopened in 2012 after being painstakingly restored to their pre-war glory. Illustrative are the beautifully illuminated domes at the Marunouchi north and south entrances.

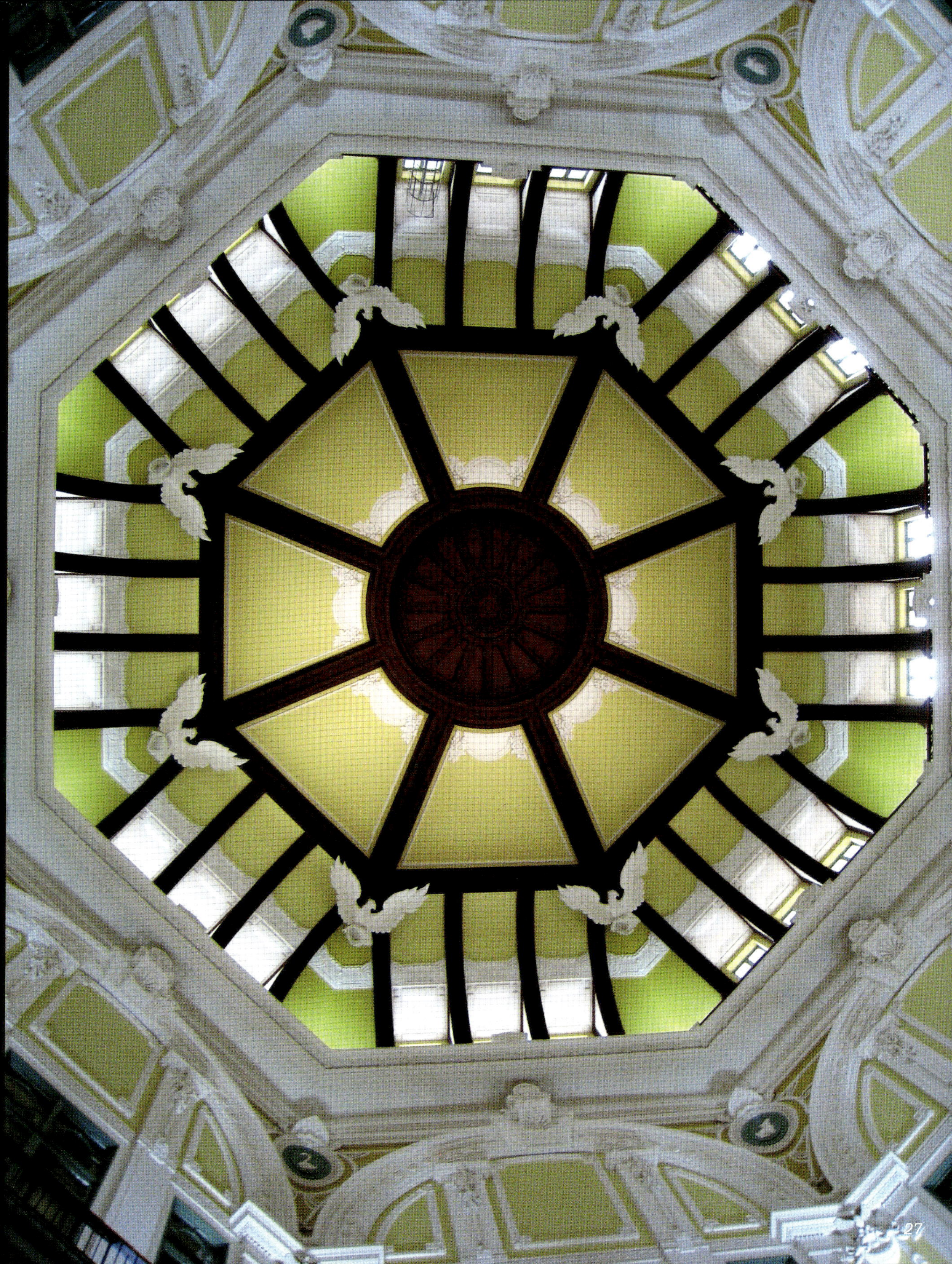

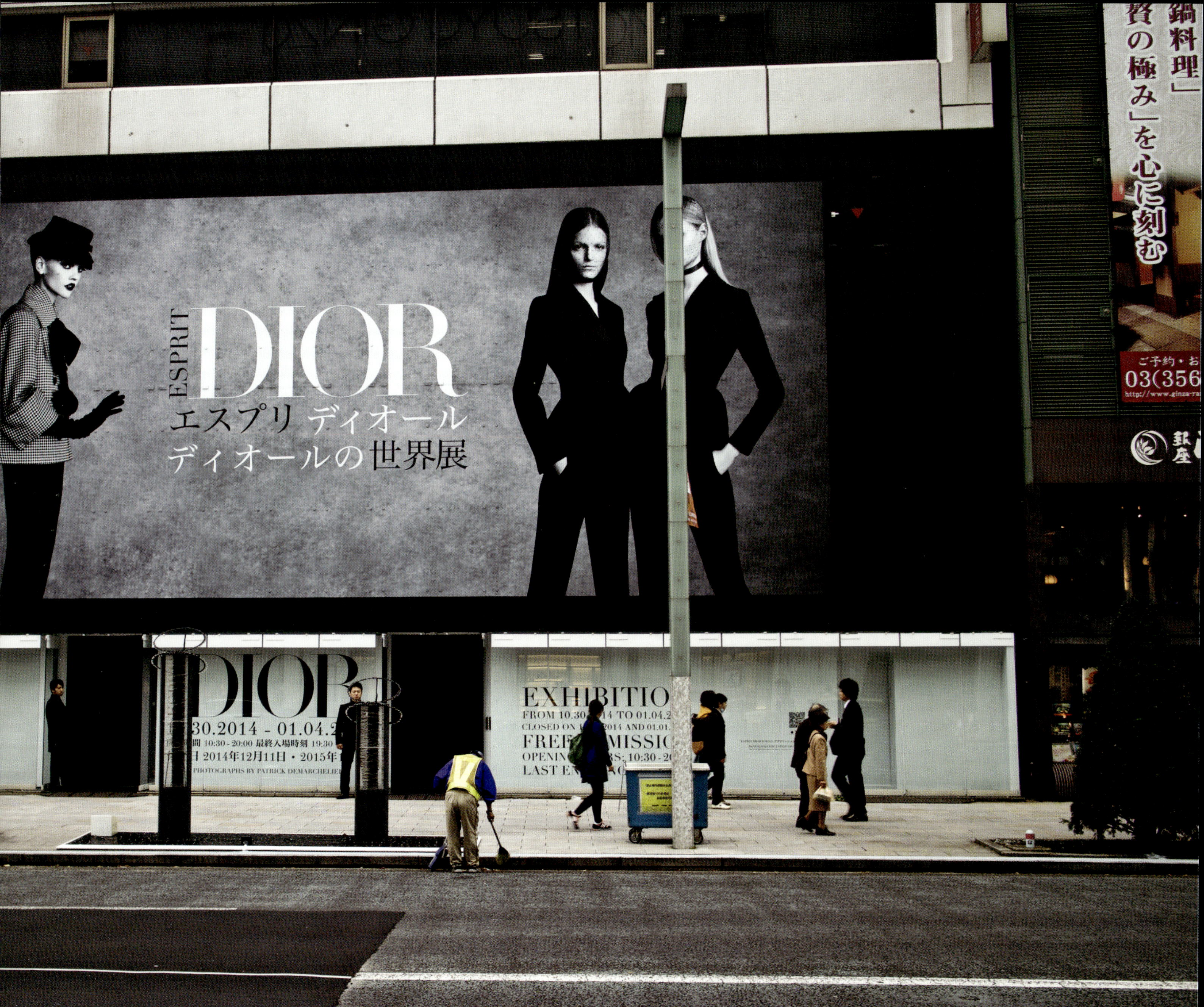
ESPRIT
DIOR
エスプリ ディオール
ディオールの世界展
PHOTOGRAPHS BY PATRICK DEMARCHELIER

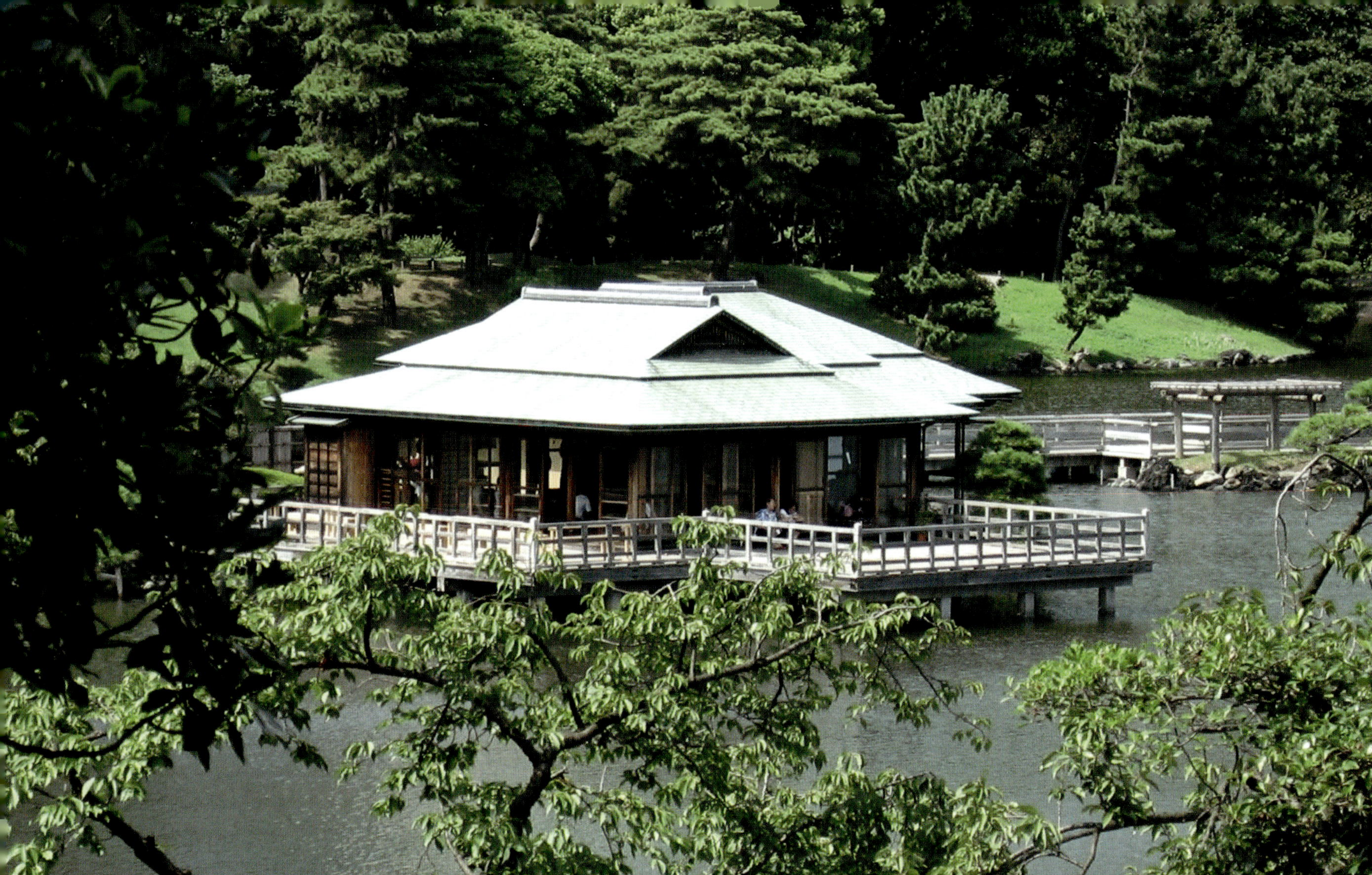

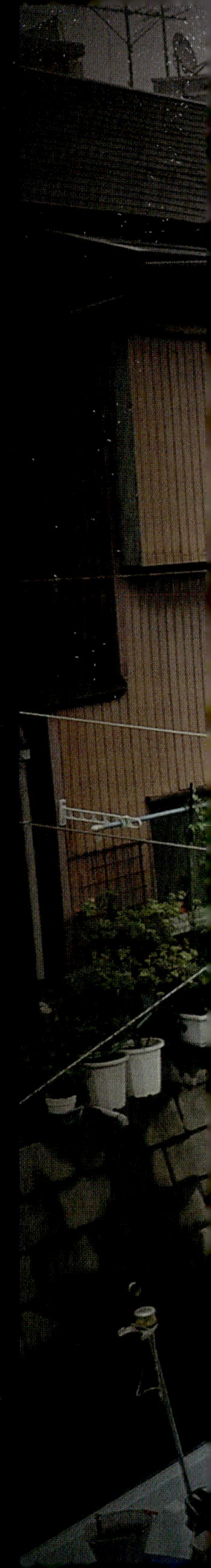

## Hama-Rikyū Gardens

A short walk from JR Shimbashi station one can find the Hama-Rikyū Gardens. A well-hidden oasis of tranquility right in the center of Tokyo which sharply contrasts with the surrounding Shiodome skyscrapers. This large beautiful park is one of the best-preserved examples of an Edo era garden. Located next to the Sumida River and the ocean, the gardens have a tidal pond. Even today it is still visible how the area for many centuries was used for duck hunting.
At times the garden's teahouse is being used to welcome statesmen, kings and queens on official visit in Tokyo. Otherwise it is open to the public and ideal to escape for a moment from the hectic of the city.

## Shinagawa

Being close to Haneda airport Shinagawa is a very important transportation hub and Shinkansen station in Tokyo. In 1601 it was designated as the first station of the Tōkaidō, the most important road in the Edo period connecting Nihonbashi in Edo with the imperial capital Kyoto.

Only a 15-minute walk from Shinagawa station, one of the busiest in Tokyo, one stumbles upon a maze of small canals and tiny harbors from where it is possible to take a pleasant old-fashioned harbor cruise.

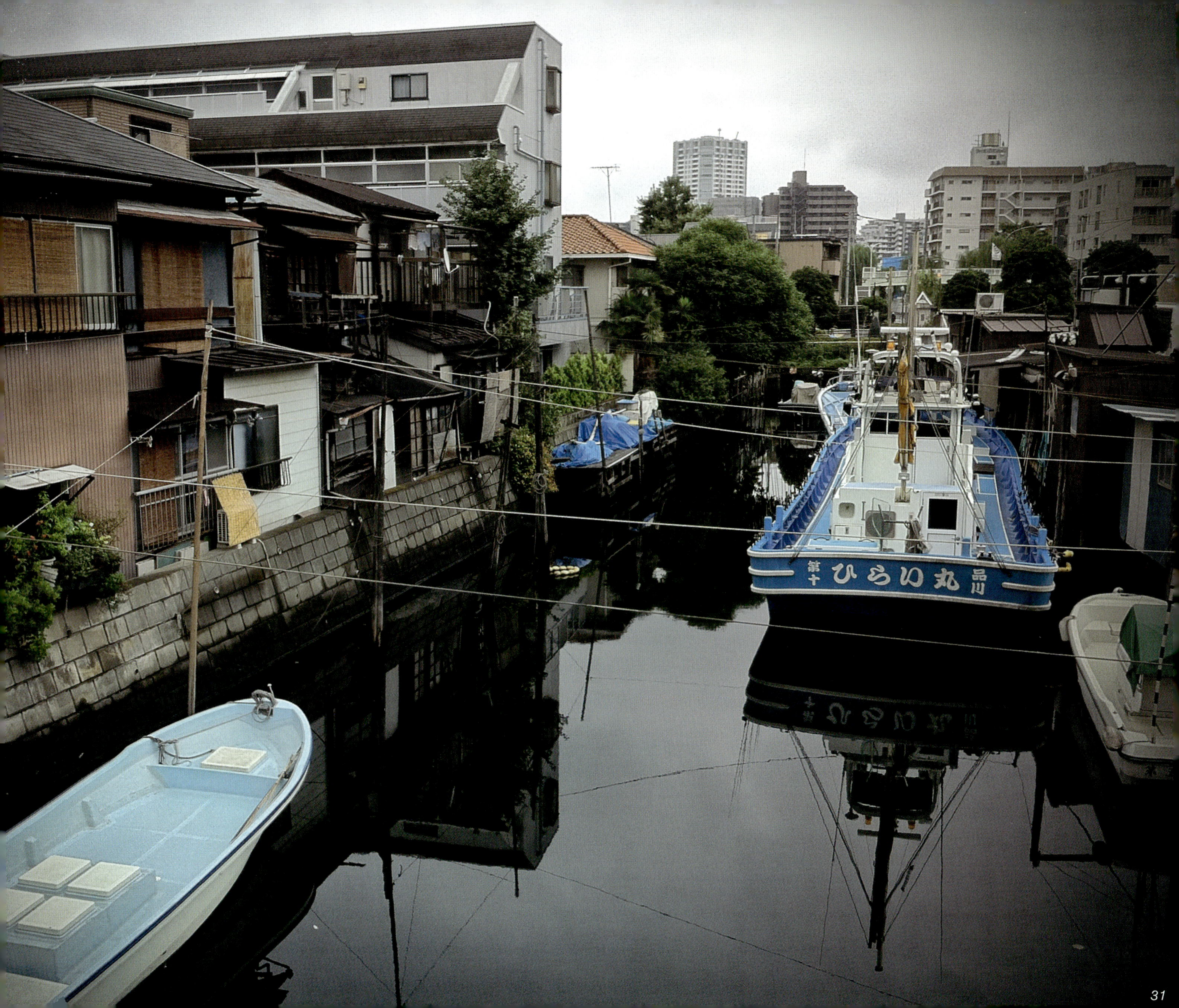
第十
ひらい丸
品川

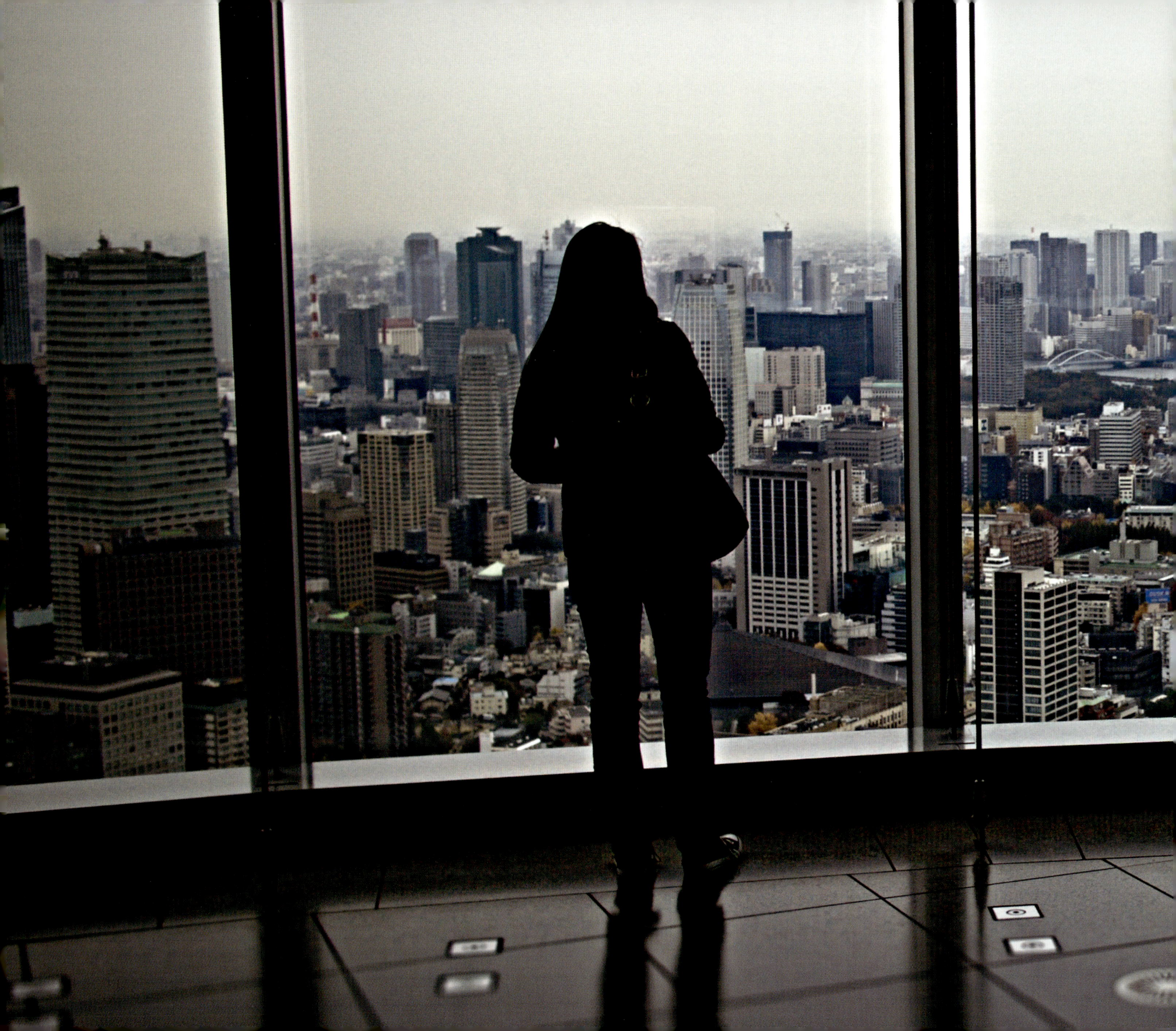

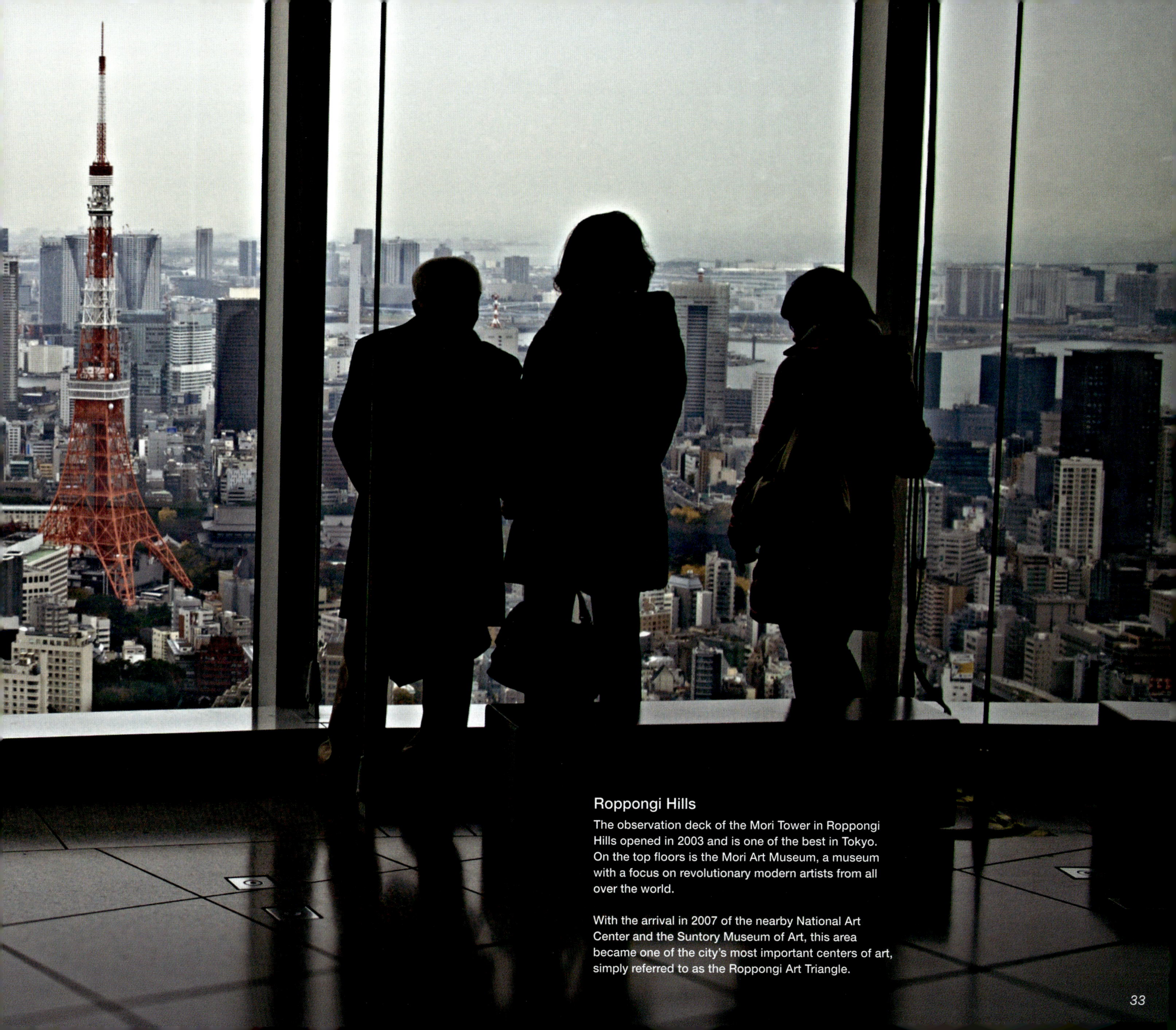

## Roppongi Hills

The observation deck of the Mori Tower in Roppongi Hills opened in 2003 and is one of the best in Tokyo. On the top floors is the Mori Art Museum, a museum with a focus on revolutionary modern artists from all over the world.

With the arrival in 2007 of the nearby National Art Center and the Suntory Museum of Art, this area became one of the city's most important centers of art, simply referred to as the Roppongi Art Triangle.

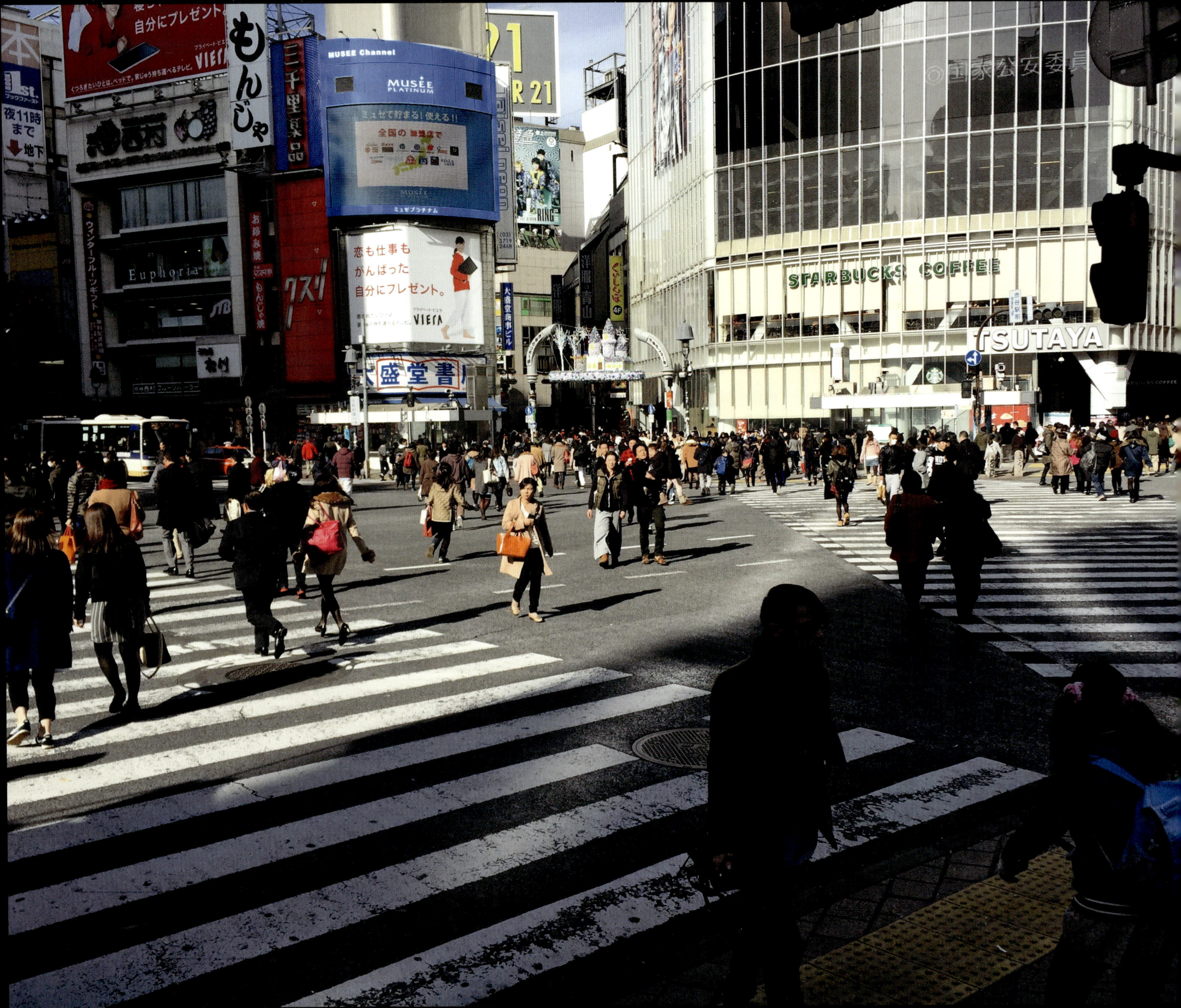
自分にプレゼント
VIERA
もんじゃ
MUSEE Channel
MUSEE PLATINUM
ミュゼで貯まる！使える!!
ミュゼプラチナム
恋も仕事も
がんばった
自分にプレゼント。
VIERA
クスリ
Euphoria
夜11時
まで
地下
大盛堂書
STARBUCKS COFFEE
TSUTAYA

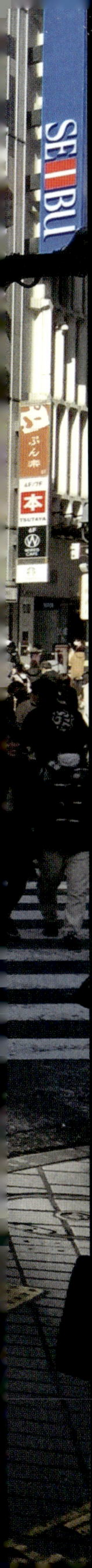

## Shibuya

The crossing just outside Shibuya station's Hachikō exit, is said to be the world's busiest and is often featured in movies, TV shows and news broadcasts. Try to get a window seat in the Starbucks and enjoy the orderly chaos every time the traffic lights turn green for the pedestrians. The statue commemorating the story of the dog Hachikō on the square is a very popular place to meet up with friends and colleagues.

## Harajuku

Near Harajuku station is Meiji-jingū, an important Shintō shrine dedicated to Emperor Meiji and his spouse. The shrine is right at the center of a beautiful forest of more than 100,000 trees that makes you forget you are in one of the busiest areas of Tokyo. If you are lucky you may see the solemn procession of a Shintō wedding passing by.

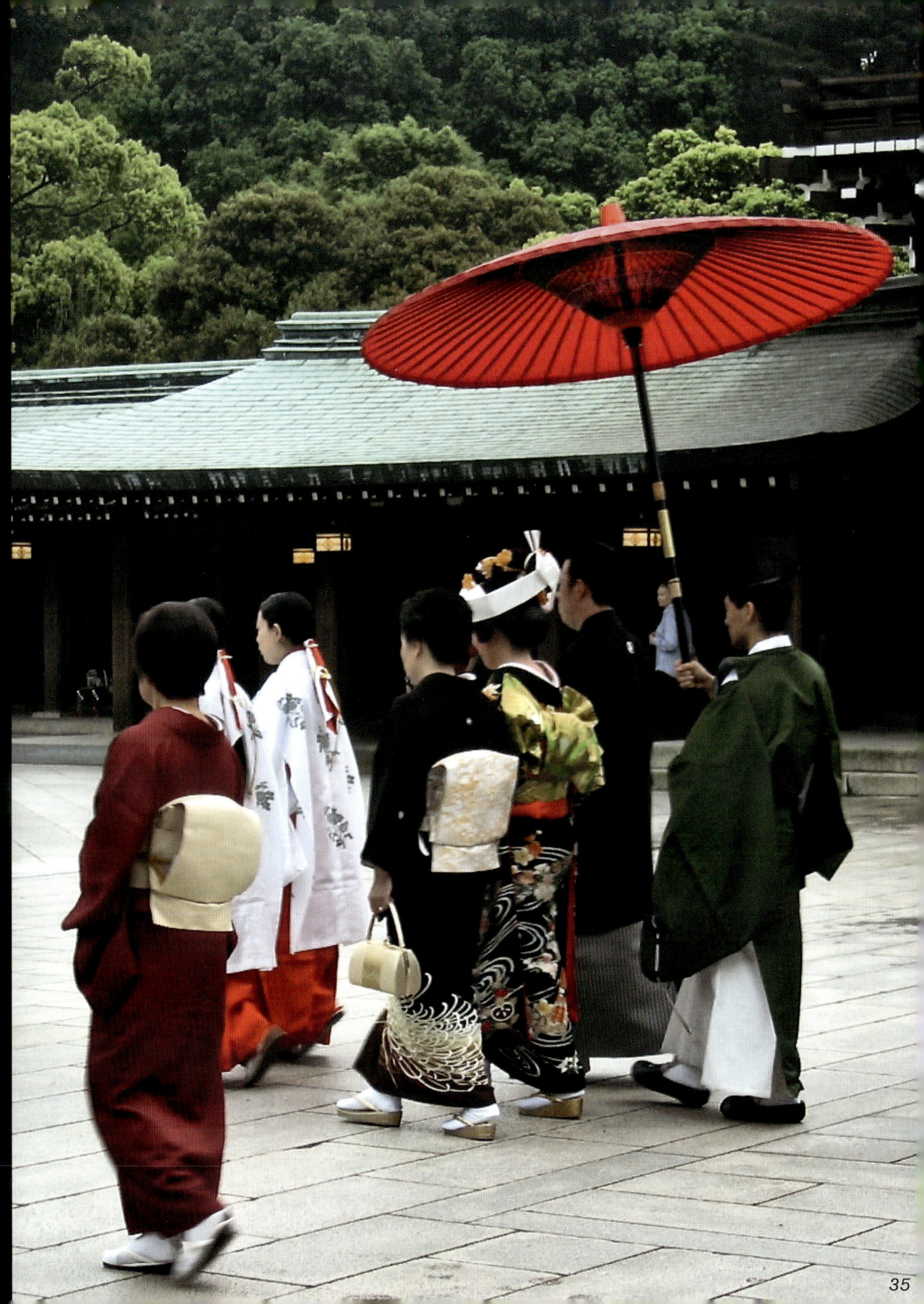

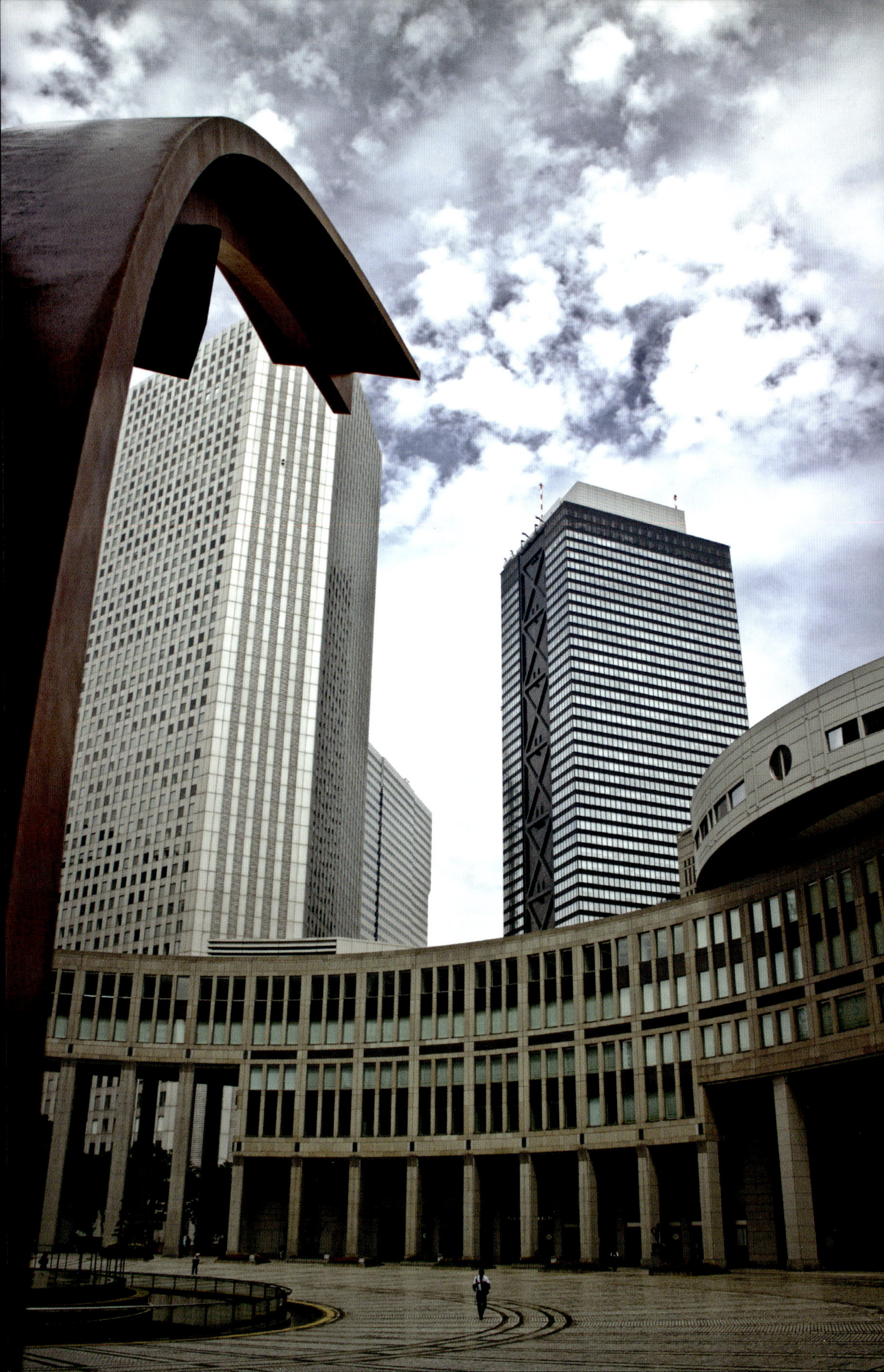

## Shinjuku

*Tokyo Metropolitan Government Buildings*
In the center of the skyscrapers west of Shinjuku station is the Tokyo Metropolitan Government Building complex, seat of the Governor of Tokyo and famous for its futuristic design by Tange Kenzō.

The 48 story and 243 meter high twin towers of the main building have excellent observation decks open to the public.

*Kabukichō*
A night part of Shinjuku transforms into a nightlife and adult entertainment hotspot. Popular places are Golden Gai and Kabukichō. Golden Gai is a cluster of tiny bars packed together in a grid of narrow streets. Prices for drinks are fairly expensive and some bars are strictly 'locals only'. In sharp contrast with the vintage look of Golden Gai is the neon glitter of Kabukichō, the red light district. Hostess bars, theme hotels, pubs, karaoke bars, Pachinko parlors all rival for the (often foreign) customer. The area is relatively safe since all parties involved – customers, police, shop tenants and the Yakuza – understand the unwritten rules of conduct.

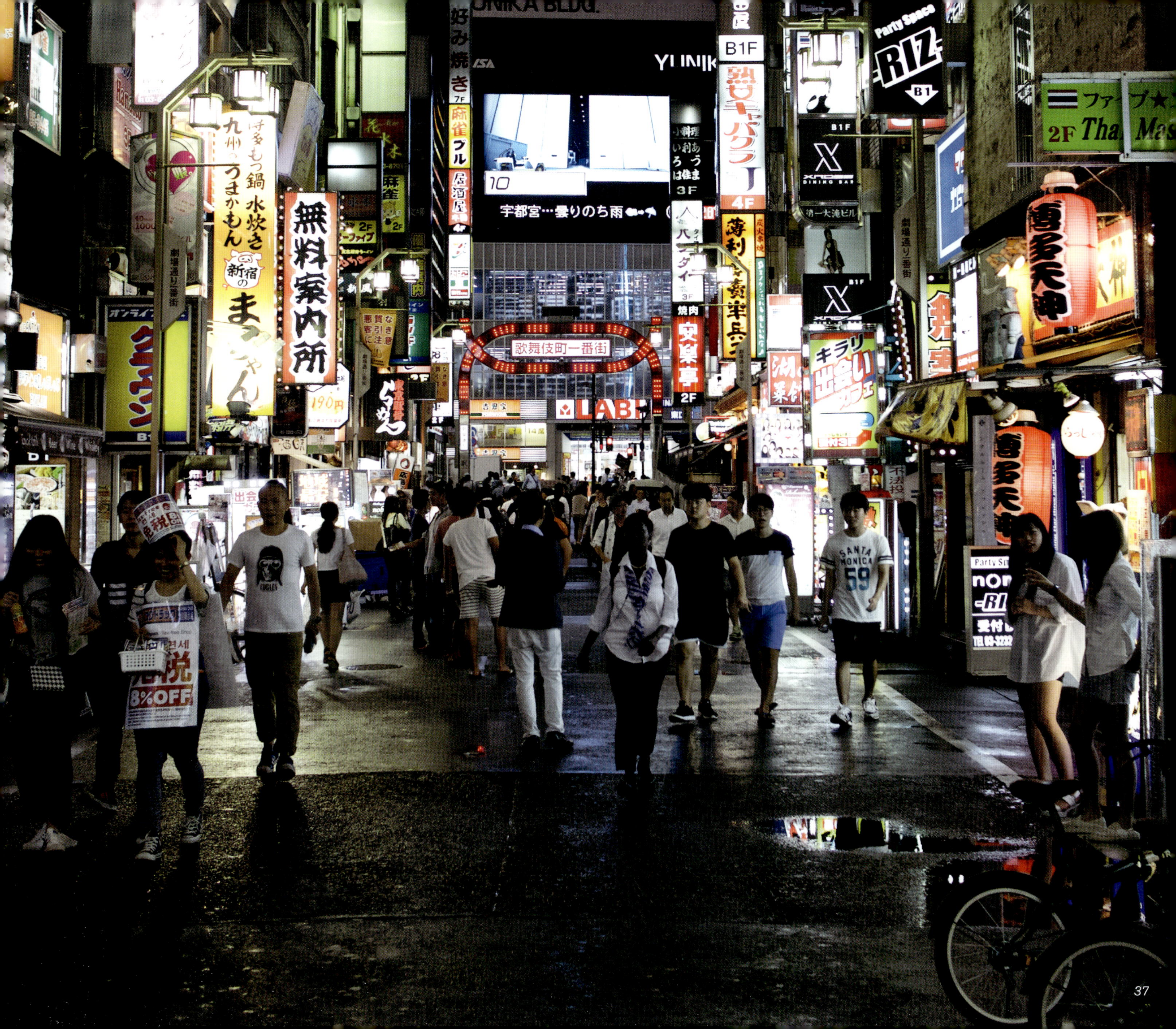
歌舞伎町一番街
無料案内所
宇都宮…曇りのち雨
LABI
Party Space
RIZ
B1
B1F
4F
3F
2F
九州のうまかもん
水炊き
SANTA MONICA 59
8%OFF

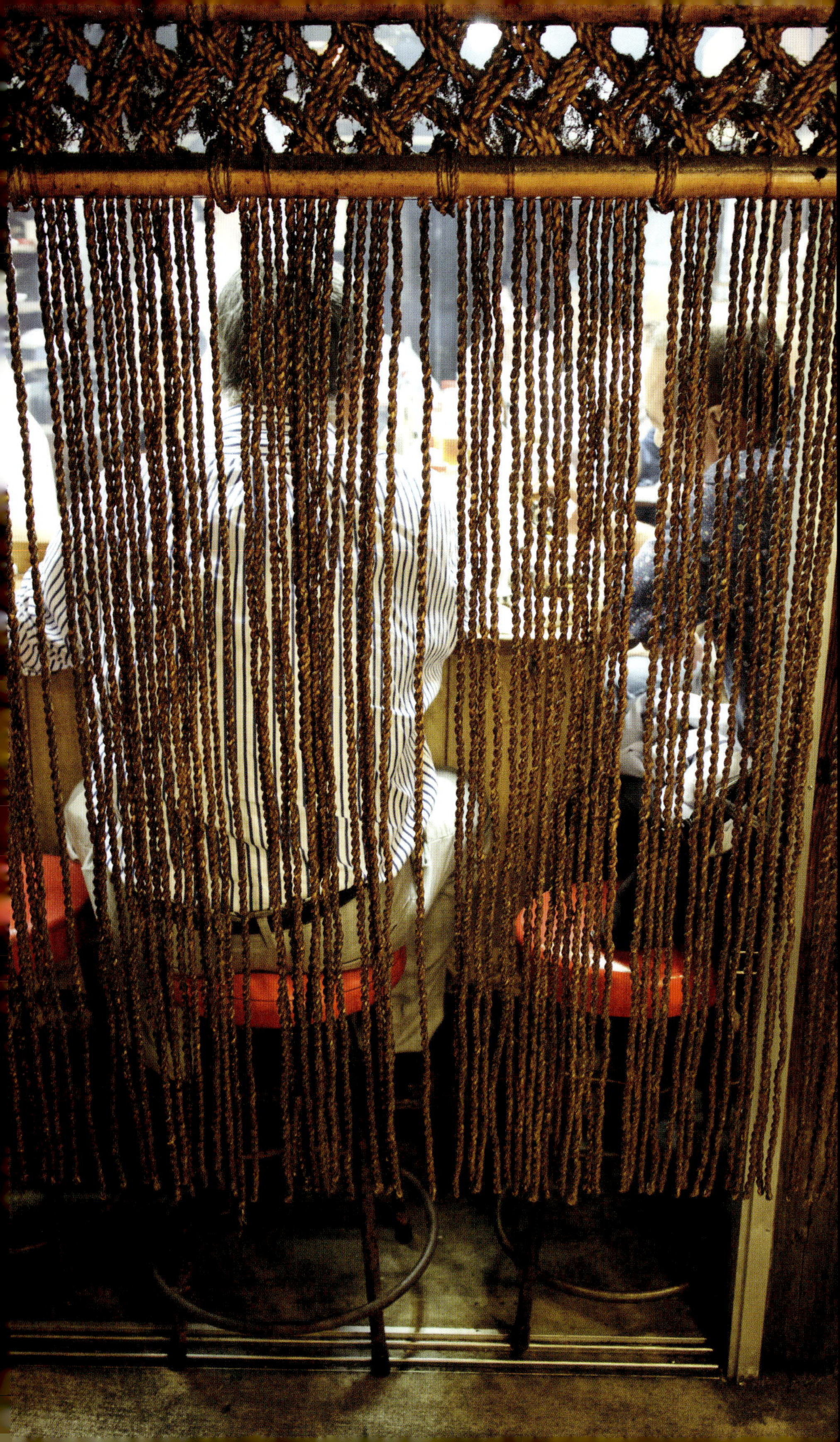
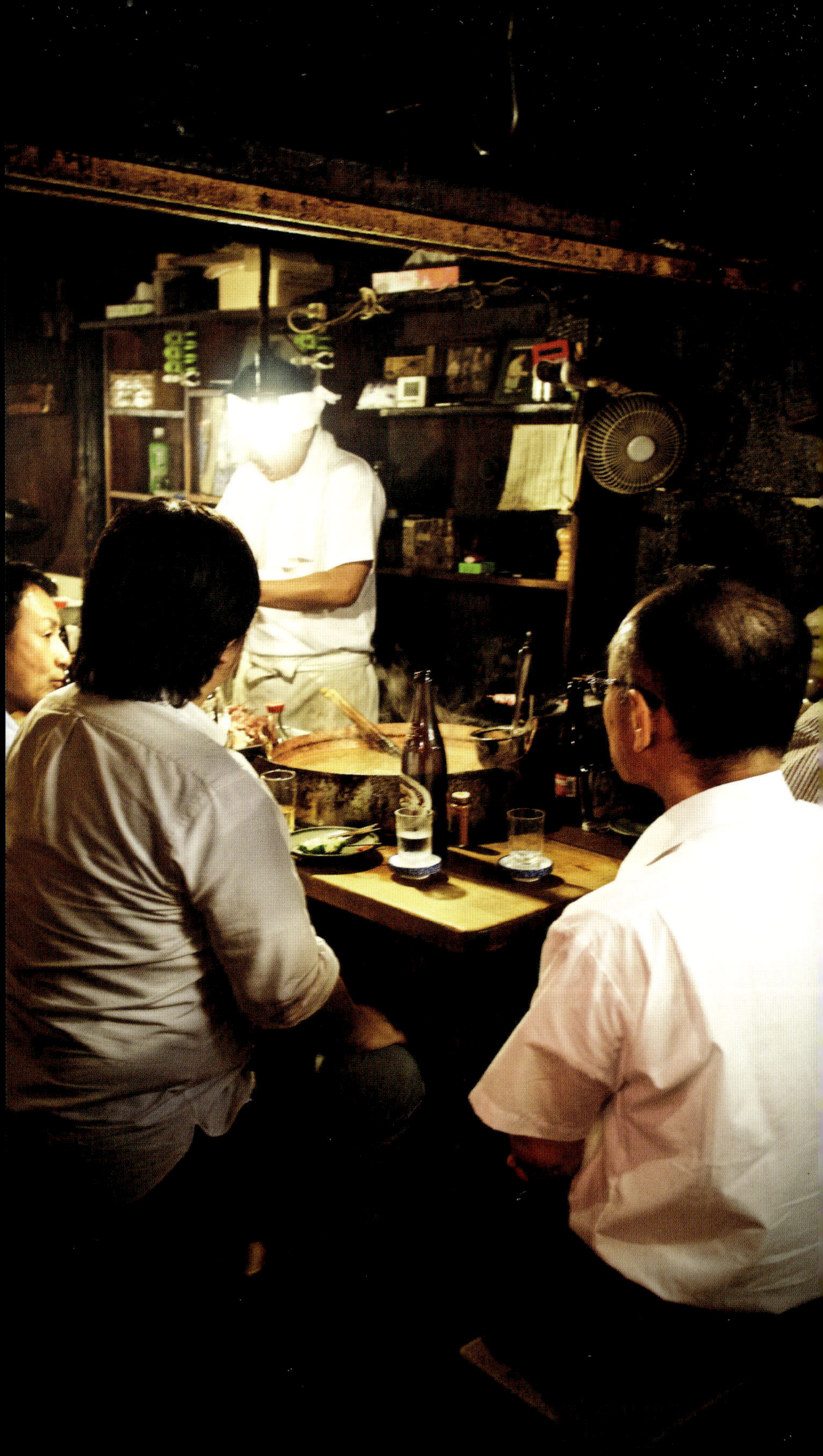

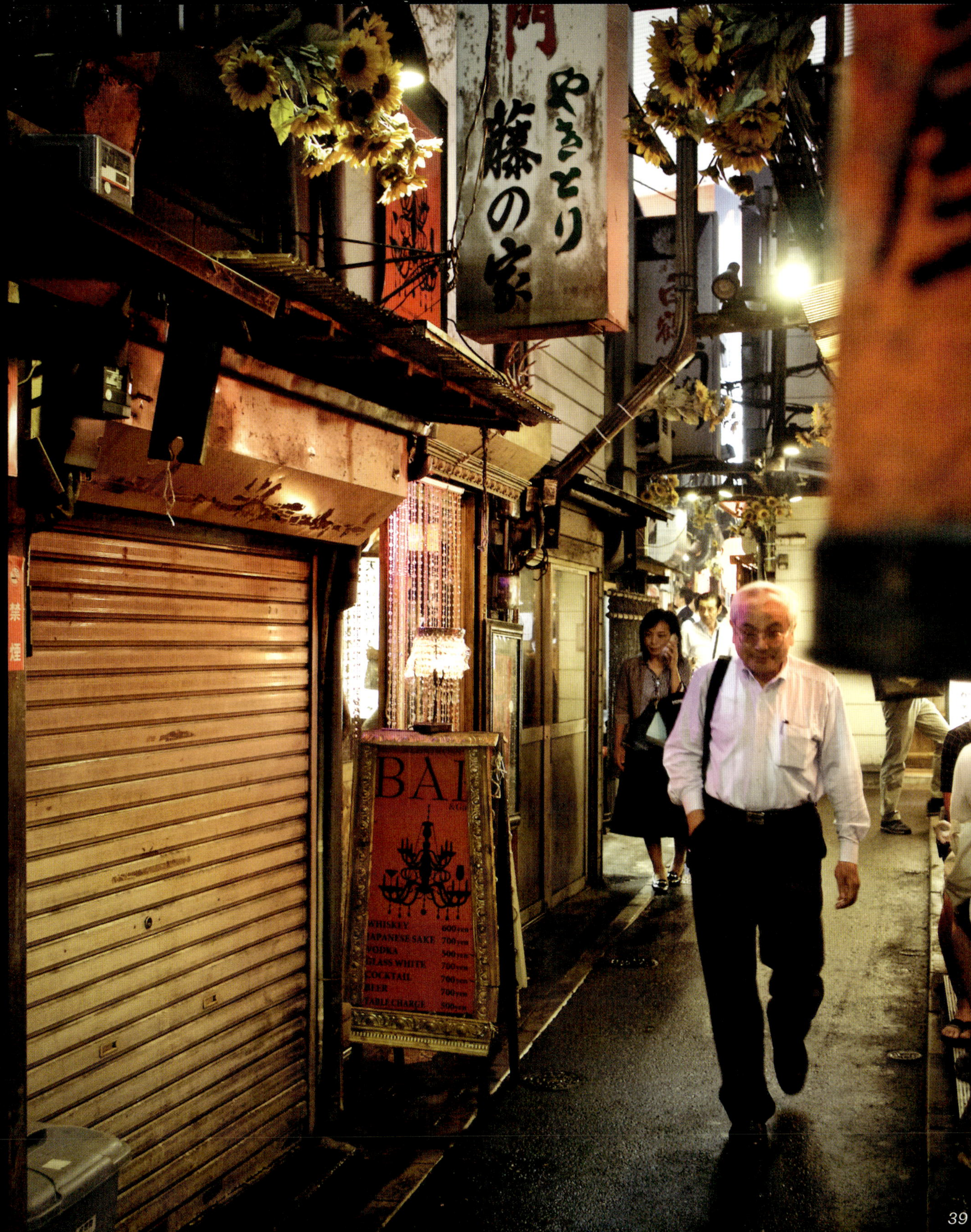


*Omoide Yokochō*

Omoide Yokochō, which can be translated as Memory Alley, is a little street near the west exit of Shinjuku station that is often overlooked by tourists. This area of Tokyo used to be the black market quarter just after the war. The street's old clandestine shops and drinking taverns were often without toilets, hence it was mockingly called 'piss alley' until most of the street burned down in the nineties.

The alley was rebuilt and is still a popular place for salarymen enjoying after work drinks and traditional dishes. Unlike Kabukichō the scene is very much local and basically no English is spoken. In this way the alley has been able to keep its nostalgic atmosphere and is much less frequented by tourists. The wooden facades of the taverns, the smoke rising from the yakitori grills and the smell of the motsu all help to evoke the atmosphere of post war Shinjuku.

Just after World War II the poor population was desperate to find food and the entrails of cows and pigs not used by the occupation forces were traded. With the guts a popular stew named 'motsu' was made. As shown in the middle picture motsu is still being served. Unfortunately this small neighborhood is under pressure and commercial development will likely turn these pictures in nostalgic souvenirs.

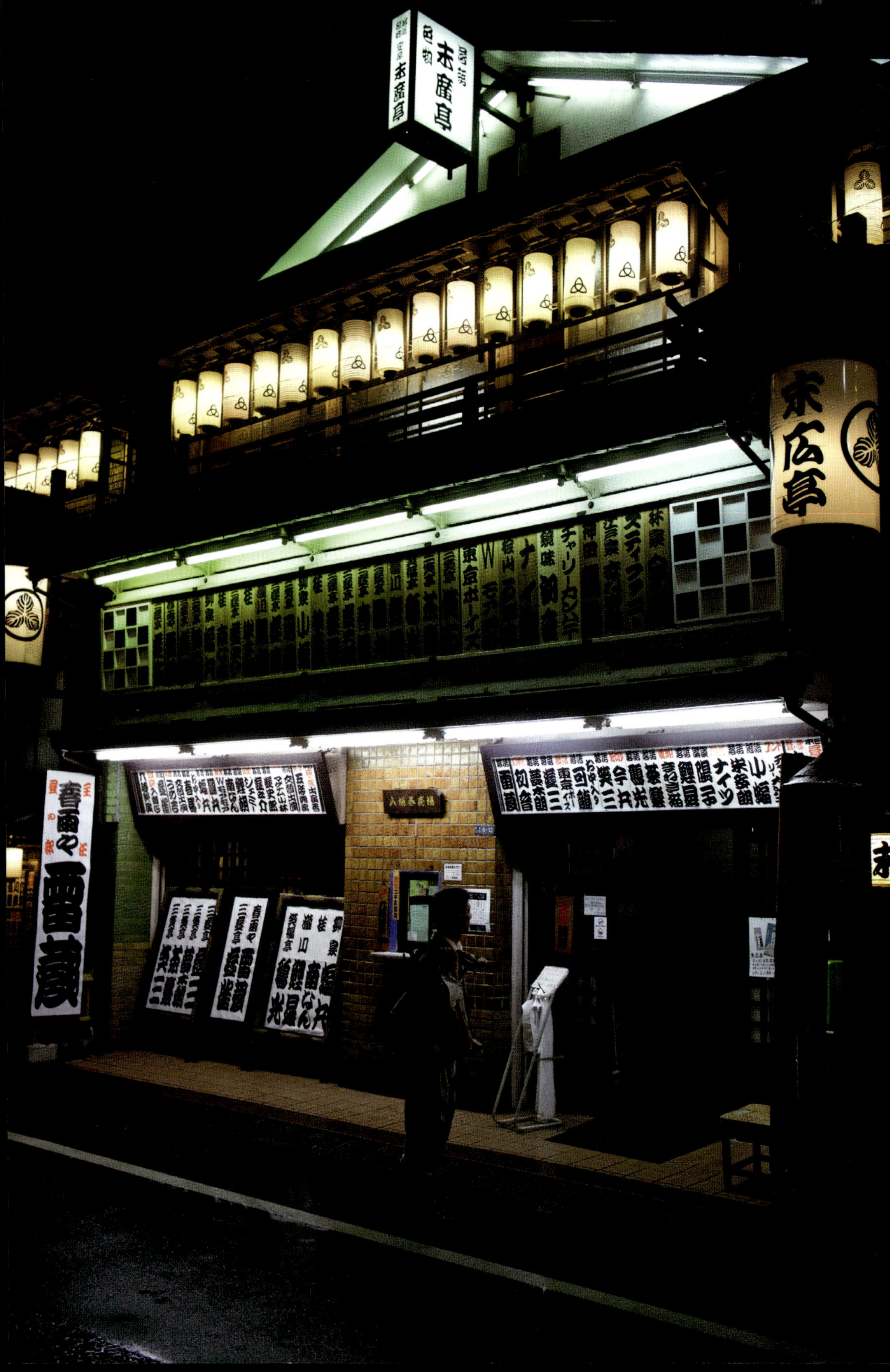


*Suehirotei theatre*
The beautiful Suehirotei theatre was built just after World War II. Next to chairs, it still has the original tatami seating as well. Recently it has been completely renovated and it is one of the few places where rakugo or traditional Japanese comic storytelling is performed.

## Matsuri

Fireworks and all kinds of festivals, named Matsuri, are held across Japan throughout the year. Most if not all have their roots in the native Shintō or Buddhist religion. Some festivals take the shape of performances or religious processions like the impressive Gion Matsuri in Kyoto, whereas others focus more on music and dance. The rhythmic Eisa parade in Naha (Okinawa) or the Awa Odori Festival that started in the 16th century in Tokushima (Shikoku) are some of the best examples.

In summer the Awa Odori Festival in Kōenji near Shinjuku attracts one million spectators to watch more than 10,000 dancers parade and dance to the rhythm of drums and classical instruments. Especially during twilight, the lanterns, the colorful costumes, the quick beat of the music combined with the loud singing and clapping add to the excitement.

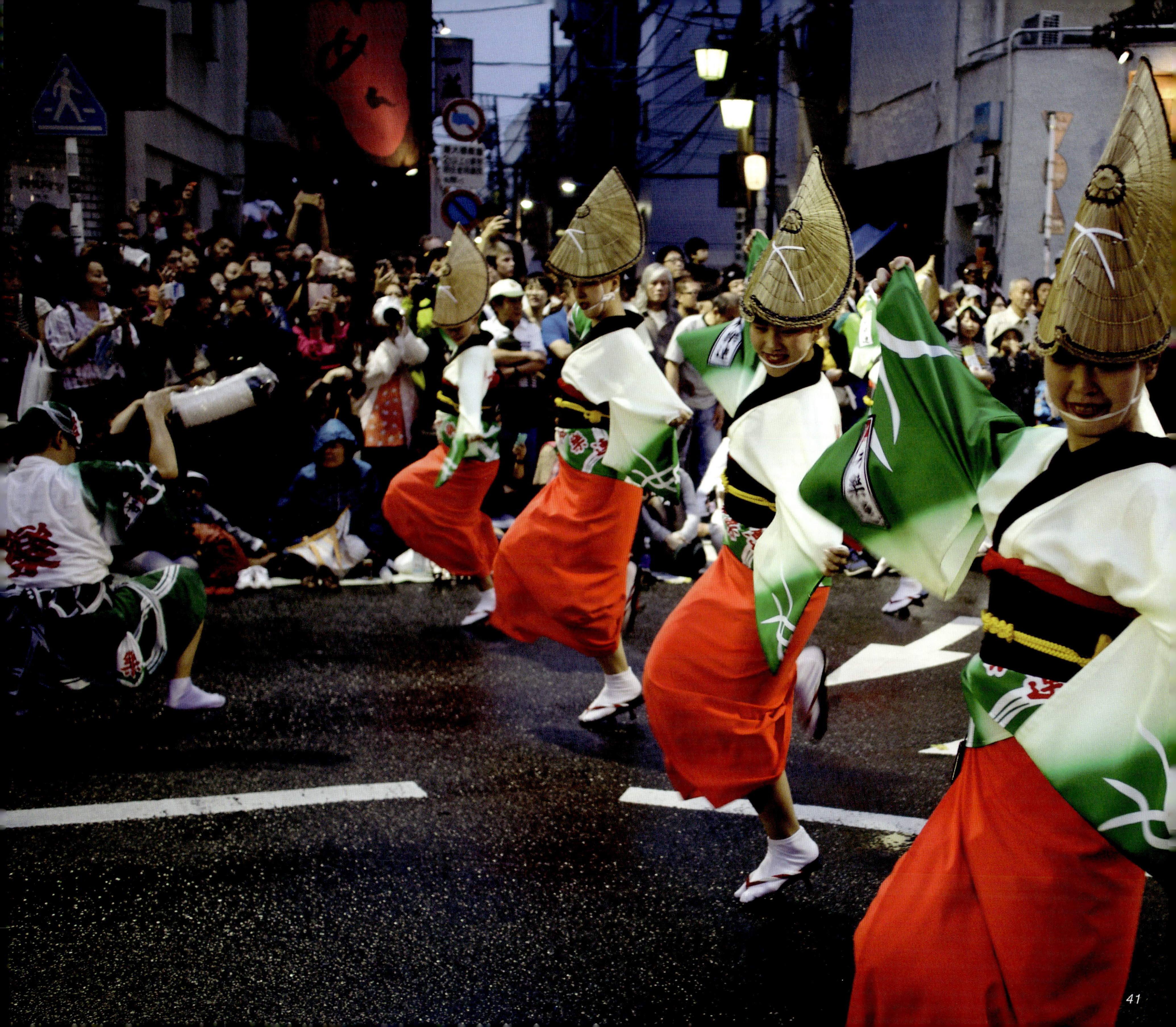

関東

# KANTŌ

If your time in Japan is limited and you stay in Tokyo, then Kantō offers the best chance of seeing an attractive part of the country without the need for rushing to other main cities and touristic areas further away.

Kantō is Japan's largest plain and encompasses the Tokyo Metropolis and the prefectures Kanagawa, Saitama, Gunma, Tochigi, Ibaraki and Chiba.

Unlike the Kansai area that is considered to be the cradle of the Japanese culture, the development of the Kantō region only really started when Japan's first shogunate took its seat in Kamakura in 1192. Much later in the early 17th century when Edo, present day Tokyo, was made the stronghold of the Tokugawa shogunate, Kantō became the leading political and economic area of Japan. A position the Kantō region still holds today.

In this chapter one will find some inspiration for day trips in the Kantō region all within the vicinity of Tokyo. In less than two hours by train from the city center of Tokyo it is possible to hike in beautiful national parks with superb views of Mount Fuji, visit stunning Nikkō and Kamakura reminiscent of the shogunate era, or take a stroll in Yokohama, Japan's second largest city.

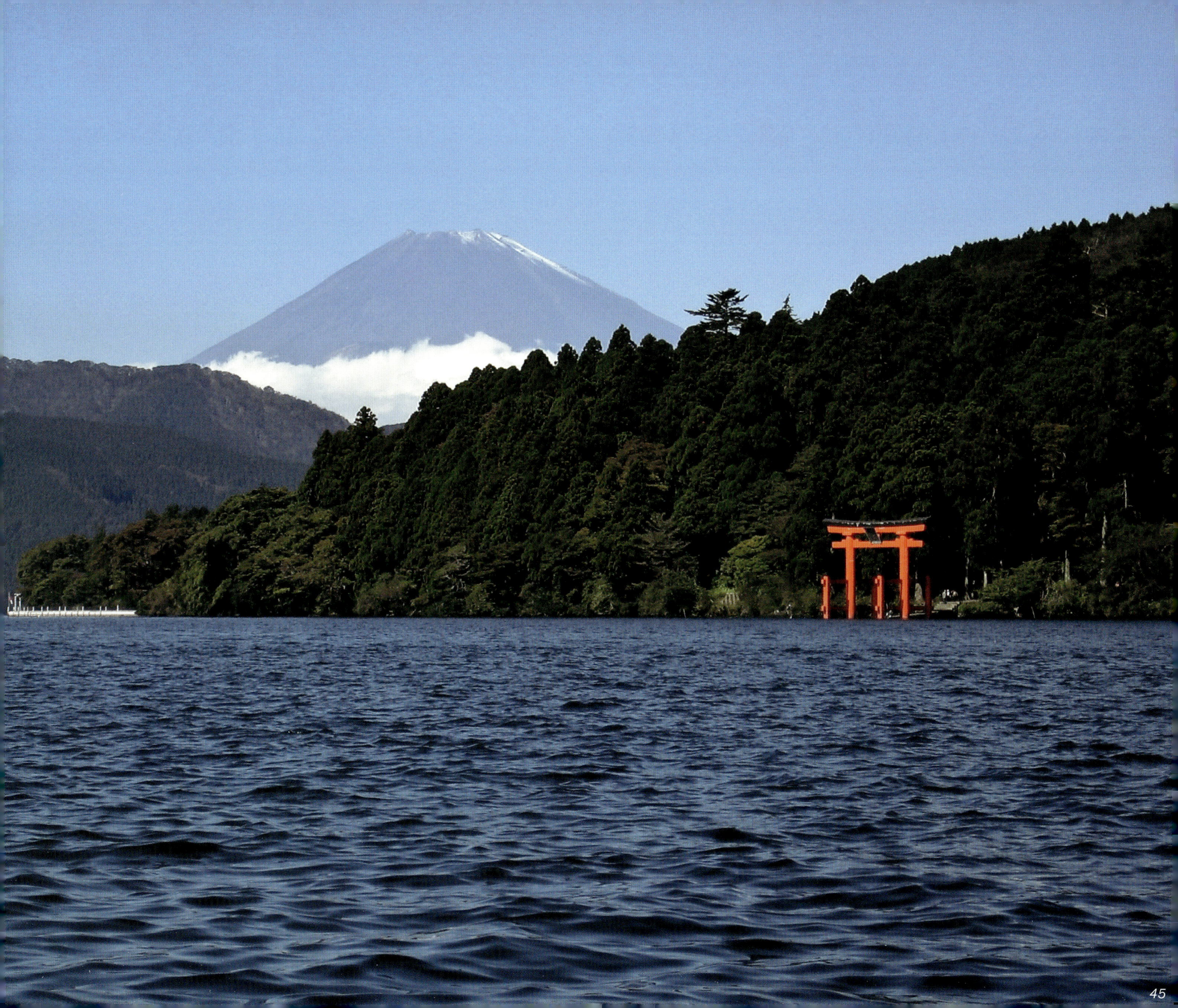

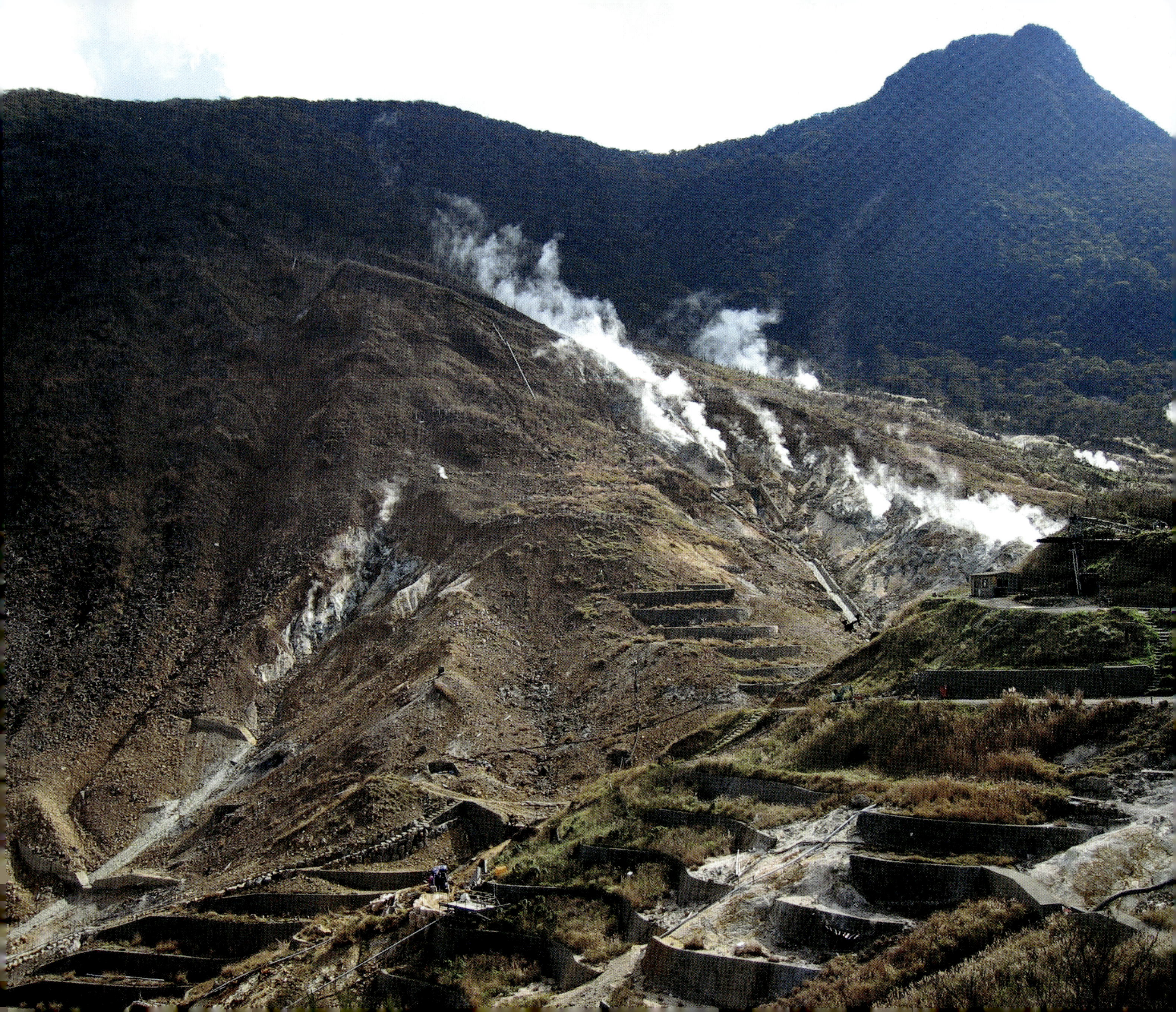

## Ōwakudani

Ōwakudani is an interesting stop on the Hakone ropeway. Apart from being an excellent viewpoint for Mount Fuji the place is synonym for the highly active volcanic activities in the region. The wells with boiling water and steam leaving the mountain and the constant smell of sulfur and volcanic gas make the setting unreal. Be aware that when danger looms the area is a no go zone.

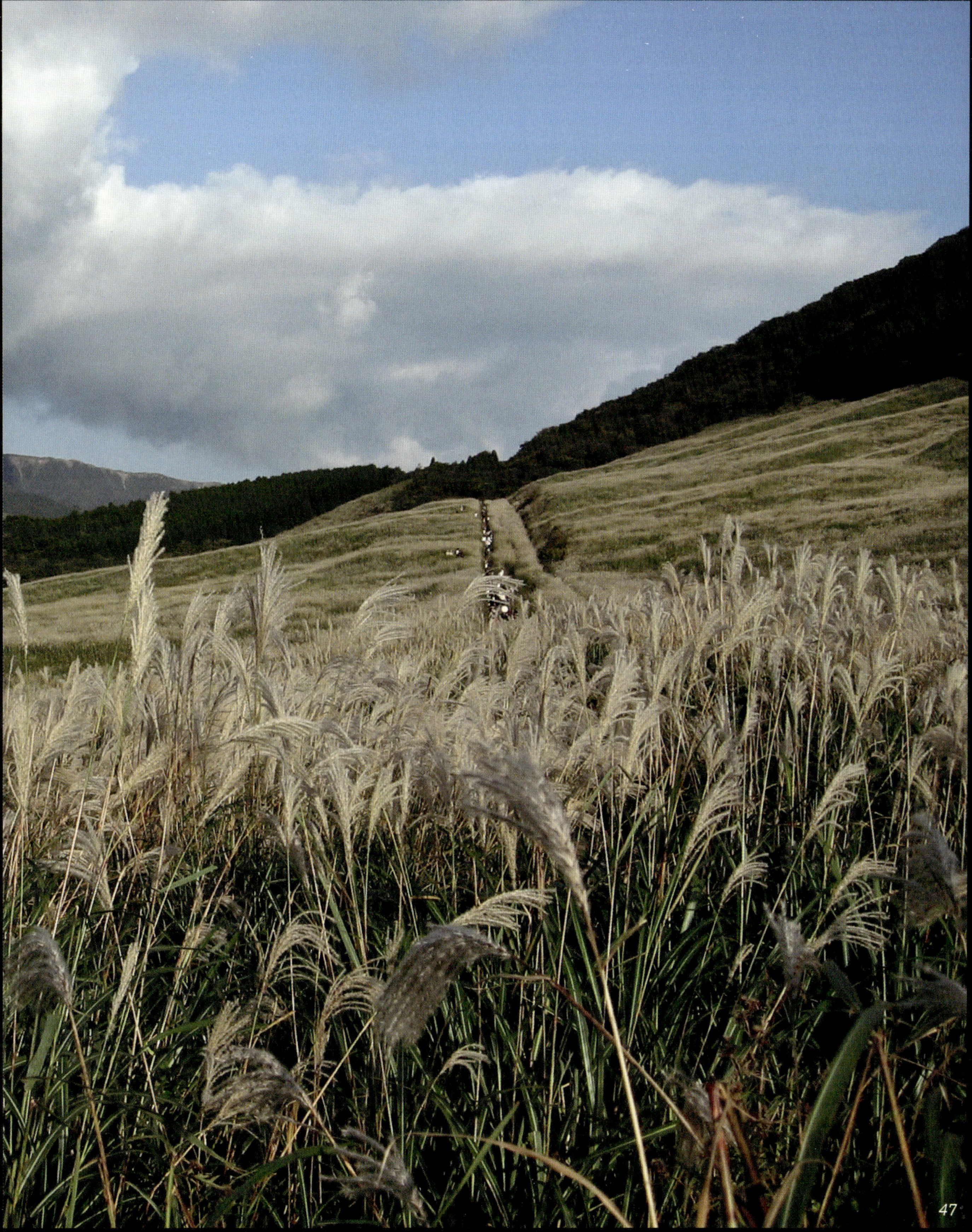

## Sengokuhara

In autumn Japanese tourists come from all over the country to the plateau at the foot of Mount Daigatake in Sengokuhara to hike through the golden-colored Japanese pampas grass.

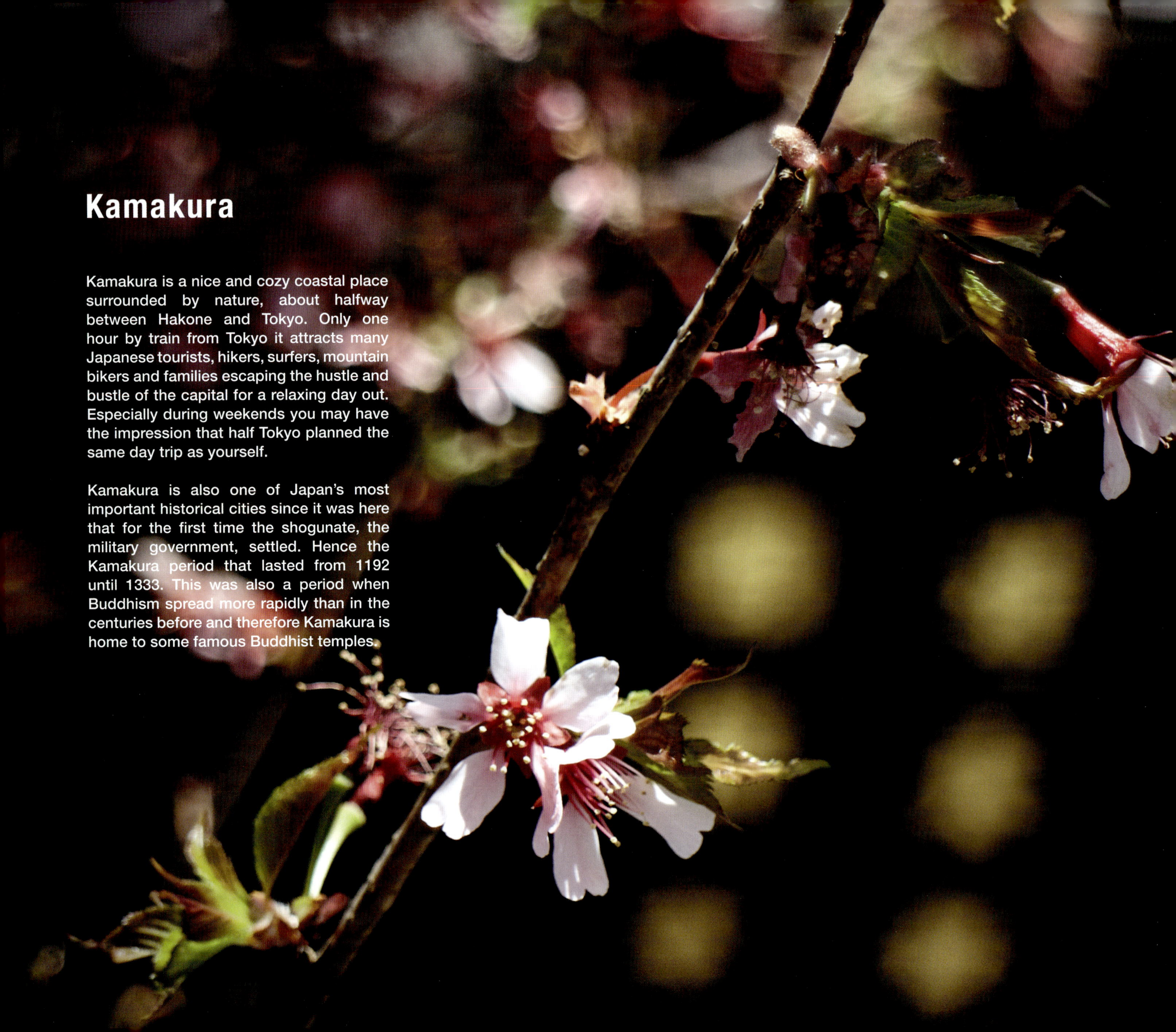

# Kamakura

Kamakura is a nice and cozy coastal place surrounded by nature, about halfway between Hakone and Tokyo. Only one hour by train from Tokyo it attracts many Japanese tourists, hikers, surfers, mountain bikers and families escaping the hustle and bustle of the capital for a relaxing day out. Especially during weekends you may have the impression that half Tokyo planned the same day trip as yourself.

Kamakura is also one of Japan's most important historical cities since it was here that for the first time the shogunate, the military government, settled. Hence the Kamakura period that lasted from 1192 until 1333. This was also a period when Buddhism spread more rapidly than in the centuries before and therefore Kamakura is home to some famous Buddhist temples.

## Kenchō-ji

Kenchō-ji was established in 1253 and is Japan's oldest Zen temple. Today visitors can still participate in the regularly scheduled meditation sessions. It is by far the largest of the Zen temples in the Kamakura area. The path leading to the massive San-mon, the entrance gate, is an impressive way of approaching the large temple complex especially during the sakura (cherry blossom) season.

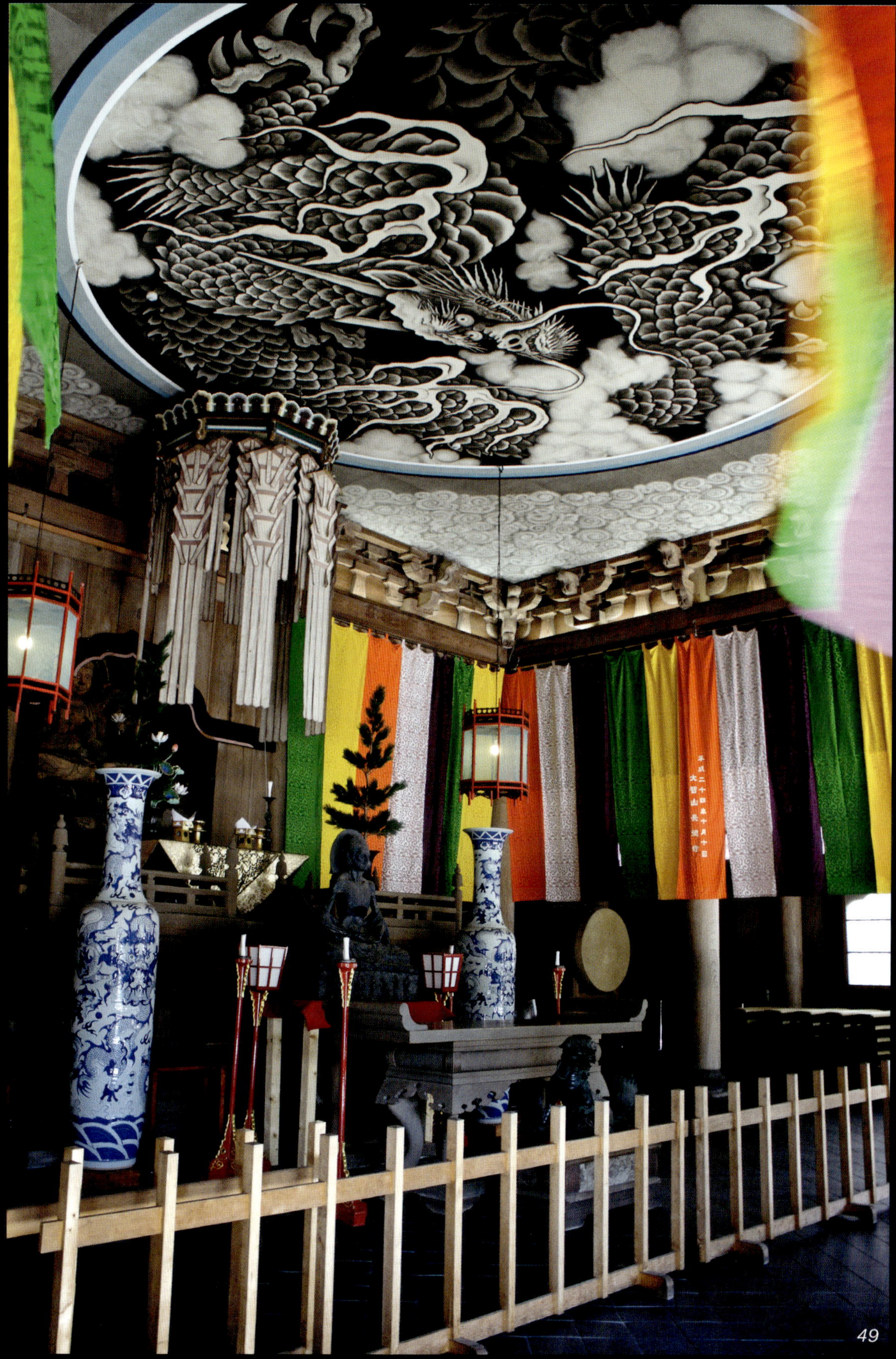

Behind the Butsu-den or main hall is the lecture hall, Hattō. Very special is the ceiling with the legendary dragon in the clouds, Unryū, that was commissioned for the 750th anniversary of the temple and made by a local artist.

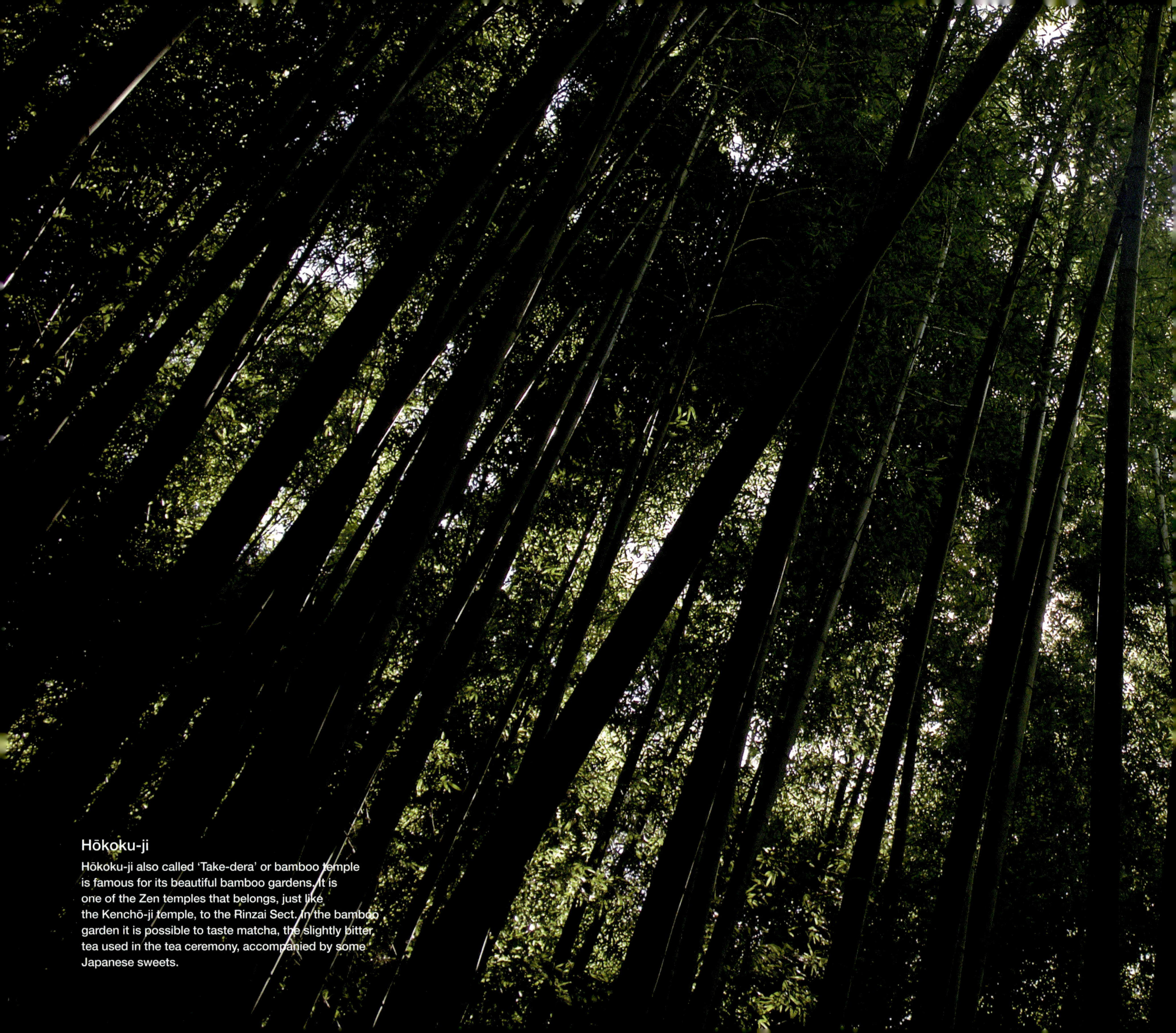

### Hōkoku-ji

Hōkoku-ji also called 'Take-dera' or bamboo temple is famous for its beautiful bamboo gardens. It is one of the Zen temples that belongs, just like the Kenchō-ji temple, to the Rinzai Sect. In the bamboo garden it is possible to taste matcha, the slightly bitter tea used in the tea ceremony, accompanied by some Japanese sweets.

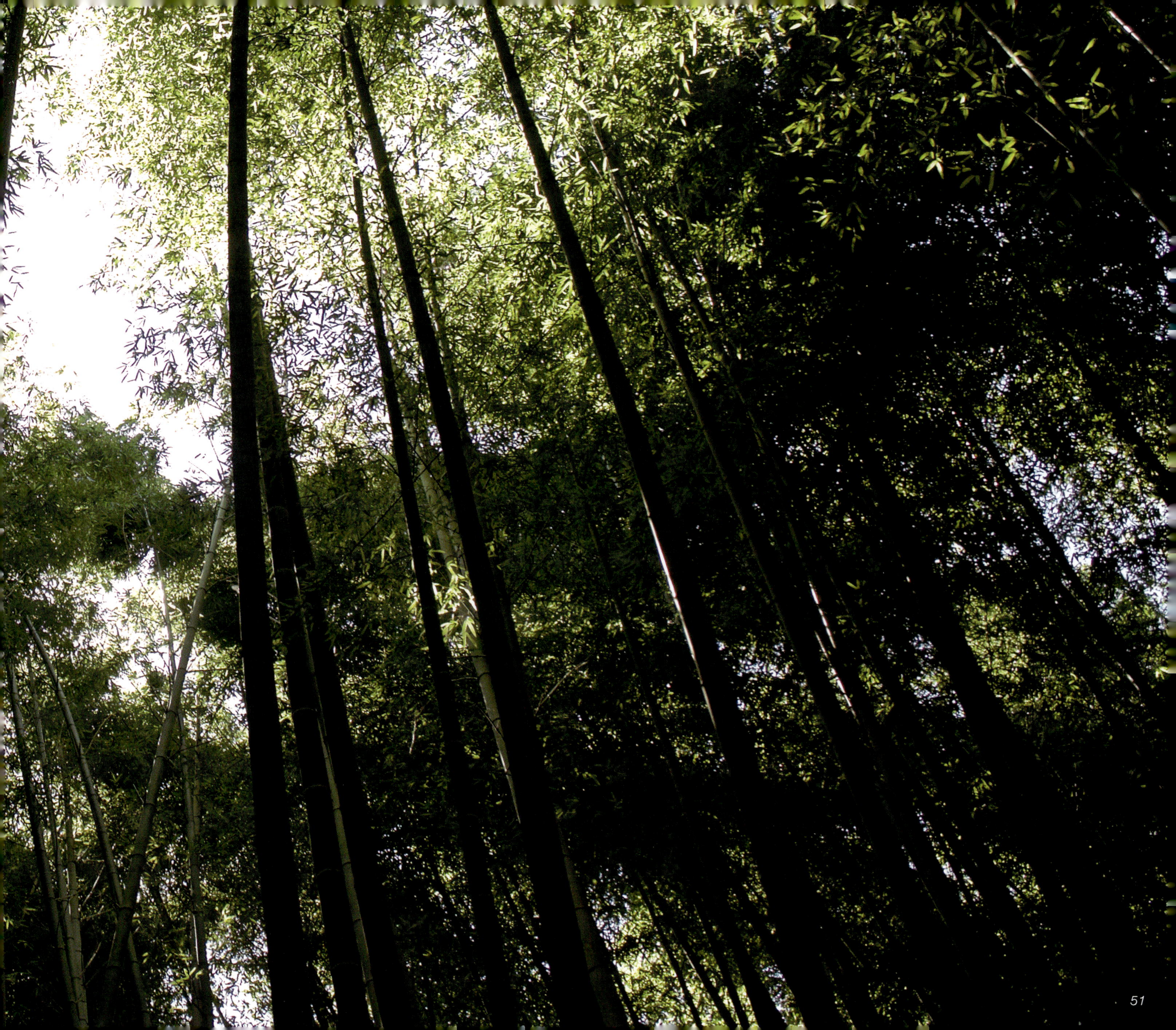

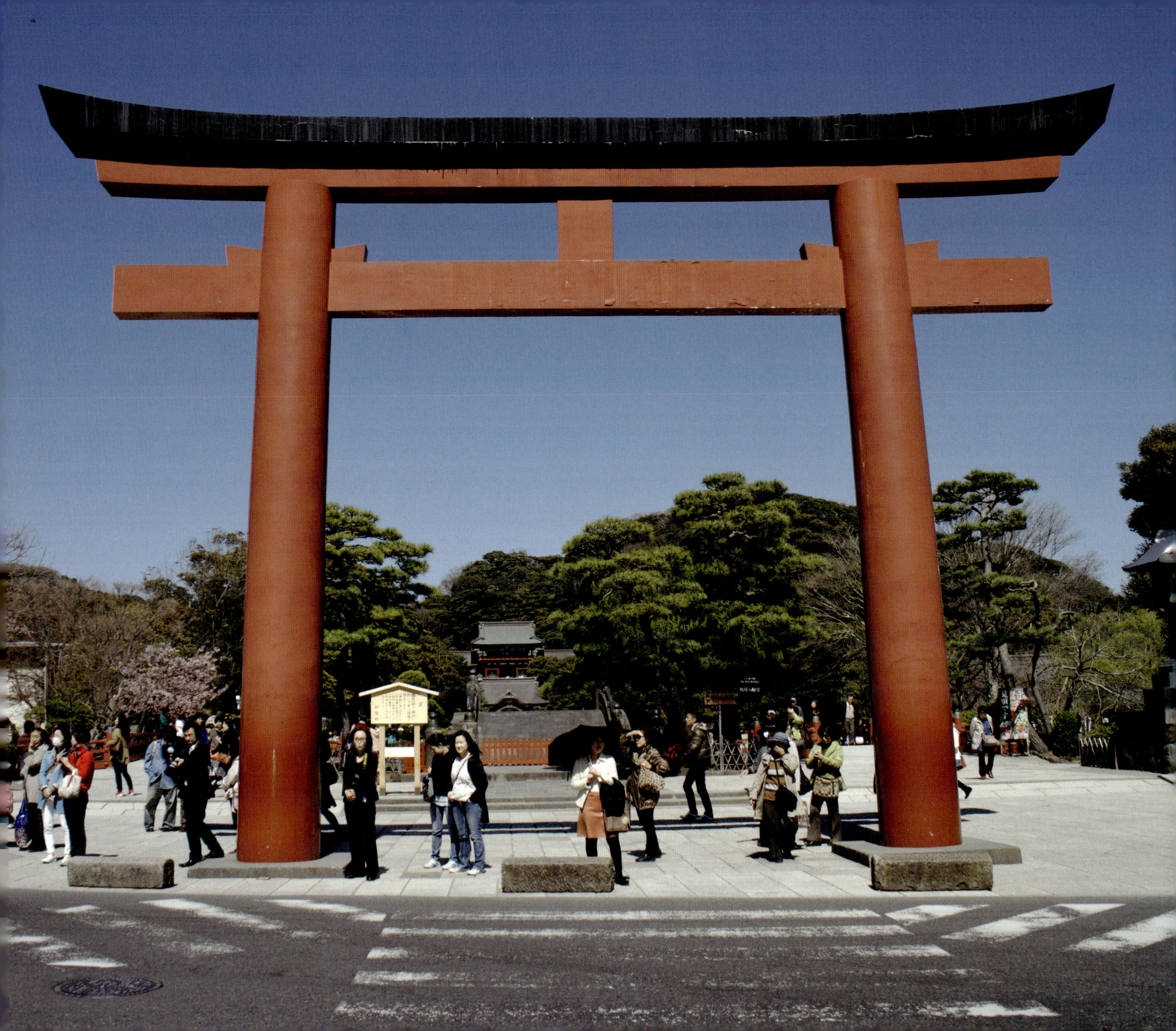

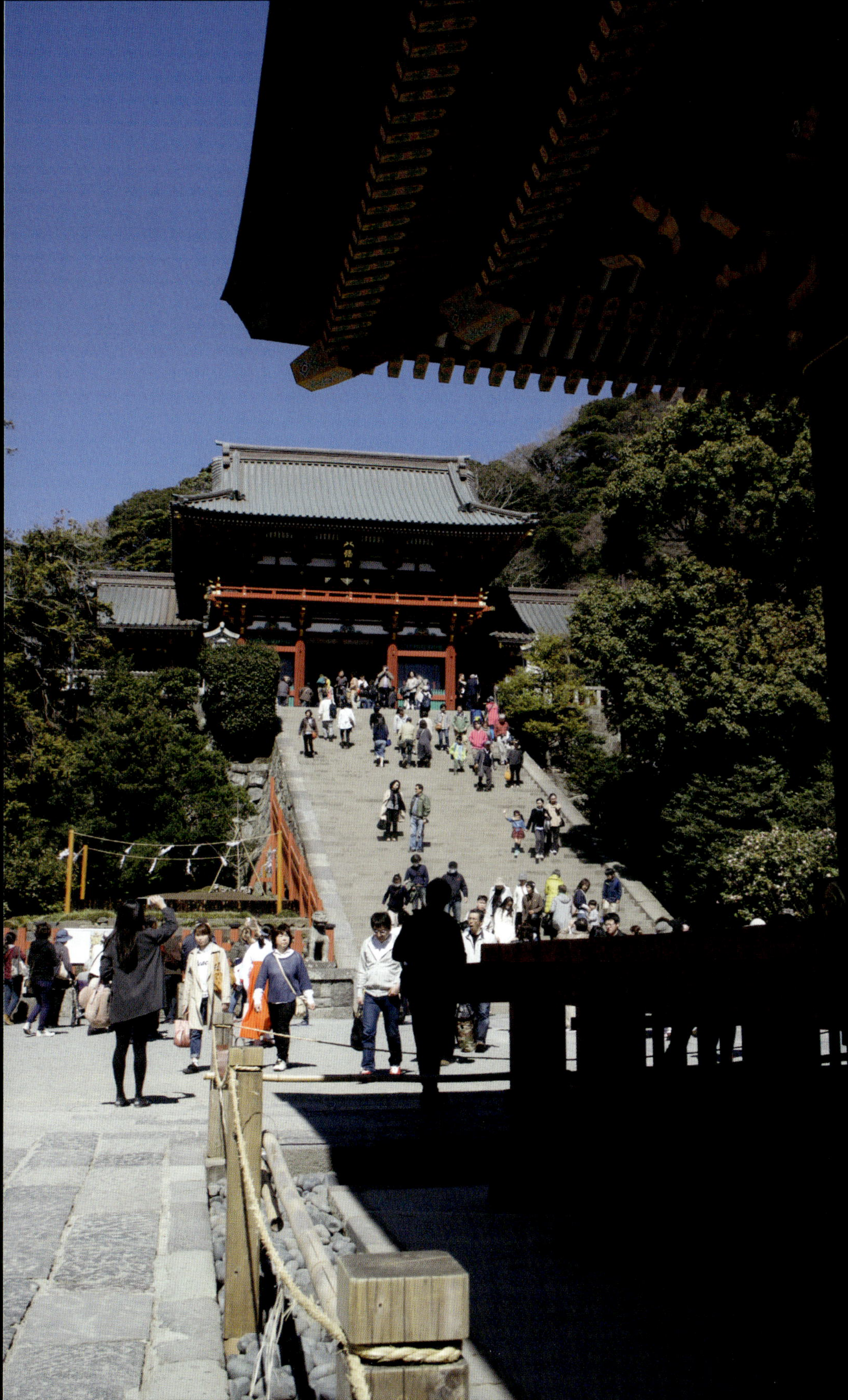

## Tsurugaoka Hachimangū

In sharp contrast with the sober Zen temples is the magnificent red lacquered and splendidly ornate Tsurugaoka Hachimangū. It is Kamakura's most important Shintō shrine and dedicated to Hachiman, the kami, deity of war. It was Minamoto no Yoritomo the famous head of the Minamoto clan who moved the shrine to its present location right in the center of Kamakura. Yoritomo, appointed in 1192 by the Emperor in Kyoto as Japan's first shogun, made Kamakura de facto the capital where the political, but especially the military power was vested. This period was the dawn of the samurai, the famous warriors that would become one of the dominant players in medieval Japan until Emperor Meiji restored the imperial rule in the 19th century.

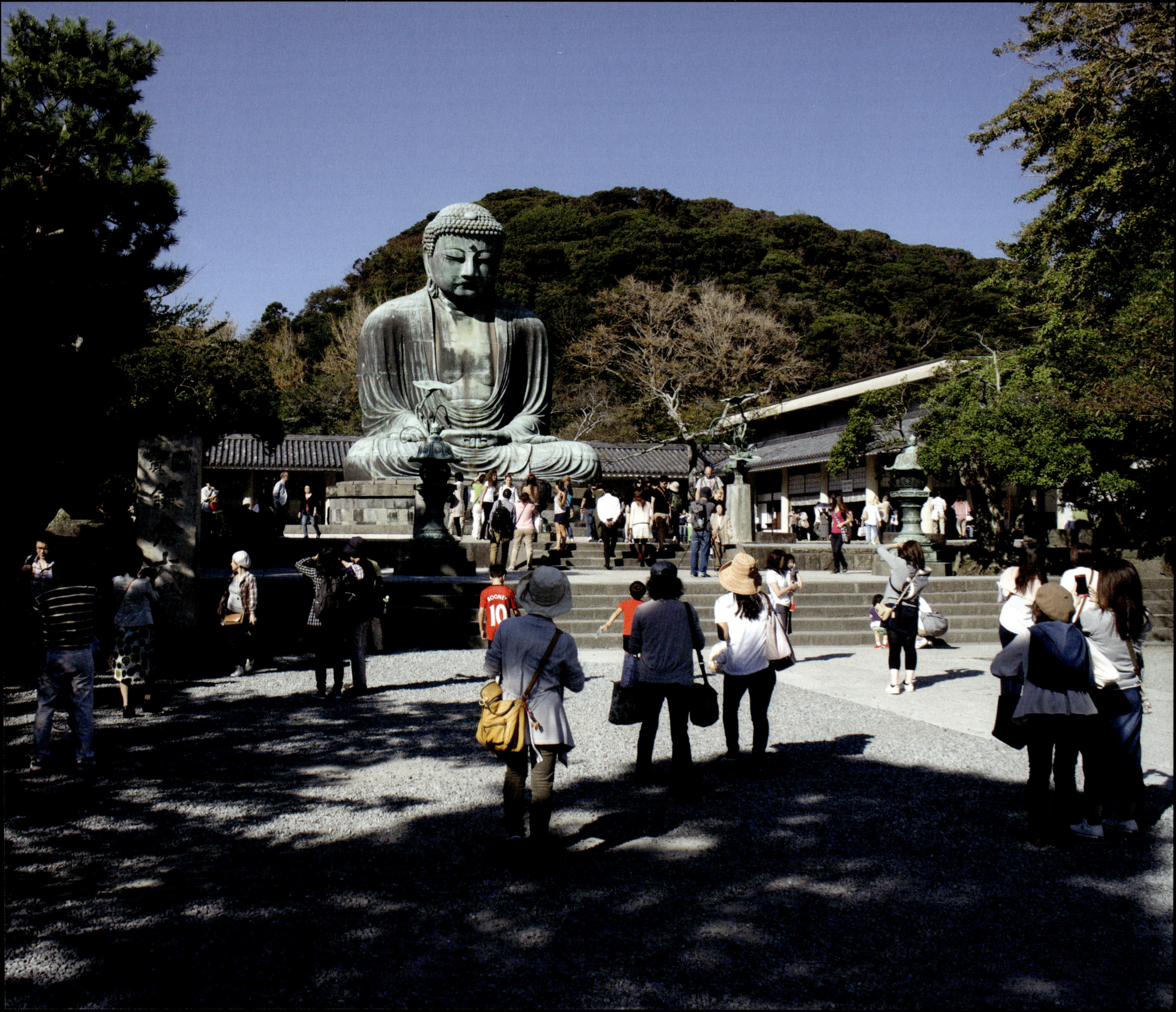
ROONEY
10

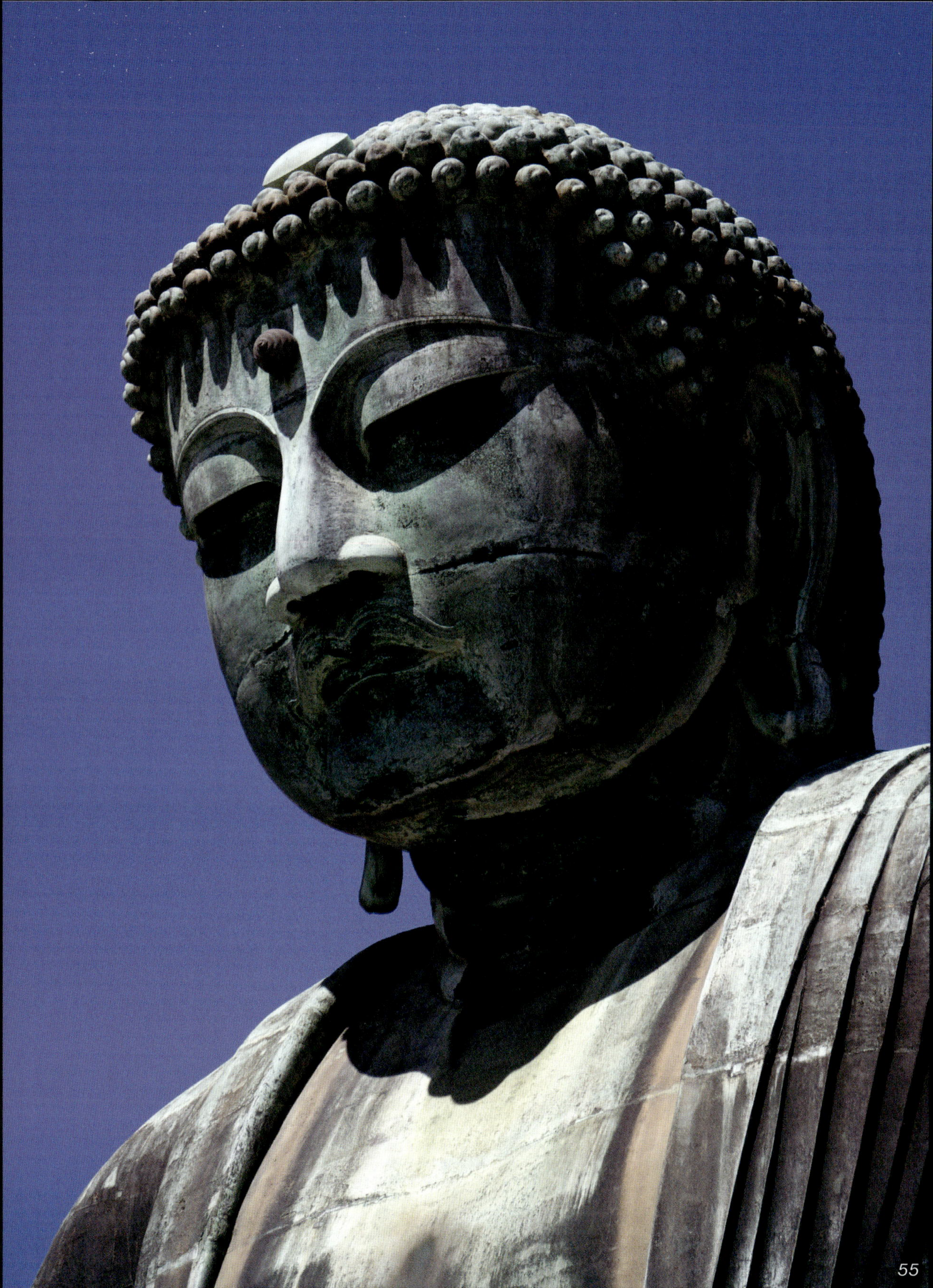

## Daibutsu

One of Kamakura's most famous sights is the colossal Daibutsu, 11.4 m tall and weighing more than 120 ton. The Great Buddha is of a serene beauty and is one of Japan's best-preserved examples of Buddhist art. The statue stands in the premises of Kōtoku-in just east of the city center. Dating from around 1252 the Daibutsu originally stood in a wooden hall that was damaged by typhoons and finally destroyed in the severe 1498 earthquake. Left without shelter the statue withstands the elements with success.

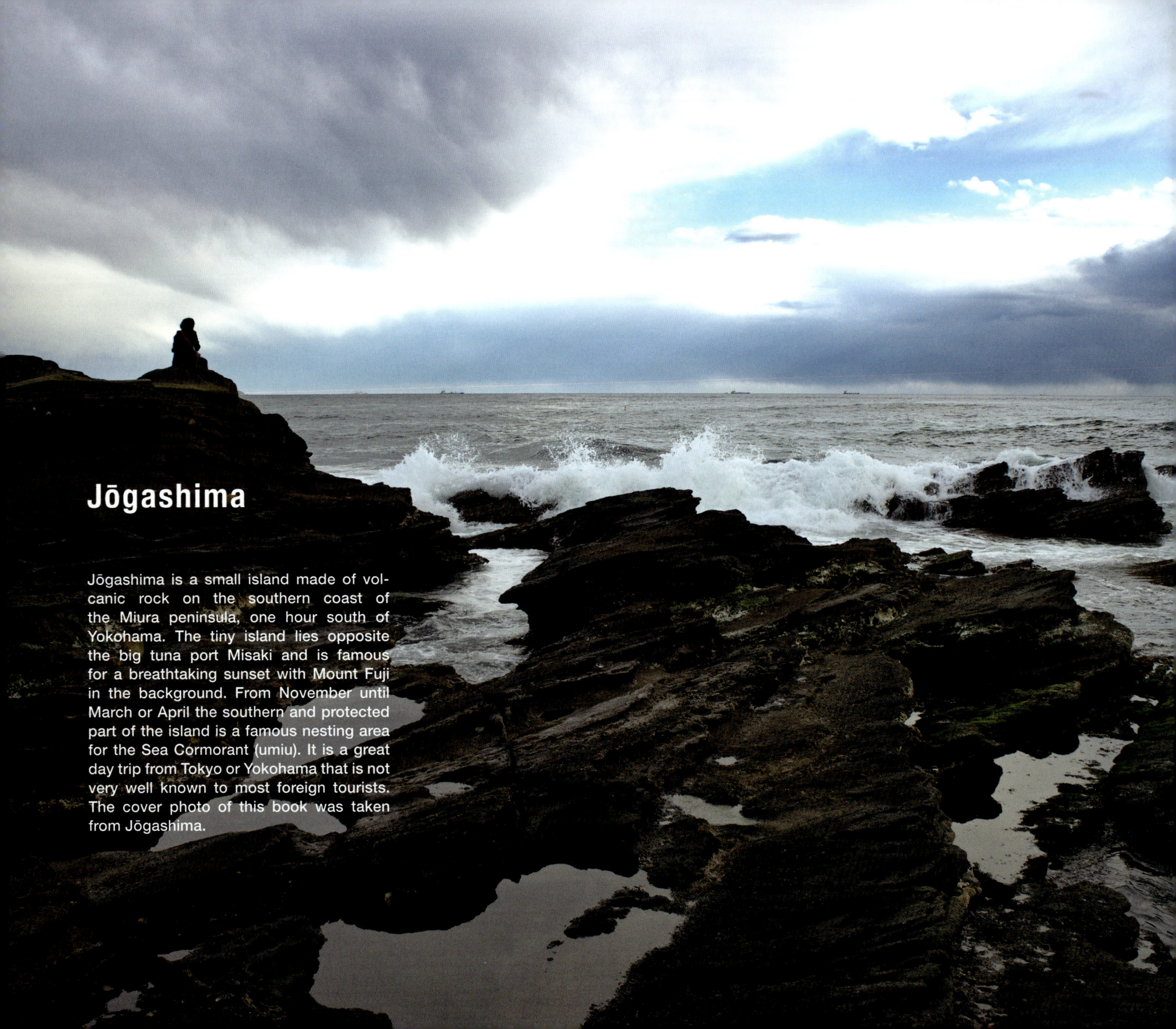

## Jōgashima

Jōgashima is a small island made of volcanic rock on the southern coast of the Miura peninsula, one hour south of Yokohama. The tiny island lies opposite the big tuna port Misaki and is famous for a breathtaking sunset with Mount Fuji in the background. From November until March or April the southern and protected part of the island is a famous nesting area for the Sea Cormorant (umiu). It is a great day trip from Tokyo or Yokohama that is not very well known to most foreign tourists. The cover photo of this book was taken from Jōgashima.

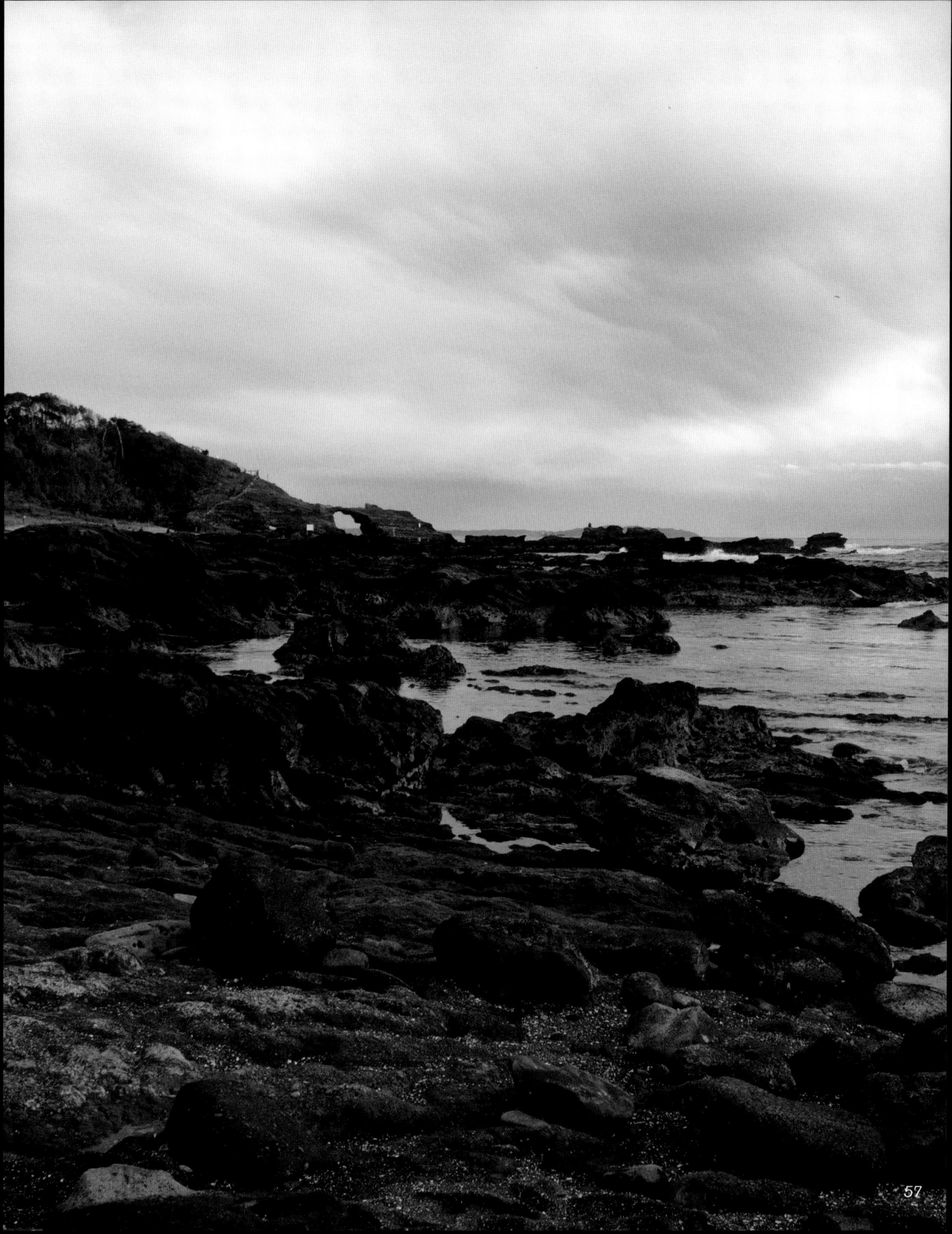

One of the popular landmarks of the island is this arch-shaped rock in the far end of the picture.

Until 1923 the rock was half-submerged and people used small boats to get through it. This coast, which was almost the exact epicenter of the great Kantō Earthquake, was lifted by 8 to 10 meters. Ever since, the rock forms a natural arch well above the sea level.

On a nice day the best way to visit Yokohama is by walking. Using the shuttle boat service that sails the three kilometers from Yokohama station to Yamashita Park Pier kicks off the day ideally. There is ample time to see the Landmark Tower, Minato Mirai, the famous red brick warehouses, Yokohama Bay Bridge and the ocean vessel Hikawa Maru passing by from the waterfront.

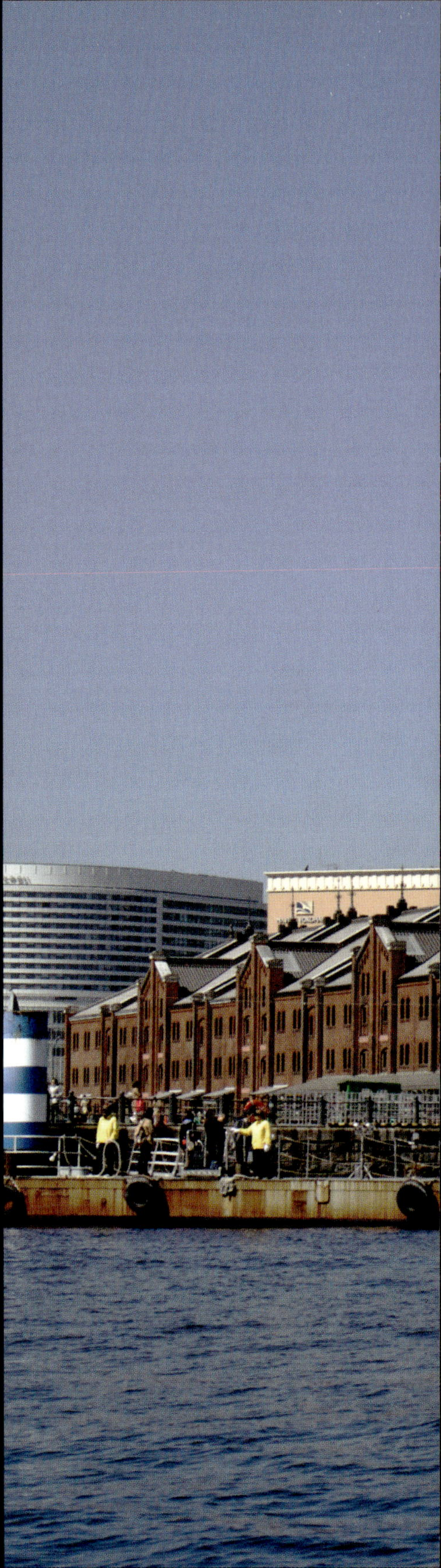

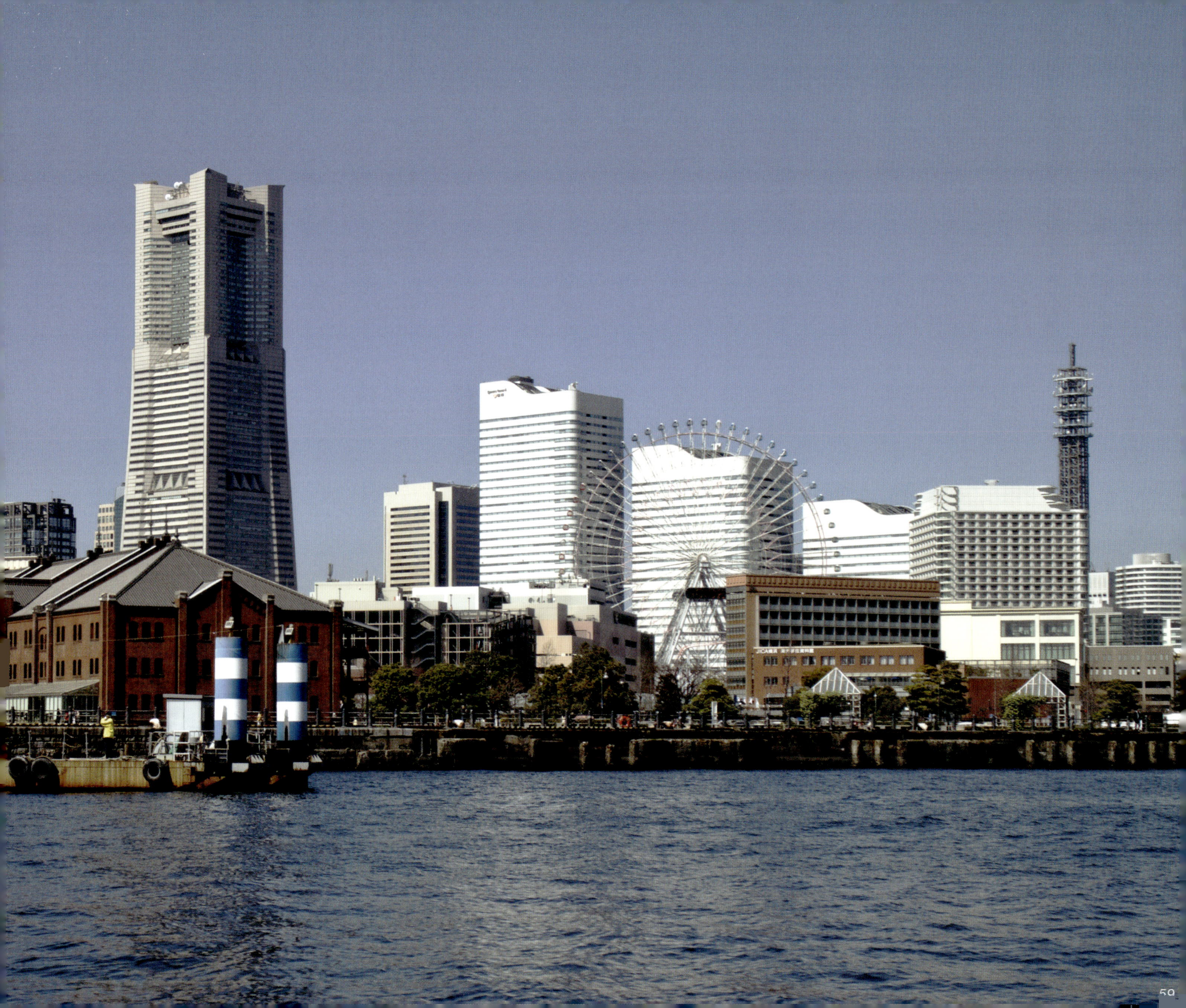

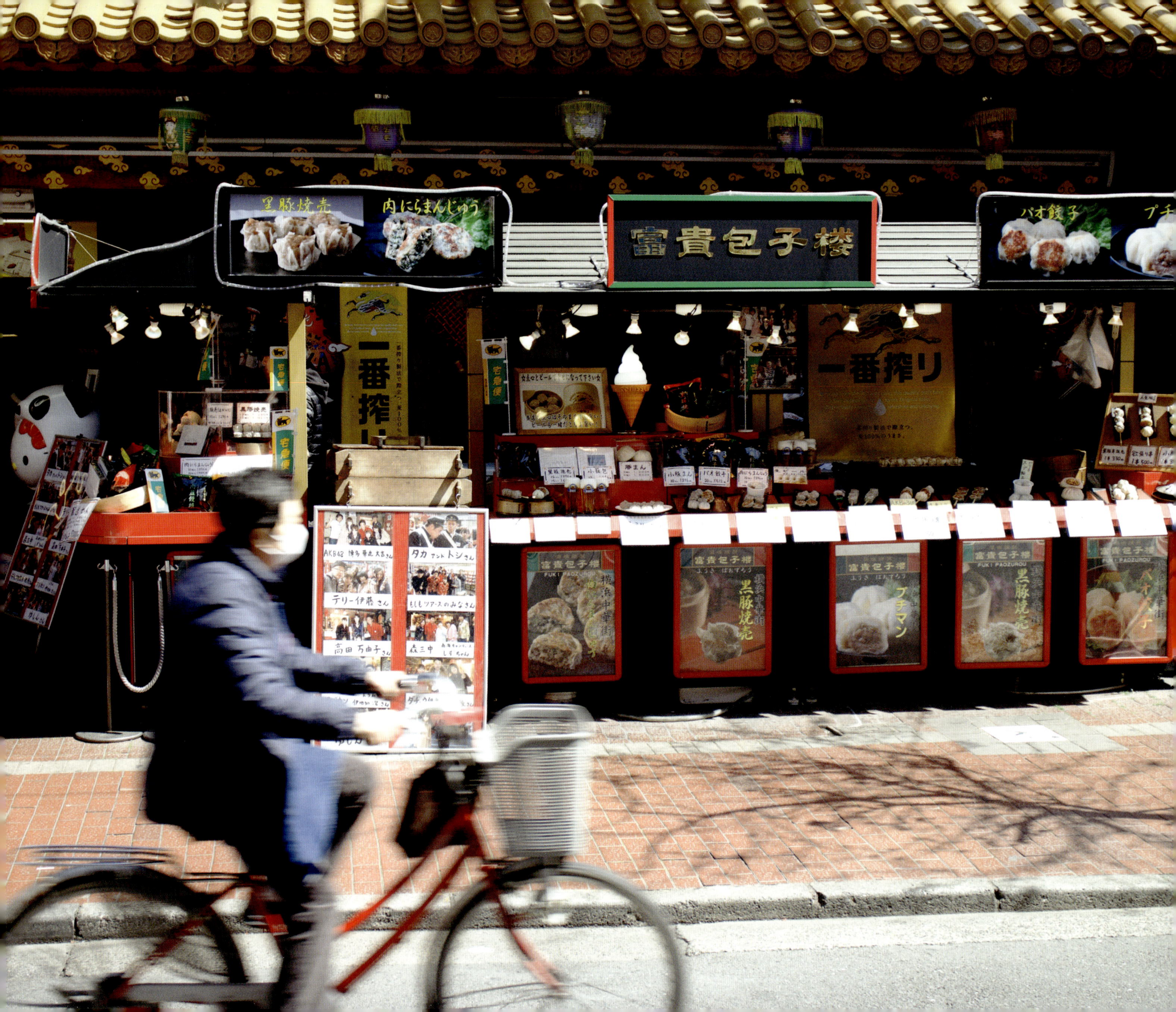
黒豚焼売
肉にらまんじゅう
富貴包子楼
パオ餃子
一番搾り
一番搾り
黒豚焼売
プチマン
黒豚焼売

## Chinatown

A visit to the city is not complete without taking a stroll in the maze of small streets of Chinatown and indulging yourself in the Chinese atmosphere. When the evening falls this quarter of the city becomes even more lively and although there are over two hundred Chinese restaurants at times it is hard to find a seat.

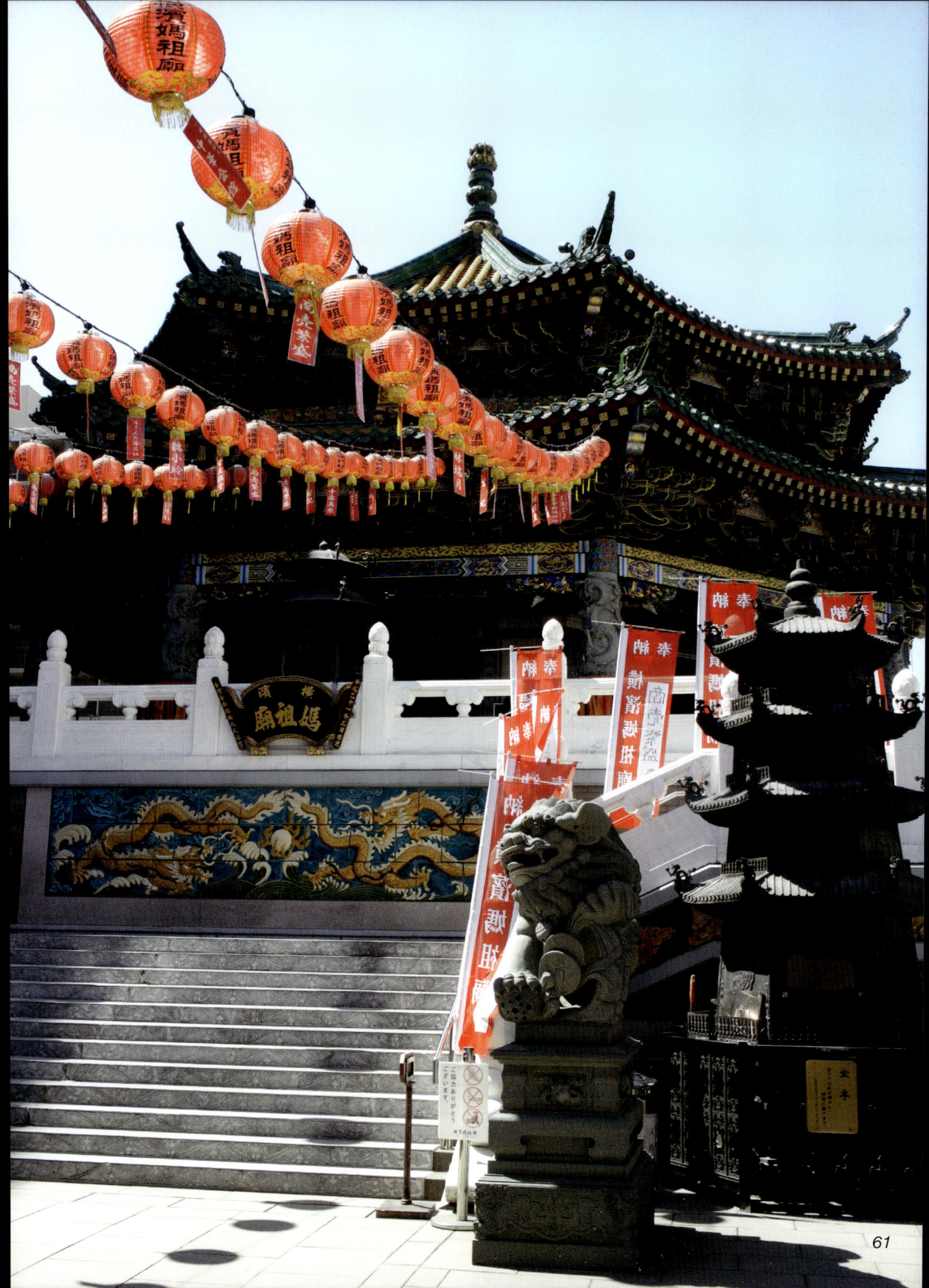


The nicely decorated Ma Zhu Miao temple was built to worship Ma Zhu, Chinese goddess of the sea and believed to protect sea travelers on their voyage.

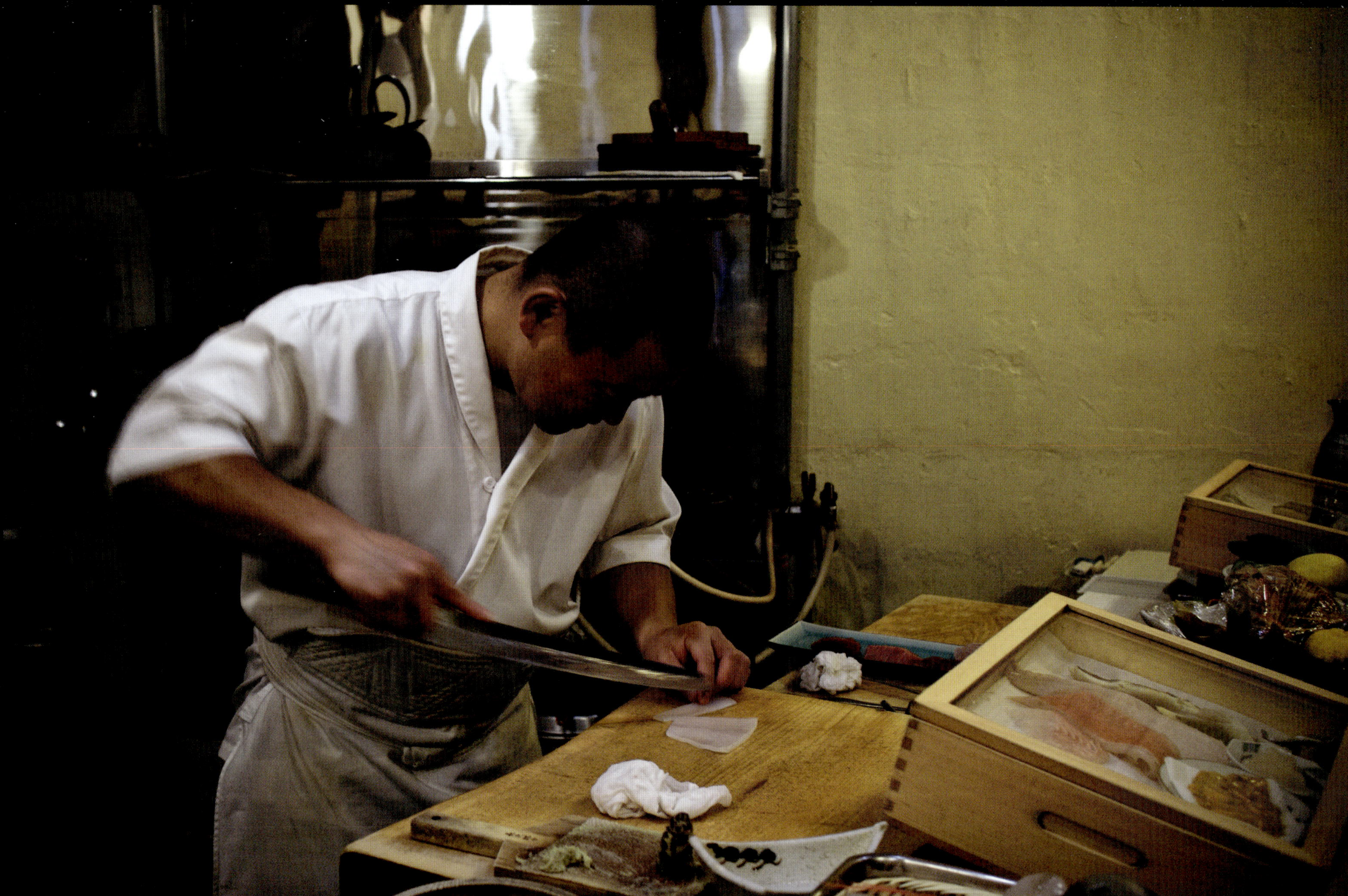

## Sushi and sashimi

Since millennia seafood has been an important element in the Japanese diet. The Japanese Archipelago is blessed with both warm and cold sea currents ensuring that in every season there is a great variety of fresh seafood. The origins of sushi go back to the ancient populations of Southeast Asia who were salting fish in rice allowing it to ferment so that the fish could be preserved in the warm climate. Gradually over time this became the Edo style nigiri-sushi we know today. For this type of sushi the chef hand-rolls vinegared rice and tops it with a bit of wasabi paste and a slice of raw fish.

Sashimi, now also appreciated more and more as a delicacy in the western world, is thinly sliced raw fish such as mackerel, tuna and salmon. It is almost always served with soy sauce and wasabi paste accompanied by thinly sliced daikon.
The chef from Sushi Hashimoto in Yokohama slices the fish in one fluent single pulling motion with a razor sharp yanagi knife. It takes years of experience to master this technique and although this comes at a price, dining while watching a chef preparing the sushi and sashimi is a great experience.

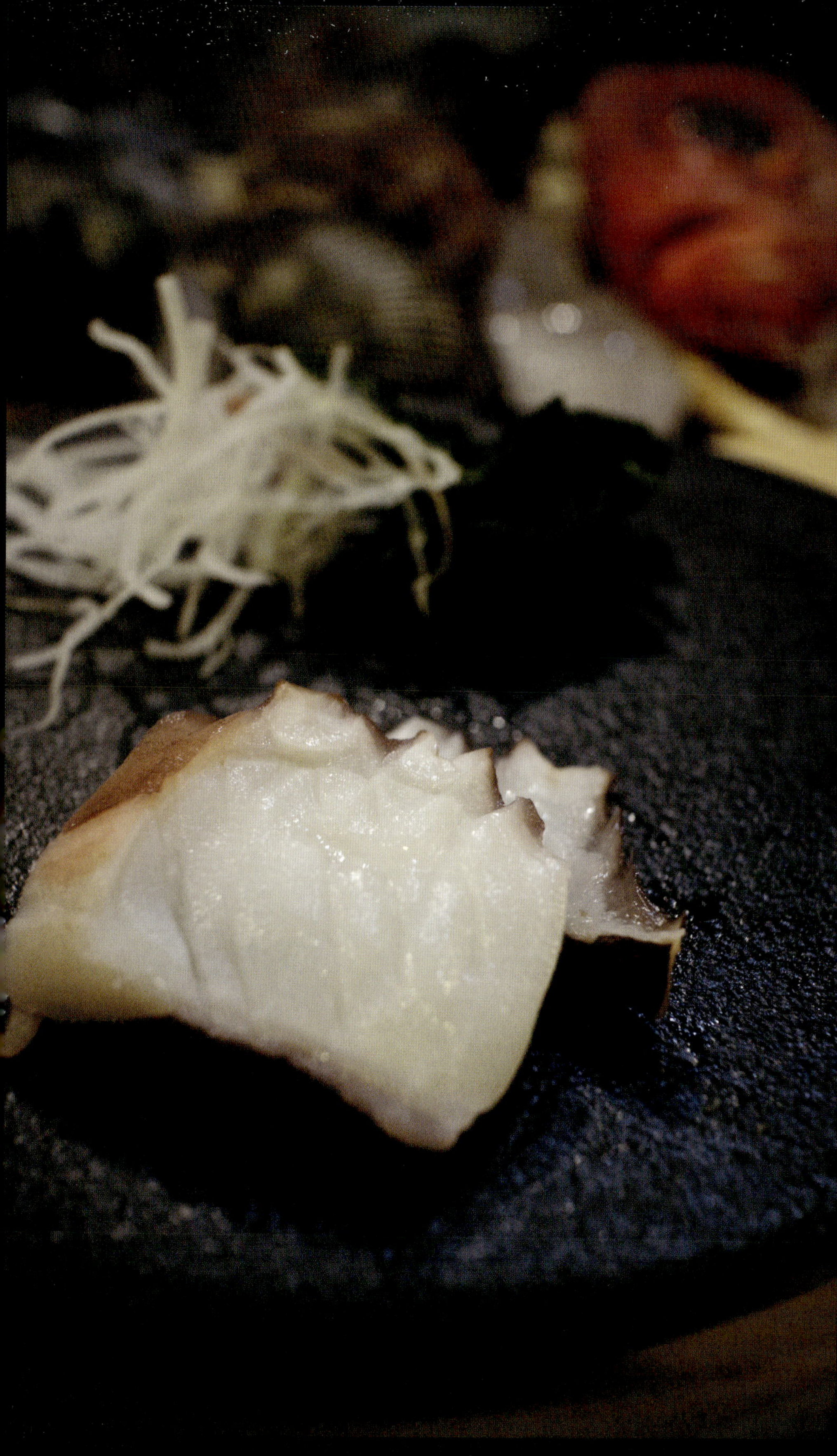

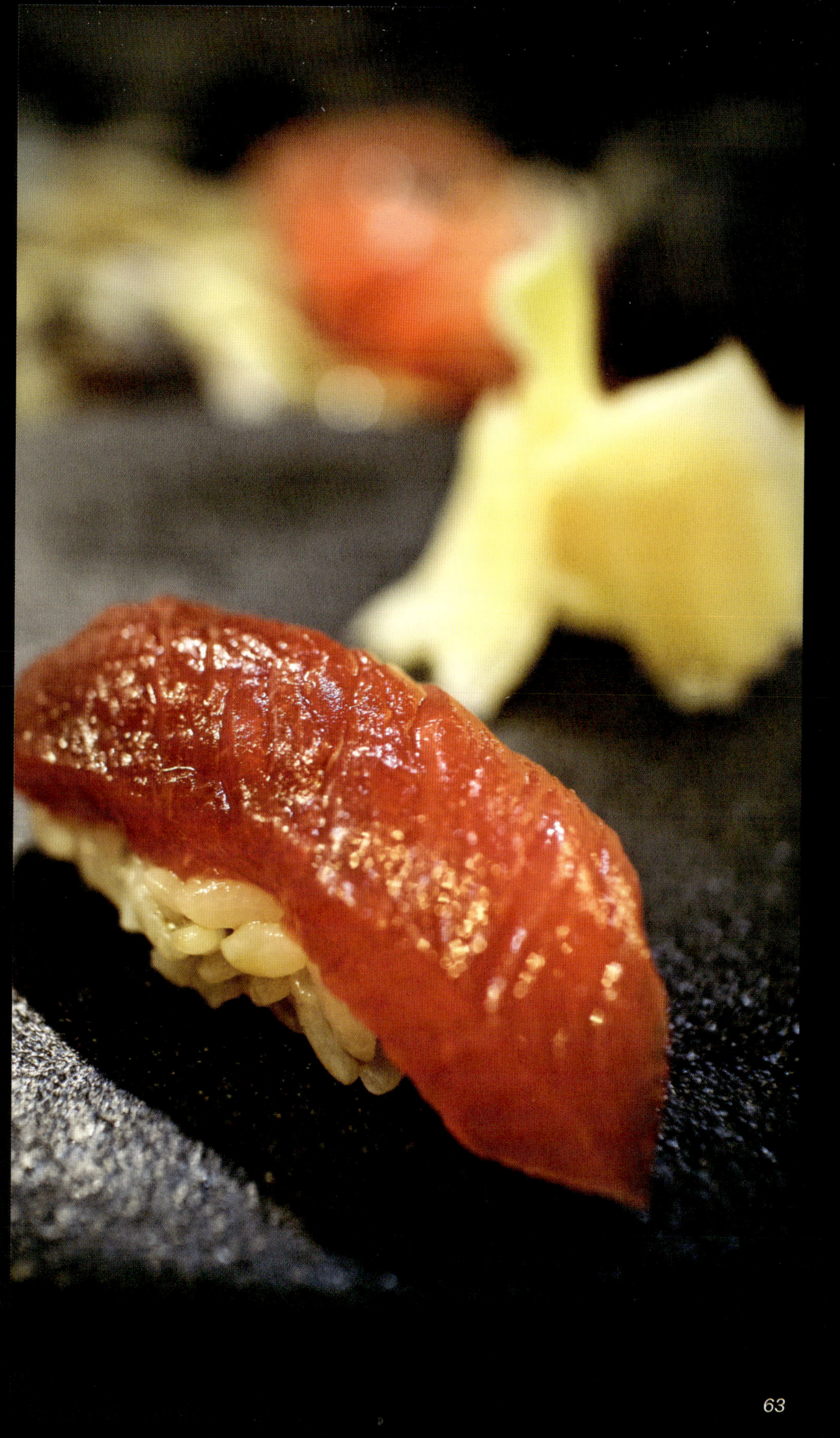

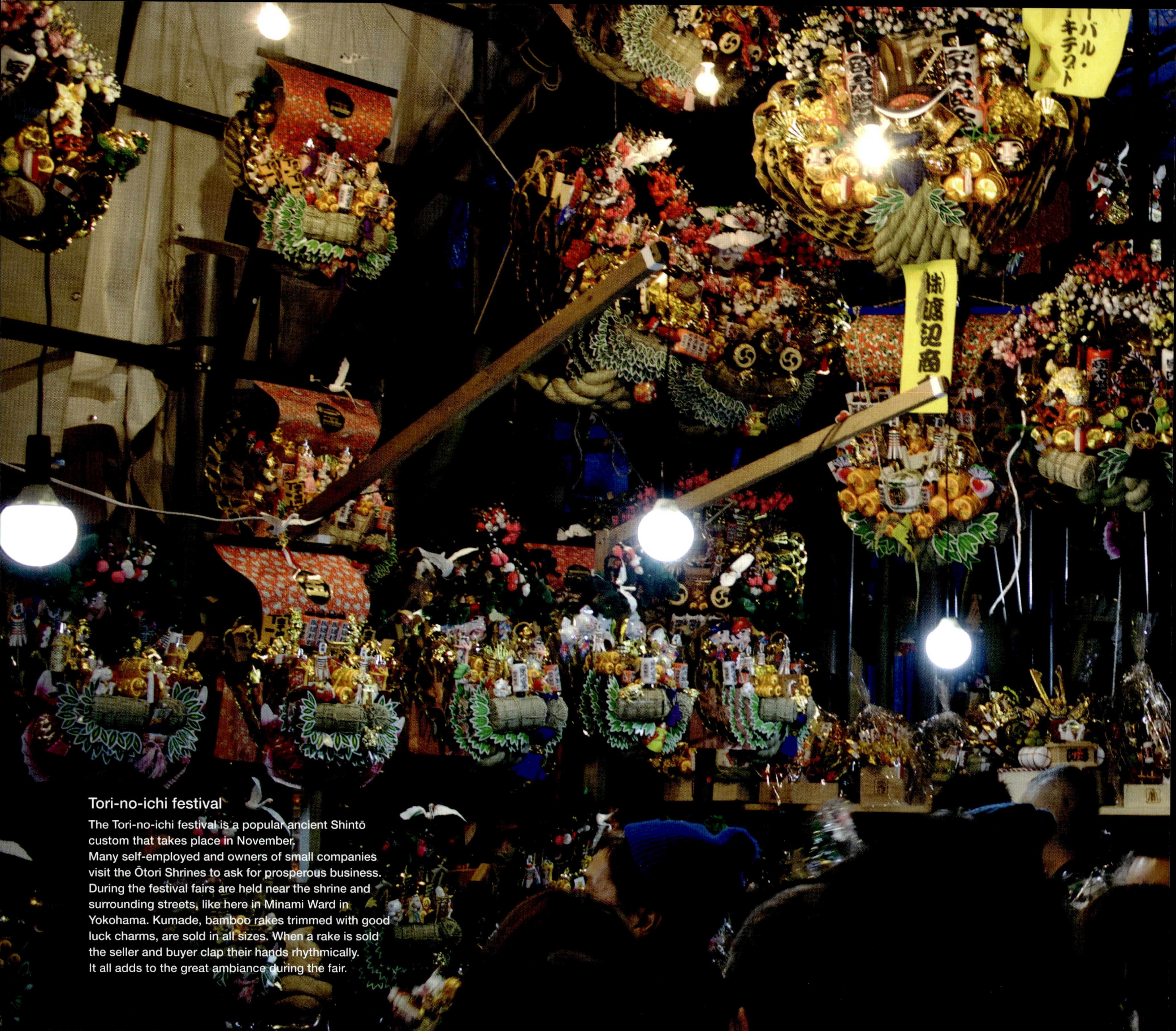

## Tori-no-ichi festival

The Tori-no-ichi festival is a popular ancient Shintō custom that takes place in November.
Many self-employed and owners of small companies visit the Ōtori Shrines to ask for prosperous business. During the festival fairs are held near the shrine and surrounding streets, like here in Minami Ward in Yokohama. Kumade, bamboo rakes trimmed with good luck charms, are sold in all sizes. When a rake is sold the seller and buyer clap their hands rhythmically.
It all adds to the great ambiance during the fair.

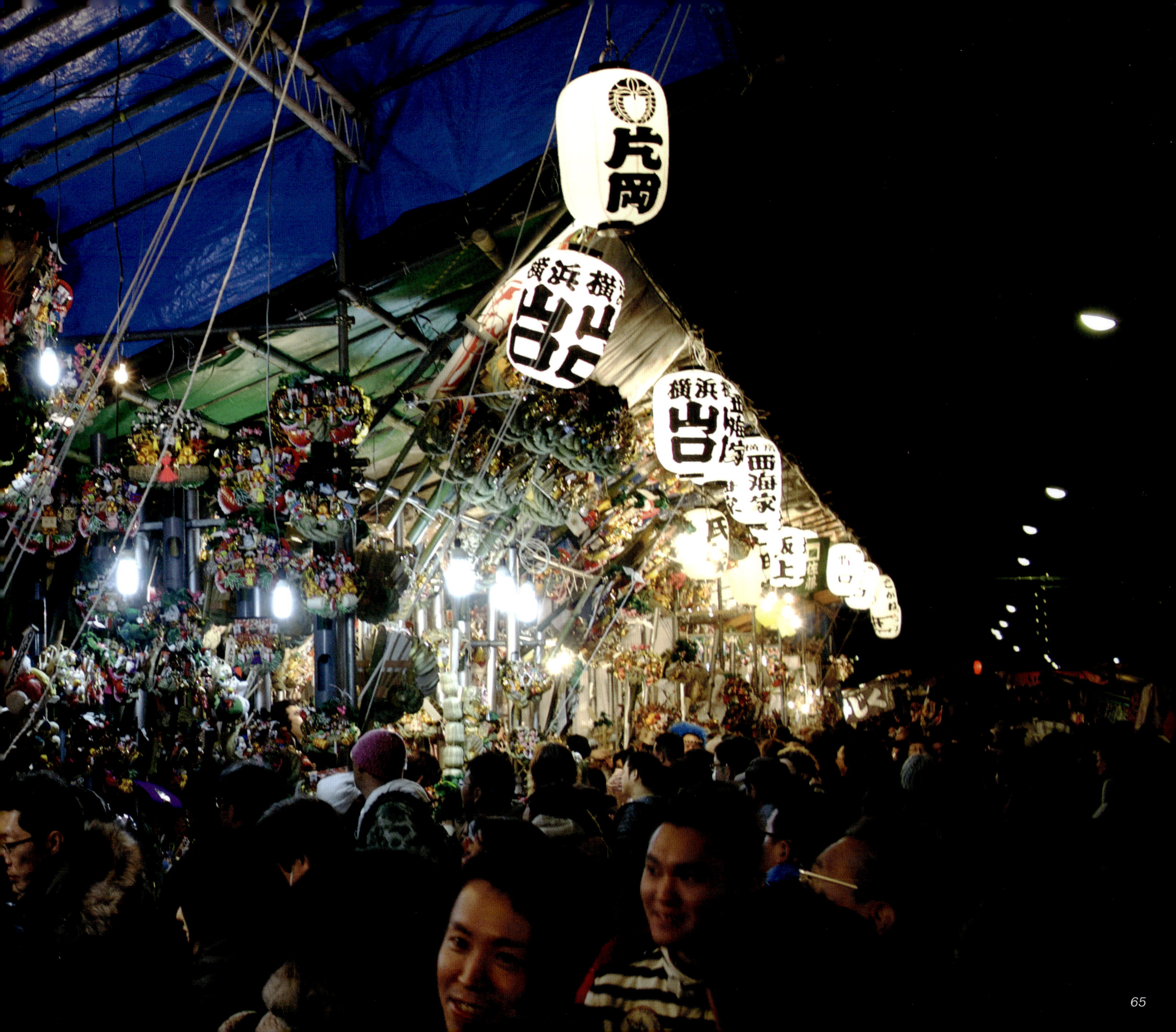
片岡
横浜
横浜

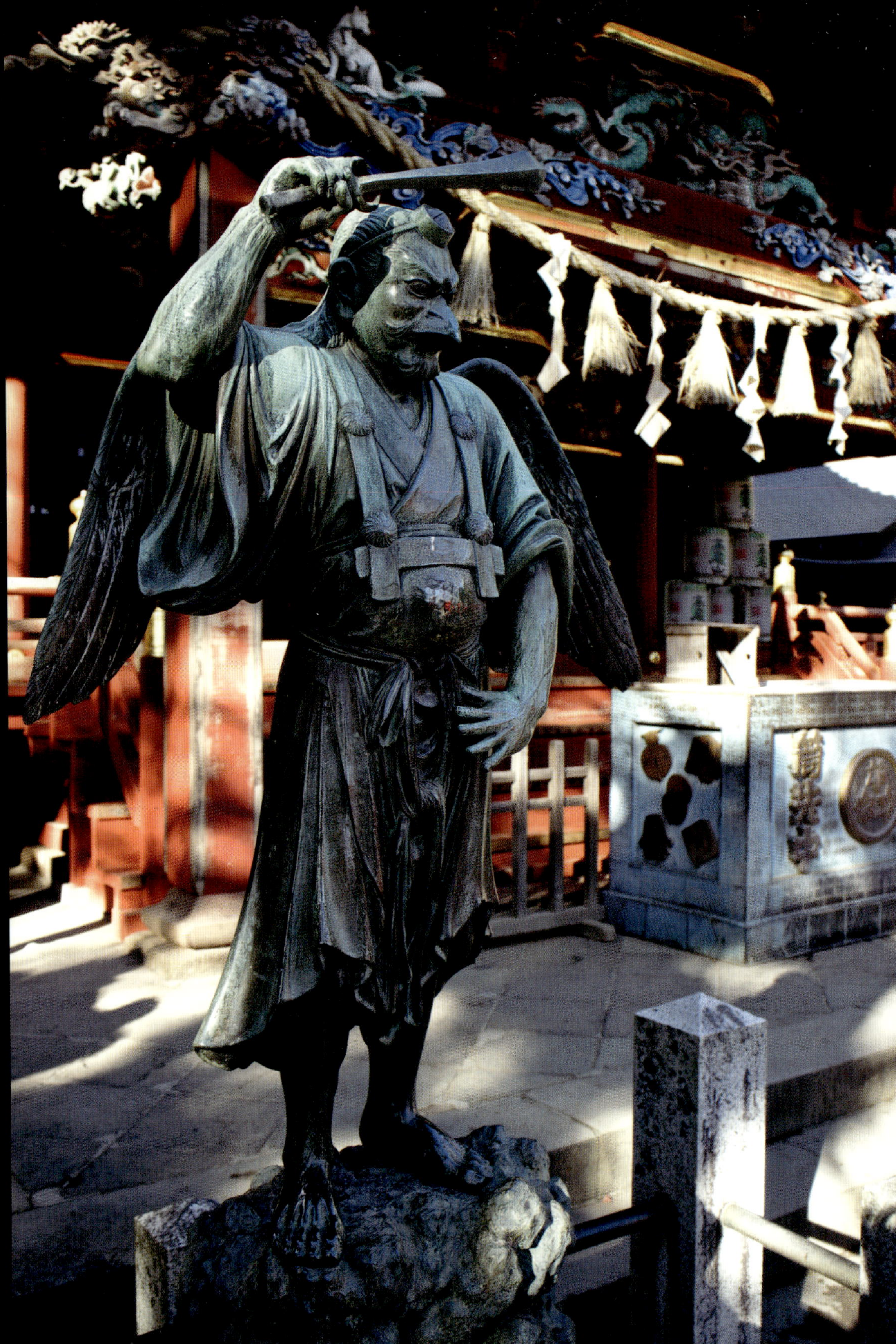

## Mount Takao

A nice easy day trip out of Tokyo leads to Mount Takao (599 m). 'Takao-san' is climbed by millions of visitors each year and has been awarded with three stars in Michelin's green guide of Japan.
A pilgrim trail takes you from the base station past a Buddhist temple to the summit in about 90 minutes. This temple, known as Takao-san Yakuo-in, is believed to have been built in 744. On their way to the top many visitors make a stop in the temple to pray for good fortune.

Mount Takao is closely associated with the devotion of Tengu, a long nosed deity. They are often depicted holding an uchiwa (Japanese fan) that sweeps away misfortune and brings good luck. Various Tengu statues can be found at the temple and other spots around the mountain.

On a clear day the top of the mountain offers great views over Tokyo, Yokohama, Mount Fuji and the Japanese Alps.

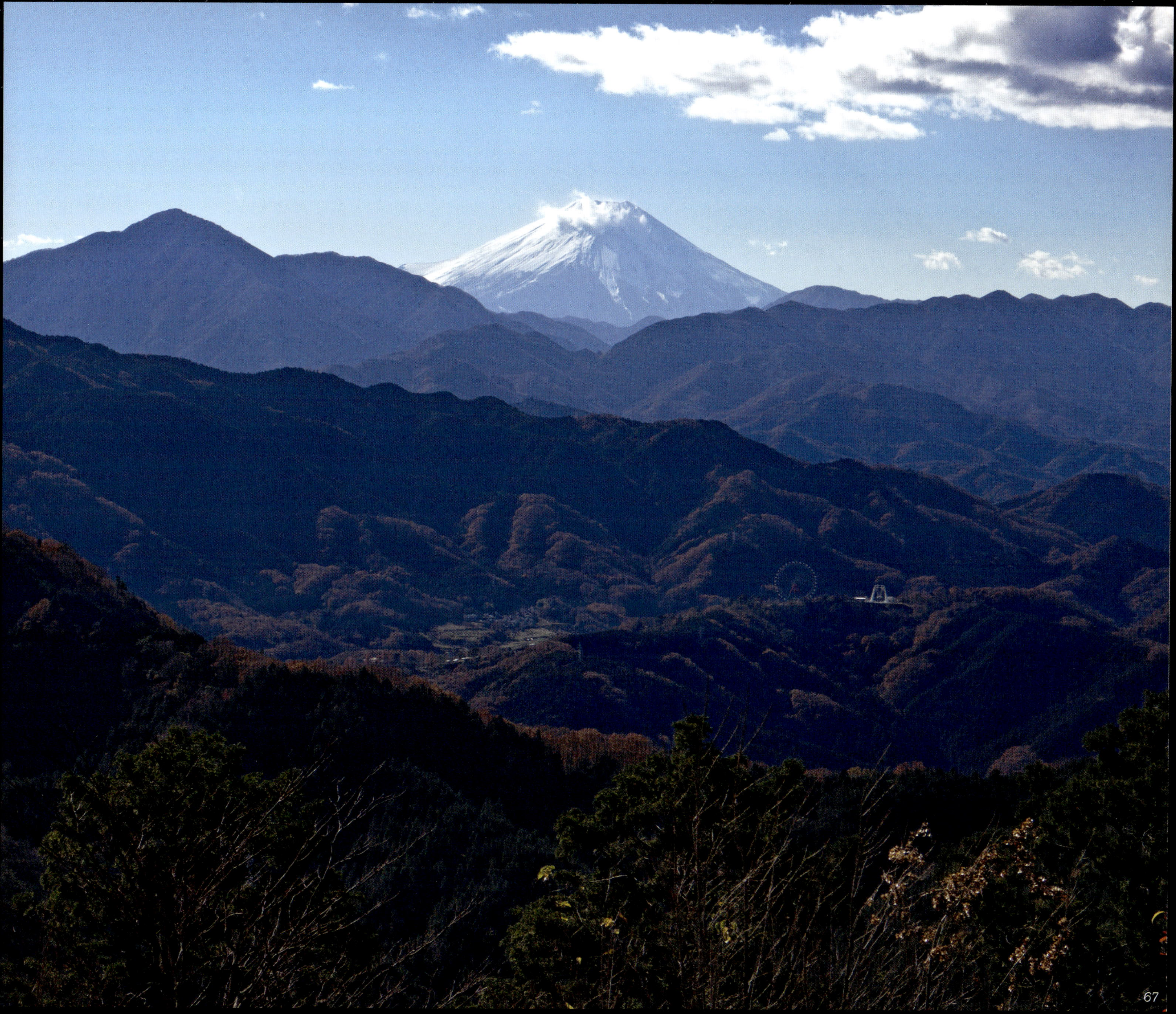

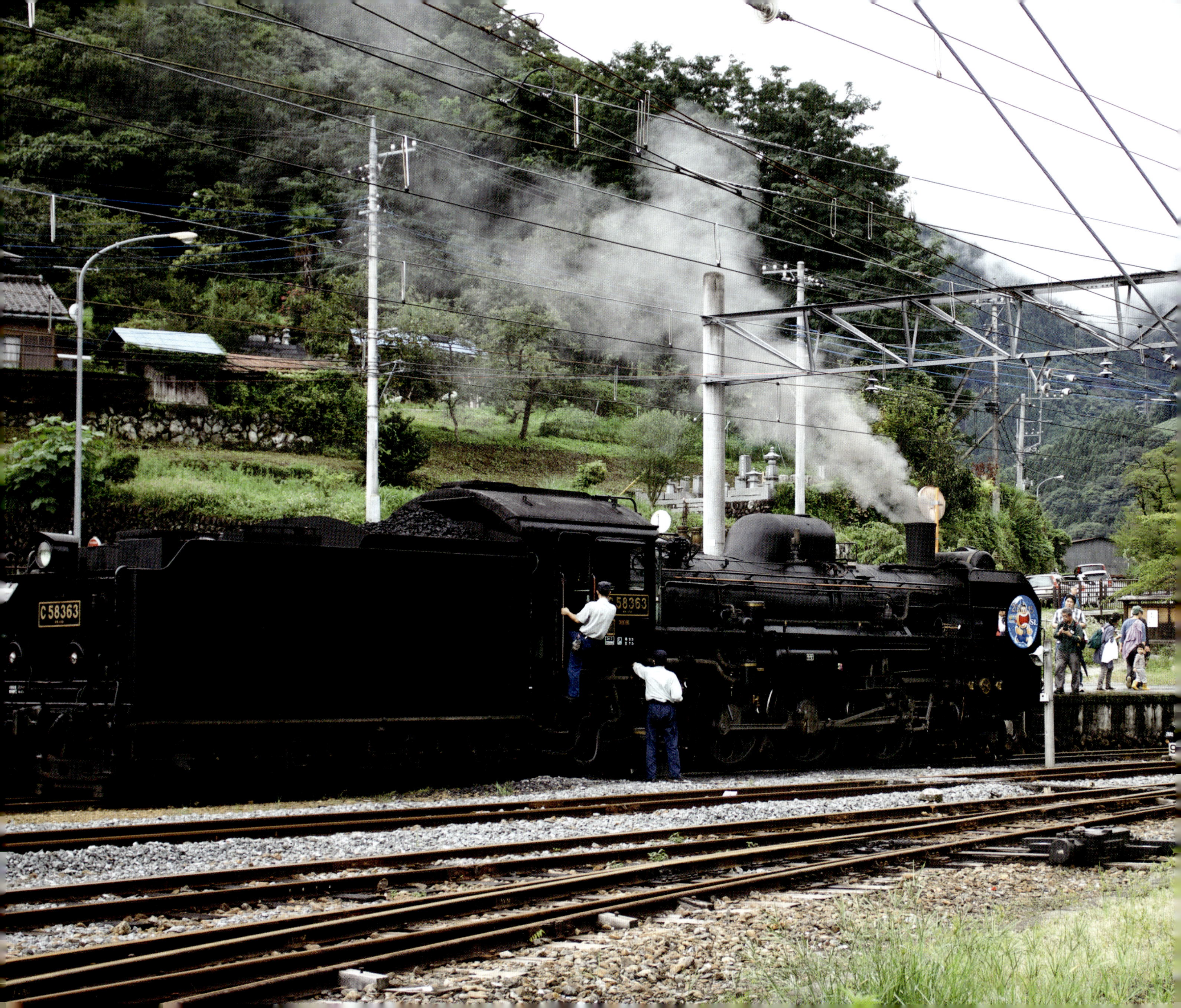
C58363

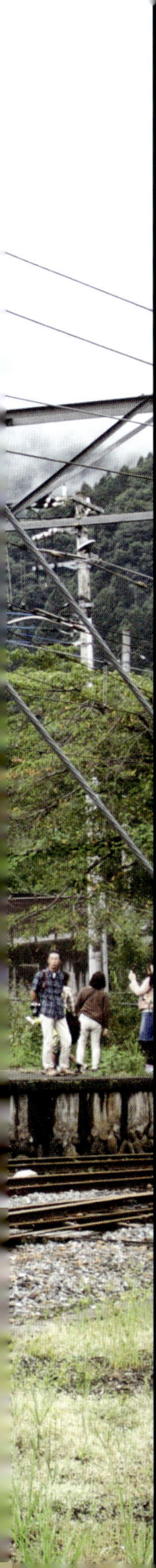

# Nagatoro

Nagatoro is a small town and train station on the Chichibu line that lies amidst a prefectural natural park in Saitama, about two hours from Tokyo. This friendly town and the surrounding area is barely known by foreign travelers, although Nagatoro has been attracting many Japanese tourists for over 100 years. Especially loved is the traditional boat tour on the Arakawa River. Combined with a ride on the steam train it is great nostalgic fun for young and old.

### The Paleo Express

Since 1988 the Paleo Express steam train runs the 57 km between Kumagaya Station and Mitsumine-guchi Station and makes a stop in Nagatoro. The locomotive is named after a genus of dinosaurs – the Paleoparadoxia – that once inhabited the area. The complete trajectory is about 90 minutes and takes you through the scenic mountainous landscape of Chichibu passing through small towns and crossing wild water rivers.

### Arakawa River Boating

Although pleasant in all seasons, nothing is more appealing than riding on the Arakawa River one of these traditional wooden Japanese long boats on a hot summer day. The tour starts and ends tranquil but be prepared for some rapids and the accompanying splash of water in the boat. Various companies also offer rafting and canoeing activities.

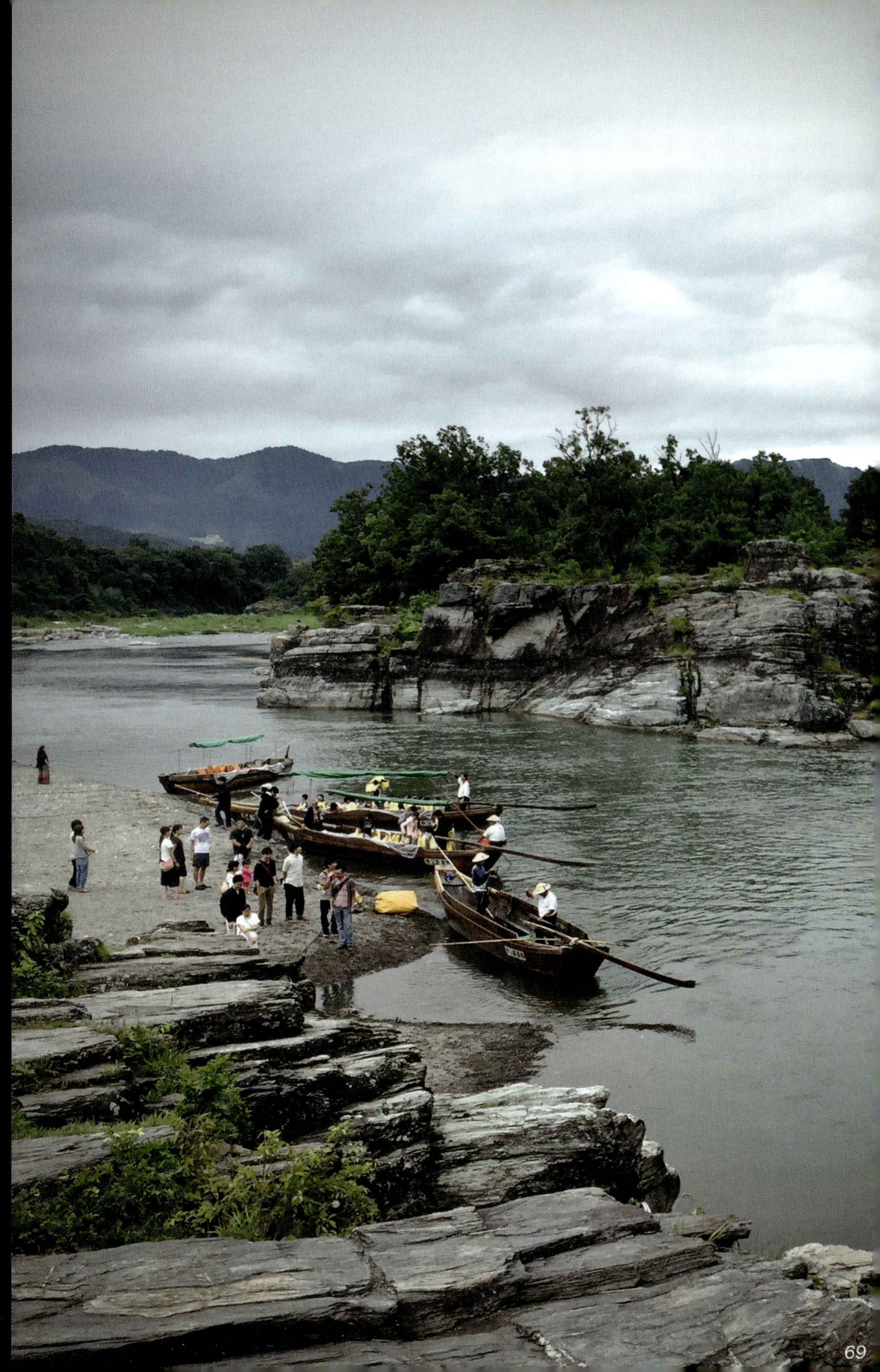

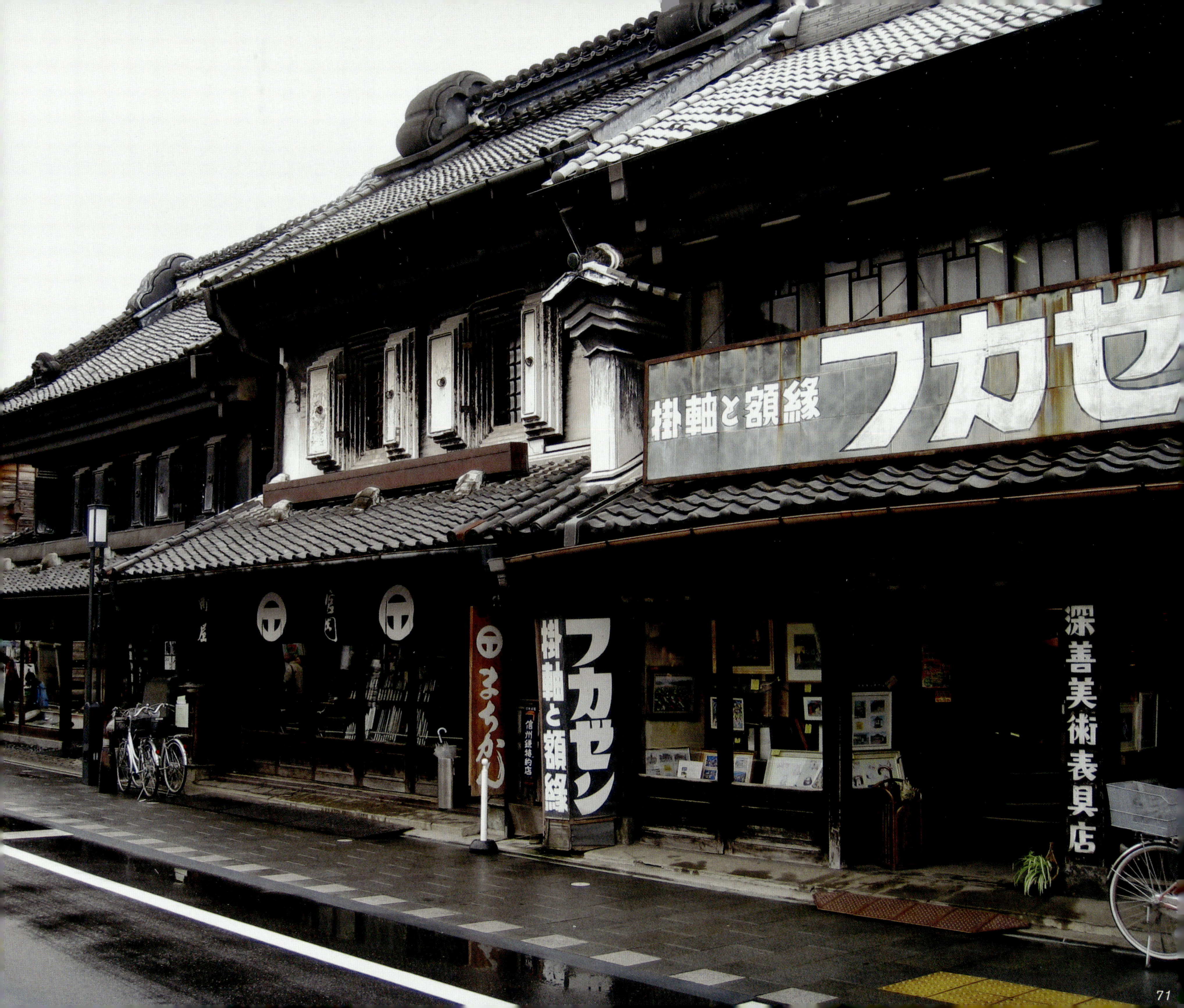
掛軸と額縁
フカゼン
掛軸と額縁
フカゼン
深善美術表具店

# Nikkō

Nikkō is the gateway to the mountains and forests of the Nikkō National Park and within living memory the area has always taken a prominent place in the Shintō and Buddhist religion.

It is in these cedar forests that the magnificent and breathtaking shrines and temples of Nikkō are located as well as the tomb of the shogun Tokugawa Ieyasu. He was one of Japan's greatest statesmen and a smart military strategist. After having won the epic battle of Sekigahara in 1600 his rule began. It laid the foundations of the Tokugawa shogunate that would remain in power over a unified Japan until the Meiji restoration in 1868.

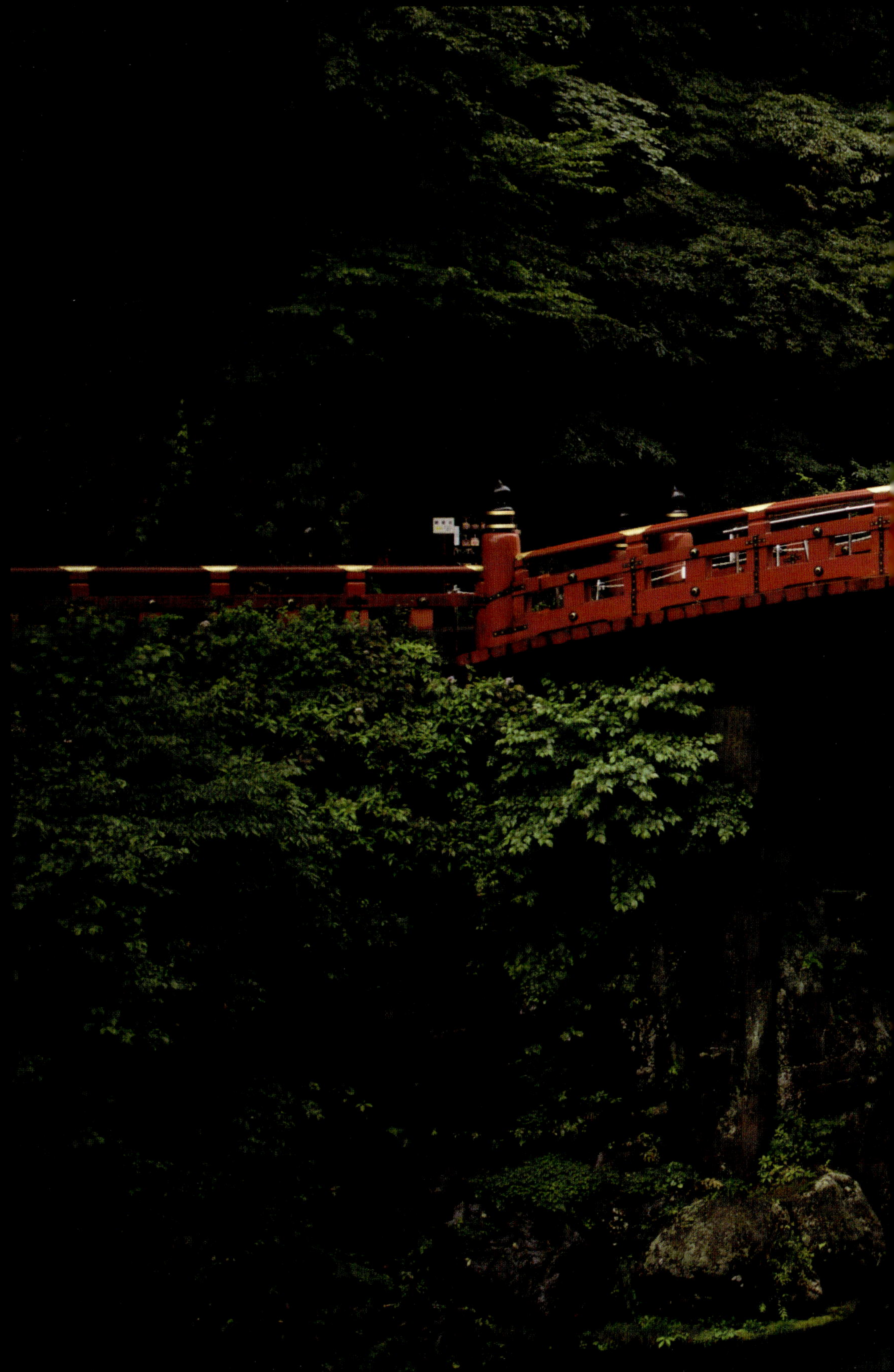

Shin-kyō Bridge

According to an old legend, it was here that, at the end of the Nara period, the Buddhist priest Shōdō Shonin could not cross the wild water river on his way to Mount Nantai. Helped by the gods, two snakes appeared forming the bridge to give way to the priest and his party. Based on this legend the original wooden bridge, from where the shogun and nobles entered the sacred premises of Nikkō, was built in 1636. Behind the bridge in the forest are world famous temples and shrines amongst which Tōshōgū. This shrine was built for Tokugawa Ieyasu, a showcase of Japanese craftsmanship built at huge cost and unequalled in its kind.

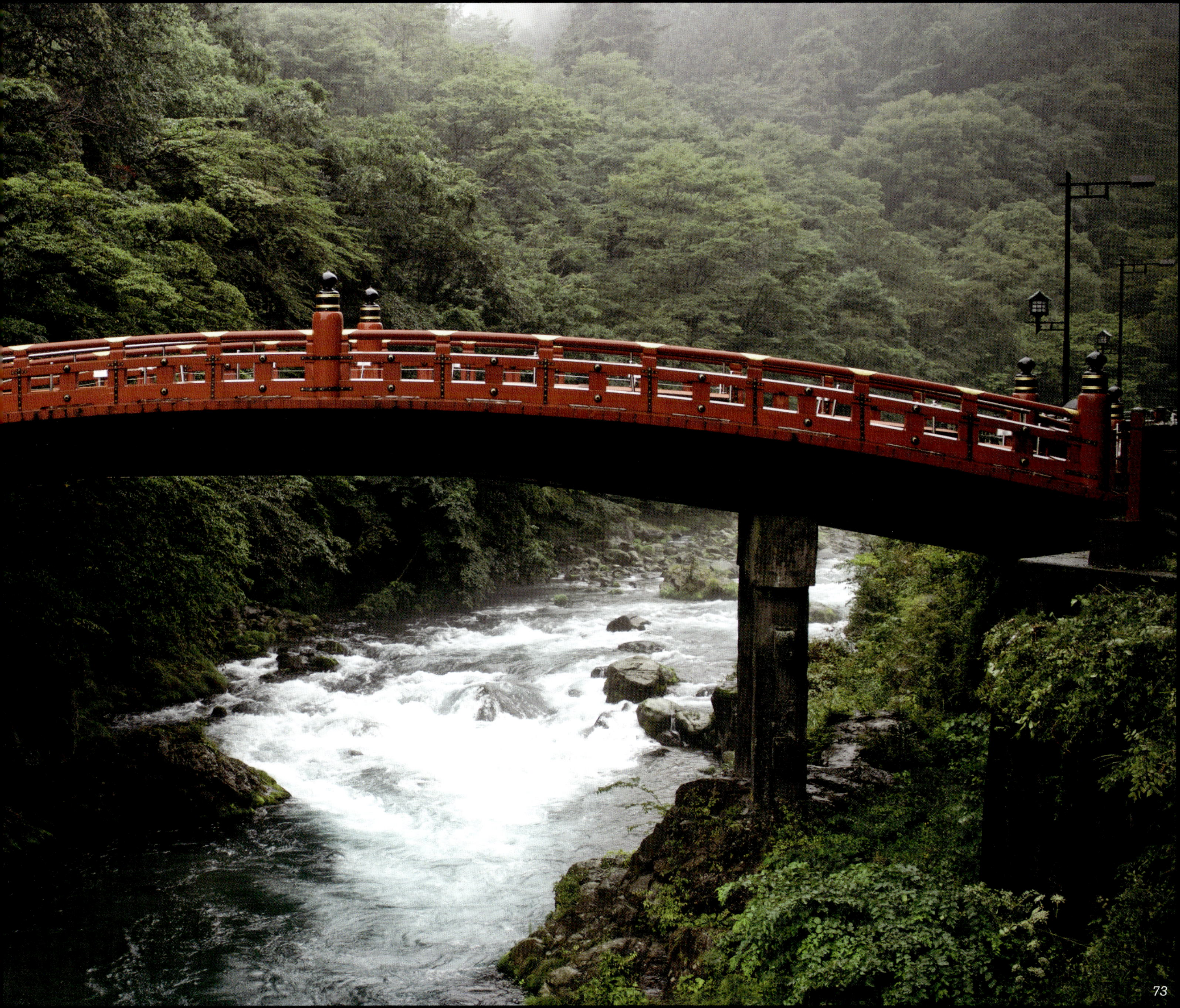

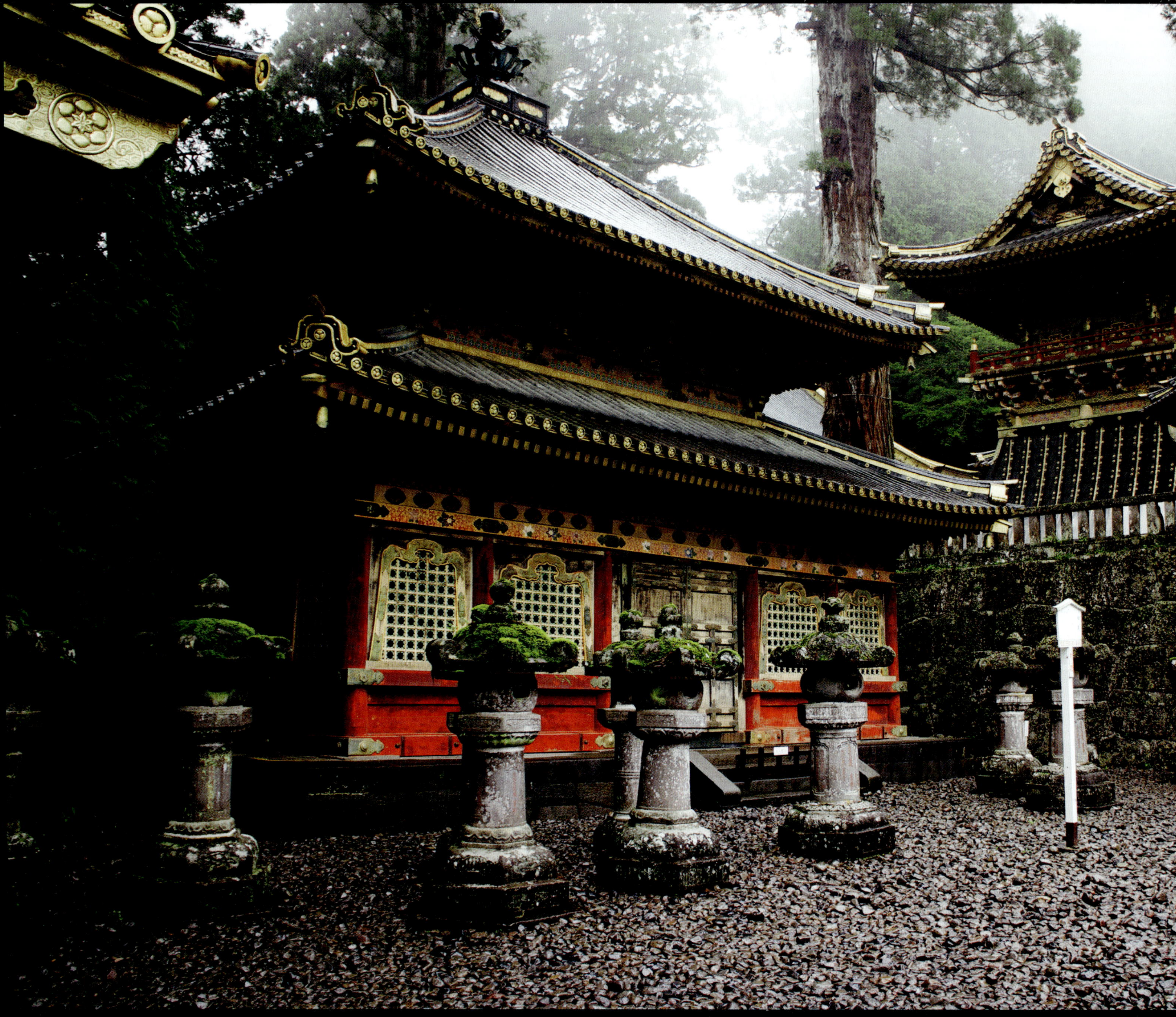

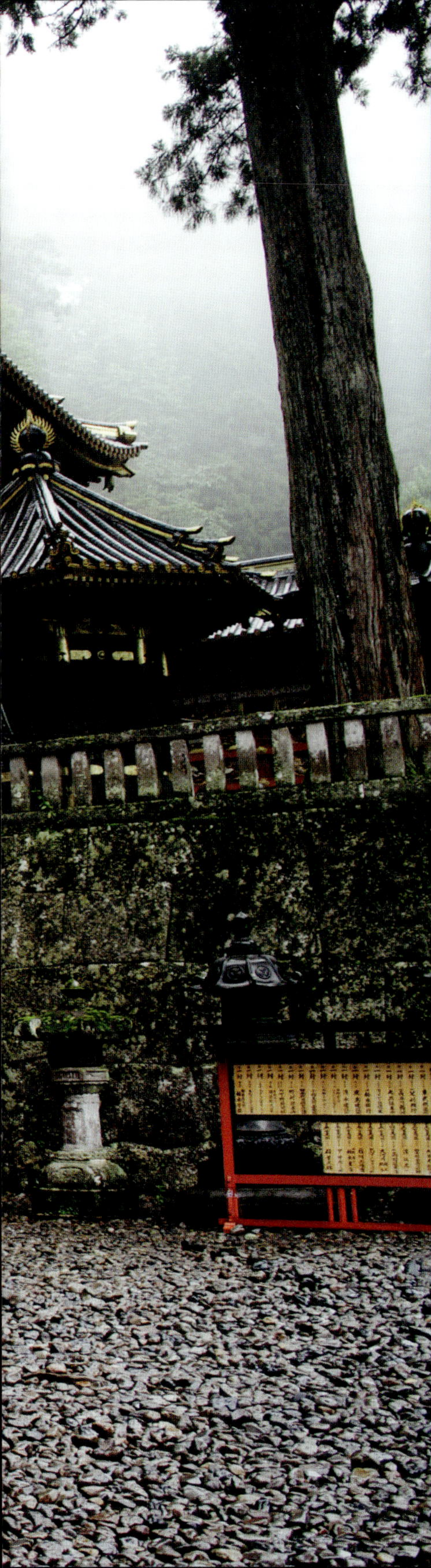

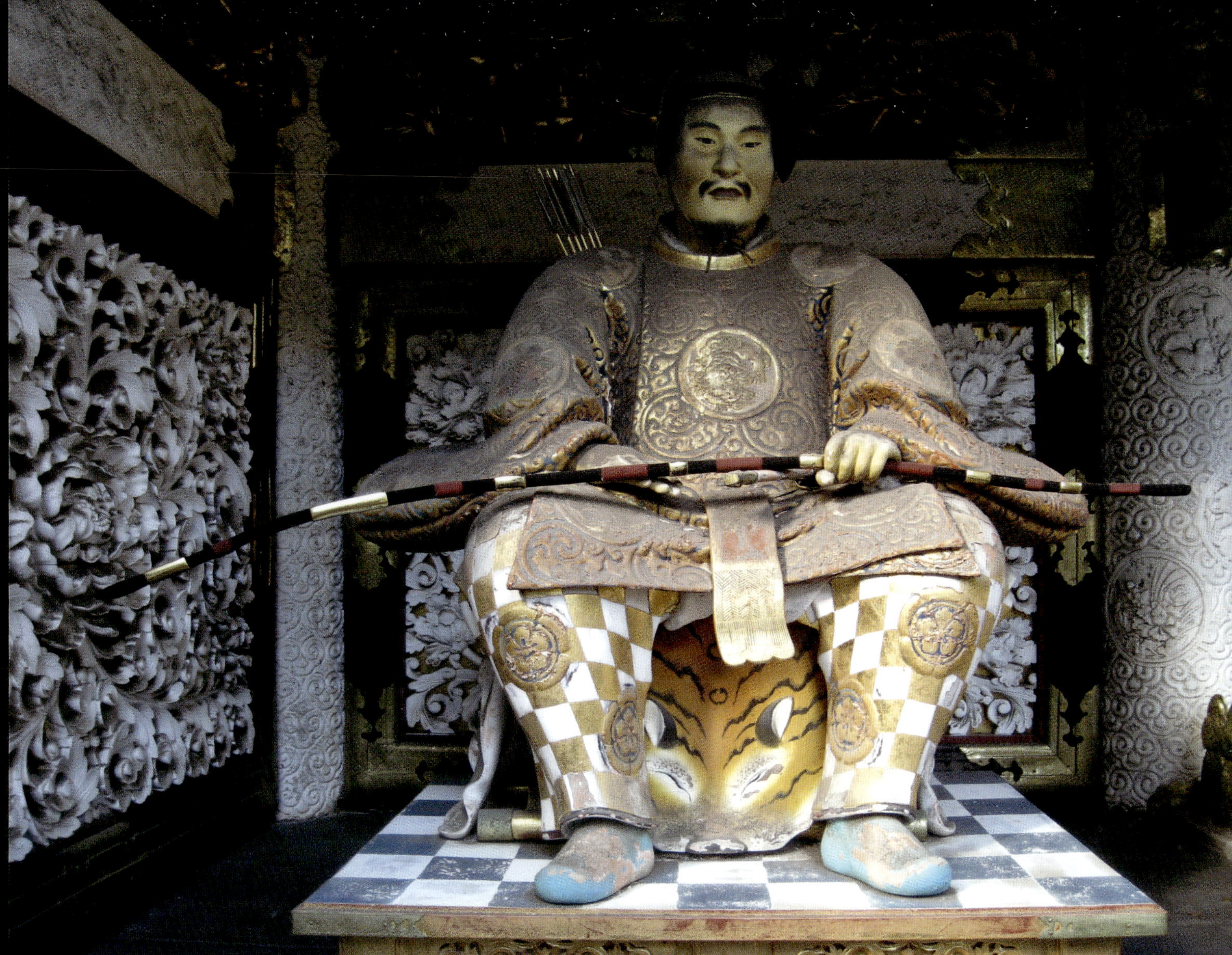

Sutra library

One of the guardians of the massive and elaborately ornate Yōmei-mon, the gate that gives access to the main hall of Tōshōgū.

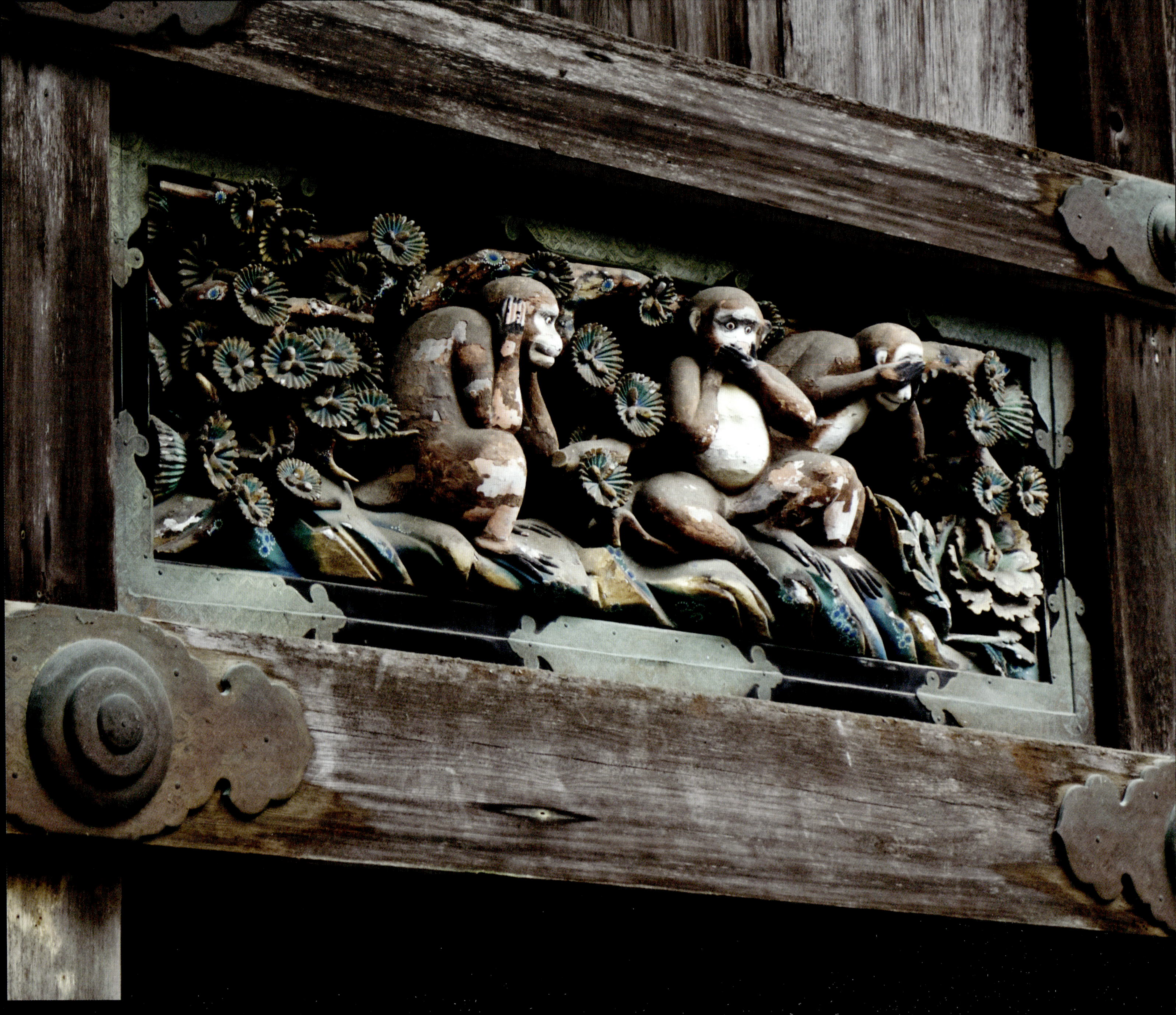

Sanzaru, the three wise monkeys, is a small carved wooden panel above the sacred stables. Monkeys are considered to be guardians of the horses. They stand for the universal proverb 'hear no evil, speak no evil, see no evil'. This is a picture no photographer wants to miss.

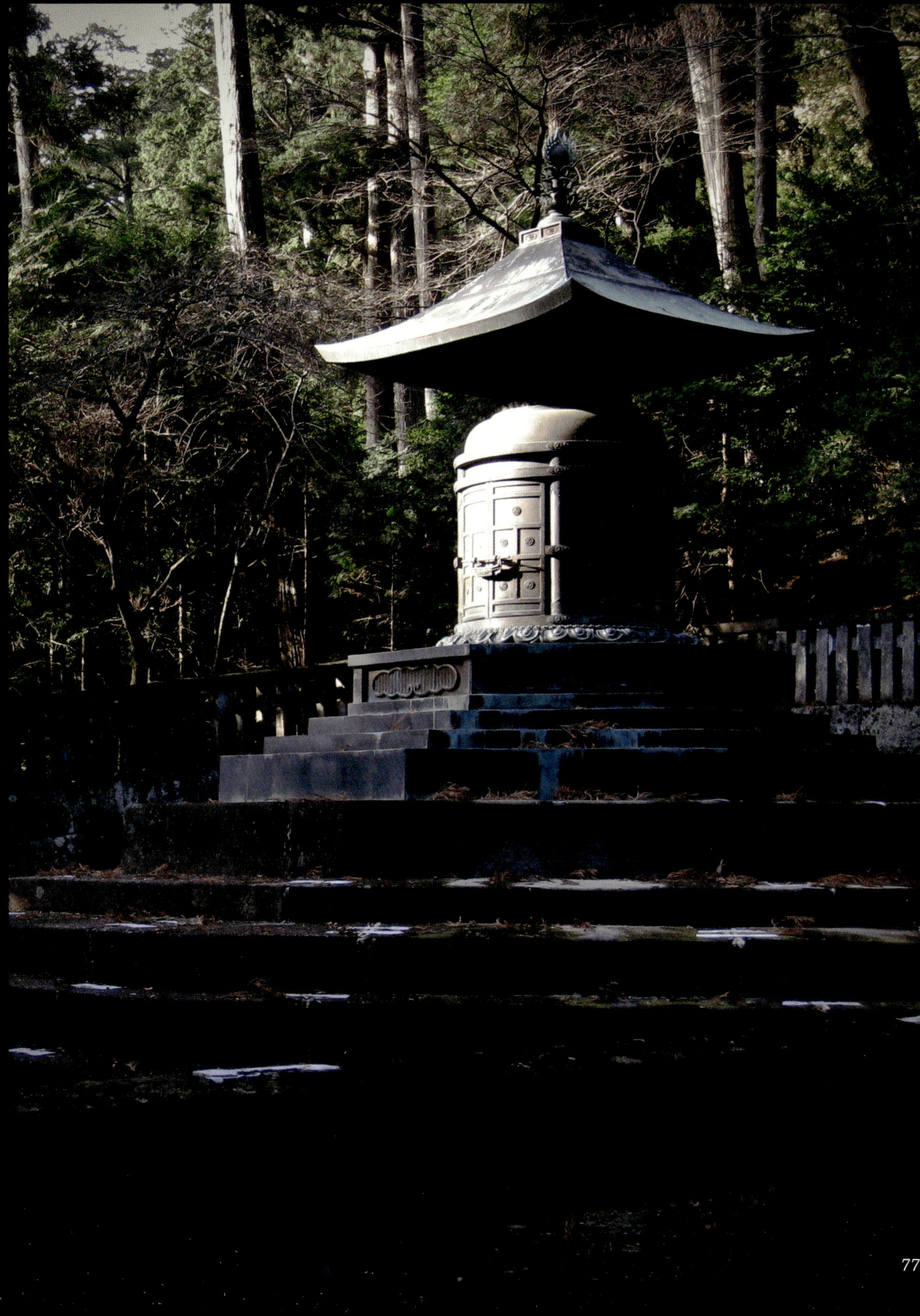

The tomb of Tokugawa Ieyasu (1542-1616) can be reached after climbing a steep path through the dark cedar forest with a seemingly endless number of steps. The setting amidst these massive century-old trees is imposing and fits the grandeur of this shogun.

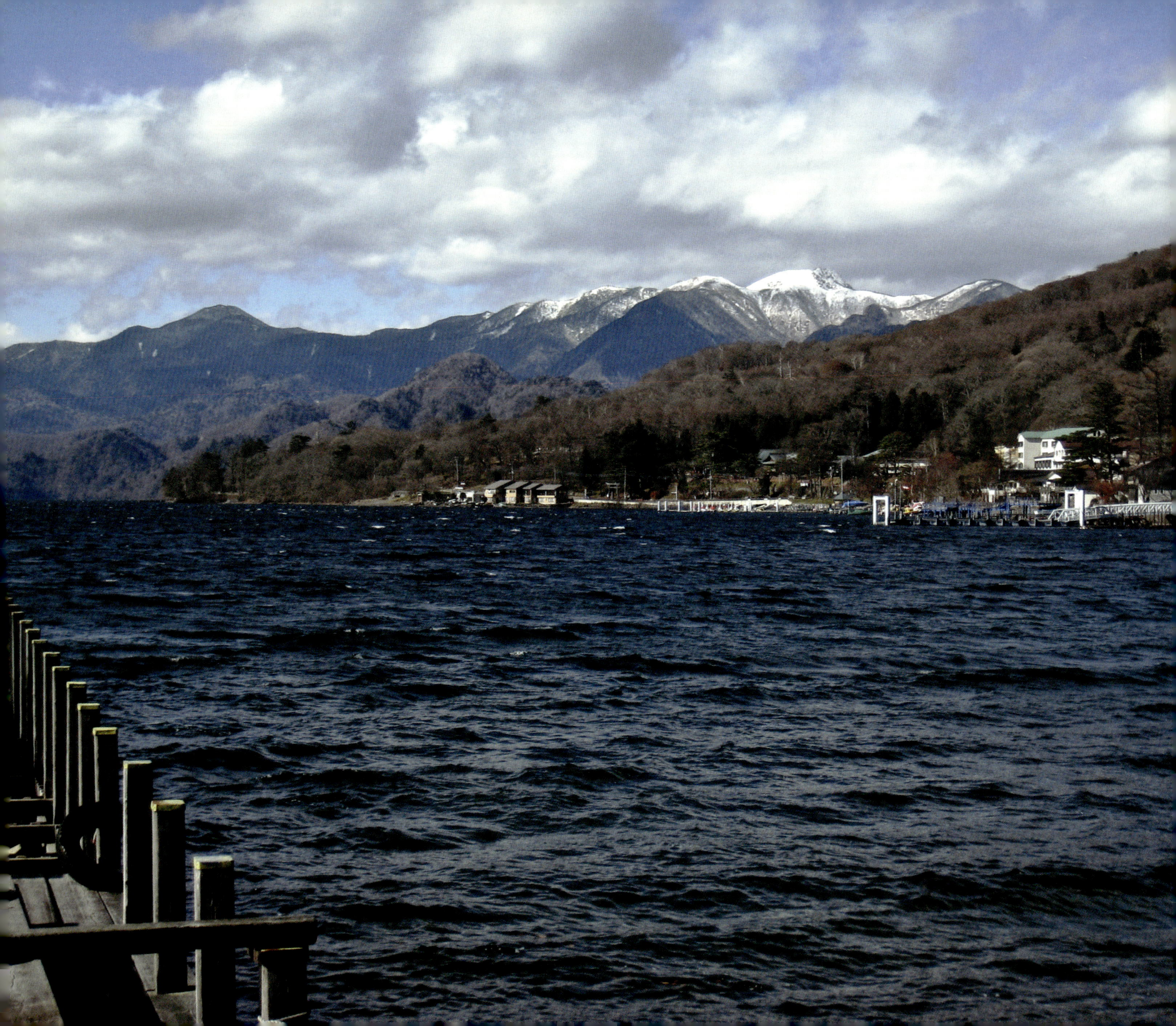

## Chūzenji

The volcanic Lake Chūzenji at the foot of the sacred Mount Nantai, just north of Nikkō, is one of the highest lakes in Japan. Especially in late autumn and winter whilst driving up the spectacular road with 48 hairpin turns from Nikkō to the lake one is rewarded with stunning panoramas.

The snowcapped peak on this photo is Mount Nikkō Shirane (2,578 m), a volcanic dome here seen from the Tochigi site with the first snow of the winter season. At the other side in the Gunma prefecture lies Marunuma Kogen a very popular ski resort that is usually open until late April.

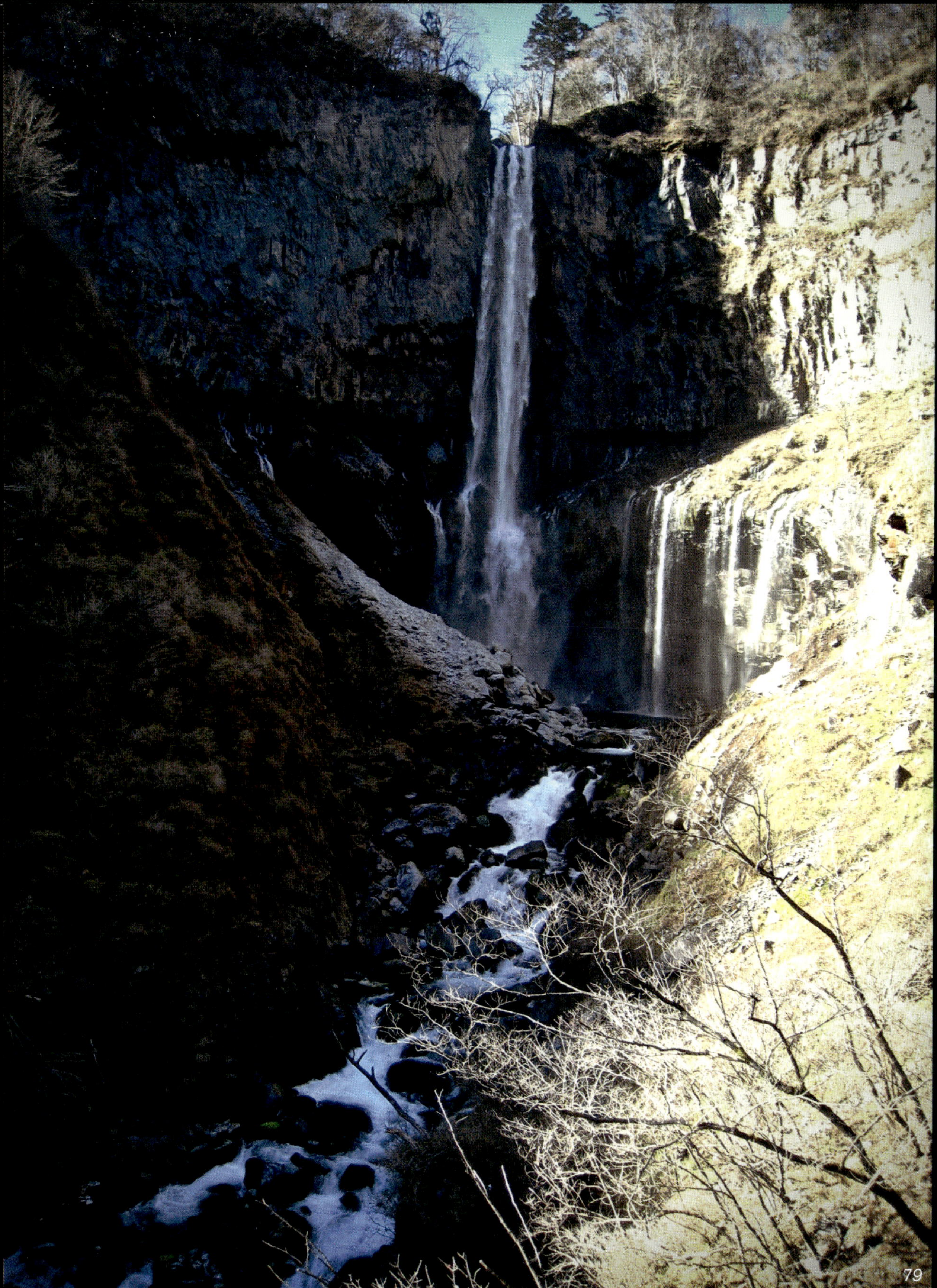

## Kegon waterfall

Located near the lake is the Kegon waterfall, 97 m high and one of Japan's most spectacular. On this photo, taken on a sunny but bitterly cold day in December, the first ice is already visible. Later in the winter season the whole waterfall becomes a blue column of ice.

# 北海道

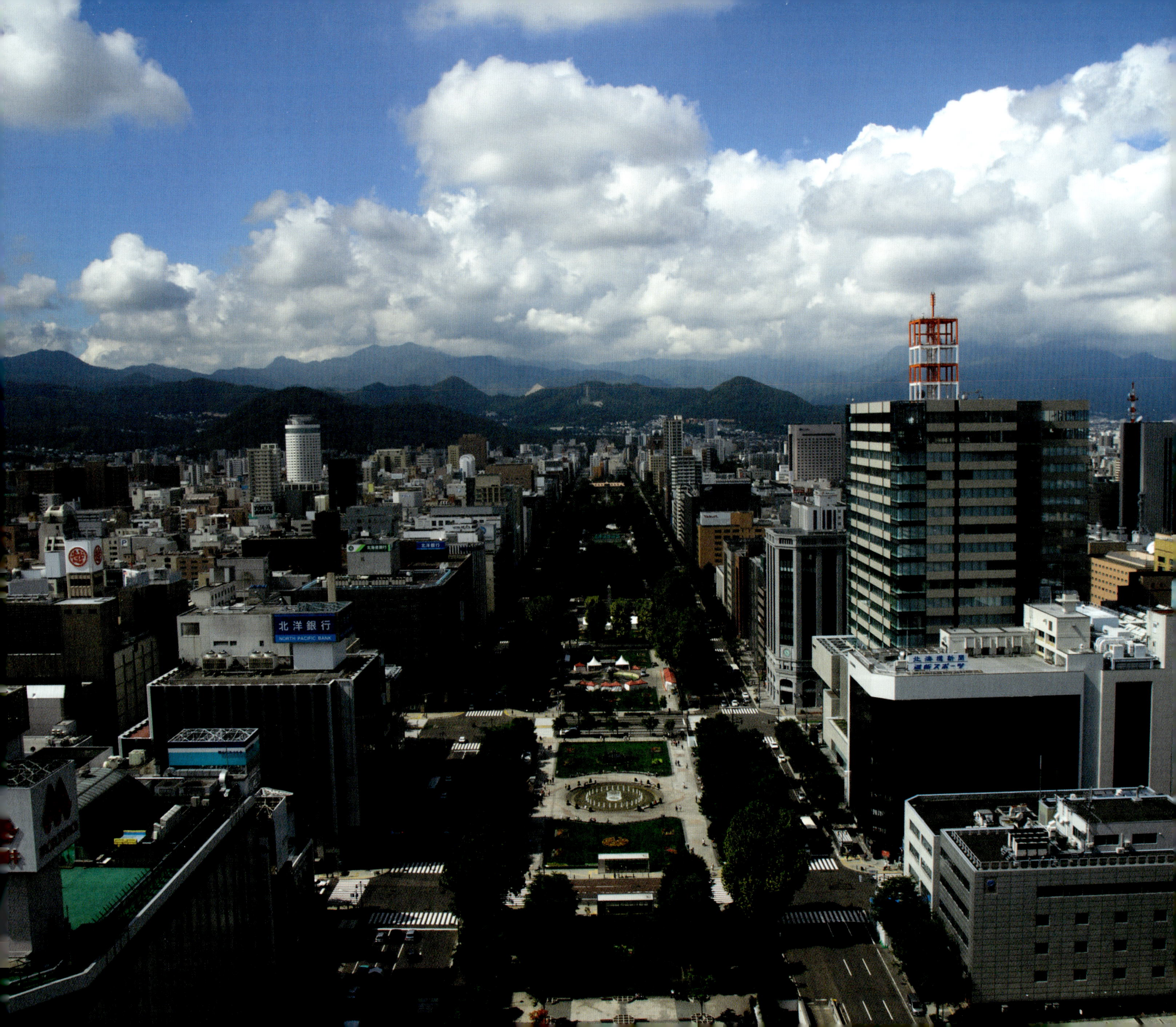
北洋銀行
NORTH PACIFIC BANK

## Sapporo

View from the 90-meter high Sapporo TV tower observation deck overlooking the city center and Ōdōri Park, one of the locations where in February the world famous Yuki Matsuri or snow festival is held.

## Furano Flower Fields

Furano is located north east of Sapporo right in the center of Hokkaidō. After the war this area of Japan specialized in the cultivation of lavender. Over time this proved to be an activity that was not very profitable and gradually the lavender farms shifted their attention to tourism. Outside the lavender season, various other types of flowers are planted and now the flower fields of Furano are a very famous tourist attraction well known by all Japanese.

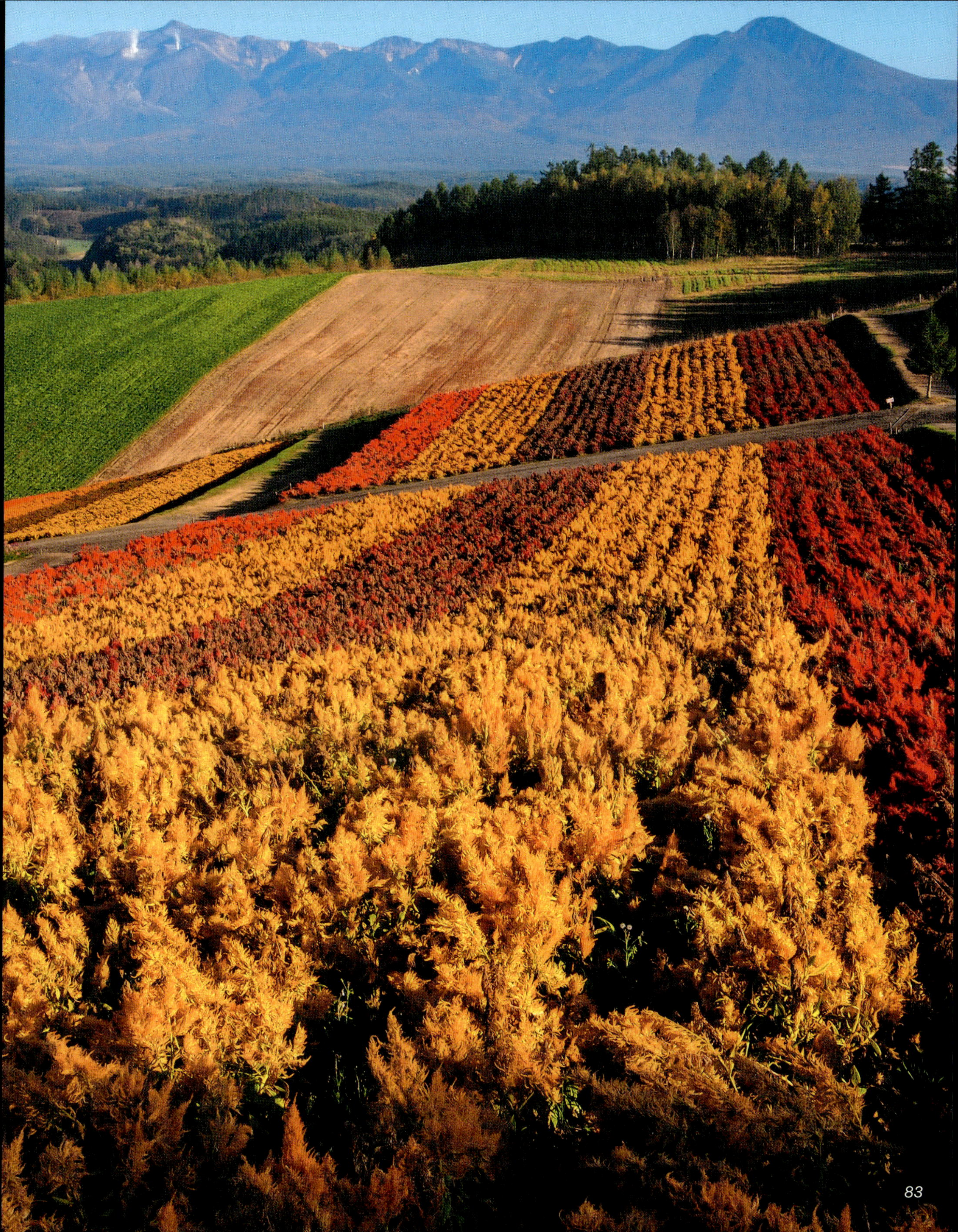

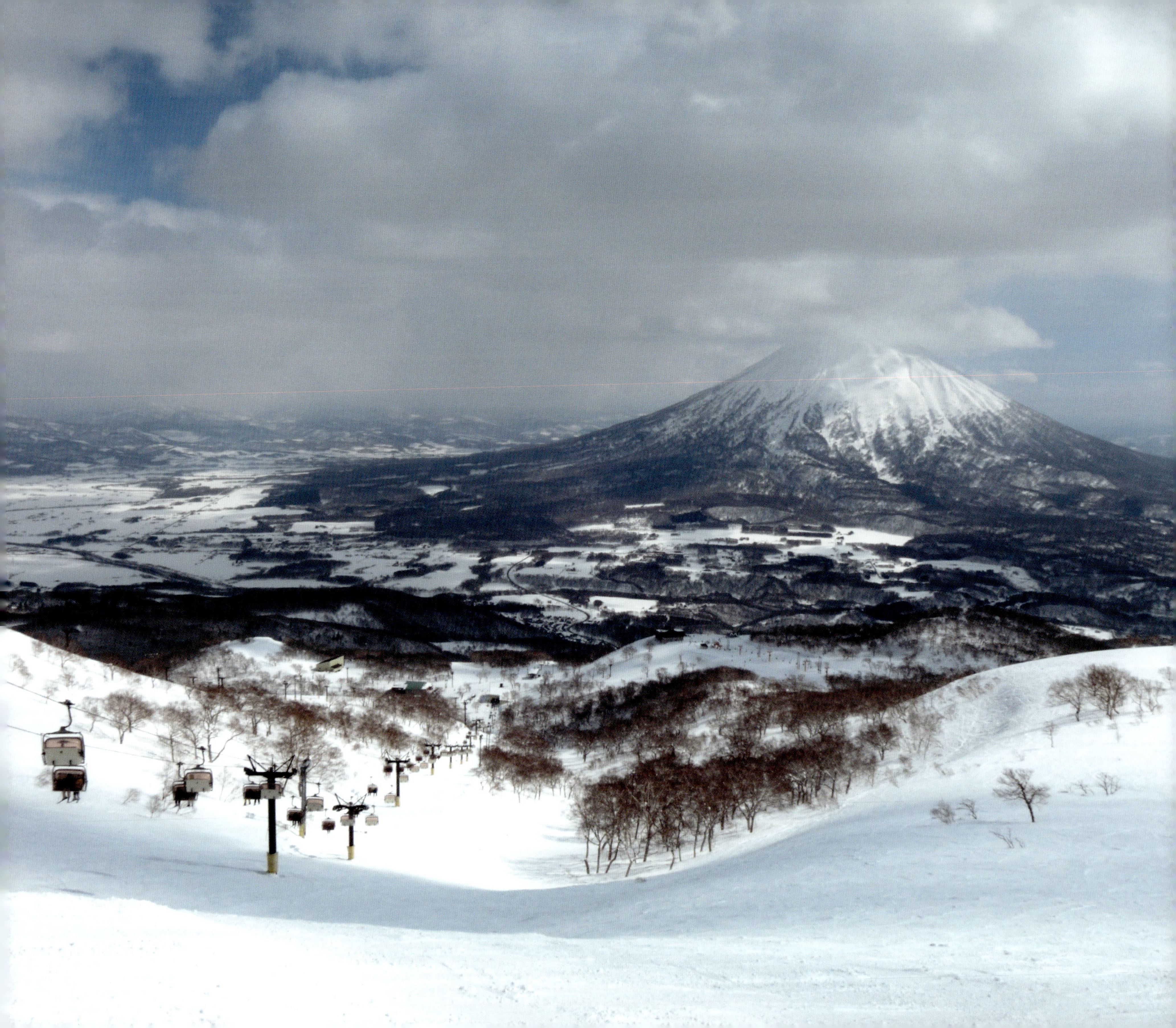

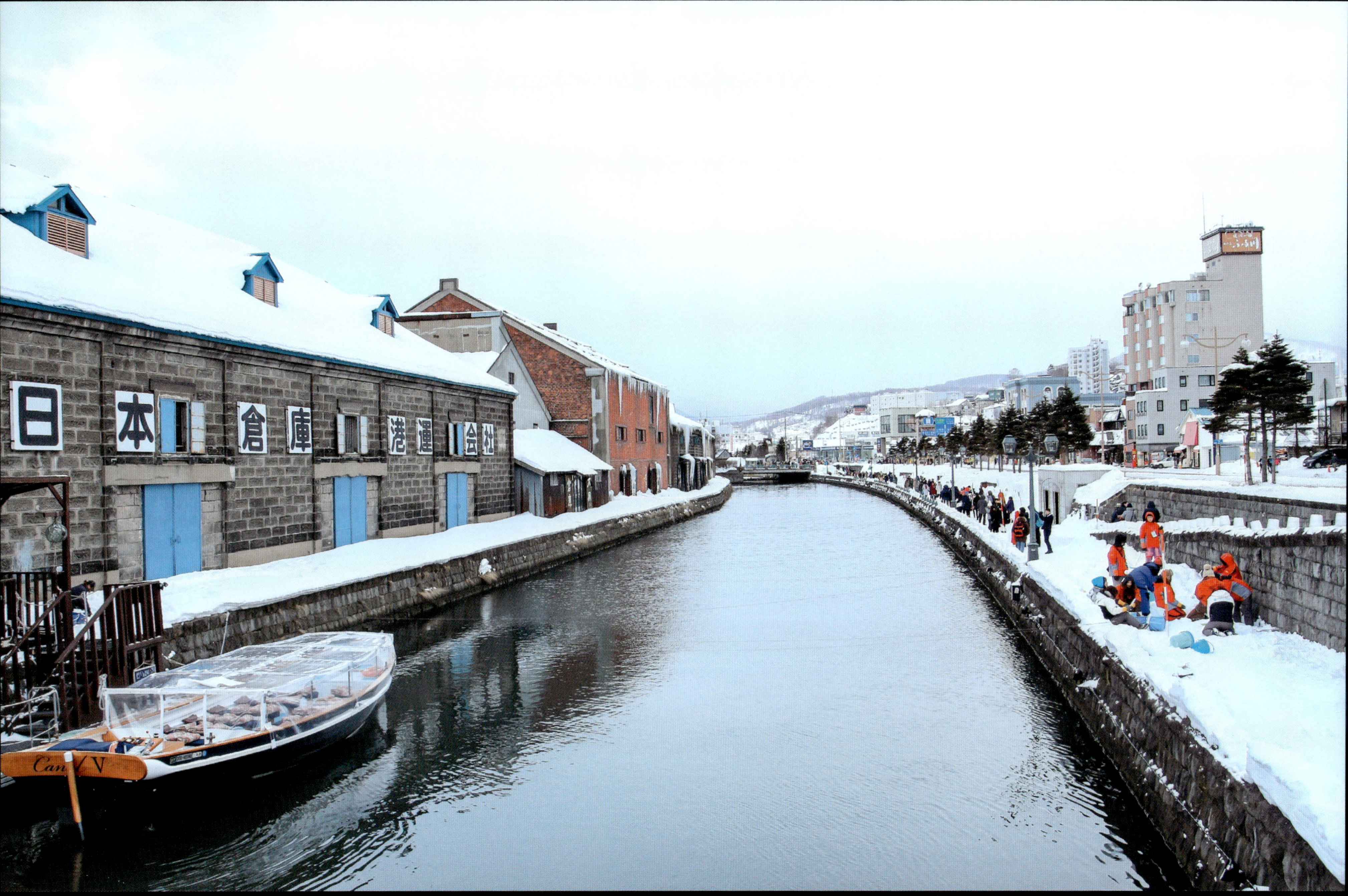


### Niseko and Mount Yōtei

The ski resort Niseko is located at the base of the dormant volcano Mount Yōtei which has a striking resemblance to Mount Fuji although it is only half as high. In winter extremely cold air from the Russian continent picks up moisture from above the Sea of Japan, which results in loads of light powder snow in this area of Japan. In search of these perfect conditions not only skiers from Japan but from all over Asia come to enjoy the ski season that lasts from end of November until the beginning of April.

### Otaru

Otaru is a romantic town about 40 km northwest of Sapporo. It is a popular place in Hokkaidō both in summer and winter. In the city center and along the canal there is a kind of oldworldly atmosphere mainly because of the well-preserved brick storage and merchant houses that are remnants of the period when this was a very wealthy fishing port.

中部

# CHŪBU

In between Kantō and Kansai lies Chūbu, which means 'central region'. As the name indicates Chūbu is located right in the center of Honshū, Japan's biggest island. Dominated by the Japanese Alps and bordered by the Sea of Japan in the north and the Pacific Ocean in the south the contrast in landscape and culture in Chūbu is unmistakable.

In the south, along the Tōkaidō Shinkansen lies Nagoya, one of the larger urban centers and the manufacturing hub of Japan as well as home of Toyota, Mitsubishi and other large multinationals.

More central the summits of the Japanese Alps set the stage for spectacular hiking and climbing routes in the summer, while offering the ultimate powder snow sensation to skiers and snowboarders in the winter. Deep inland, in the forests, lie the UNESCO World Heritage sites Shirakawa-gō and Gokoyama, famous for their 250-year-old farmhouses.

A beautiful coastline and tiny fishing and agricultural villages characterize the north, along the Sea of Japan. The major center here is Kanazawa where history is beautifully preserved in the old city districts next to the stunning 21st Century Museum of Contemporary Art.

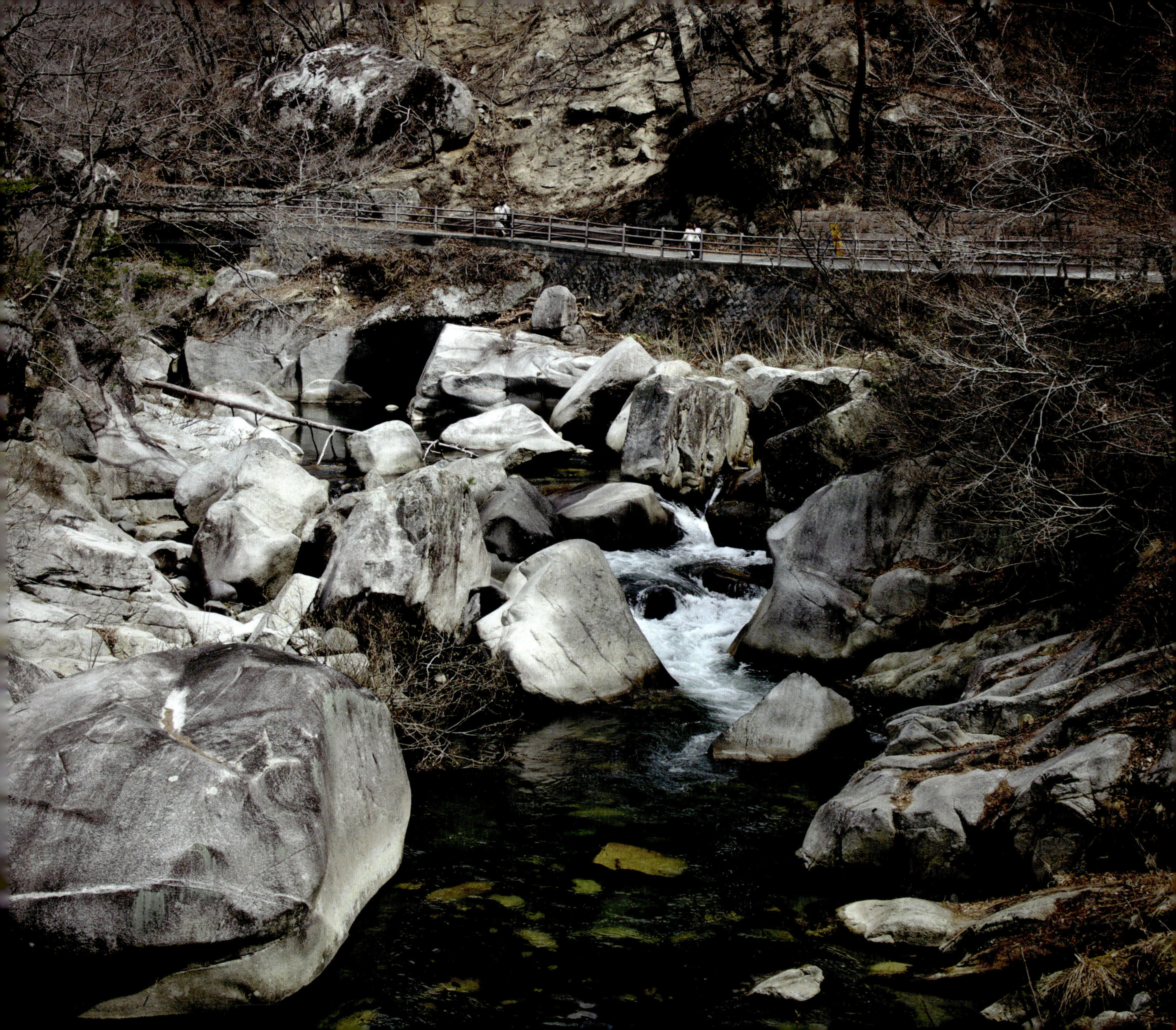

# Shōsenkyō

Mitake Shōsenkyō is a spectacular 5 km long gorge just north of Kōfu in the Chichibu mountain range. By many Japanese travel magazines it is considered to be one of the most beautiful places in the country to see autumn colors, although in all seasons it is an excellent (but to foreign tourists relatively unknown) daytrip from Tokyo.

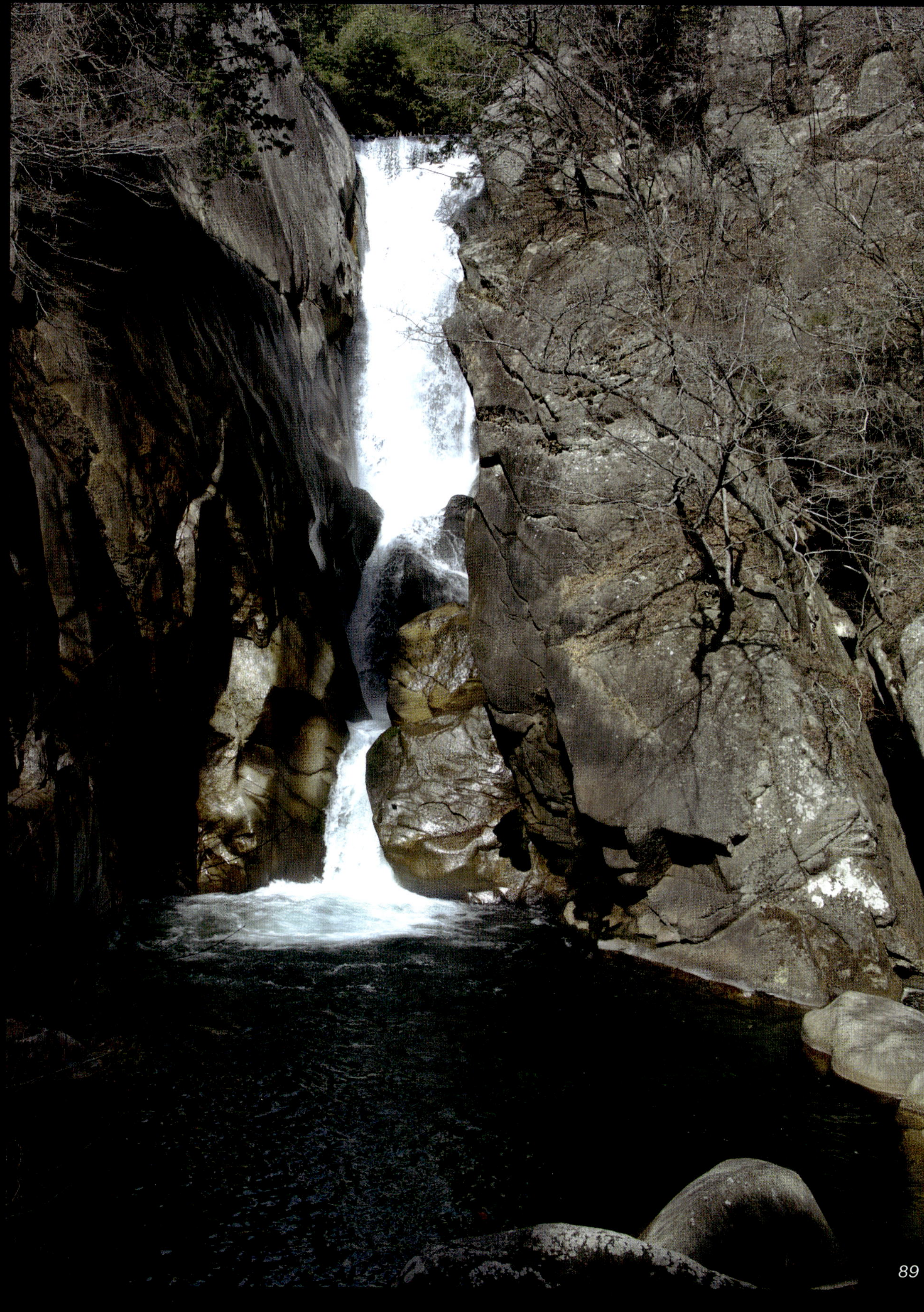

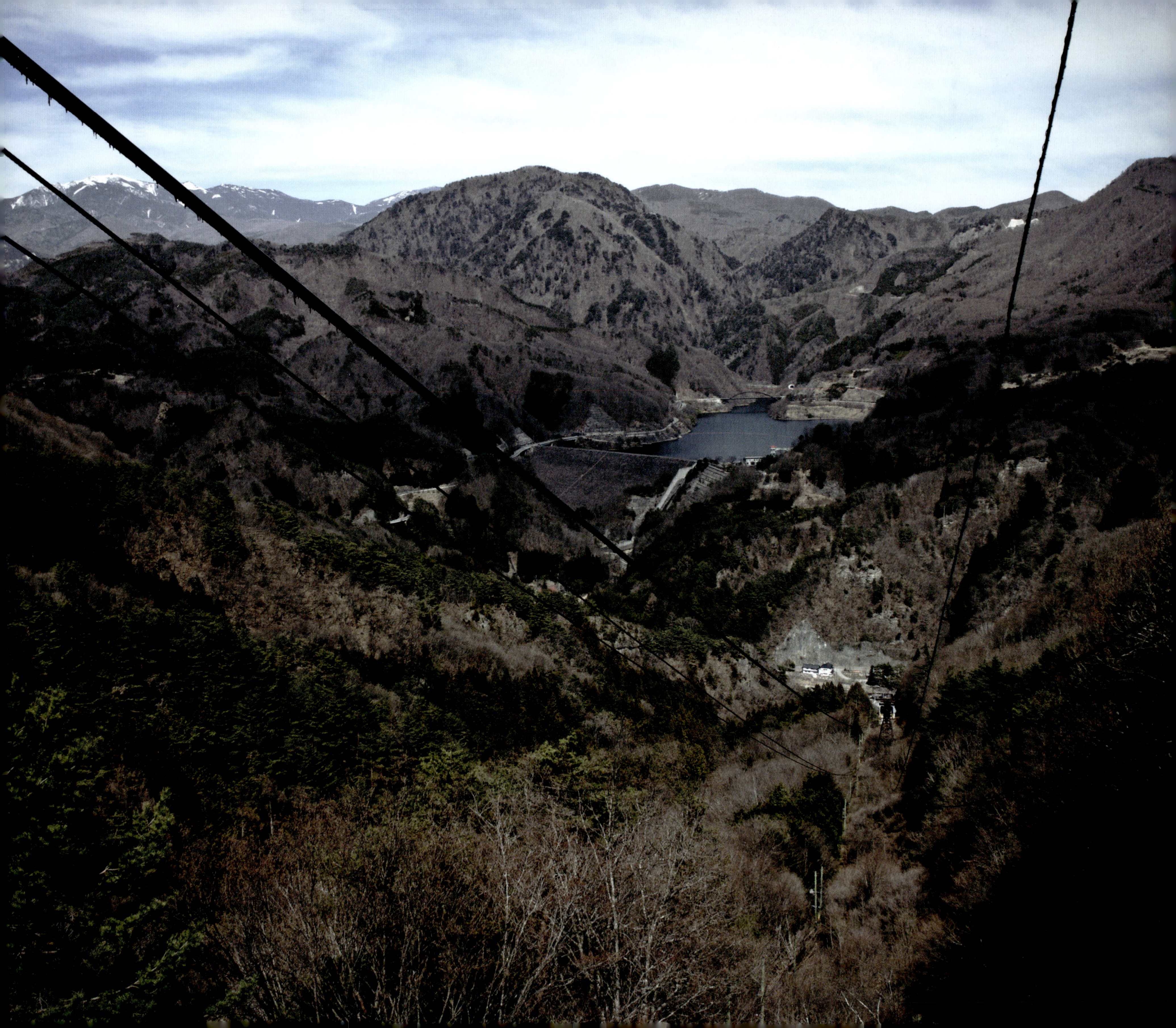

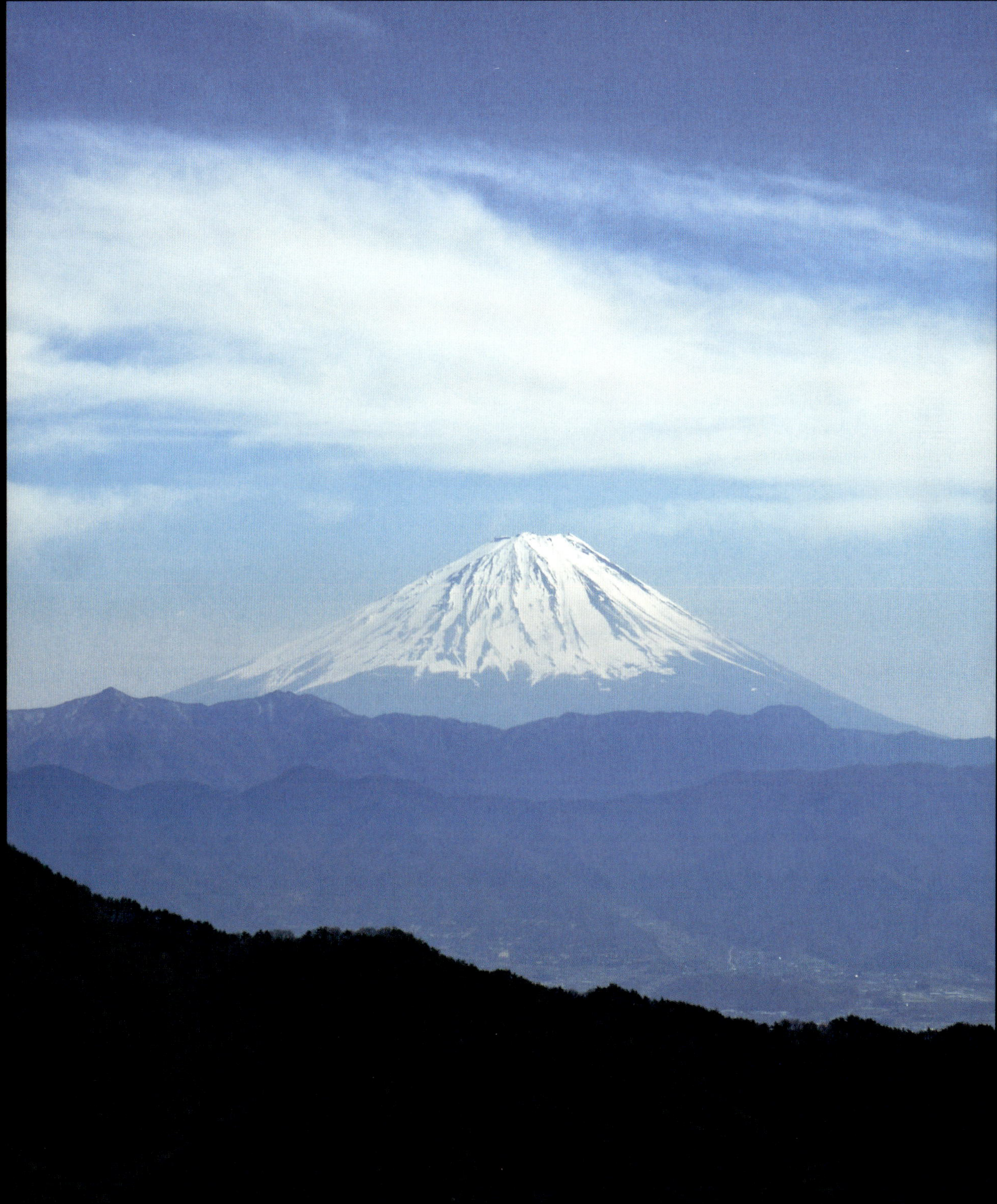

At the end of the gorge is a ropeway that takes

# Karuizawa

One hour northwest from Tokyo with the Hokuriku Shinkansen lies Karuizawa, a posh upscale mountain town. The town is situated at the foot of the majestic Mount Asama (2,568 m), an active volcano and famous for some of Japan's most violent and destructive eruptions in the past millennium.

Initially the town was a small retreat for the upper class and diplomats of Tokyo seeking the cool mountain breeze during the long hot summers. It may have stayed like that if it were not for the photos of the later emperor Akihito and his future wife Michiko Shōda on the local tennis courts that went around the world in the late 1950's.

It was really put on the map in the western world when in the seventies John Lennon and his family spent their summer vacations in the famous Mampei hotel. It is the first western hotel in Japan with a history that goes back to the 19th century.

Taking a stroll to the Kumoba pond, said to be one of the favorite places of the Emperor Akihito will not only thrill nature lovers but also photographers. The lush forest and abundant plants that change into a different color palette every season and reflect in the water are truly a delight for the eye.

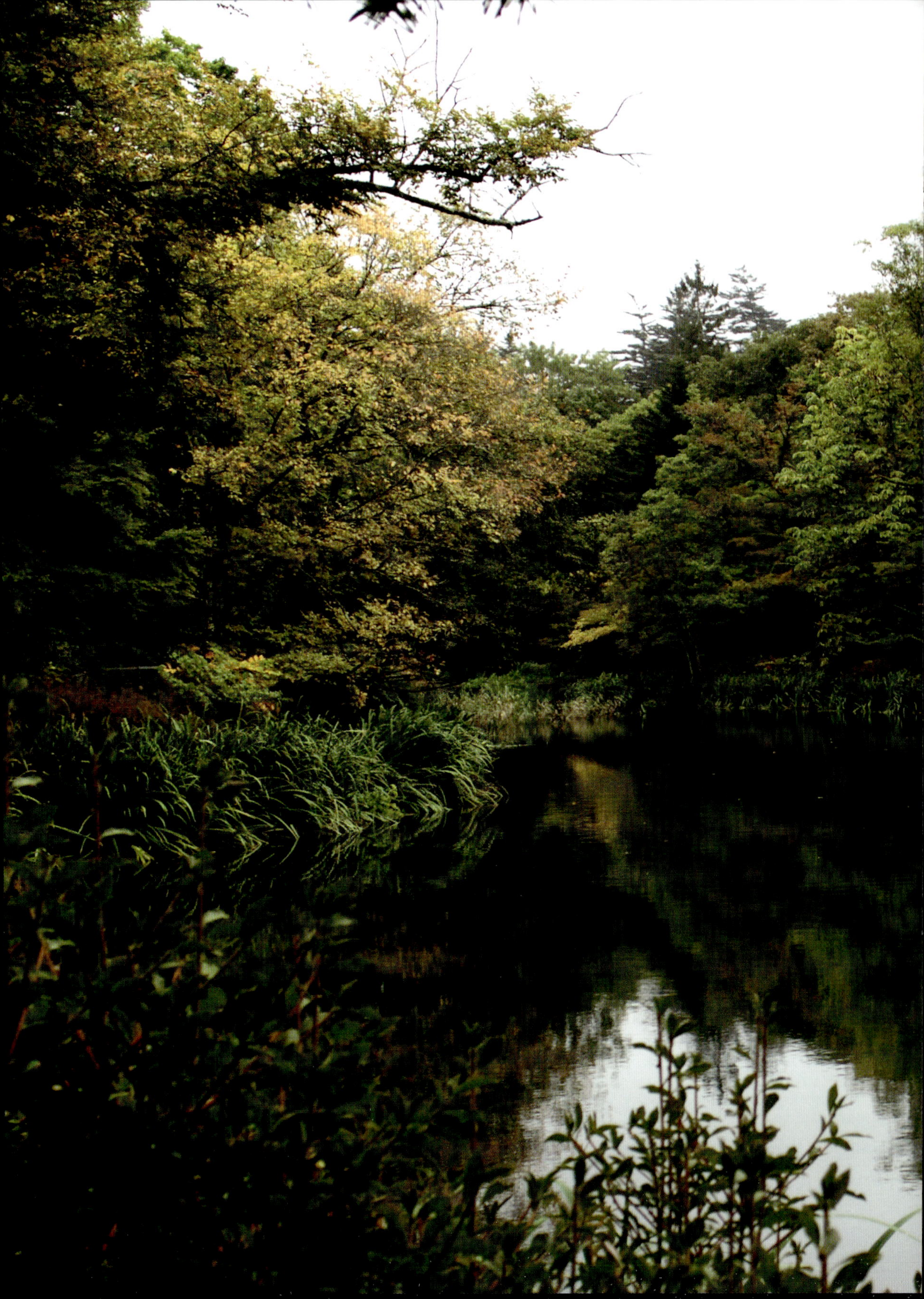

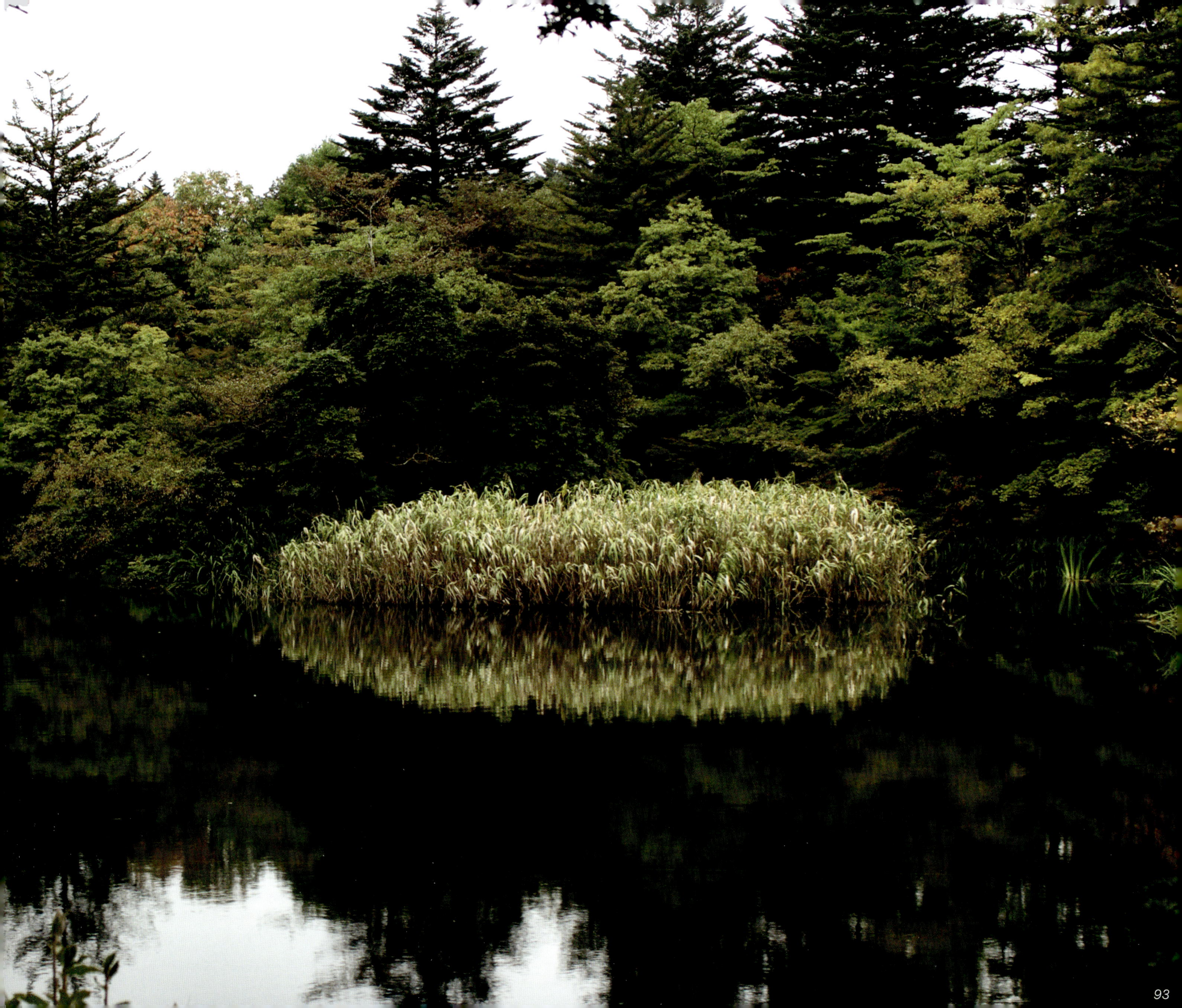

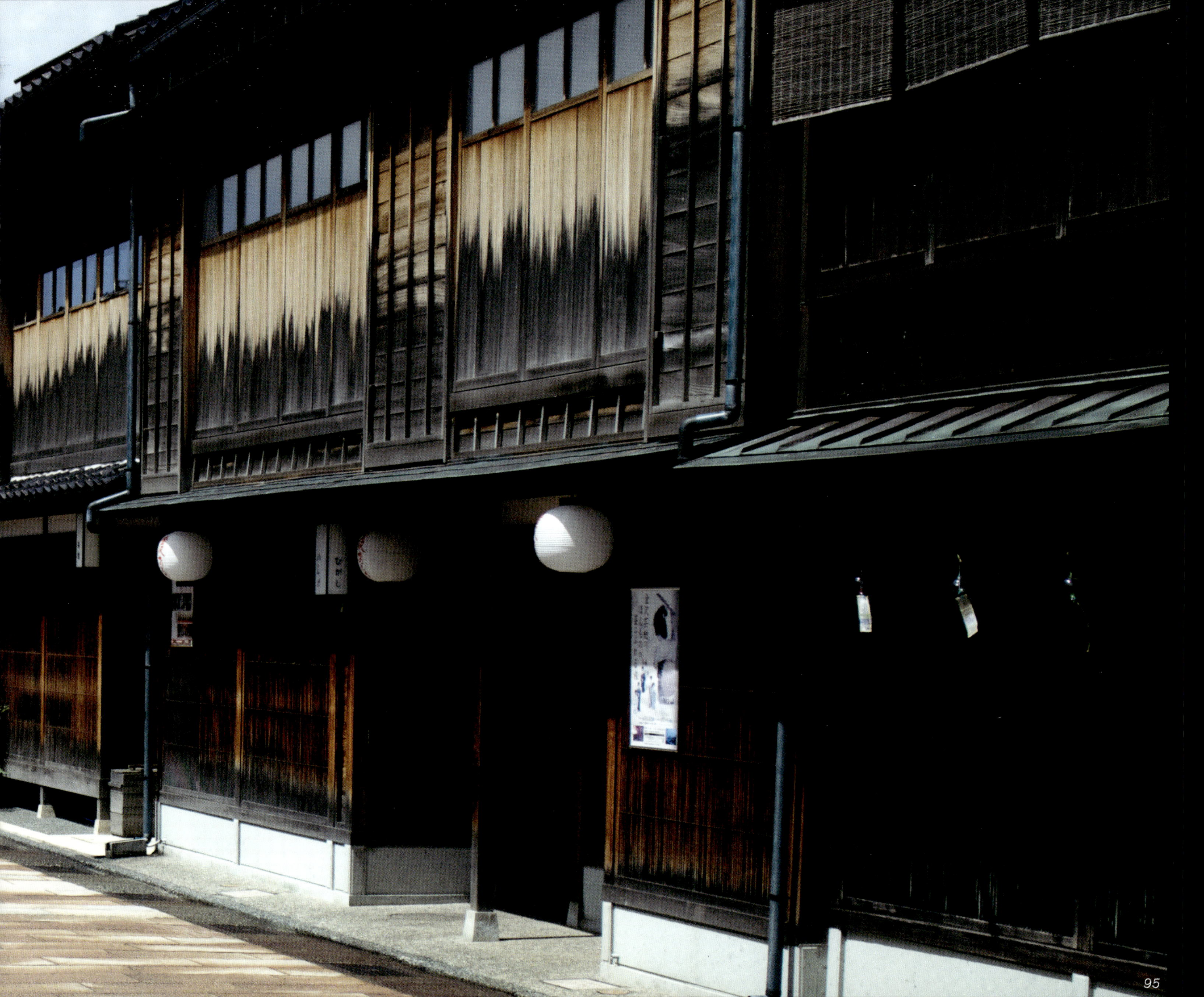

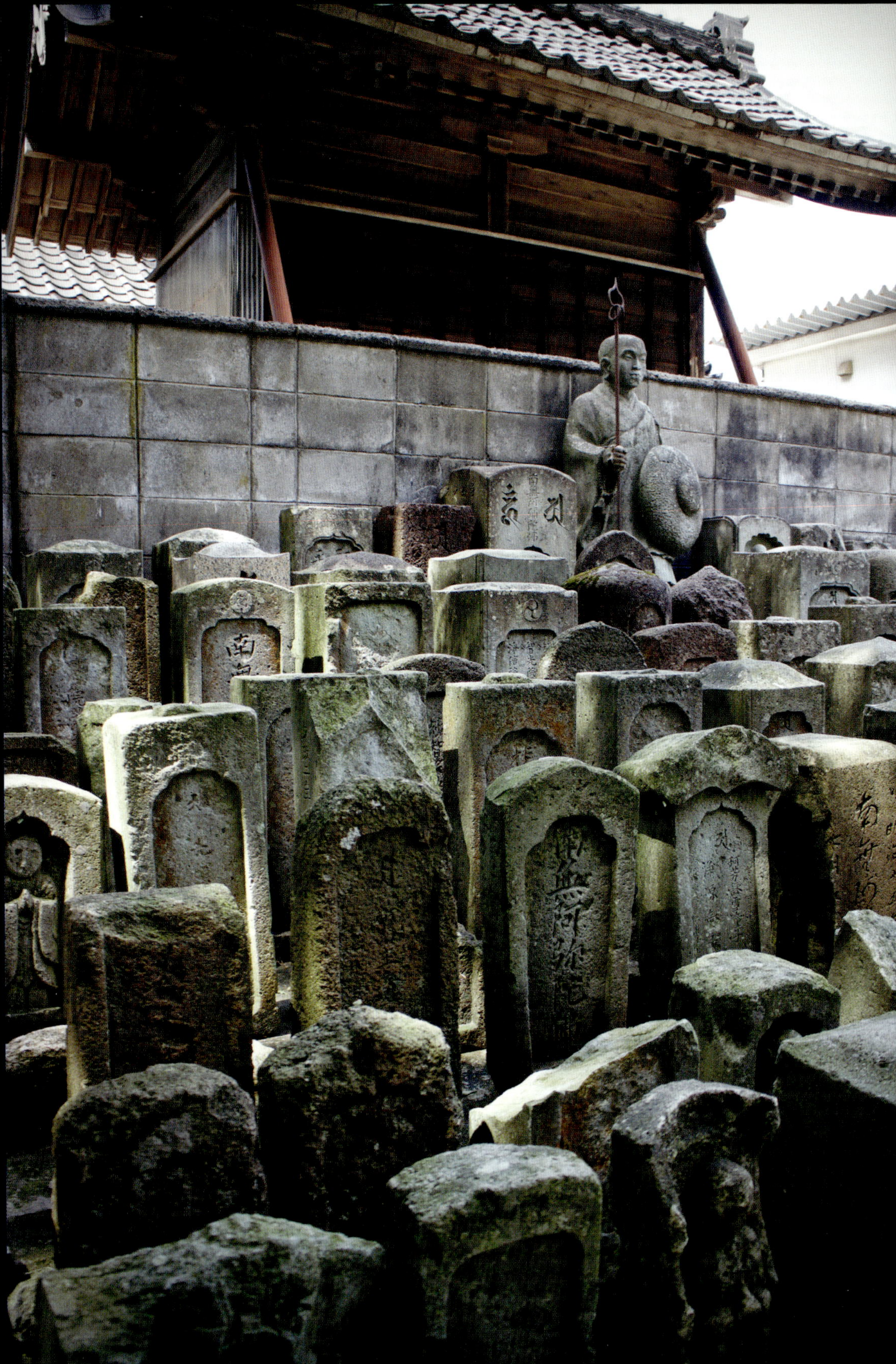

A short walk uphill from the Higashi Cha-ya district and one is immersed in the tranquility of Hōsen-ji. A small temple from where there is a viewpoint overlooking the city of Kanazawa.

### Kanazawa station

The city of Kanazawa is rightly very proud of its station. The central wooden gate named Tsuzumi-mon symbolizes Japanese hand drums or 'tsuzumi'. The station was selected as the sixth most beautiful in the world by the American magazine 'Travel Leisure'.

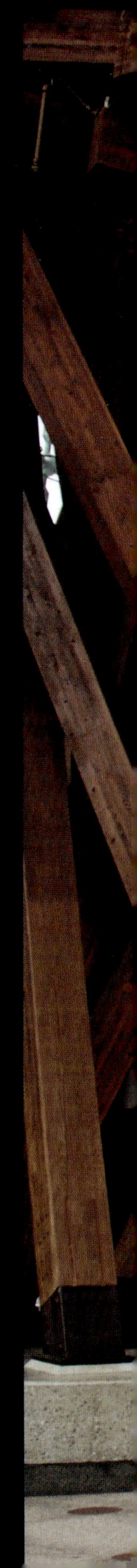

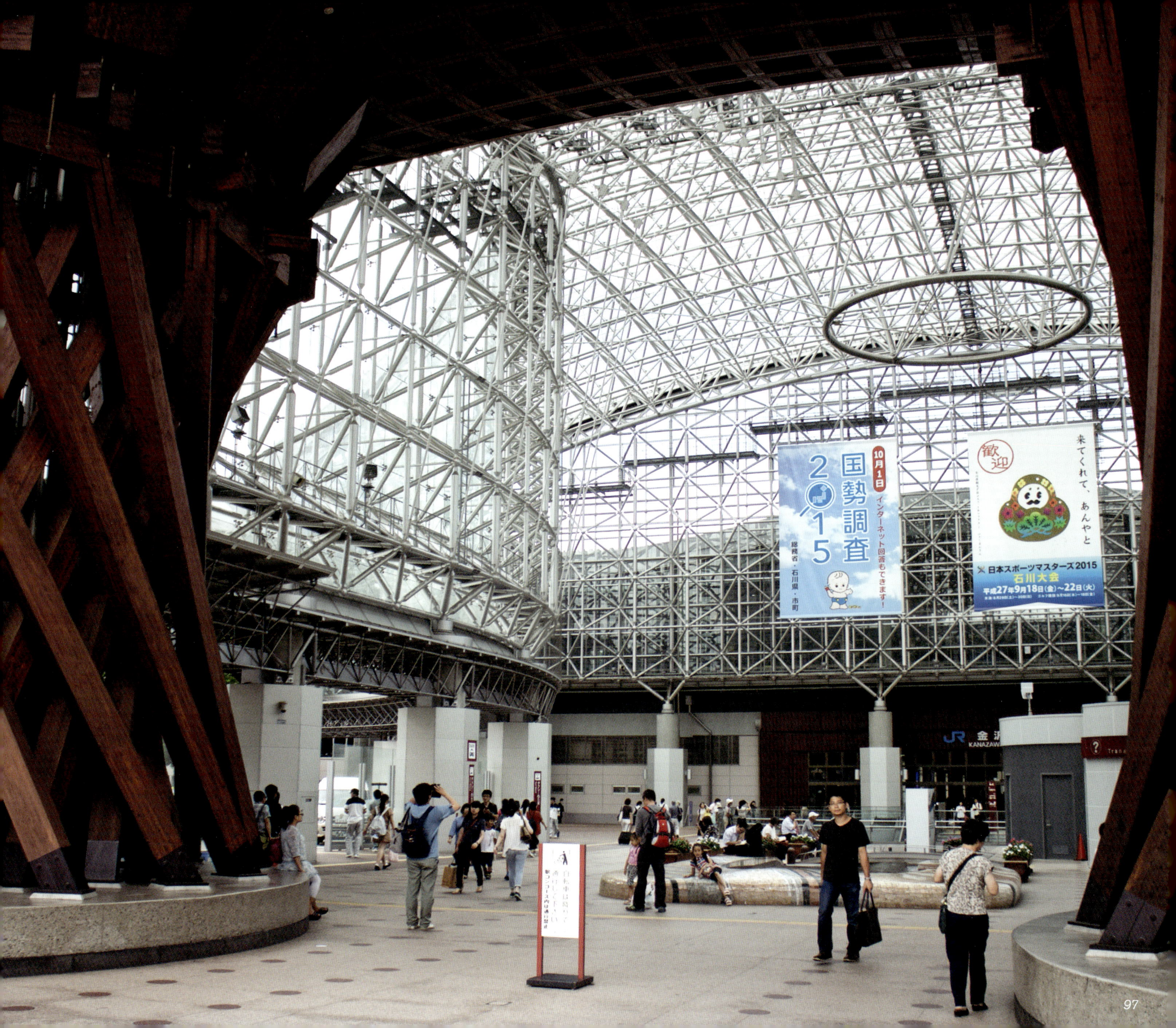
10月1日
国勢調査
2015
インターネット回答もできます！
総務省・石川県・市町
歓迎
来てくれて、あんやと
日本スポーツマスターズ2015
石川大会
平成27年9月18日(金)~22日(火)
JR 金沢
KANAZAWA

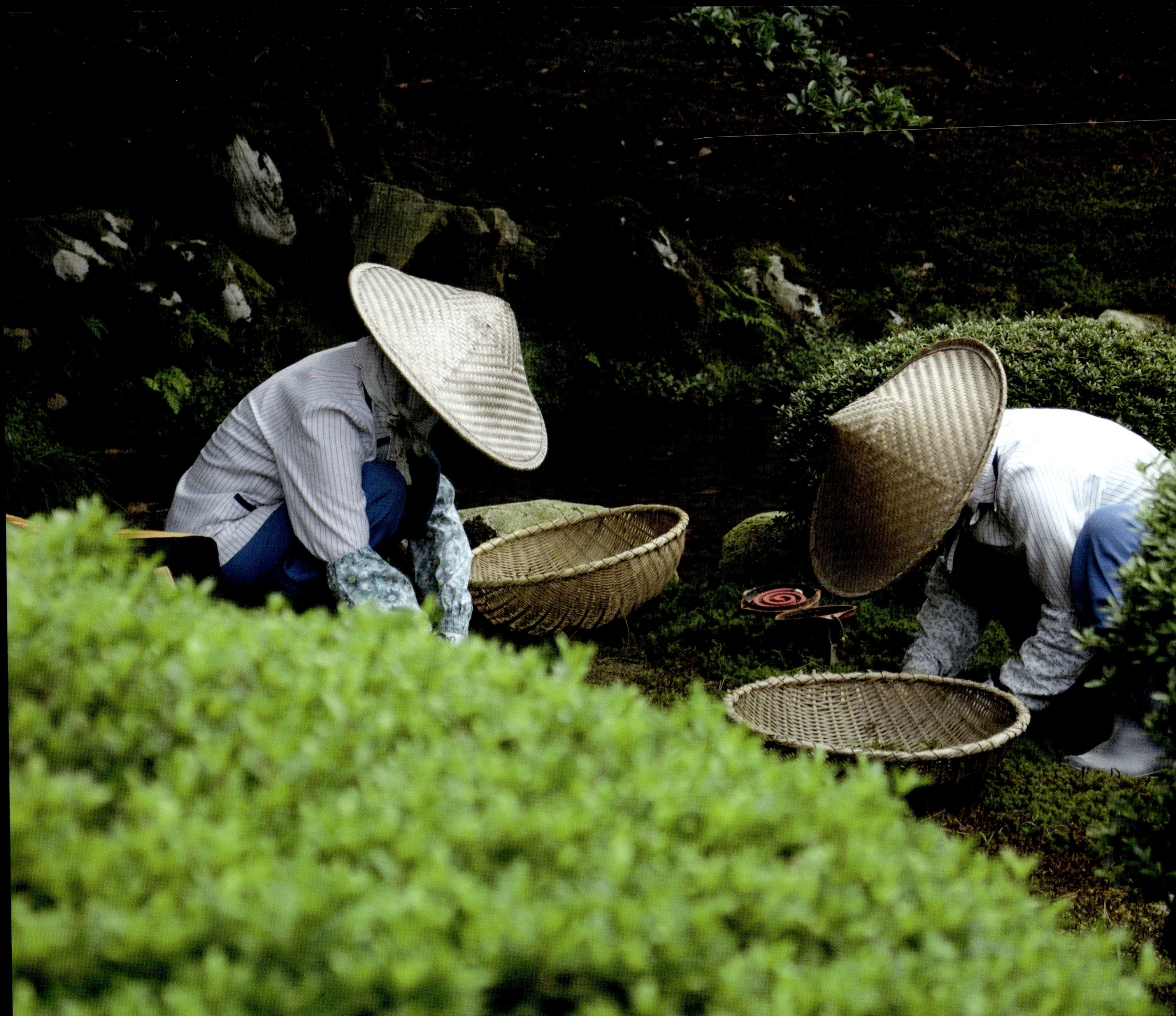

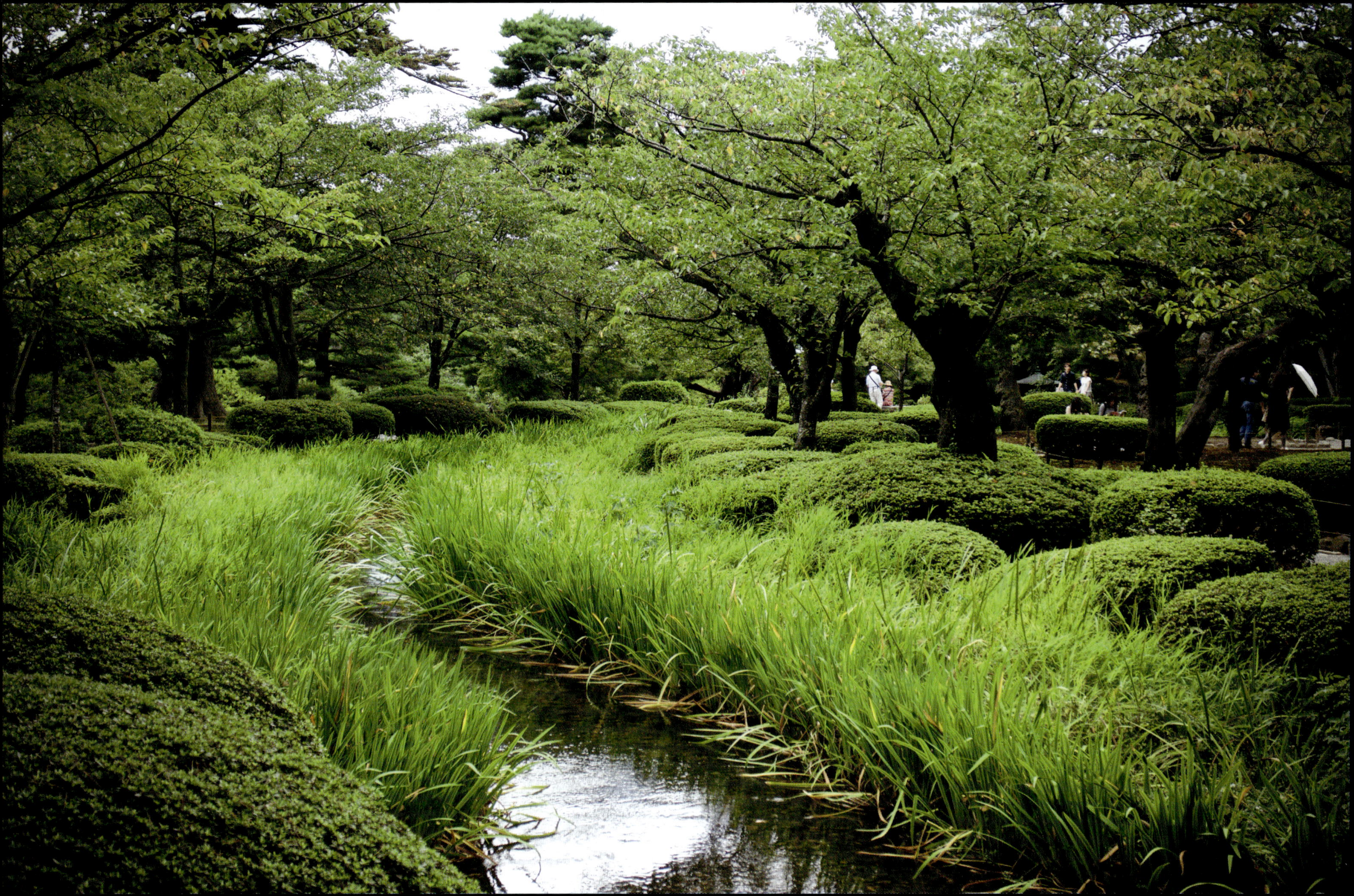

## Kenroku-en

The Edo style landscape garden Kenroku-en, located on the slopes of Kanazawa Castle, was created in 1676 and is considered to be one of Japan's three most beautiful gardens. Roku means 'six' in Japanese and the name of the garden refers to the six attributes of the perfect landscape garden: spaciousness, seclusion, artifice, antiquity, water and panoramas.

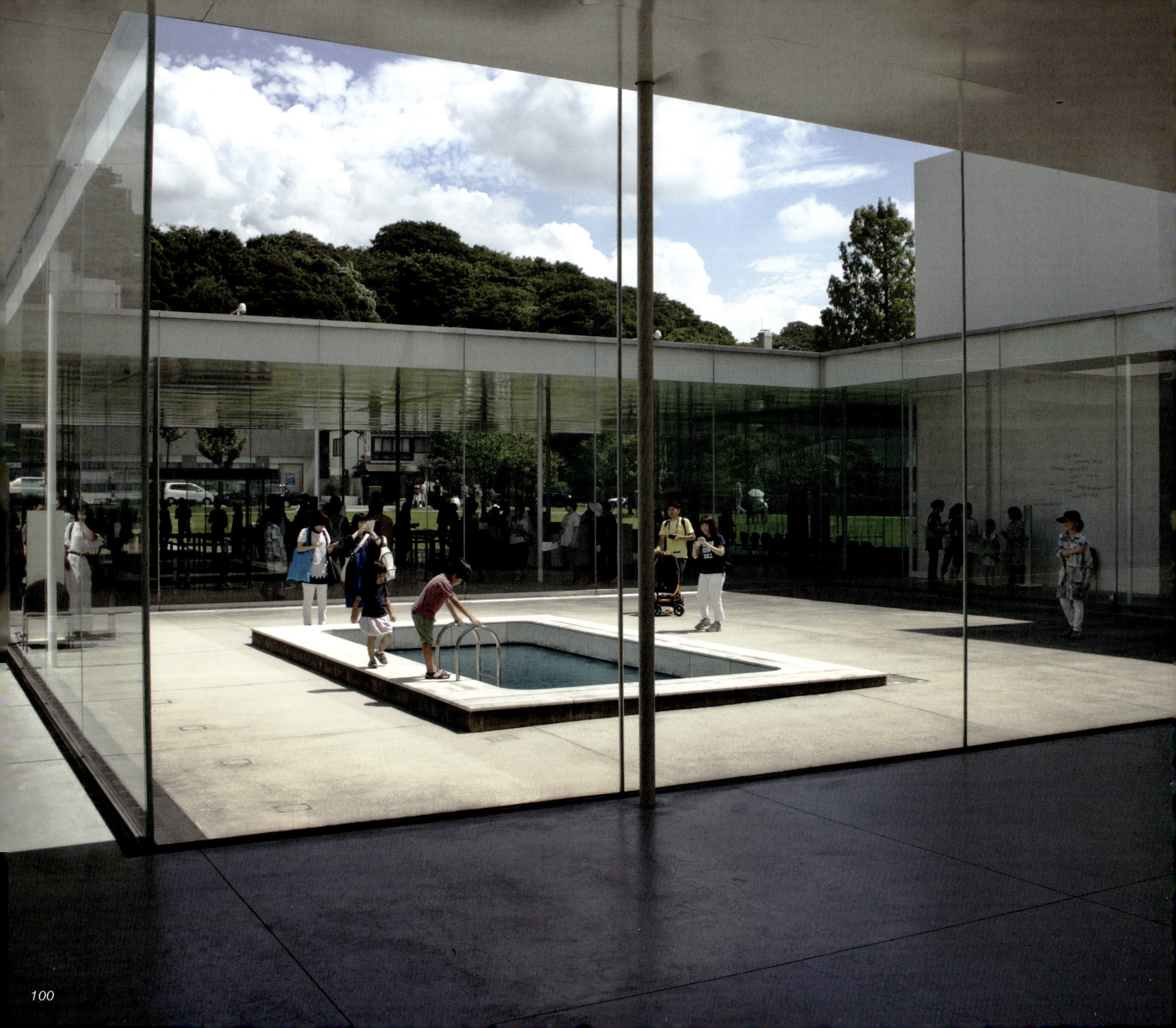

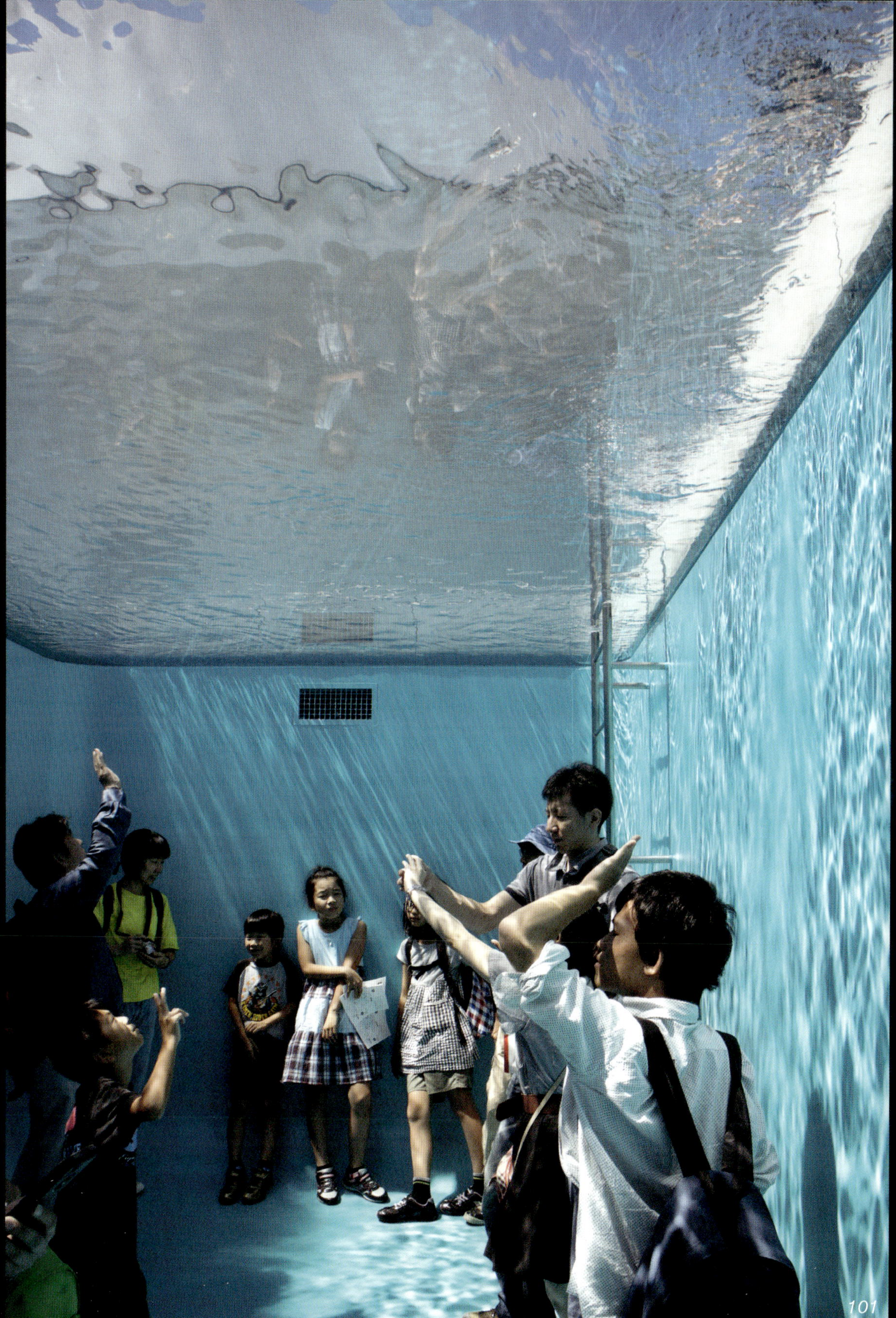

## 21st Century Museum of Contemporary Art, Kanazawa

The world-famous architects Sejima Kazuyo and Nishizawa Ryue from SANAA designed the building. This very modern museum is structured around huge, immaculate white exhibition rooms separated by courtyards. The large glazed walls create a form of transparency and see-through effect and bathe the museum in bright daylight. The permanent collection houses the modern artwork of both Japanese and internationally renowned artists including 'The Swimming Pool' (2004) from Leandro Erlich.

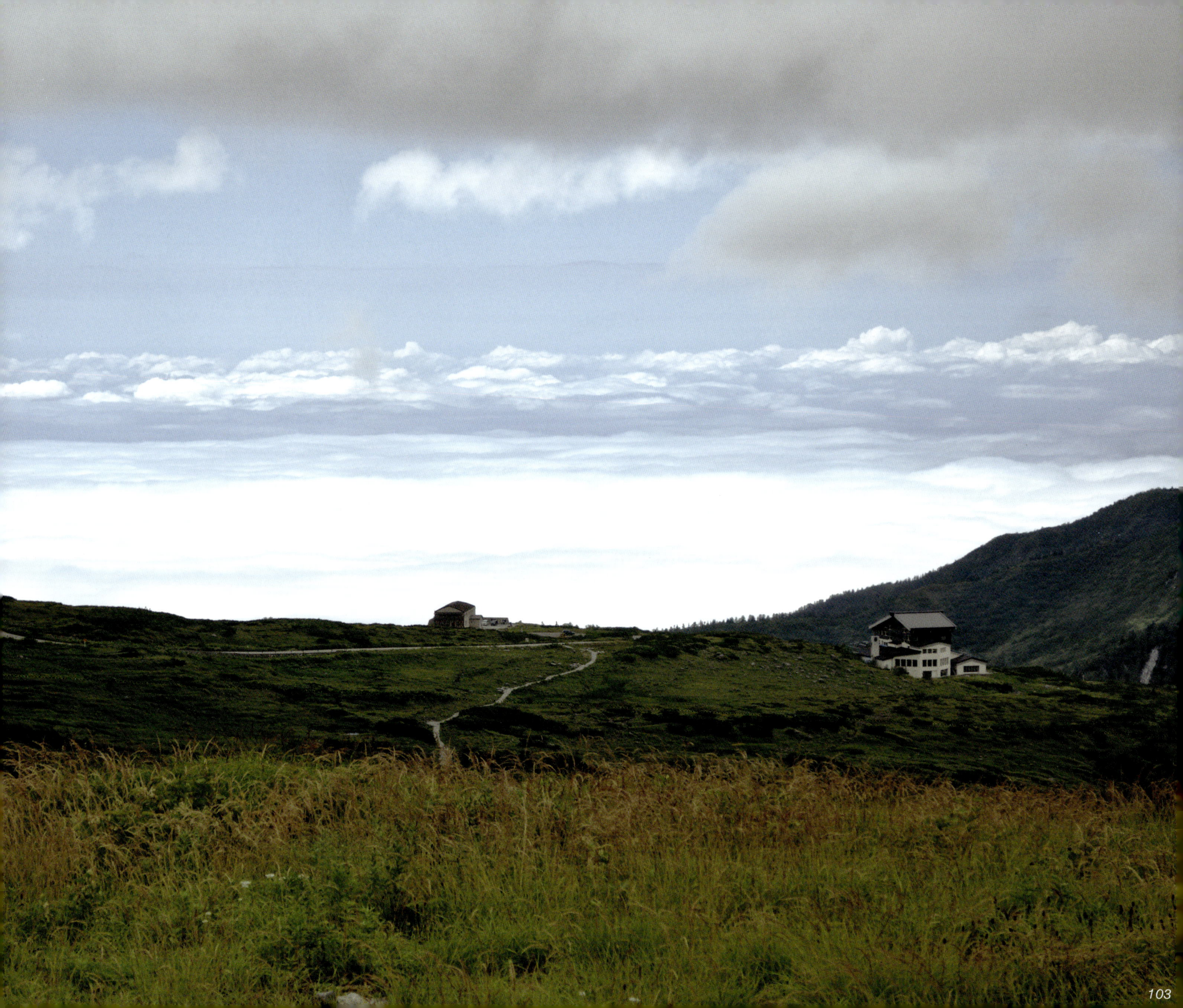

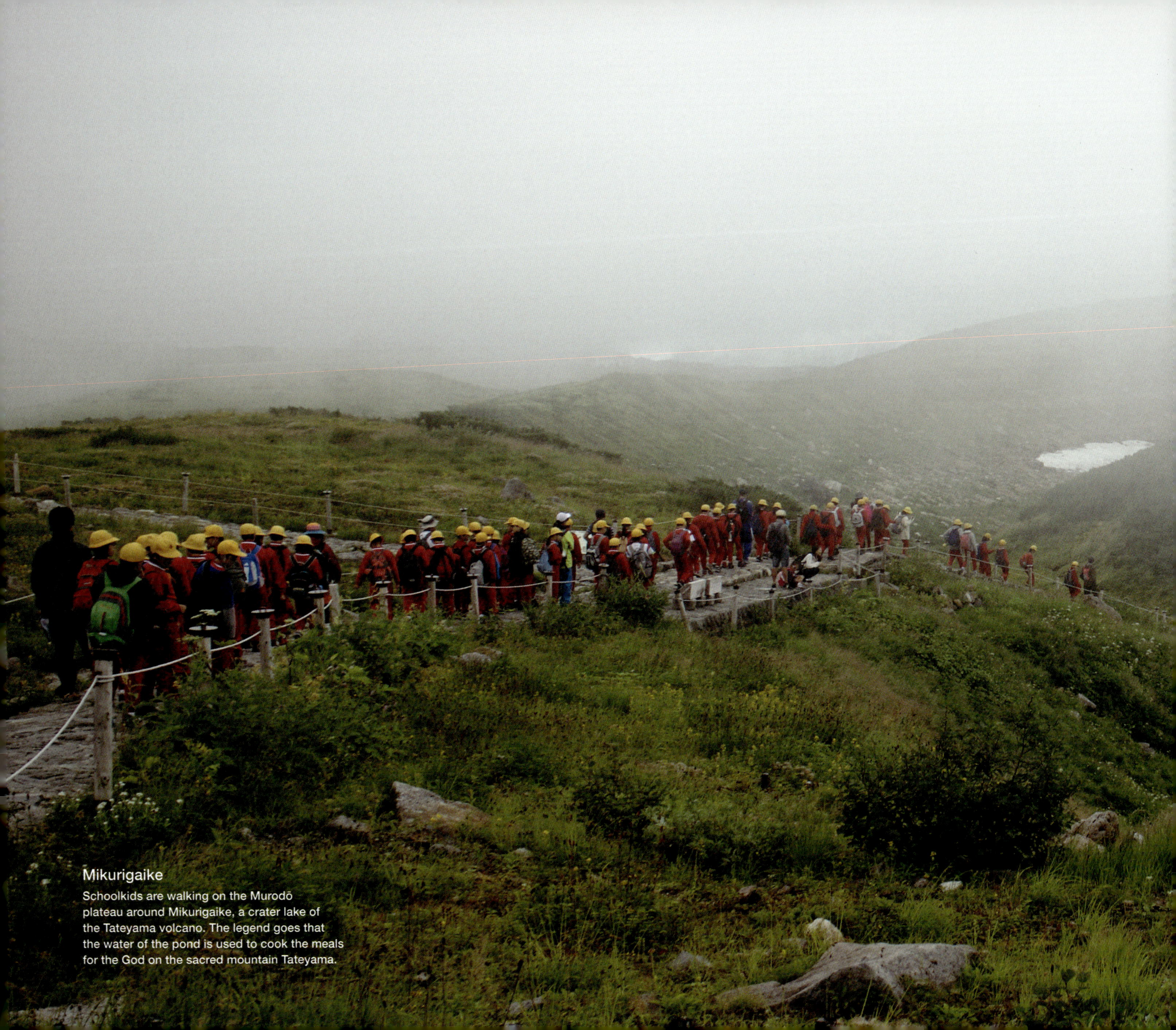

**Mikurigaike**

Schoolkids are walking on the Murodō plateau around Mikurigaike, a crater lake of the Tateyama volcano. The legend goes that the water of the pond is used to cook the meals for the God on the sacred mountain Tateyama.

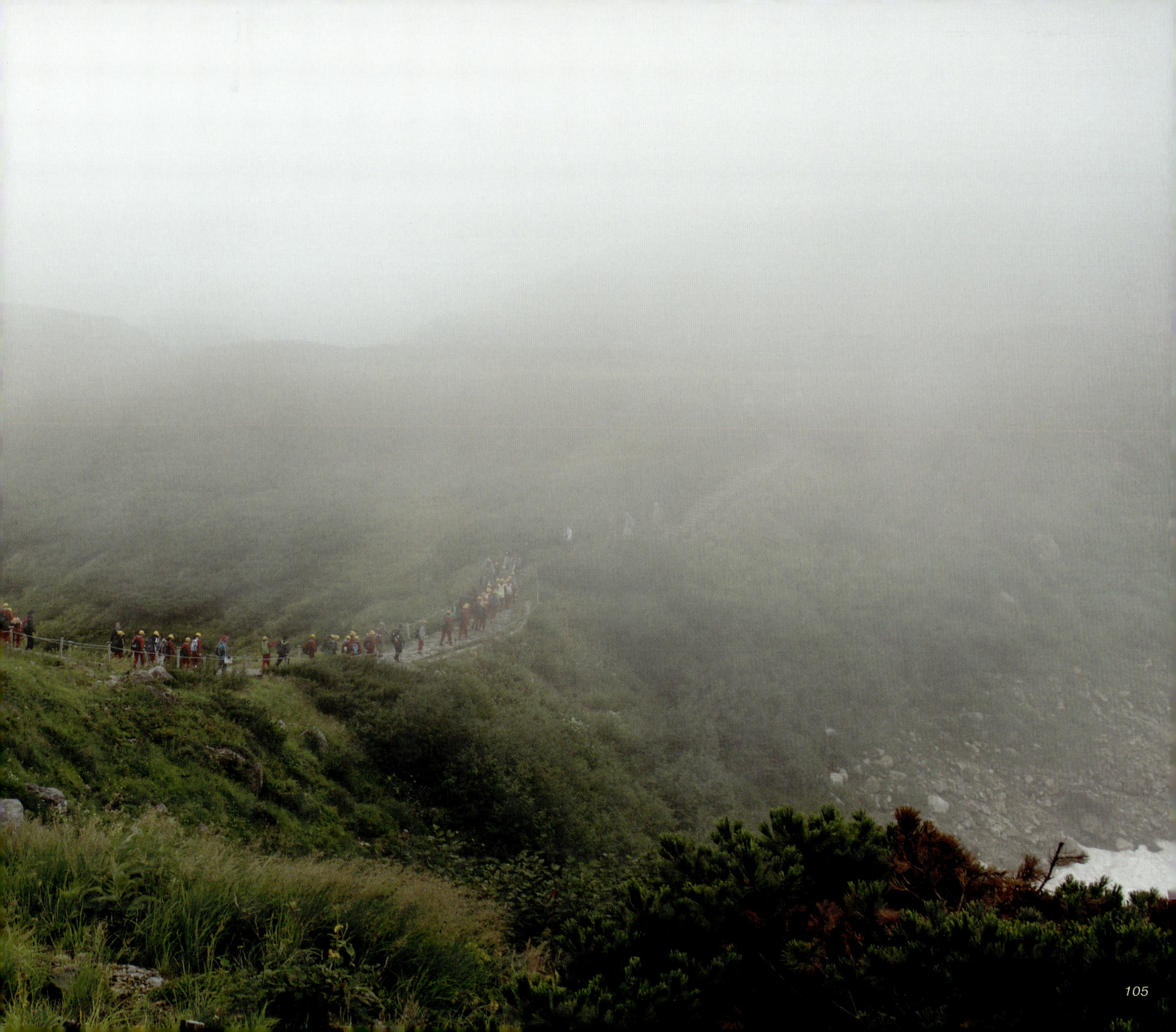

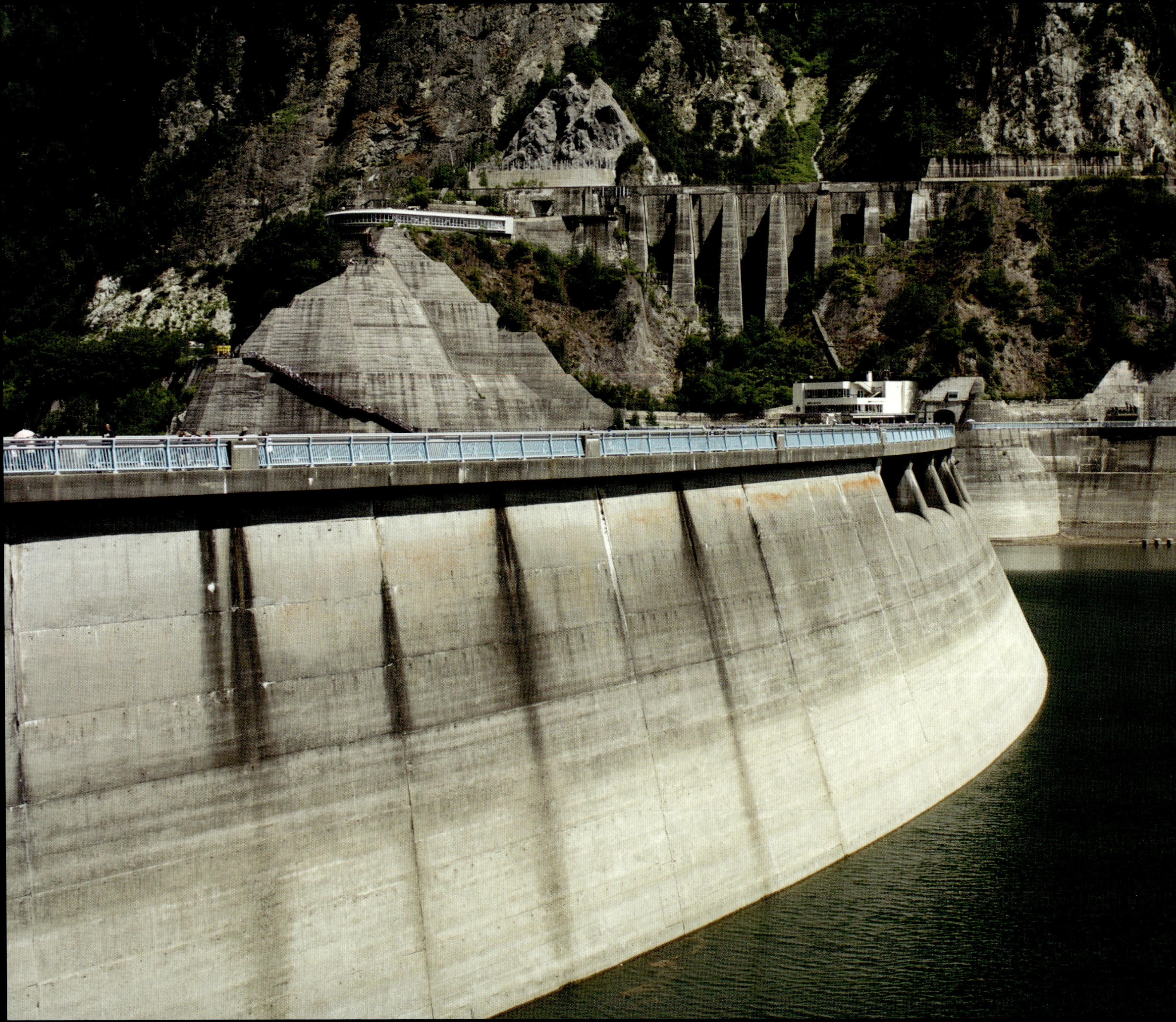

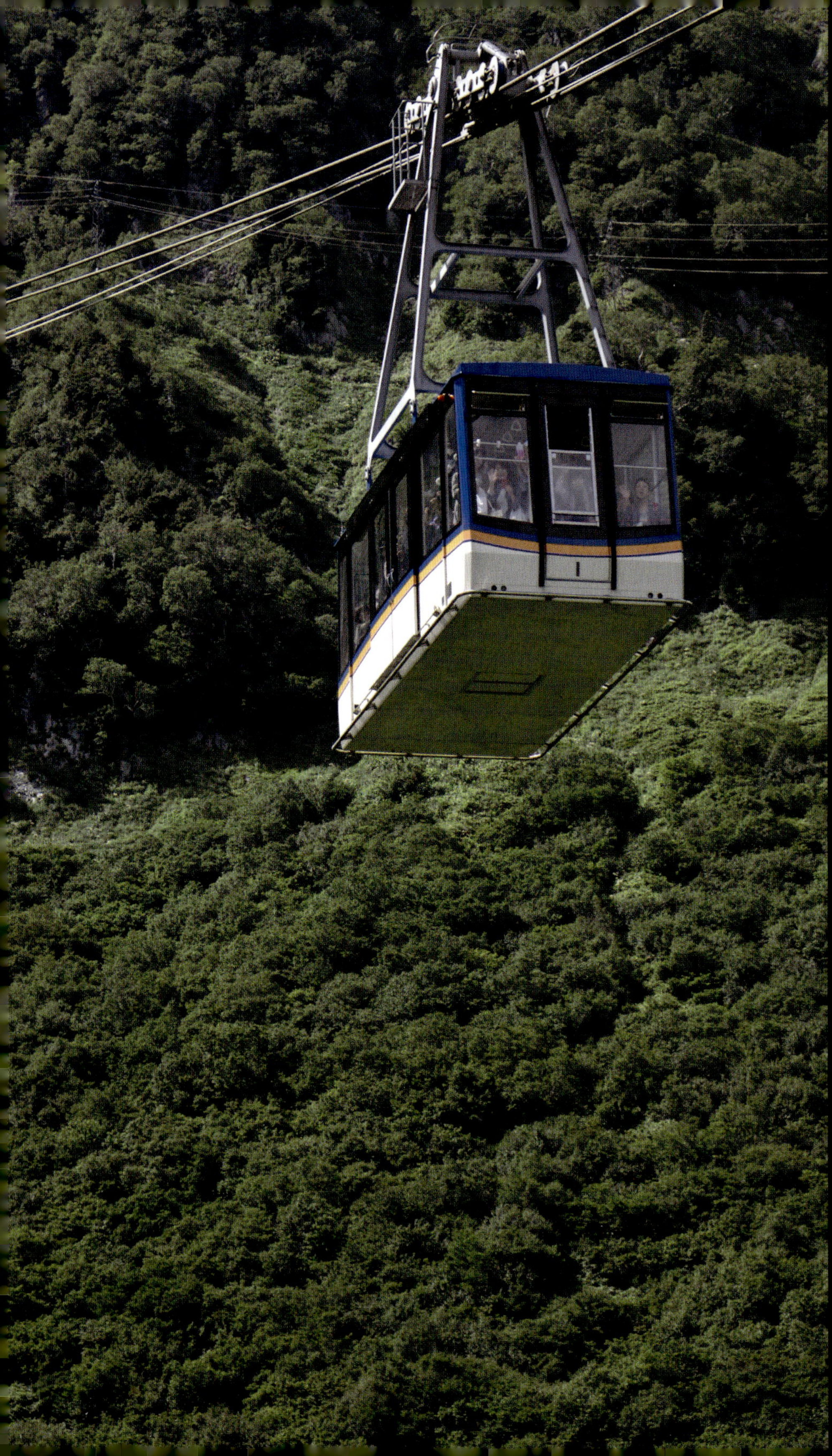

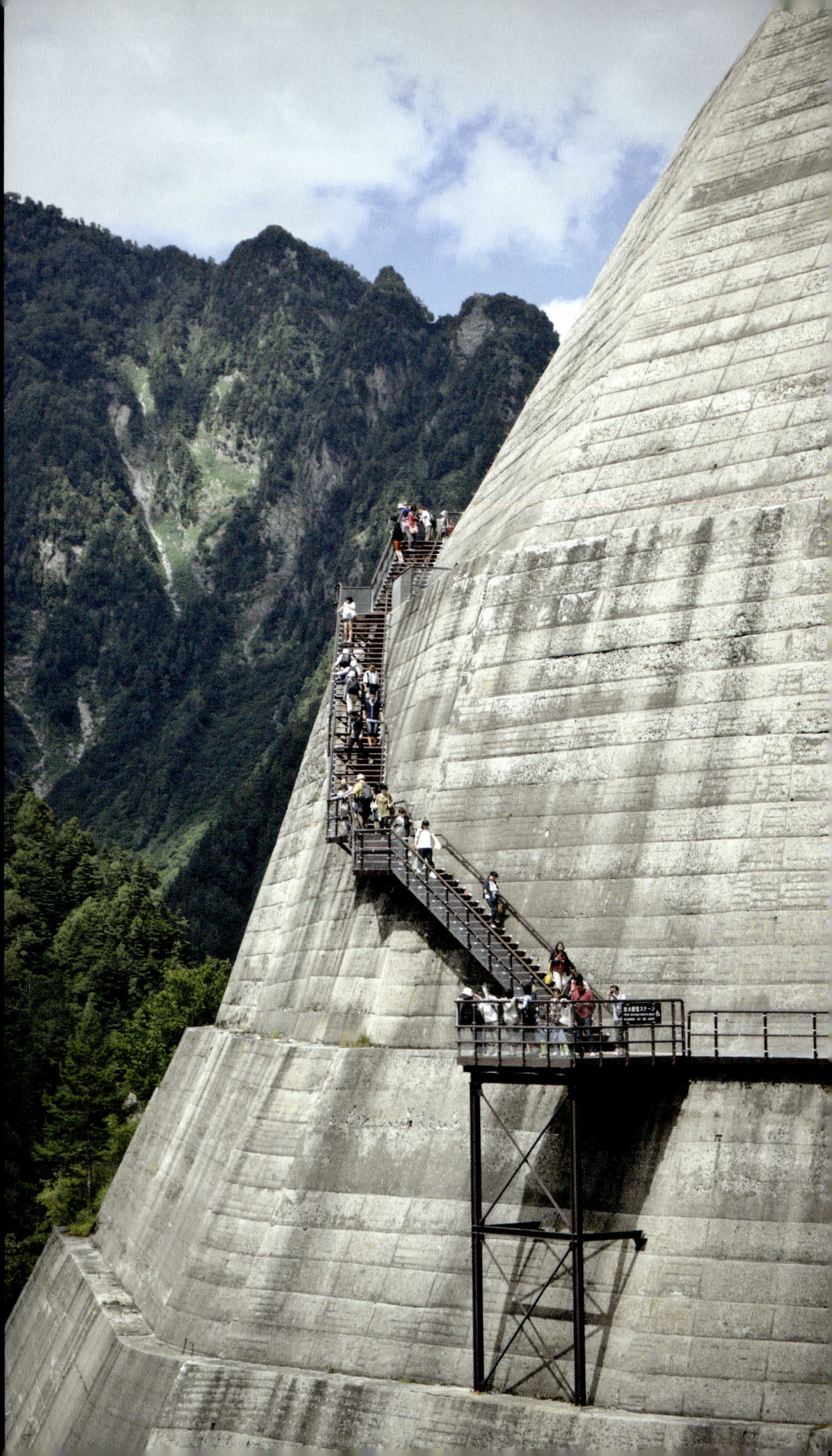

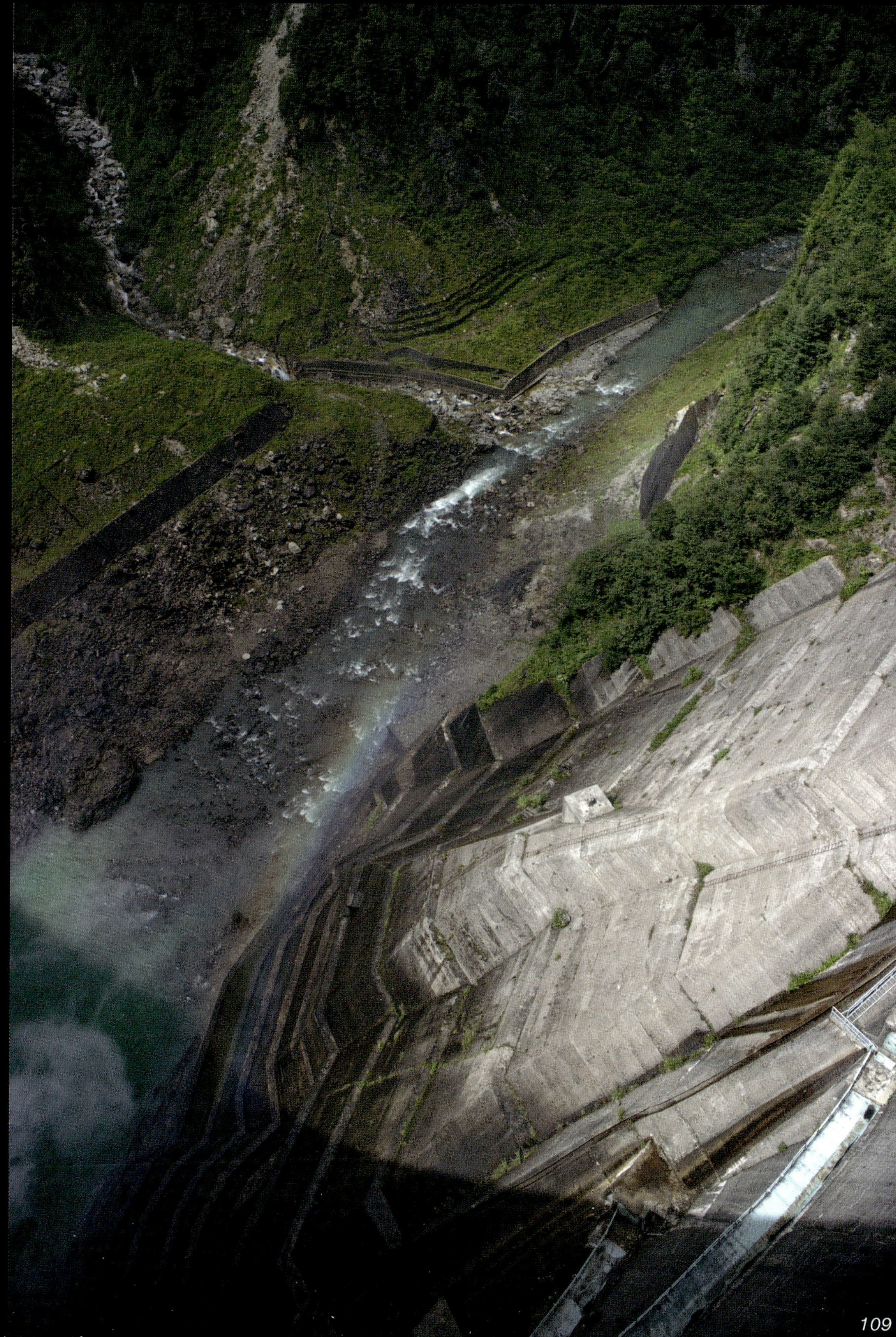

The steep descent by ropeway towards the 1,500-meter-high located dam is truly spectacular and opens a panorama on the Japanese Alps that is unforgettable. Climbing the staircase along the concrete wall of the dam is not for the fainthearted, but is definitely worth the effort. In the summer months it is possible to see a rainbow appearing when water is discharged.

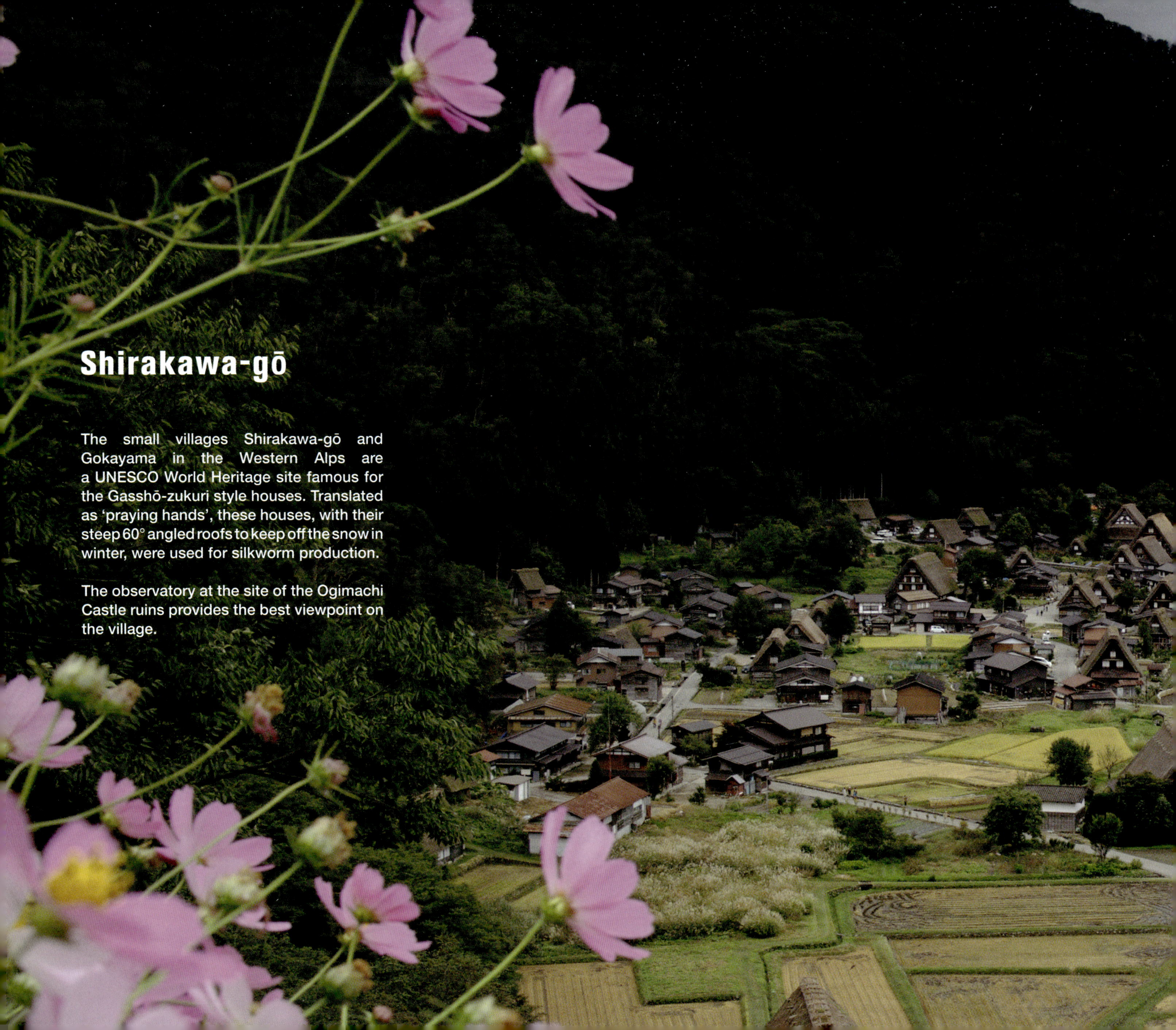

## Shirakawa-gō

The small villages Shirakawa-gō and Gokayama in the Western Alps are a UNESCO World Heritage site famous for the Gasshō-zukuri style houses. Translated as 'praying hands', these houses, with their steep 60° angled roofs to keep off the snow in winter, were used for silkworm production.

The observatory at the site of the Ogimachi Castle ruins provides the best viewpoint on the village.

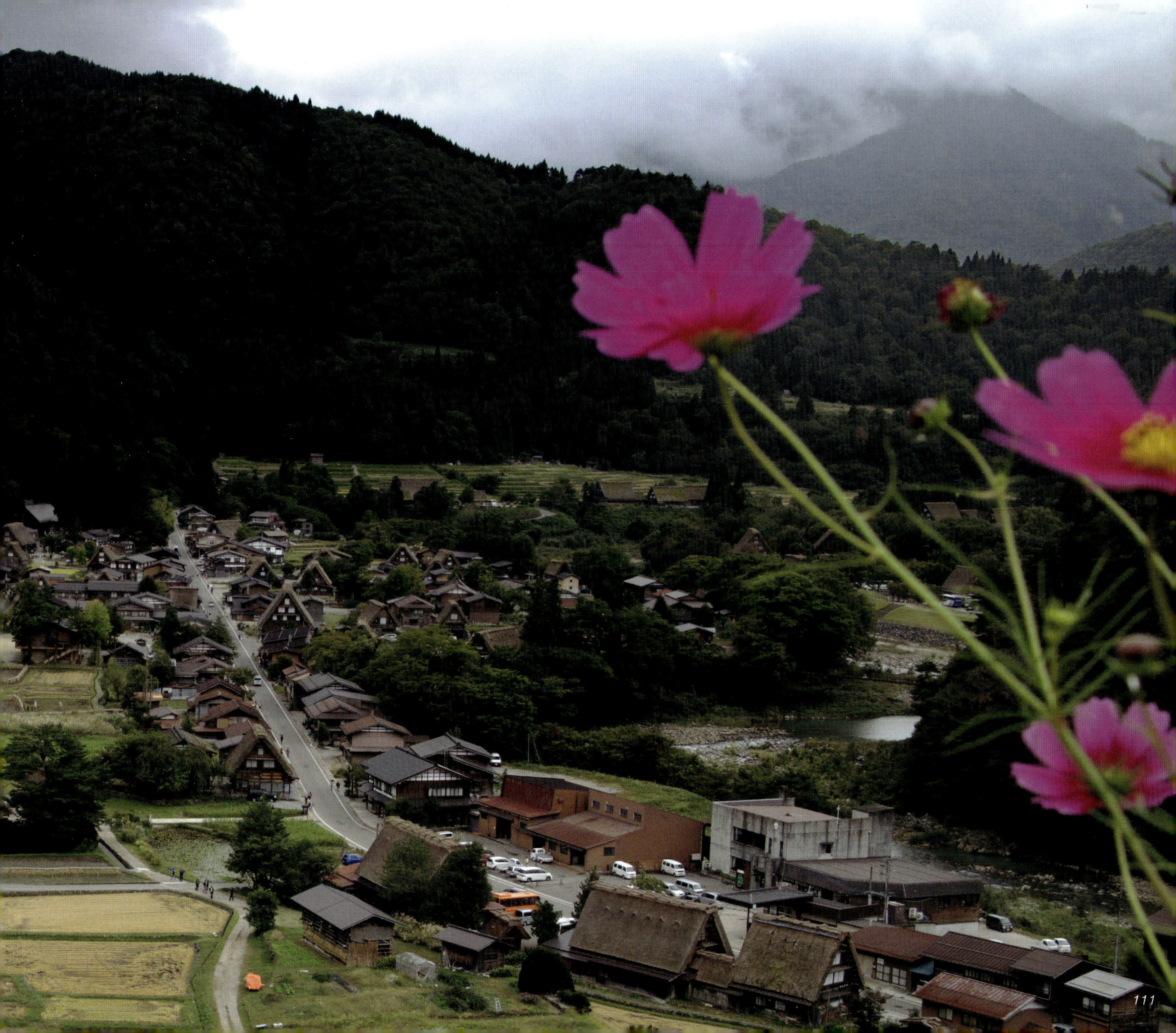

## Rice and Sake

Over 2,500 years ago rice cultivation was introduced in Japan probably from China. Recent archeological findings suggest that rice even may have been grown much earlier. Ever since, rice has become a staple of the Japanese diet and is a core element of the Japanese culture.
Most of Japan has an ideal climate for growing rice and the variety of rice that is cultivated is called the Japonica. The ordinary Japanese short-grained rice consists of short translucent grains that have a sticky texture when cooked making it ideal to eat with chopsticks.

When talking about the cultivation of rice one cannot neglect the history of Japanese sake, a rice based fermented alcoholic beverage. The technique to make a fermented alcoholic drink from rice is also thought to have originated in ancient China. The subtle taste of this light alcoholic drink goes well with sushi and is slowly becoming more appreciated in the western world.

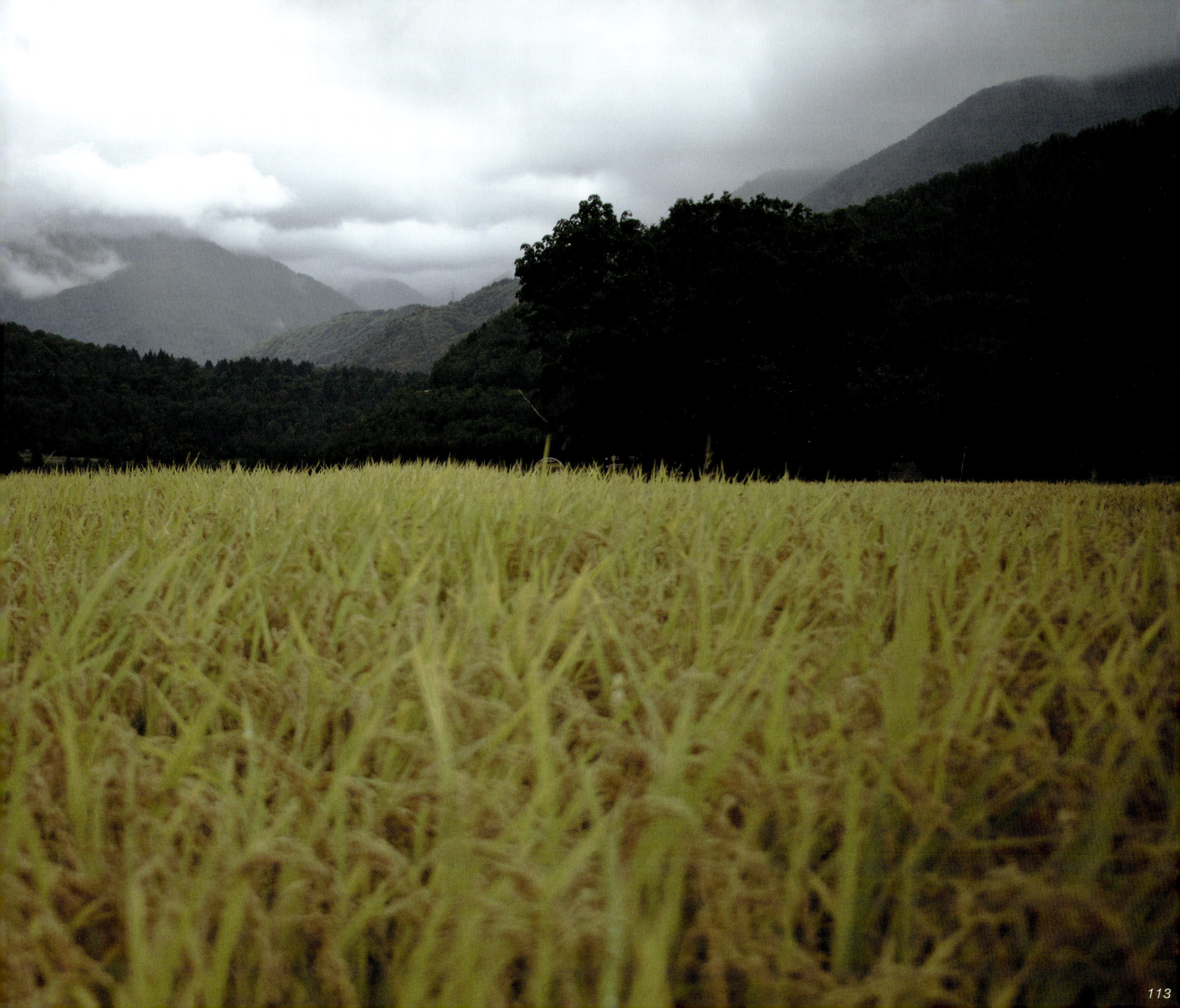

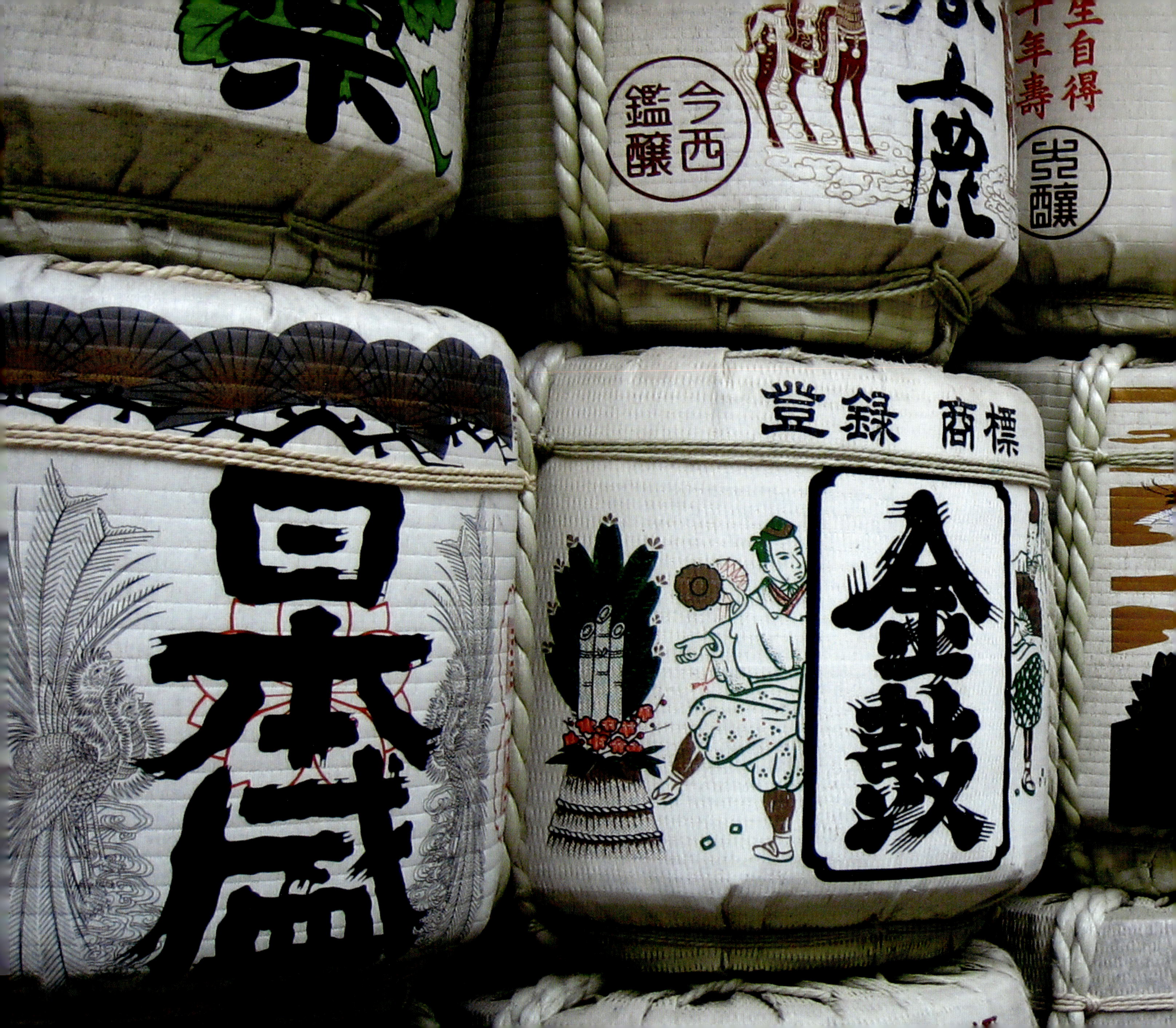

今西
鑑釀
日本盛
登録商標
金鼓

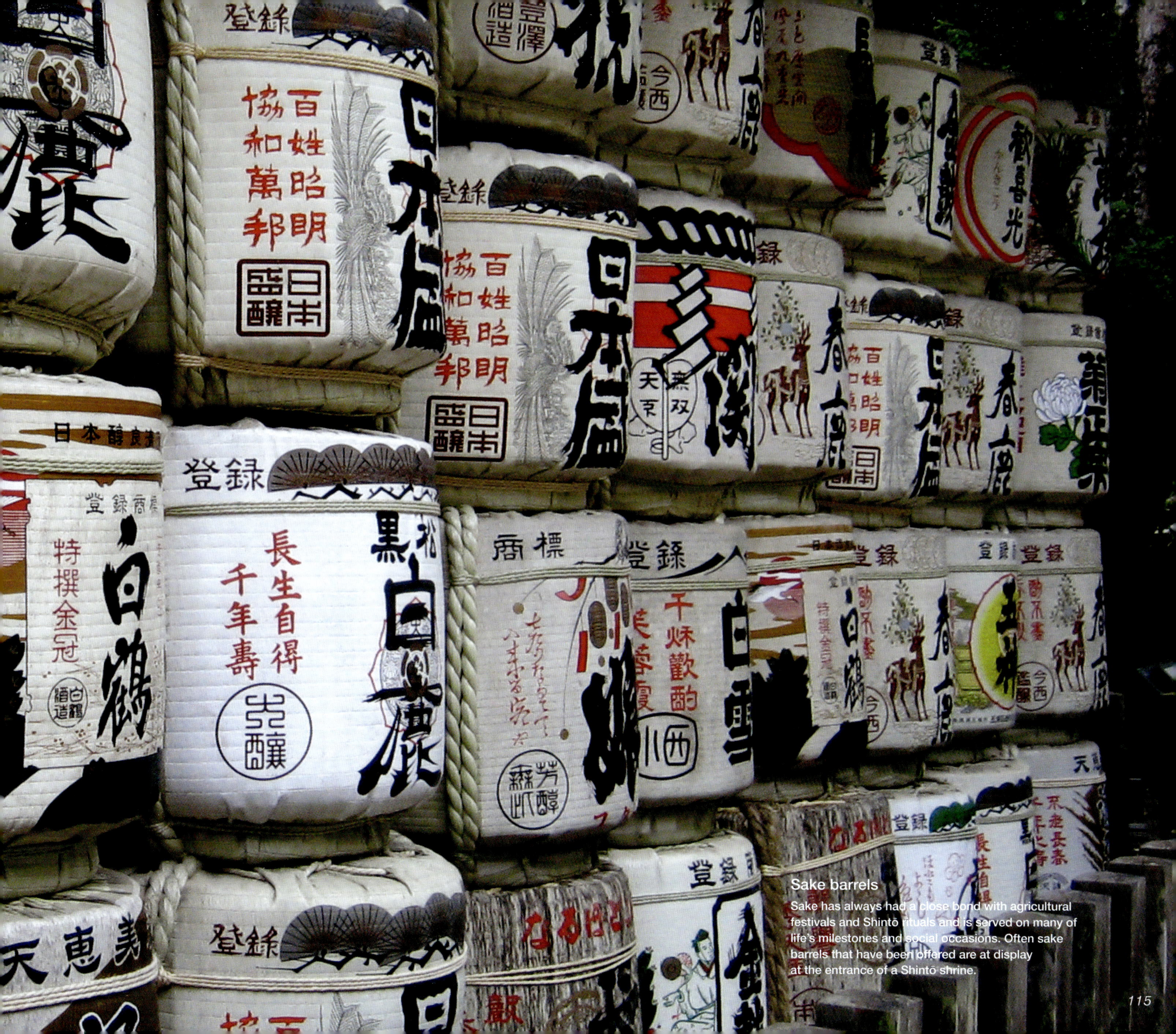


**Sake barrels**

Sake has always had a close bond with agricultural festivals and Shintō rituals and is served on many of life's milestones and social occasions. Often sake barrels that have been offered are at display at the entrance of a Shintō shrine.

京都

# KYOTO

Kyoto, centrally located in Honshū, is a large modern city with excellent restaurants, a vast tourist infrastructure and many universities. It is the home base of big technology groups such as Nintendo and Kyocera.

Kyoto however received its real fame as the imperial capital of Japan and the cultural heart of the nation. A position it held for over a millennium, until in 1868, as part of the Meiji restoration, the capital was moved to Tokyo. Kyoto, like Kanazawa, was not destroyed by the allied bombings of World War II and despite modern developments a lot of temples, shrines, gardens and traditional districts from the Edo period have been preserved.

There is so much to see, try, do and taste in Kyoto that the city and its beautiful surrounding areas justify your trip to Japan even if that would be the only place you plan to visit. Kyoto is lovely in all seasons, yet if I would be asked to make a ranking I would recommend a visit in autumn, spring, winter and summer – in that order.

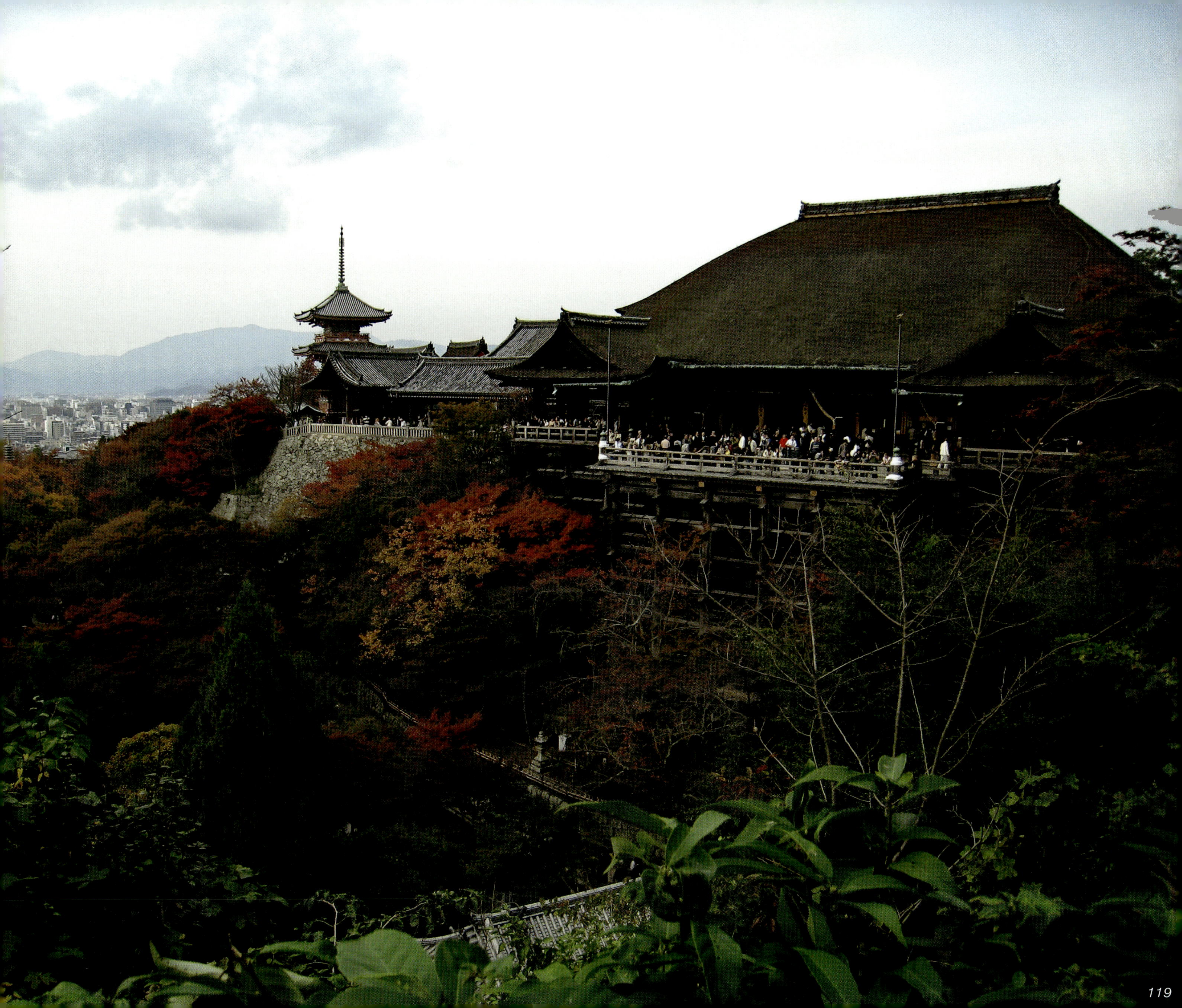

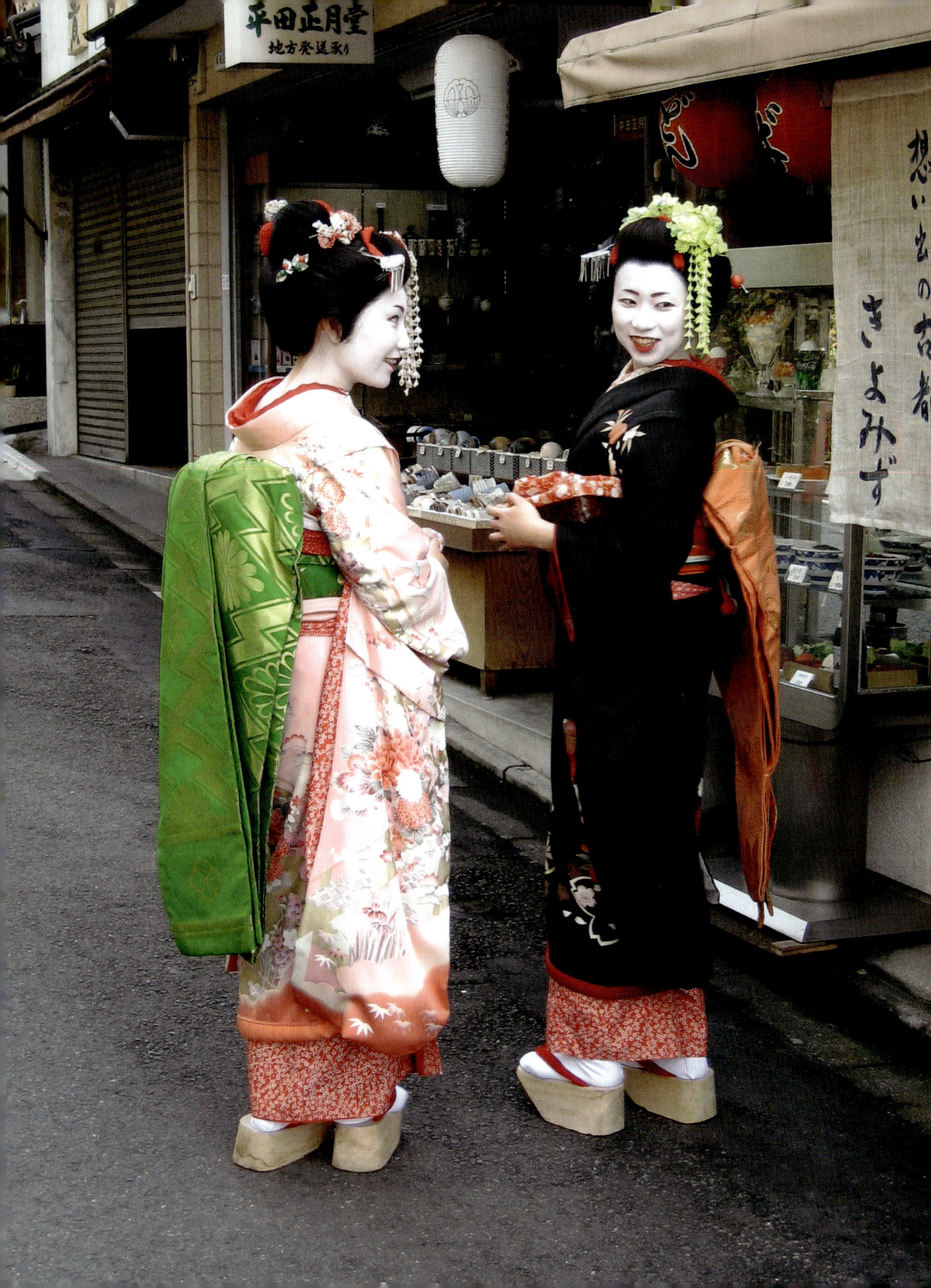


## Geisha

The origins of the geisha culture go back to the courtesans entertaining high-ranking and wealthy men in traditional Japan. Geisha are extremely well trained in a range of Japanese arts, but the community has been shrinking considerably over the last century. It is still possible to see geisha and maiko, apprentice geisha, in the Higashiyama district and Gion, the old pleasure quarter of Kyoto, although they are becoming a rare sight. The exquisite kimonos, the make-up and the mystery surrounding the profession have a strong appeal on tourists. Over the last years, the geisha community has expressed the wish not to be followed around by hordes of tourists searching for the perfect selfie.

## Higashiyama

The narrow streets in the Higashiyama district are flocked with tourists and hence not short of shops selling pottery, teacups and pots, Japanese sweets, bamboo ware, traditional dolls and other souvenirs. Most of the wooden two-story houses are over two hundred years old and give a good idea of what Kyoto may have looked like in the 18th century.

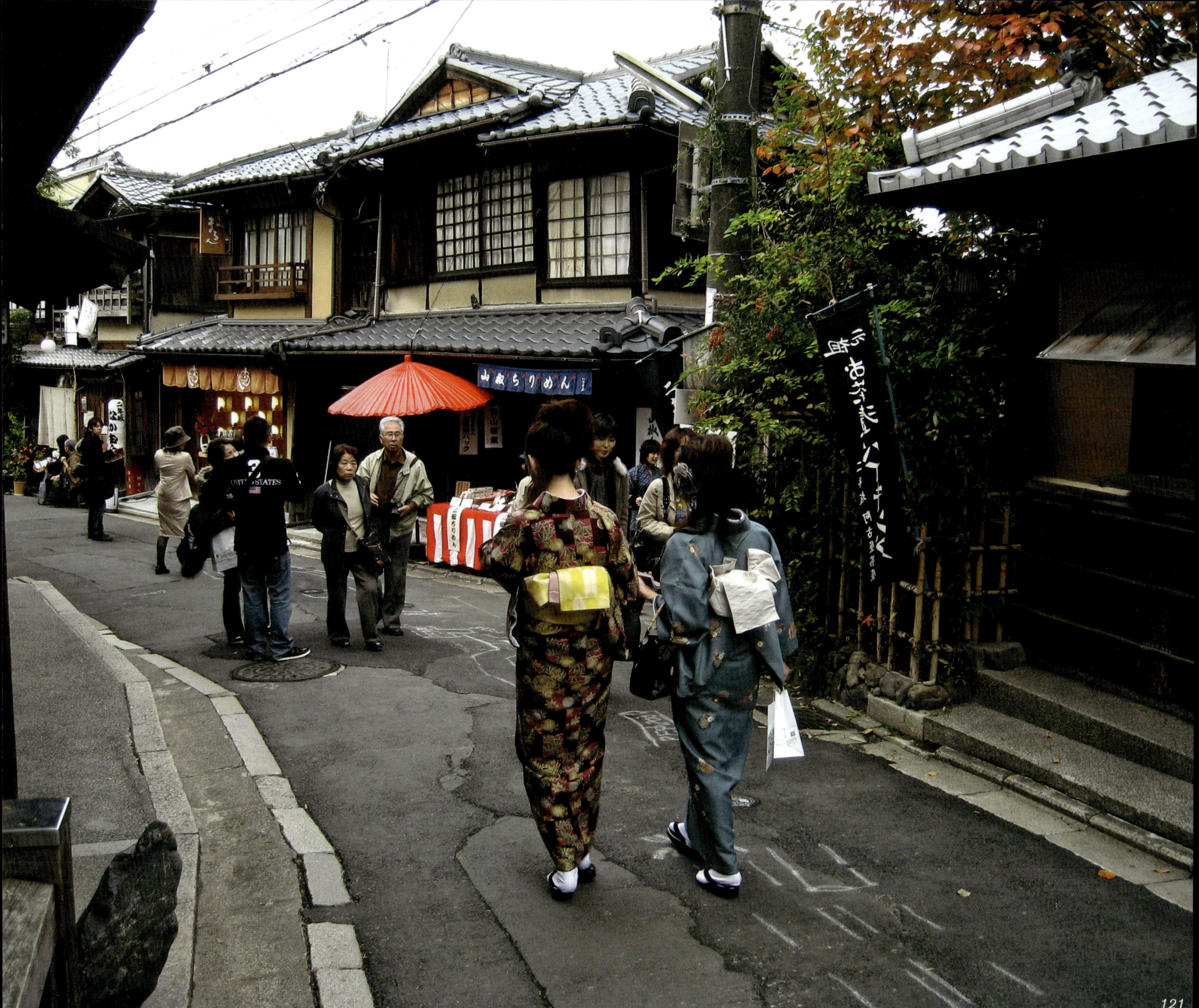
山椒ちりめん

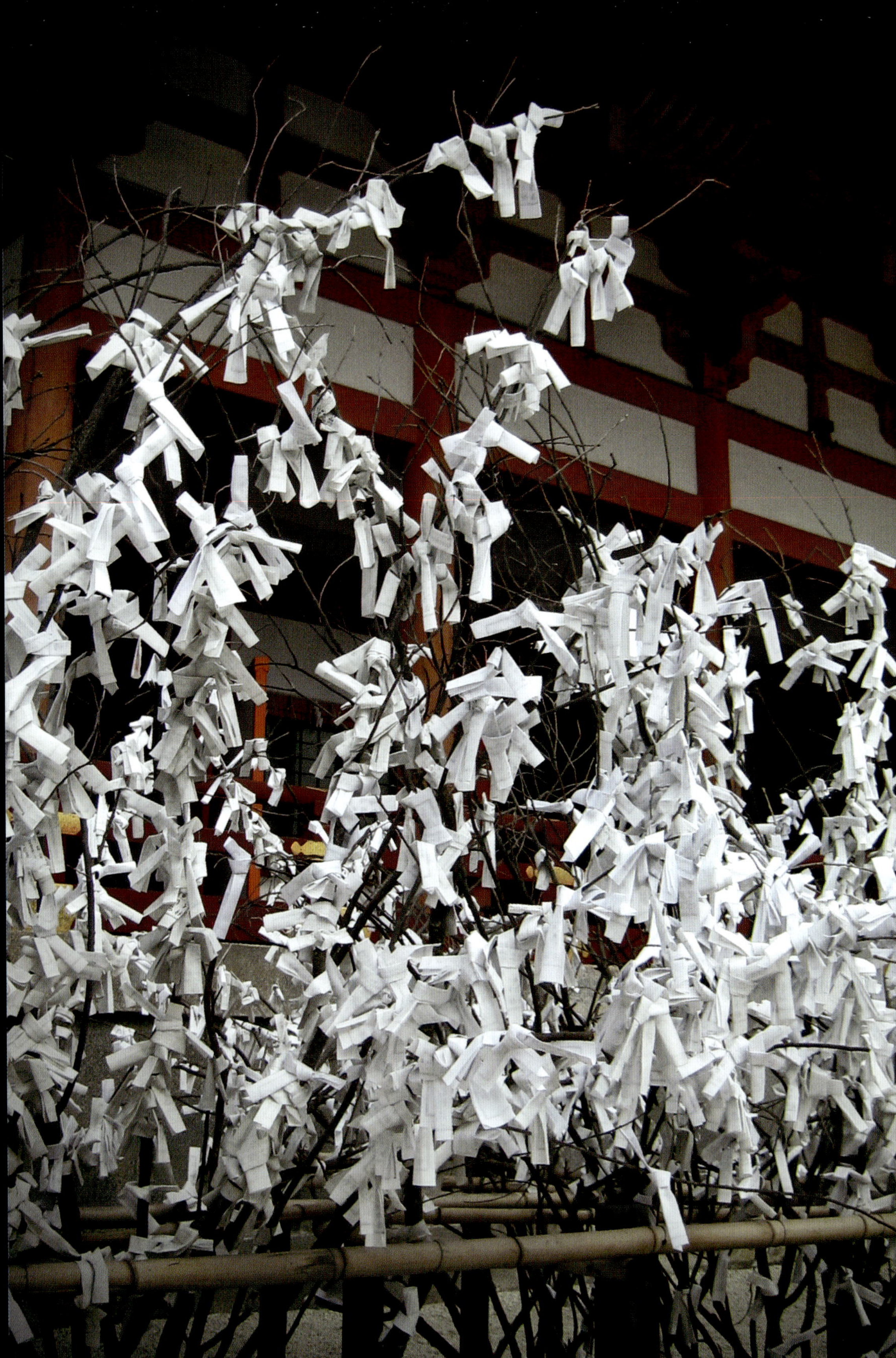

Try your luck by making a small offer which allows you to choose a fortune telling strip of paper named o-mikuji in Japanese. Should you have bad fortune waiting, then leave the bad luck at the shrine by tying the paper to a dead tree placed there for that purpose.

## Heian-jingū

The huge vermillion red Heian Shrine and the massive torii on the avenue leading to the shrine make it a landmark that cannot be missed. The Shintō shrine was completed in 1895 to commemorate the 1100th birthday of the city of Kyoto and to honor Emperor Kanmu and Emperor Komei, respectively the first and last emperors to rule Japan from Kyoto. The impressive site, including a nice Japanese garden is a replica at 60 percent of the original size of the emperor's Hall of State.

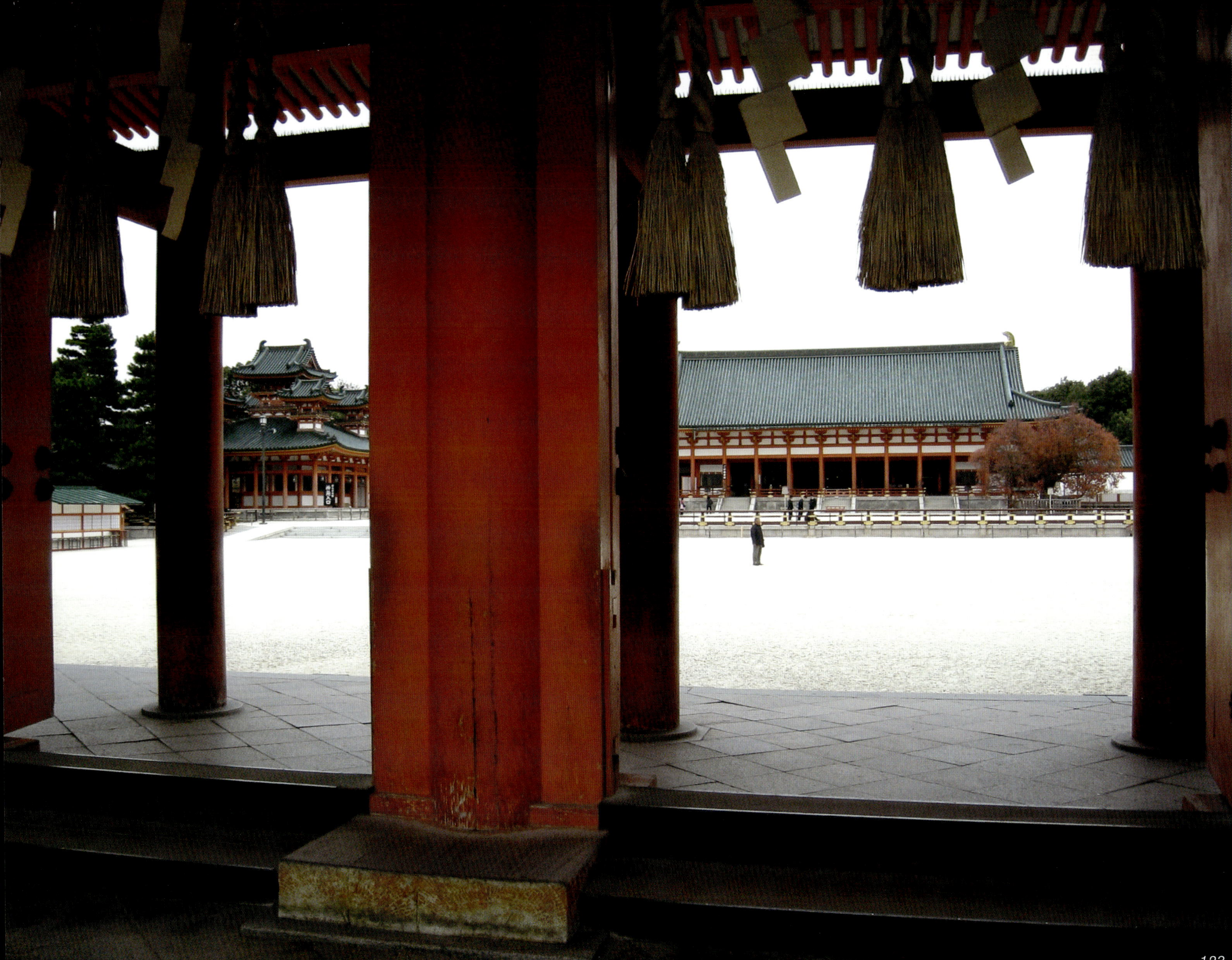

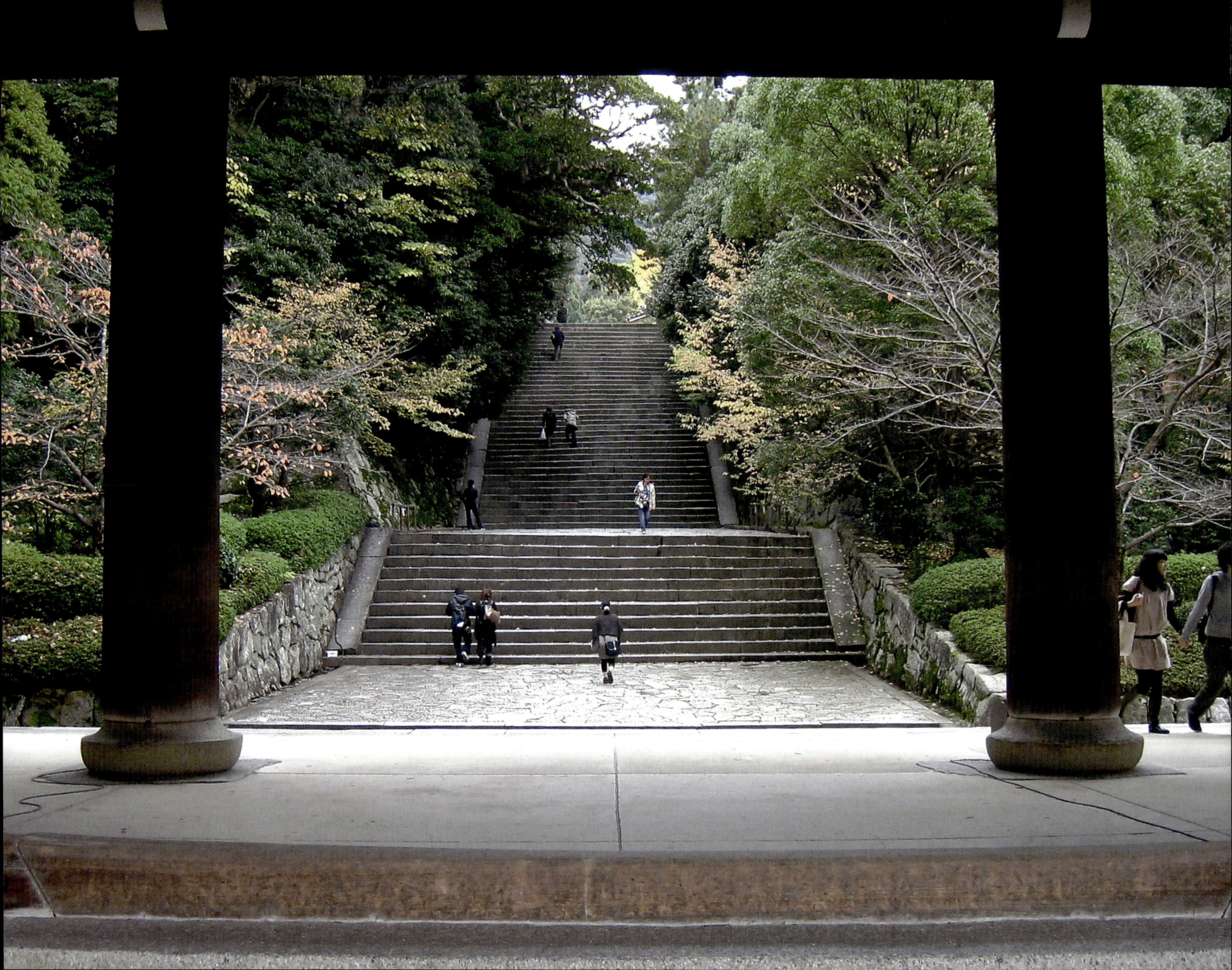

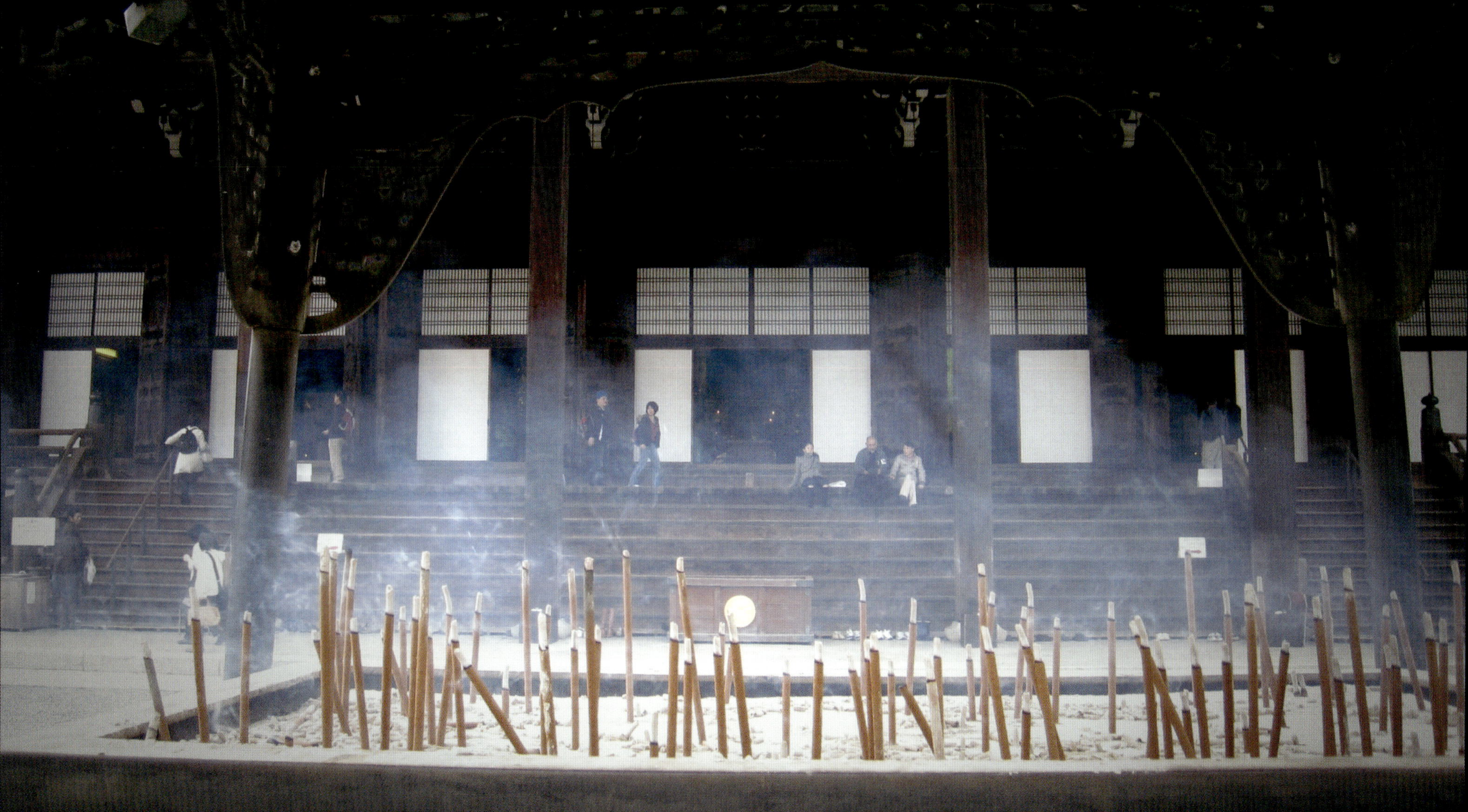

## Chion-in

In the northern area of Higashiyama lies the huge temple complex Chion-in of the Jōdo Buddhist sect founded by Hōnen in 1175. Note the vast differences in style between the Heian Shrine and this temple. Supported financially by the second and third generation of the Tokugawa shogunate, the wooden buildings are absolutely monumental. The San-mon gate was erected in 1621 and is 24 meter high and 50 meter wide and therefore one of the largest in Japan. After having climbed the steep staircase to the temple complex, the view of the main hall with the burning incense in front gives the site a kind of solemn feeling. It is in this building that the sacred image of the founding priest Hōnen is worshipped.

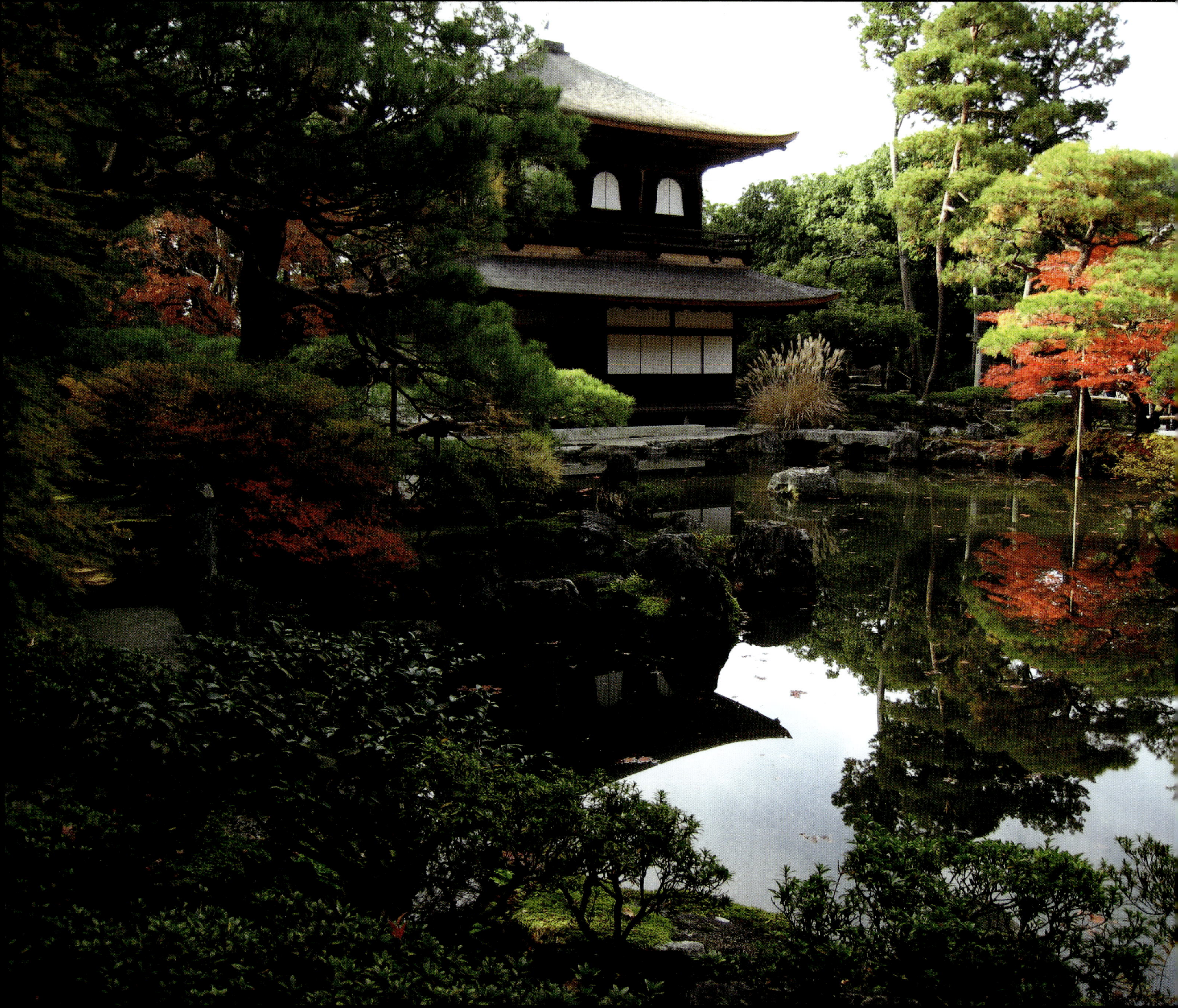

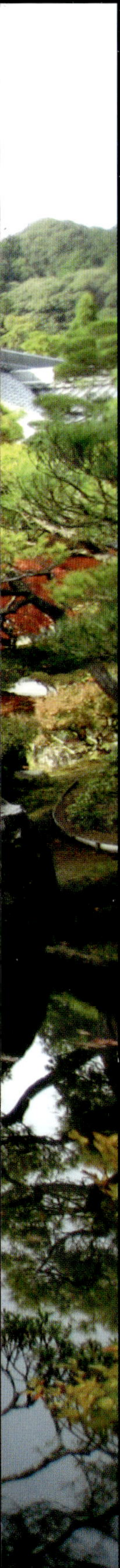

## Ginkaku-ji

The elegant beauty and gardens of Ginkaku-ji, the Silver Pavilion Temple, make it one of the top attractions in Kyoto. The popularity of the temple is immense, so – if somehow possible – plan your visit early and outside the weekends. Originally the temple was built in the 15th century as a retirement villa for shogun Ashikaga Yoshimasa. After his death the building was converted into a temple of the Rinzai Zen sect of Buddhism and became listed as a UNESCO World Heritage site in 1994.

## The Philosopher's path

The Philosopher's path is a scenic walk between Nanzen-ji and Ginkaku-ji along a small canal at the foot of the hills bordering the Higashiyama district. It is highly recommended to take this stroll on your way to Ginkaku-ji instead of the busy tarmac street leading to the temple.

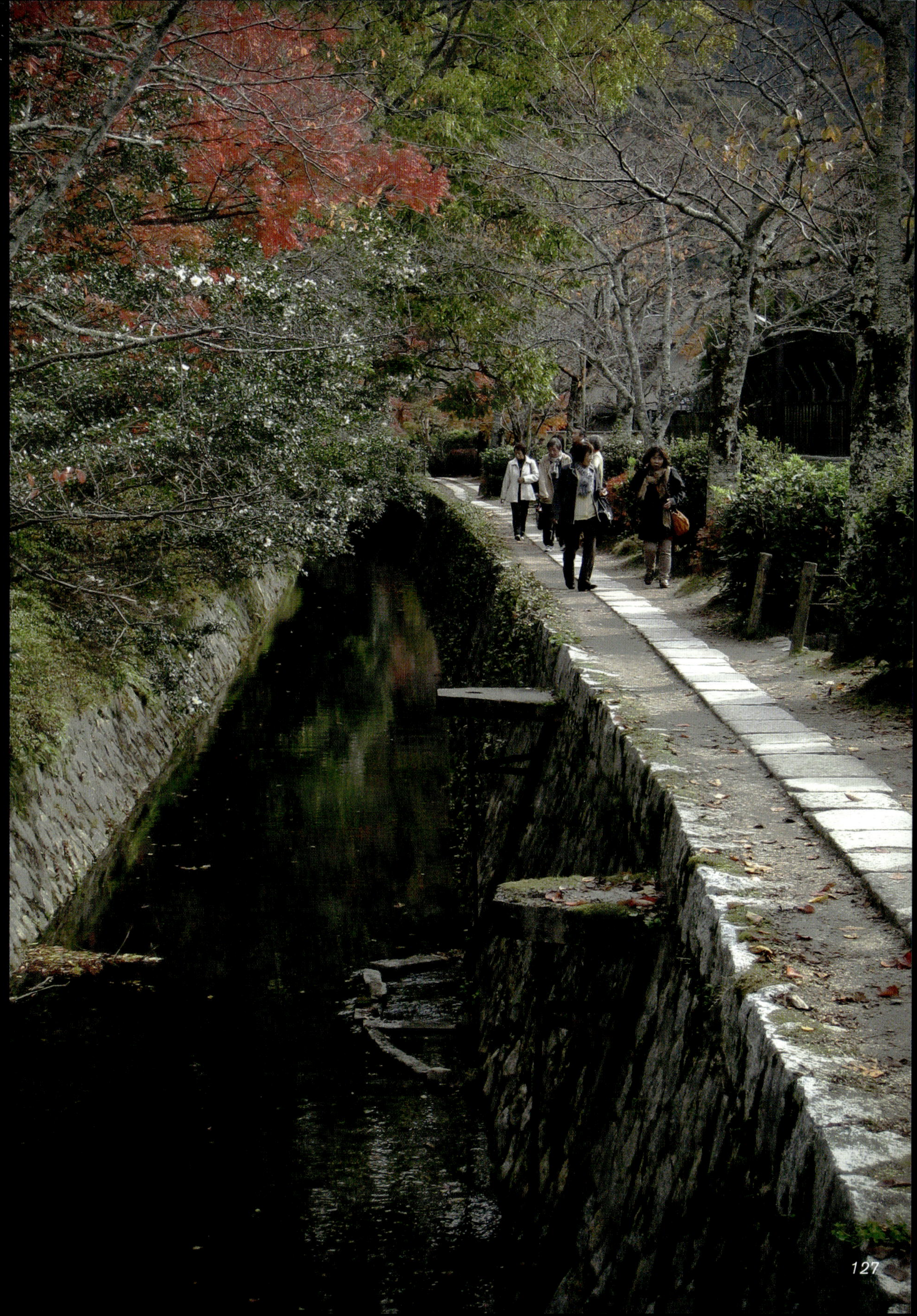

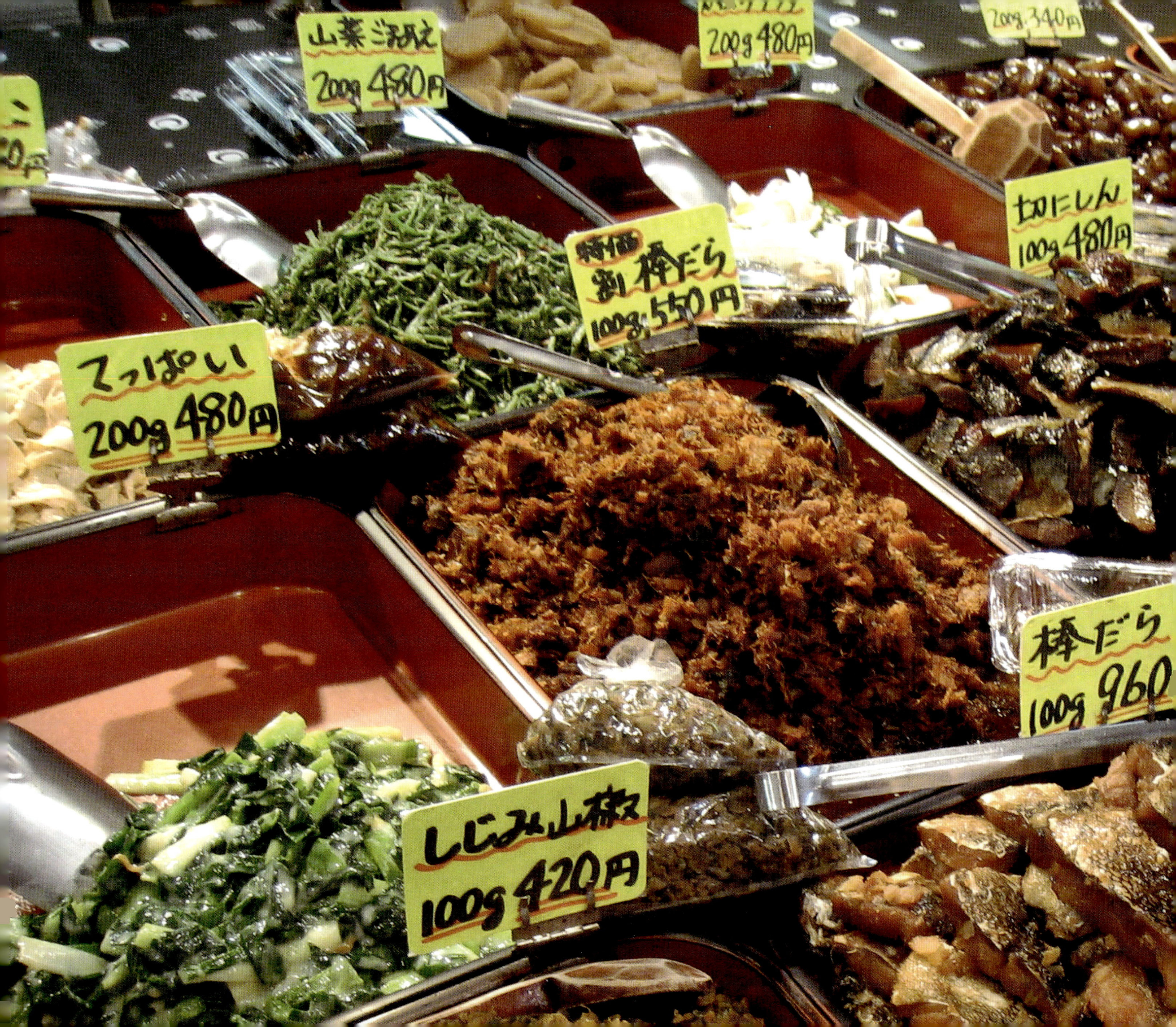
200g 480円
200g 480円
200g 340円
切にしん
100g 480円
特価
割 棒だら
100g 550円
てっぱい
200g 480円
棒だら
100g 960
しじみ山椒
100g 420円

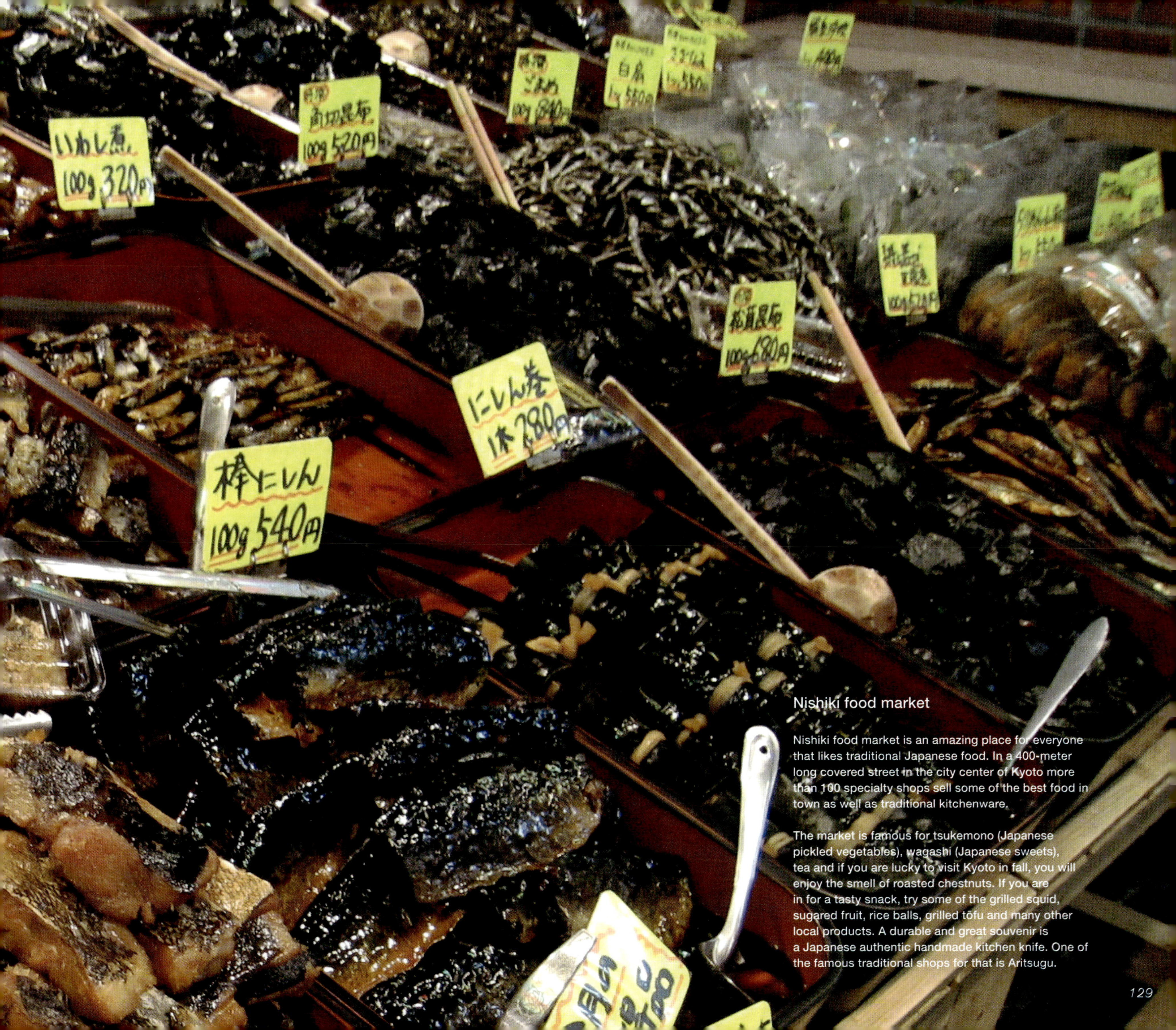


## Nishiki food market

Nishiki food market is an amazing place for everyone that likes traditional Japanese food. In a 400-meter long covered street in the city center of Kyoto more than 100 specialty shops sell some of the best food in town as well as traditional kitchenware.

The market is famous for tsukemono (Japanese pickled vegetables), wagashi (Japanese sweets), tea and if you are lucky to visit Kyoto in fall, you will enjoy the smell of roasted chestnuts. If you are in for a tasty snack, try some of the grilled squid, sugared fruit, rice balls, grilled tōfu and many other local products. A durable and great souvenir is a Japanese authentic handmade kitchen knife. One of the famous traditional shops for that is Aritsugu.

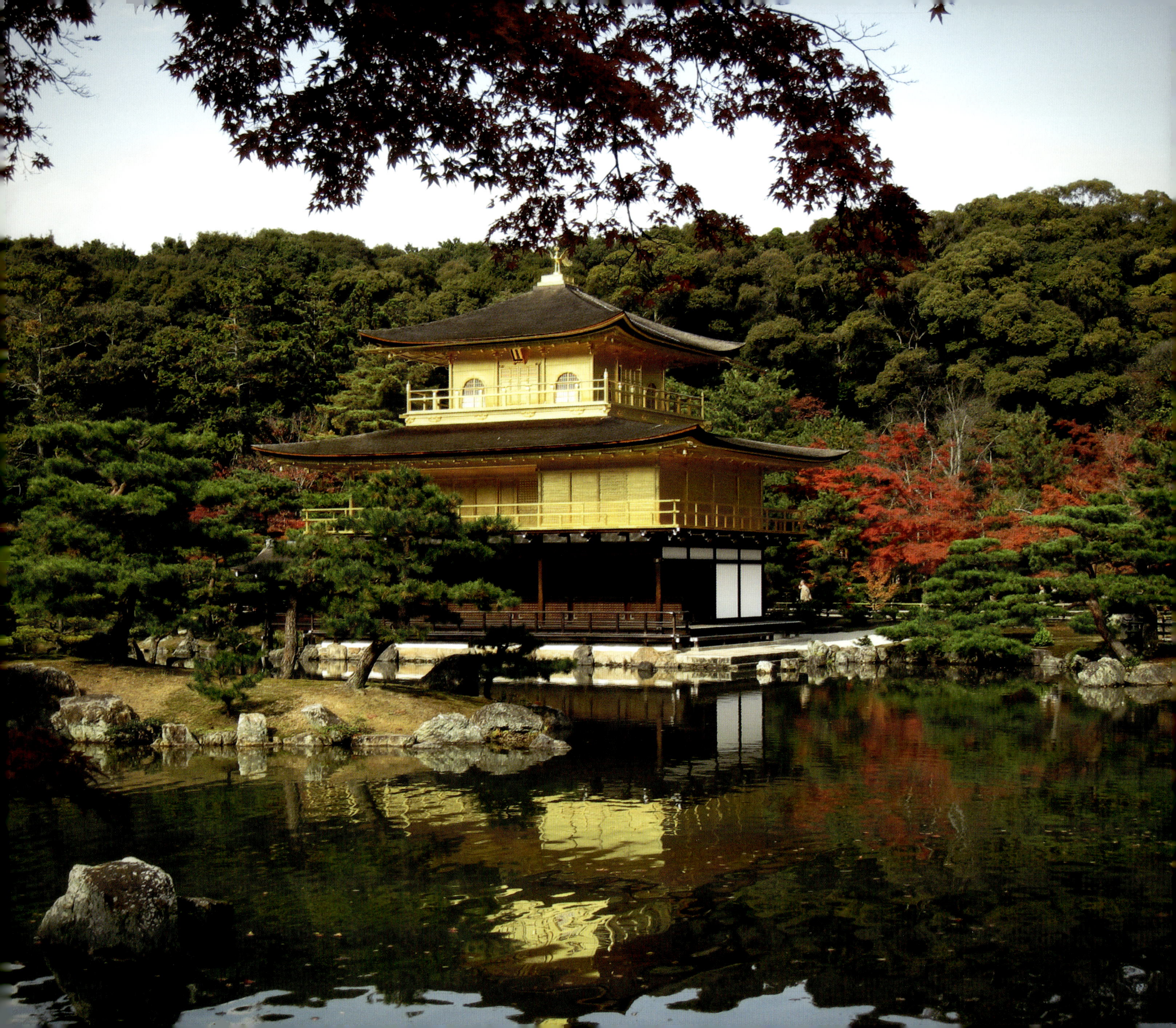

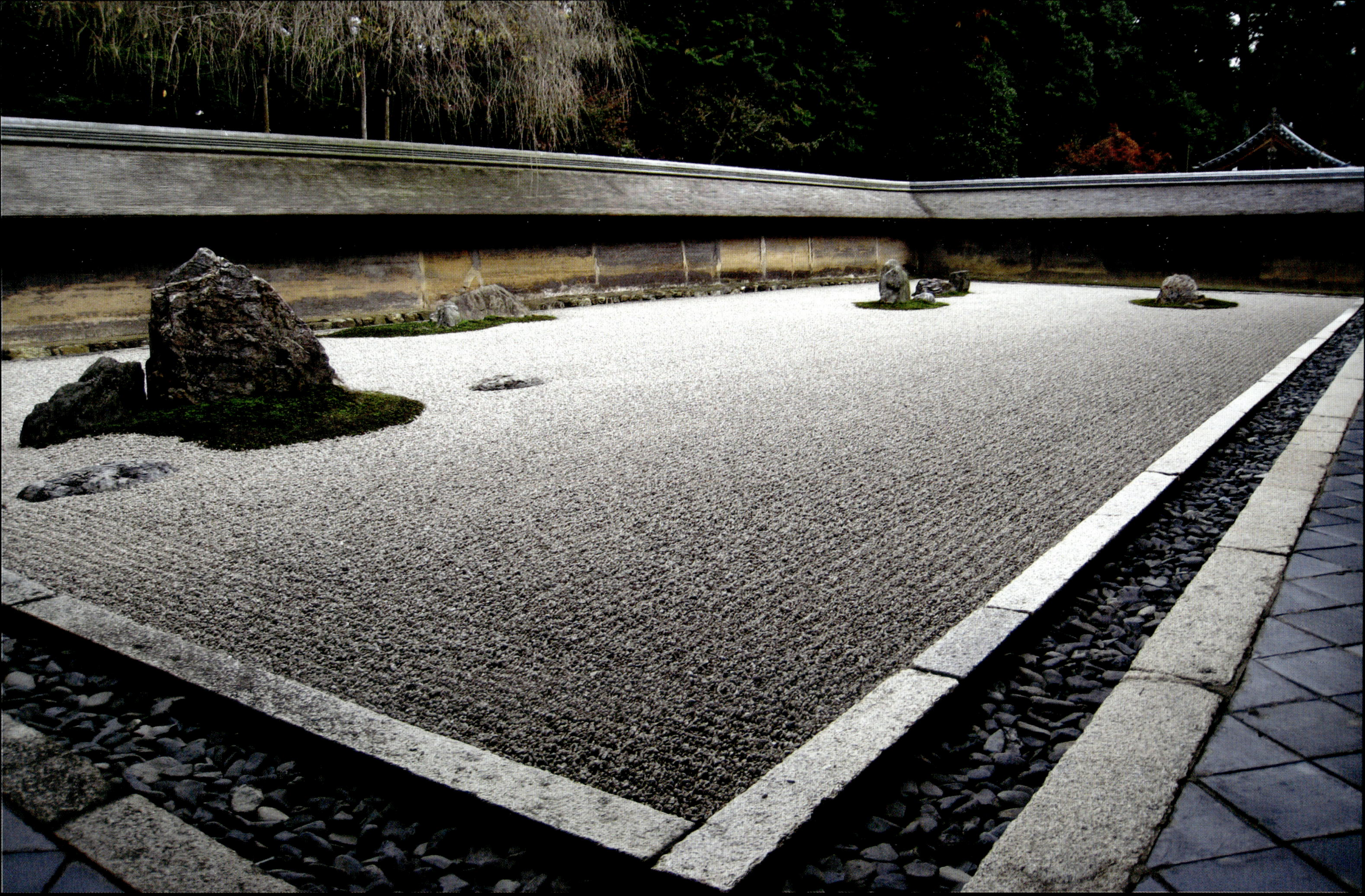

## Kinkaku-ji

Kinkaku-ji, which translates as 'Golden Pavilion Temple', is located in the north western hills of Kyoto. Originally it was a villa used by the aristocrat Ashikaga Yoshimitsu, who became a Buddhist priest by the end of the 14th century. His estate was changed into a Zen Buddhist temple according to his last will. As a mentally ill novice monk set the original afire in 1950, today's Rokuon-ji temple – as it is officially named – is actually a replica from 1955. The reflection of the garden and the gold lacquered temple in the 'mirror pond' is an awesome sight that for many justifies the trip to Kyoto. Not visible on the photo is the huge popularity of this epic setting. You will be surrounded by schoolkids and tourists arriving by bus every minute, so be prepared to wait for your turn to take a good photo.

## Ryōan-ji

A small walk from Kinkaku-ji, in the hills of Kitayama, one can find Ryōan-ji, probably Japan's most famous stone garden. This minimalist, abstract Zen rock garden's history goes back to the Muromachi period and is surrounded by mystery as the designer nor his intentions are known. The layout of the 15 stones in the gravel appears to be in such way that the stones cannot be seen all together.

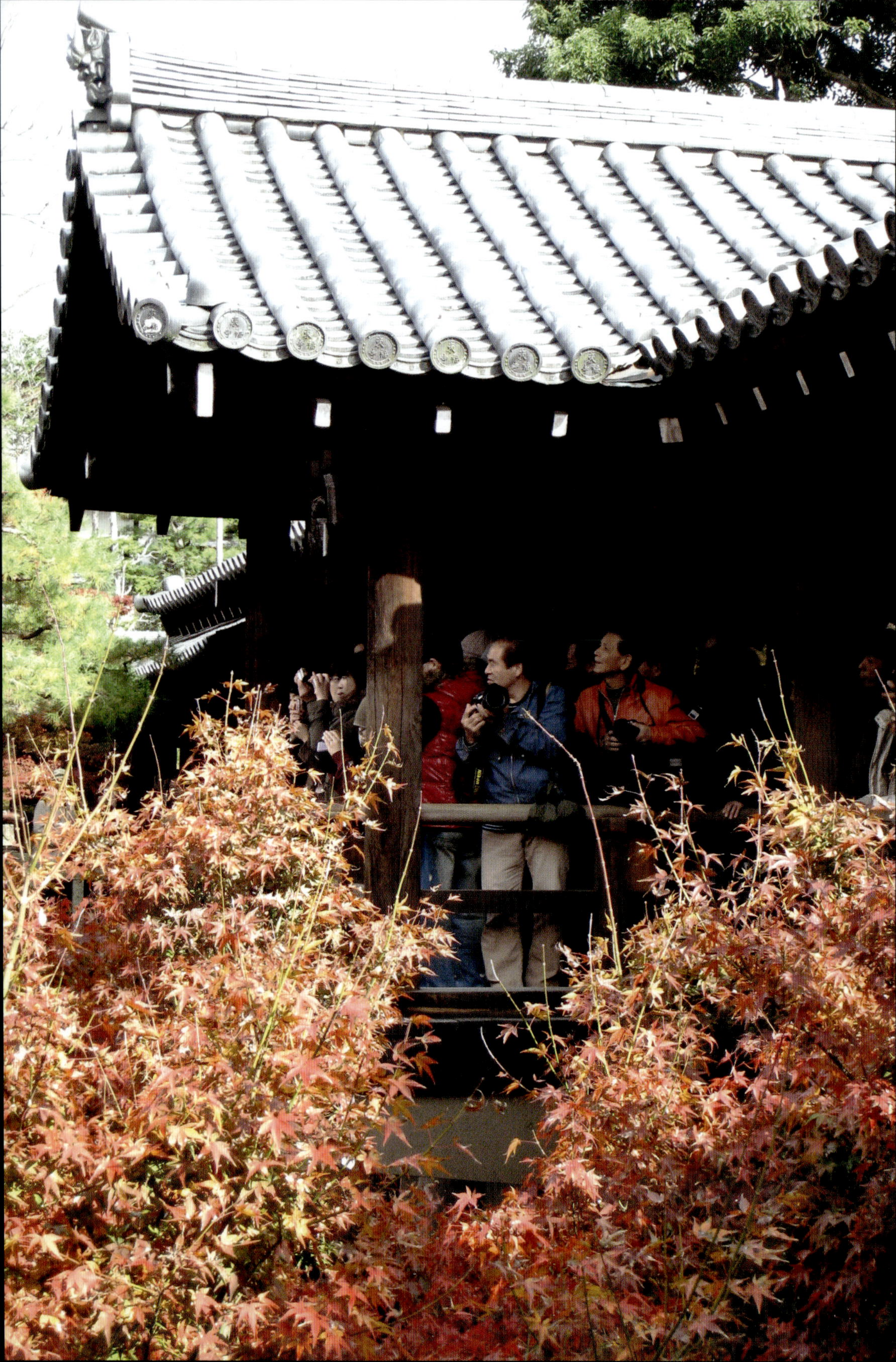

## Tōfuku-ji

Tōfuku-ji is the head temple of the Rinzai sect of Zen Buddhism and dates from 1236. It is not only the largest but also the oldest temple in Kyoto. The tall San-mon gate and the many different gardens are worth the visit, although the temple is probably most famous for the spectacular view of the maple leaves from the Tsuten Bridge in autumn.

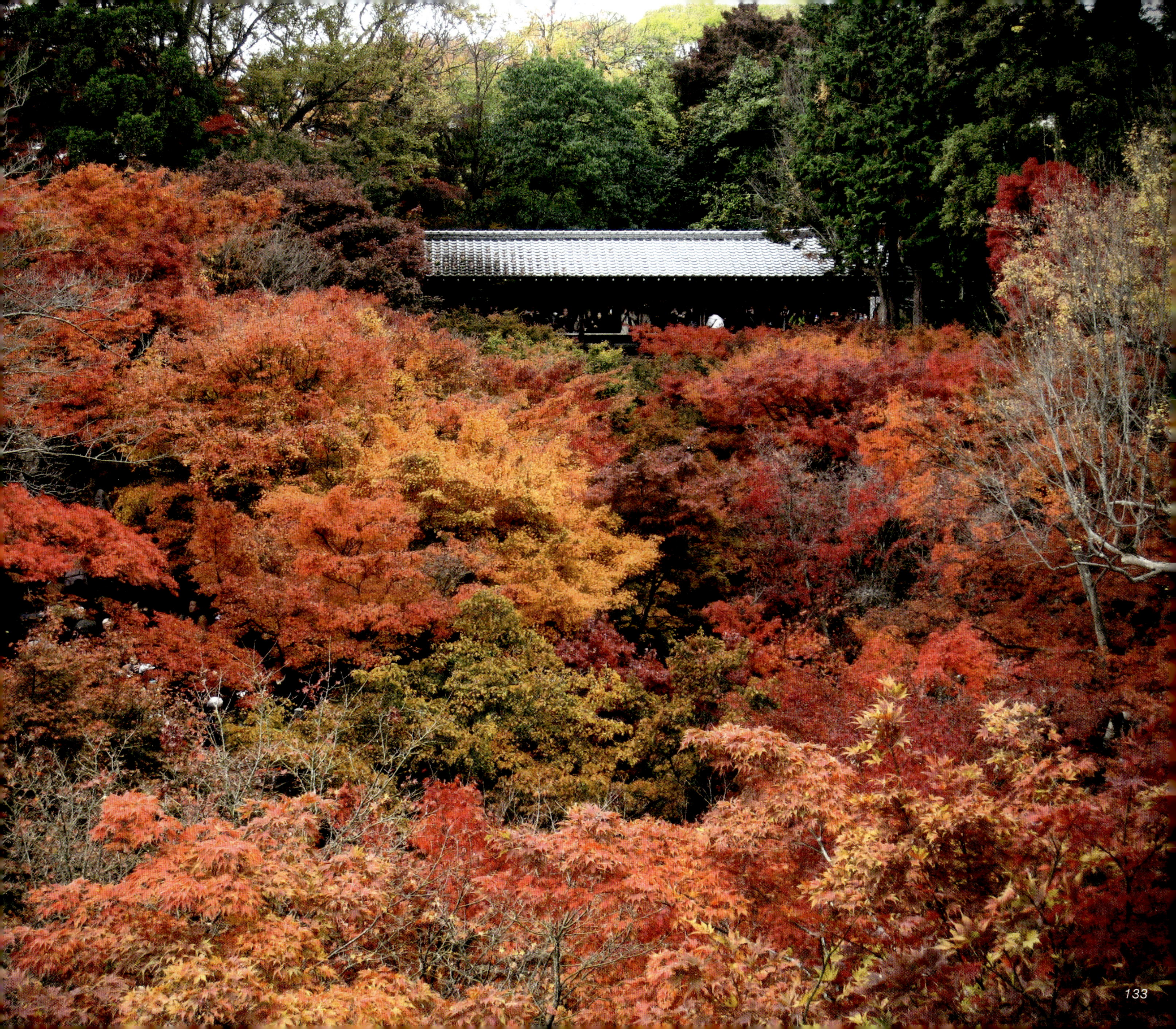

関西

# KANSAI

There are few places in the world with so many UNESCO World Heritage sites as the Kansai region. Home of the former imperial capital cities Kyoto and Nara, Kansai was at the dawn of Japan's long history as the cultural center of the nation.

Often overlooked by tourists is that the Kansai region has always been playing an important maritime and merchant role in Japan thanks to the ports of Kobe and Osaka.

Kansai was politically, culturally and economically important but also spiritually, as the roots of Japanese Buddhism and Shintō, Japan's native spiritual belief, are deeply imbedded in the Kansai area. Especially in the southern area of Kansai are some of Japan's most important spiritual and religious centers such as the Buddhist temple complex of Kōya-san and Ise-jingū, the Shintō shrine dedicated to Amaterasu, the sun goddess, from whom it was believed that all Japanese emperors descended.

Finally, at the border of Kansai and Chūgoku is the castle town of Himeji, home of Japan's most impressive feudal castle.

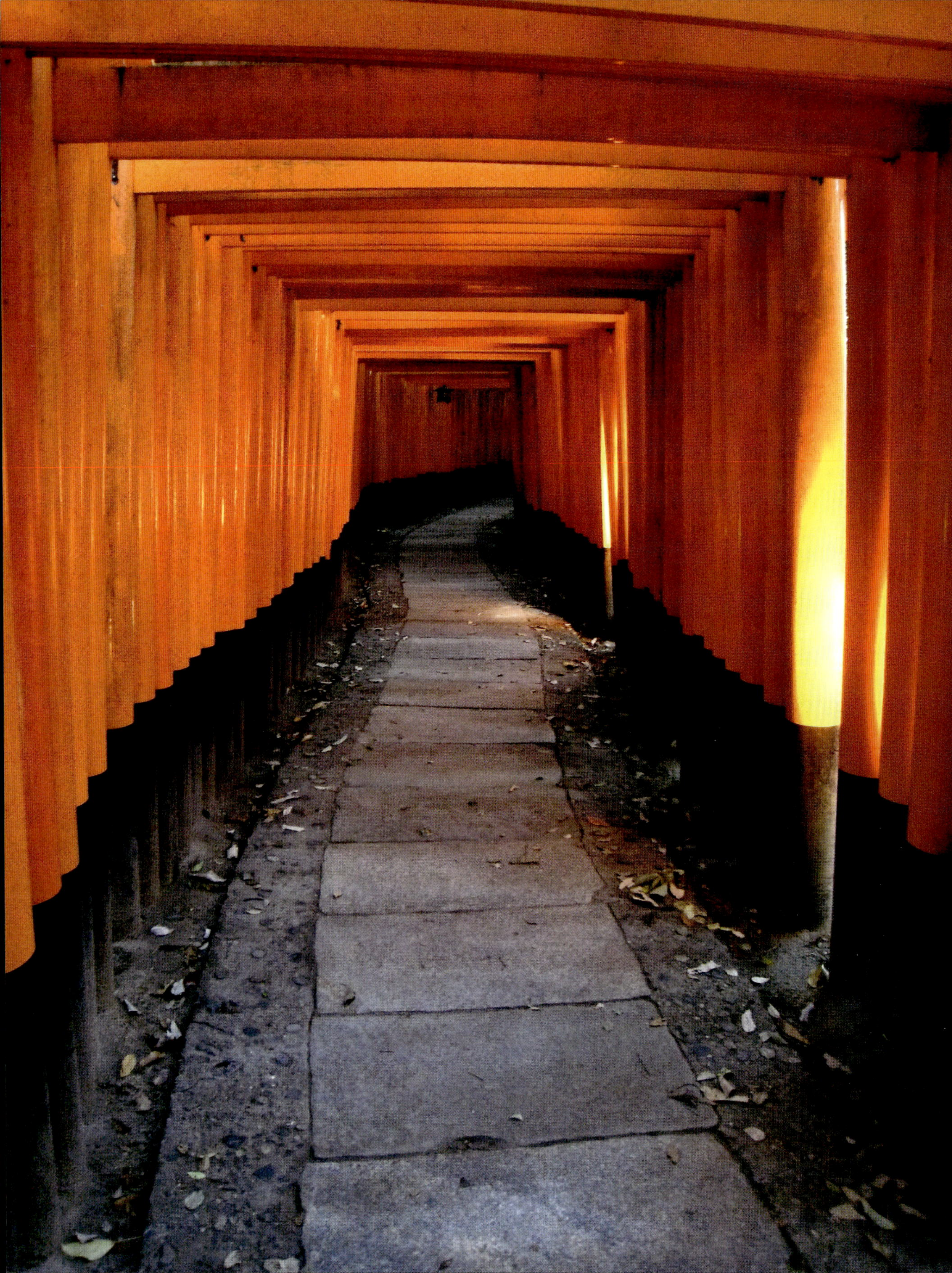

# Nara

Nara was Japan's first permanent imperial capital in the 8th century and is by many scholars considered as the cradle of the Japanese culture. Some magnificent buildings and artefacts from that era survive and being only one hour away from Kyoto by train, both places are often combined in one trip.

### Fushimi Inari

Just outside the city center of Kyoto, on your way by train to Nara lies the splendid Shintō complex Fushimi Inari. It dates from the 10th century and is dedicated to Inari, the god of rice and sake. What makes this shrine unique and appealing are the thousands of red torii that form a kilometers long arcade from the temple all the way up the mystical hill behind it. One may recall the setting from the scene where little Chiyo runs through the torii in the film Memoirs of a Geisha.

### Hōryū-ji

The temple Hōryū-ji, established by the great statesman and Buddhist Prince Shōtoku, dates from the early 7th century and many of the structures are original. It is not only the oldest Buddhist temple in Japan but also one of the world's oldest wooden structures. It became a UNESCO World Heritage site in 1993. The five story pagoda and the main hall at the center of the almost 200,000 m² large temple grounds give a historically accurate view of the splendor of Nara during the Asuka Period.

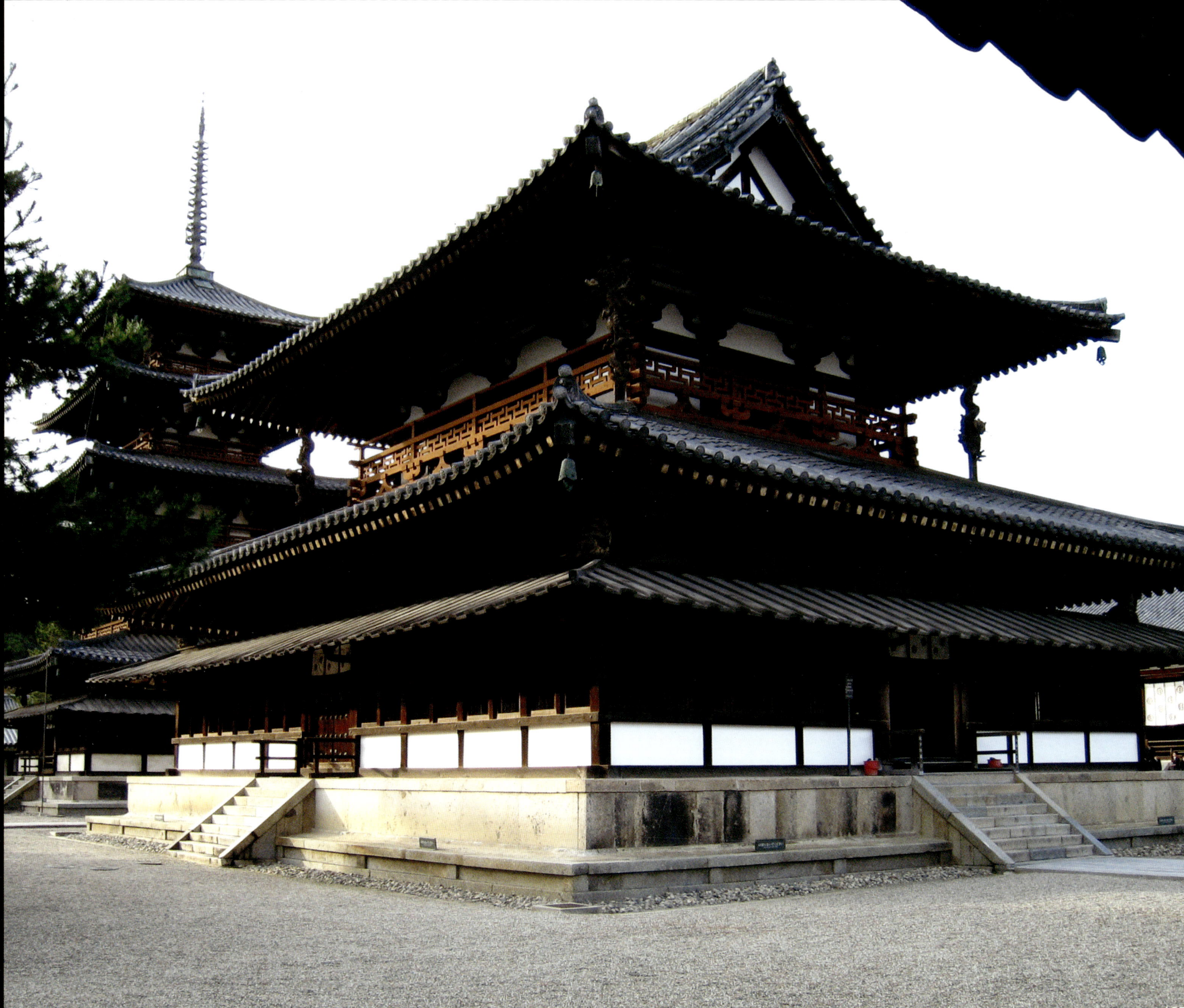

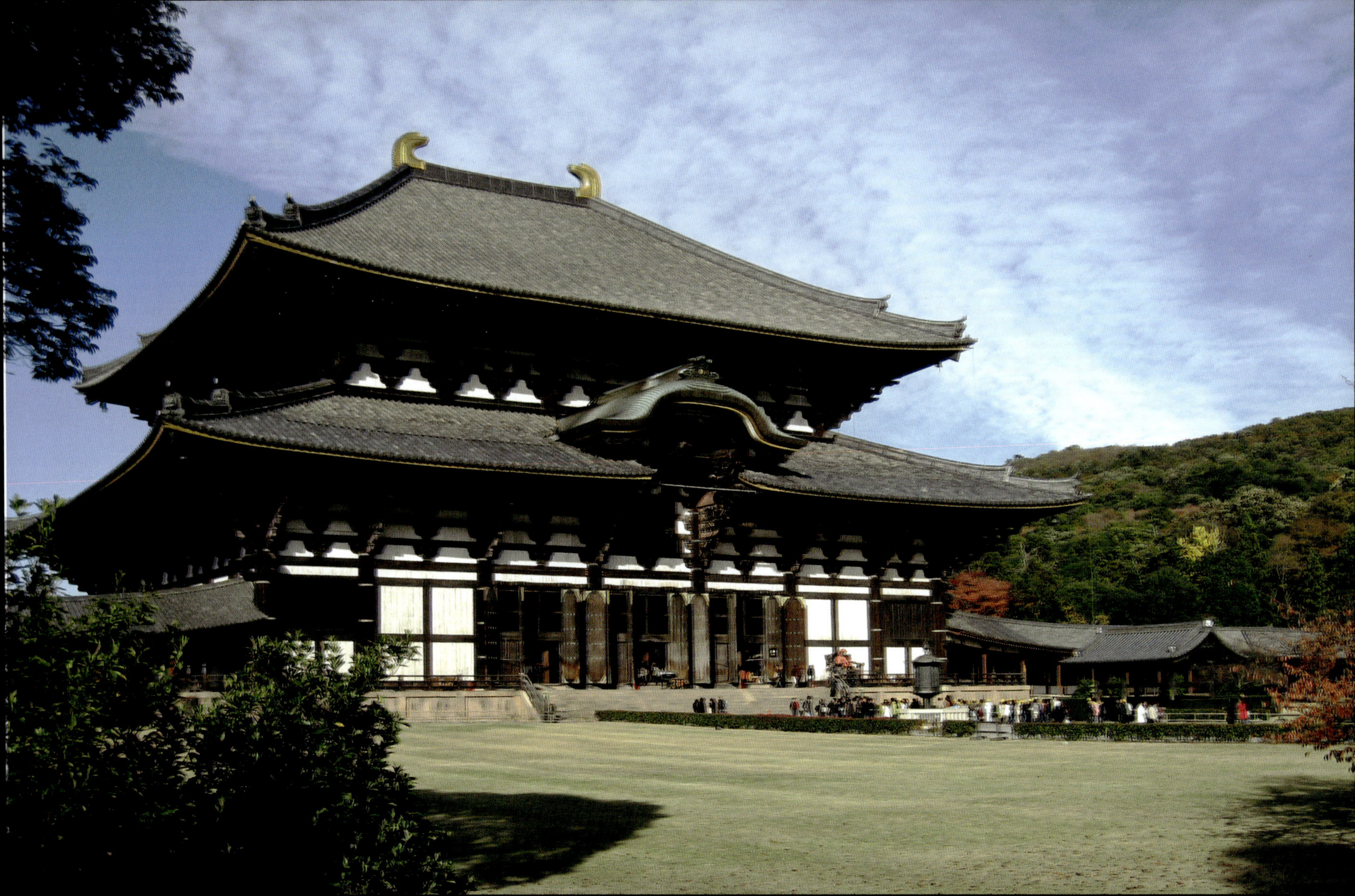

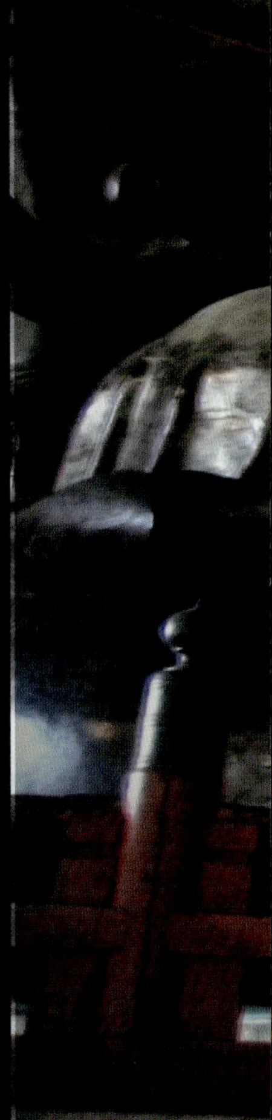

## Tōdai-ji

Tōdai-ji is without a doubt the most famous landmark of Nara. This Buddhist temple was founded by Emperor Shōmu in the mid 8th century. The original great Buddha Hall has been destroyed various times by war and fires. The present structure shown on the photo is a replica from 1709 at two-thirds of the size of the original building. Yet it is still considered to be one of the largest wooden buildings in the world.

## The great Buddha

This bronze statue of Buddha on a lotus throne is 15-meter high and the largest statue of its kind in Japan. It was unveiled in 752 in the presence of many dignitaries and representatives from other Asian countries. In that period it must have been a colossal undertaking that consumed massive resources in terms of labor and funds. Over time the statue has been repaired and recast because of serious damage caused by earthquakes and fires. Nevertheless, when standing in the main Buddha Hall it is hard not to be impressed by the sheer size of the statue and the stunning work of art that the craftsmen in the Nara period were capable of.

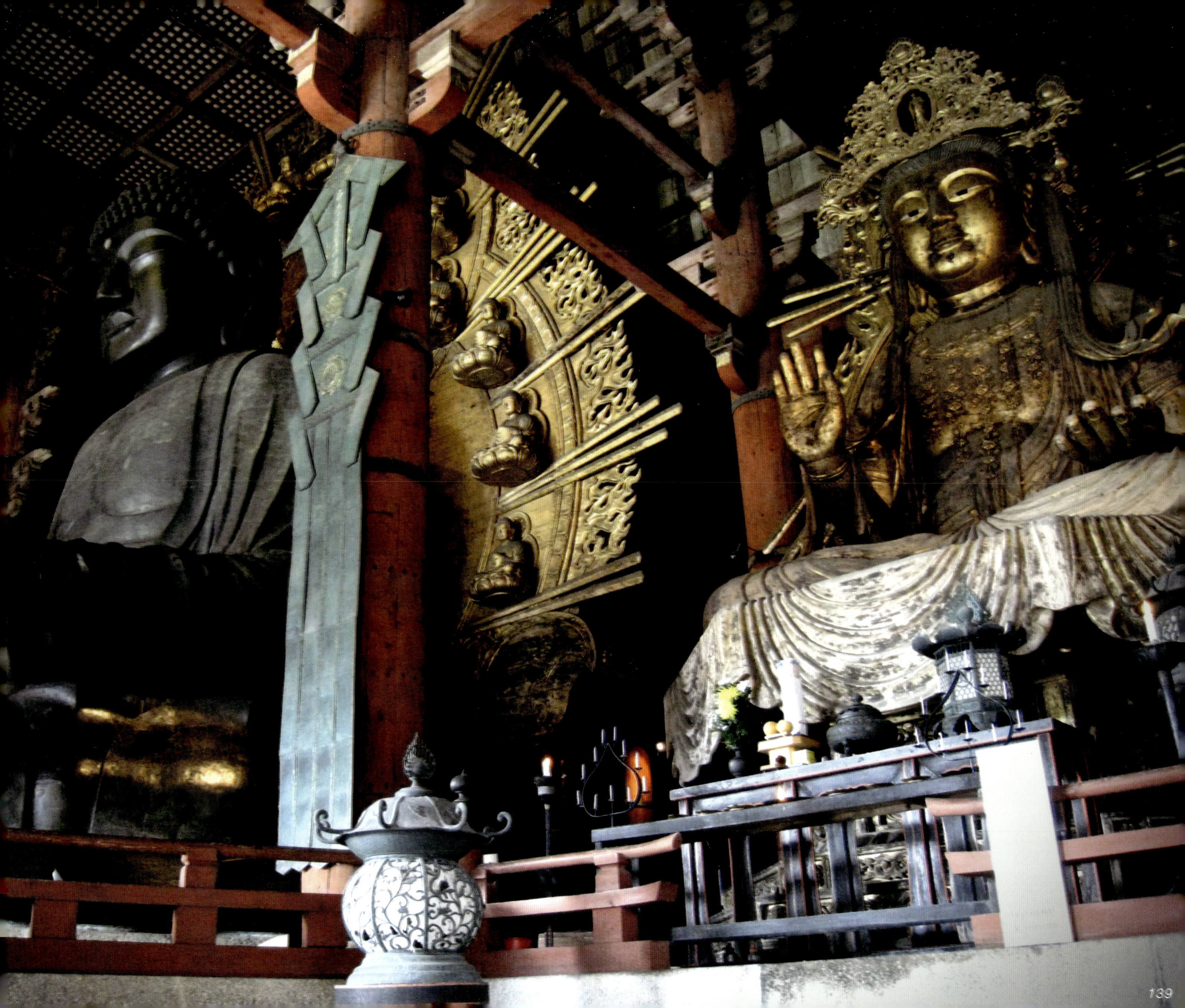

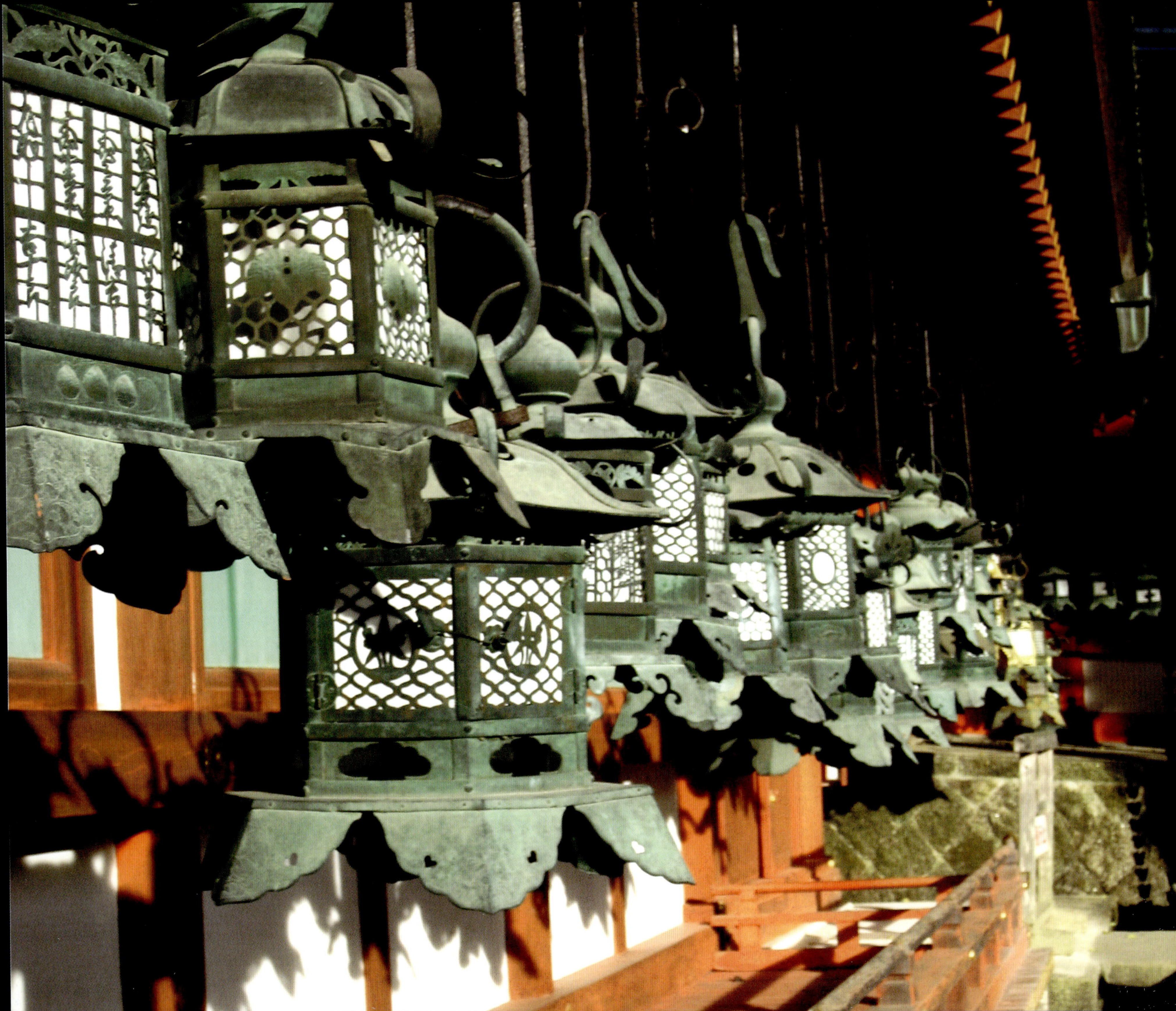

## Kasuga Taisha

From the deer park there is a path through the forest that is bordered with thousands of stone lanterns and that leads to this Shintō shrine. Kasuga Thaisha was established by the powerful Fujiwara family in 768. Outside the shrine are hundreds of bronze lanterns that, combined with the vermillion red colours, give the sanctuaries a very special look. During the famous o-bon festivities in mid-August all the lanterns are lit up.

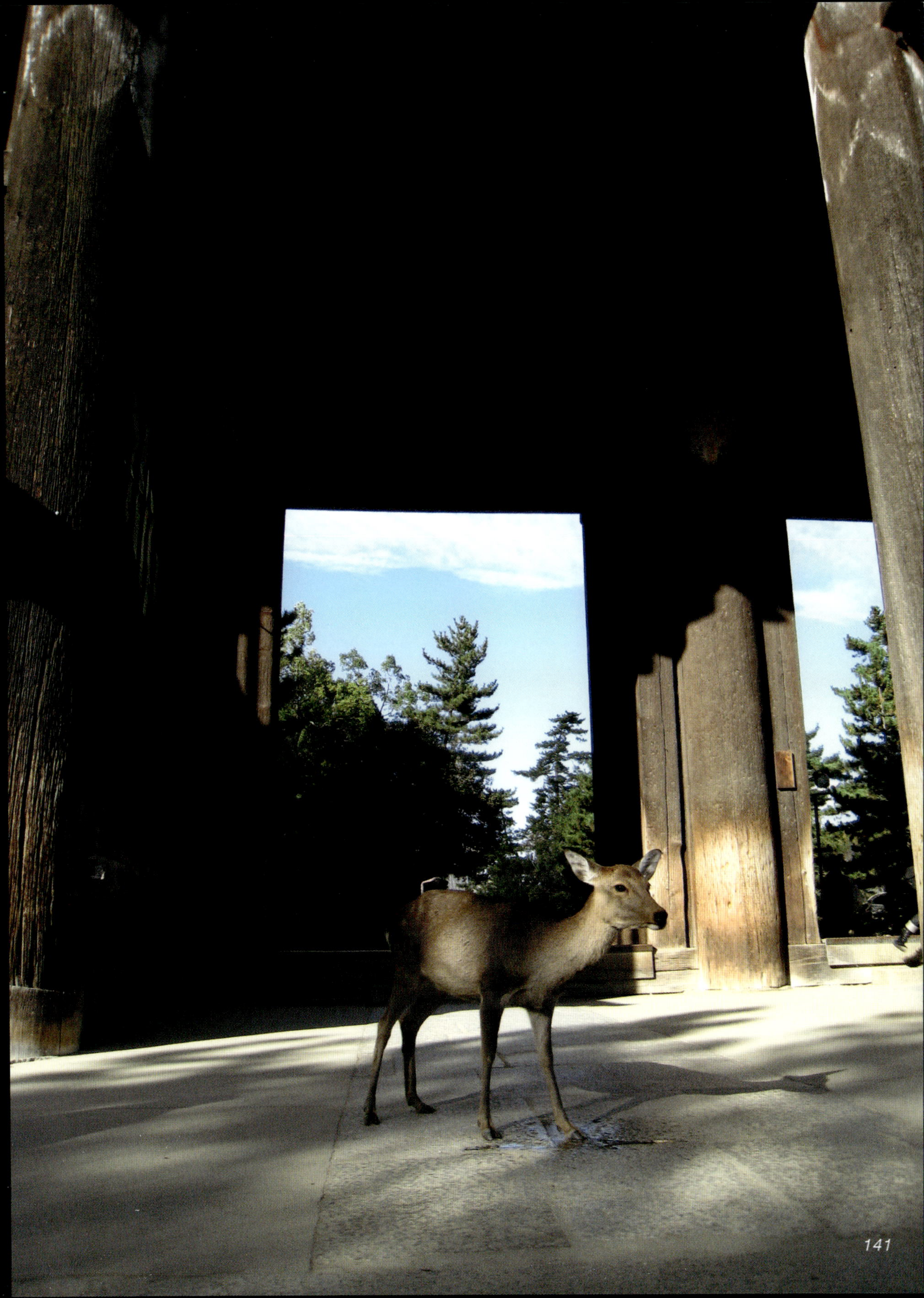

## The Nara deer

One of the popular attractions for young and old around the temples are the relatively tame deer that walk freely in the streets and parks and eat out of your hand pretty much anything including your bentō lunch. It is believed that the deer bring luck and although the death penalty for killing a deer was abolished centuries ago and they are 'officially' no longer considered as sacred they still behave accordingly.

# Miho museum

The impressive Miho Museum is one of Japan's architectural highlights and houses a breathtaking collection of ancient artifacts. The museum lies hidden in the densely forested rocky landscape near Shigaraki, about one hour by train and bus from Kyoto. The magnificent building is designed by I.M. Pei, one of the world's leading modern architects who also designed the pyramid of the Grand Louvre in Paris and the modern wing of the National Gallery of Art in Washington DC.

Entering the tunnel under the hill that leads to the museum may give you the impression of an interstellar passageway from the Star Trek saga. The end of the tunnel gives way to a hanging bridge over a gorge from where you get to see the entrance of the museum. The art displayed in the south wing of the museum mainly covers the old civilizations from present day Egypt, Greece, the Middle East over Afghanistan and Pakistan to China. The north wing of the museum focuses on Japanese art and also has a periodically changing collection.

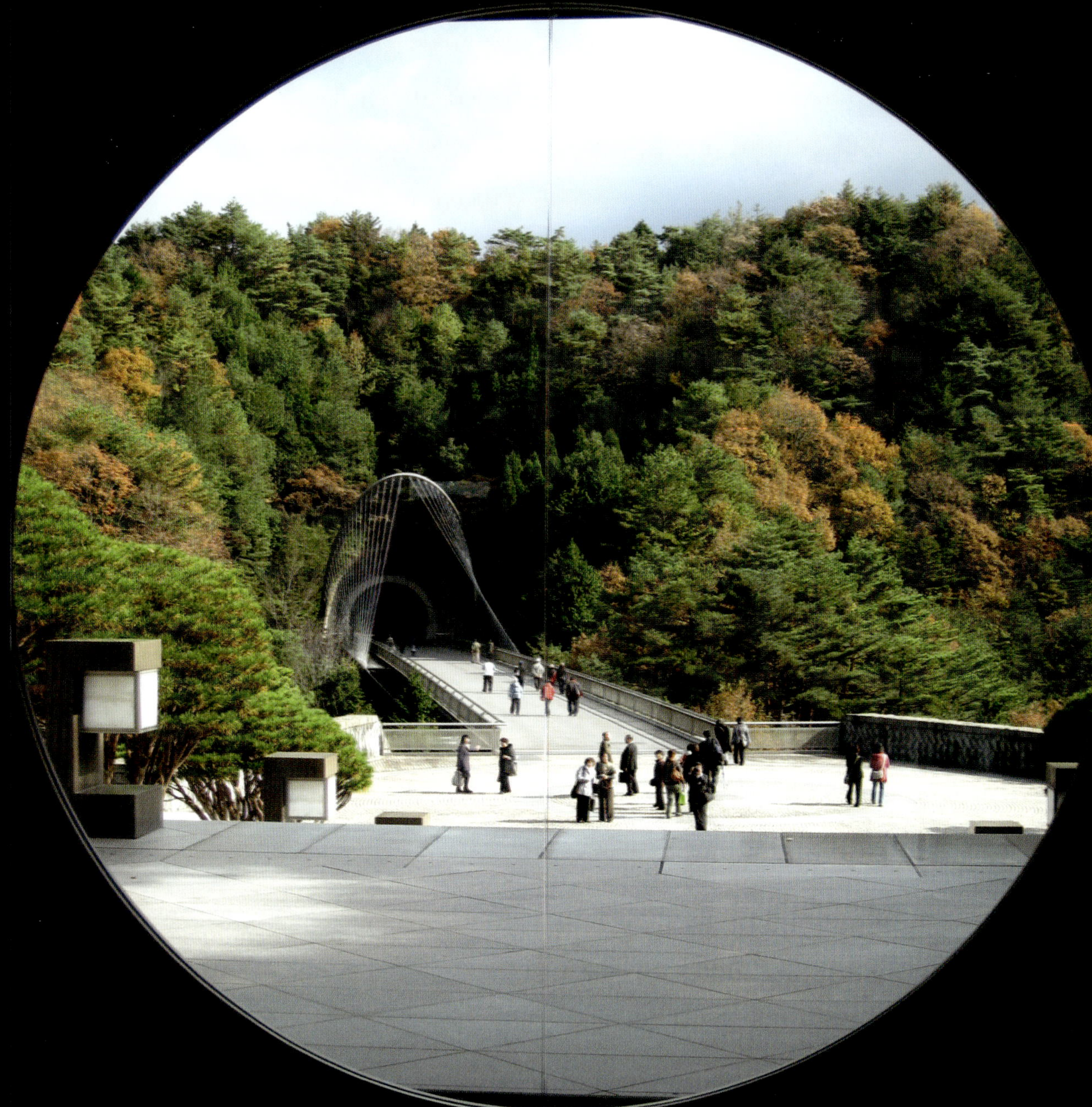

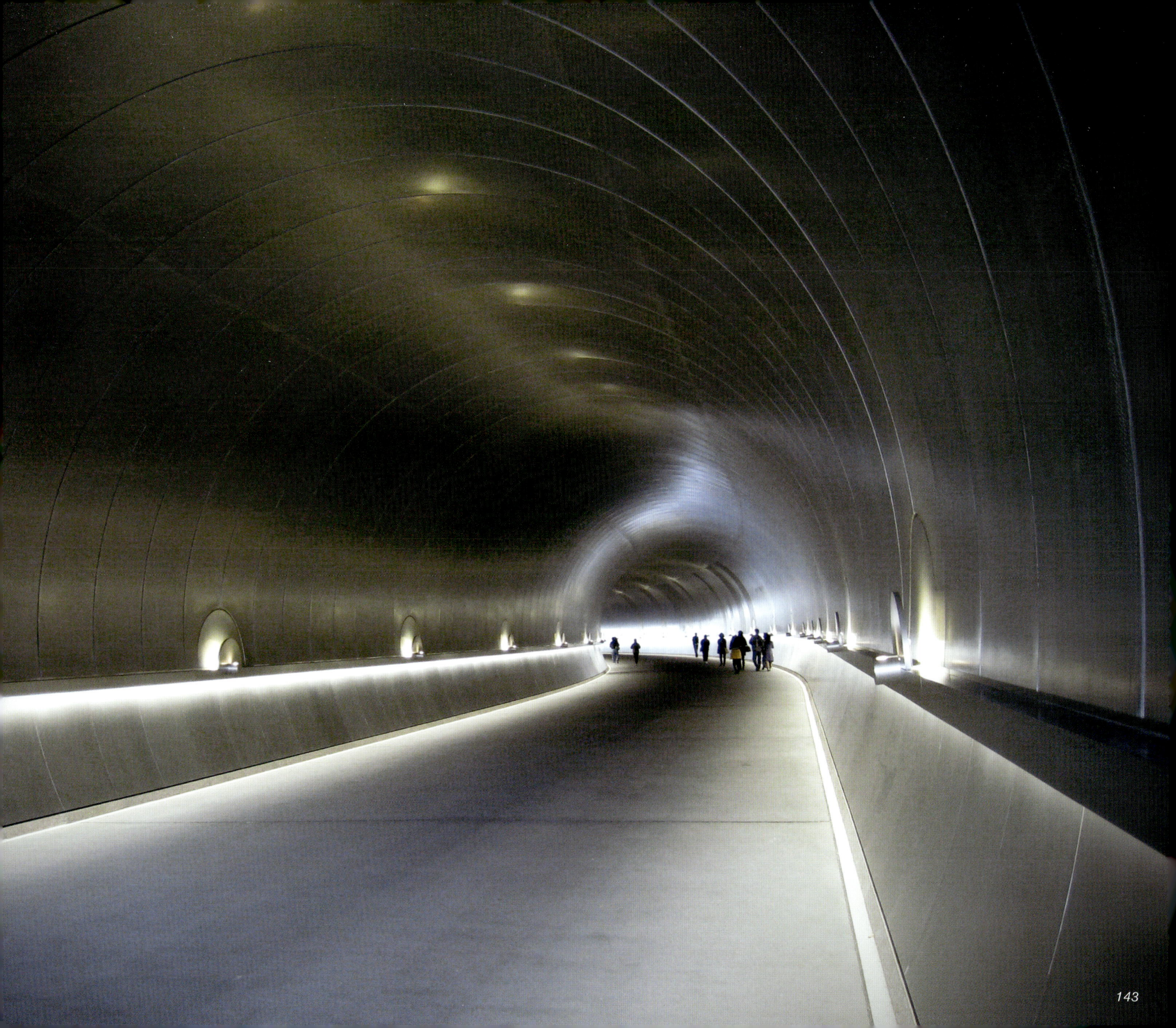

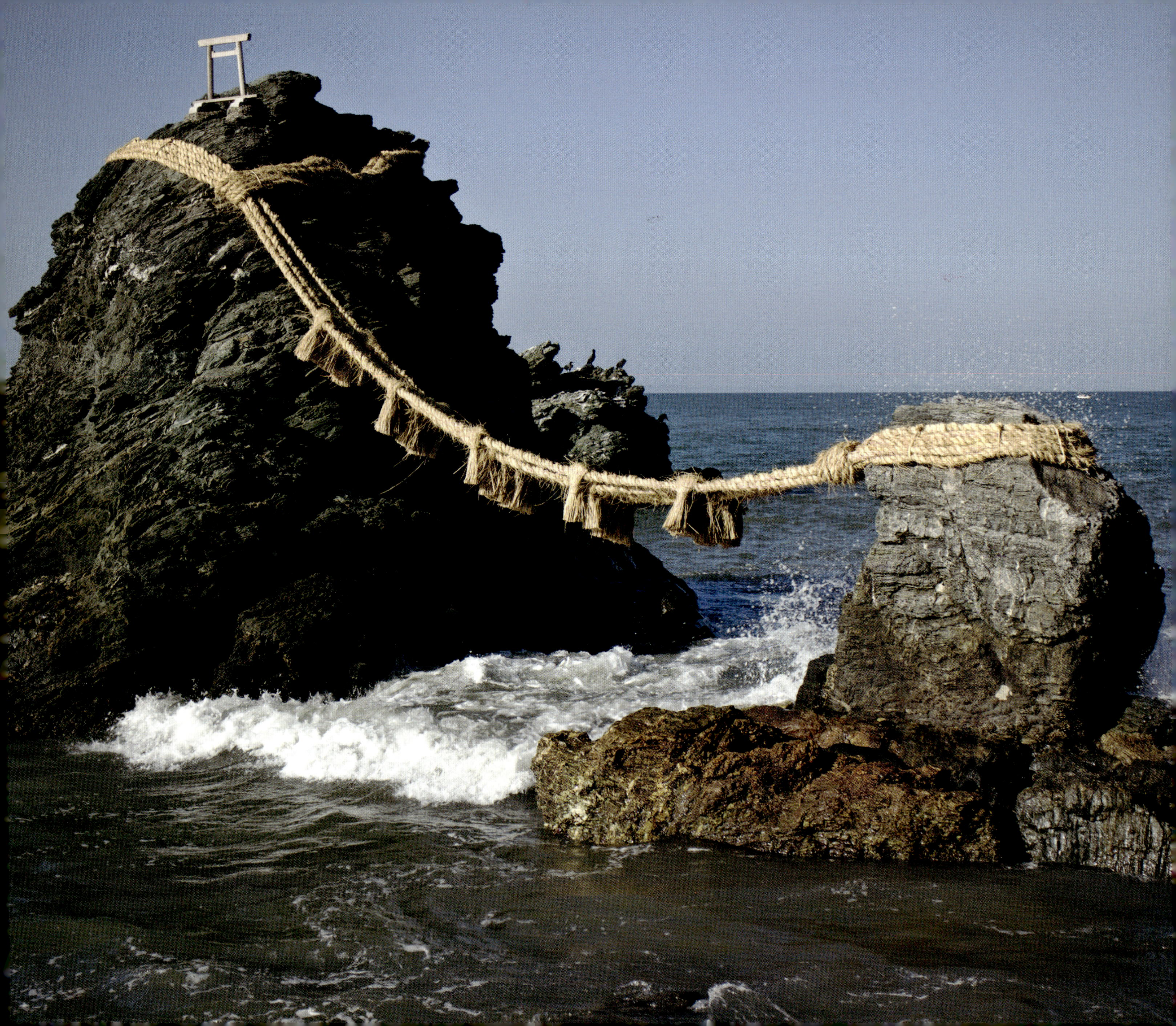

# Ise

## Meoto-Iwa

Meoto-Iwa, the pair of wedded rocks, in Ise-shima has a very special place in the Japanese mythology. Meoto means couple in Japanese. The larger rock with the small Shintō torii symbolizes the husband named Izanagi. The smaller rock to the right is his spouse named Izanami. According to the ancient Shintō legends, the islands in the Japanese archipelago were born from this couple. Based on information provided by the nearby shrine, the ropes around the rocks, weighing one ton, were hung at least as early as the 14th century. They are replaced in a special ceremony held by the local people three times a year (May, September and December). Judged by the number of tourists visiting the place, the wedded rocks are without doubt the most photographed pair of rocks in the country.

## Naikū, Ise-jingū

The inner shrine of Ise-jingū named Naikū is dedicated to the Sun Goddess and is Japan's most sacred Shintō shrine. Only the Emperor, the Empress and some high-ranked Shintō dignitaries can enter the inner shrine. It is here that a mirror is stored that according to the legends was passed in direct family line from the Sun Goddess to the first Emperor Jinmu. Every 20 years since the 7th century the inner shrine buildings are rebuilt on grounds adjacent to the old one. This rare picture was taken in the fall of 2013. The roof of the new sanctuary can be seen adjacent to the old premises. The next re-installation of the deity will take place in 2033.

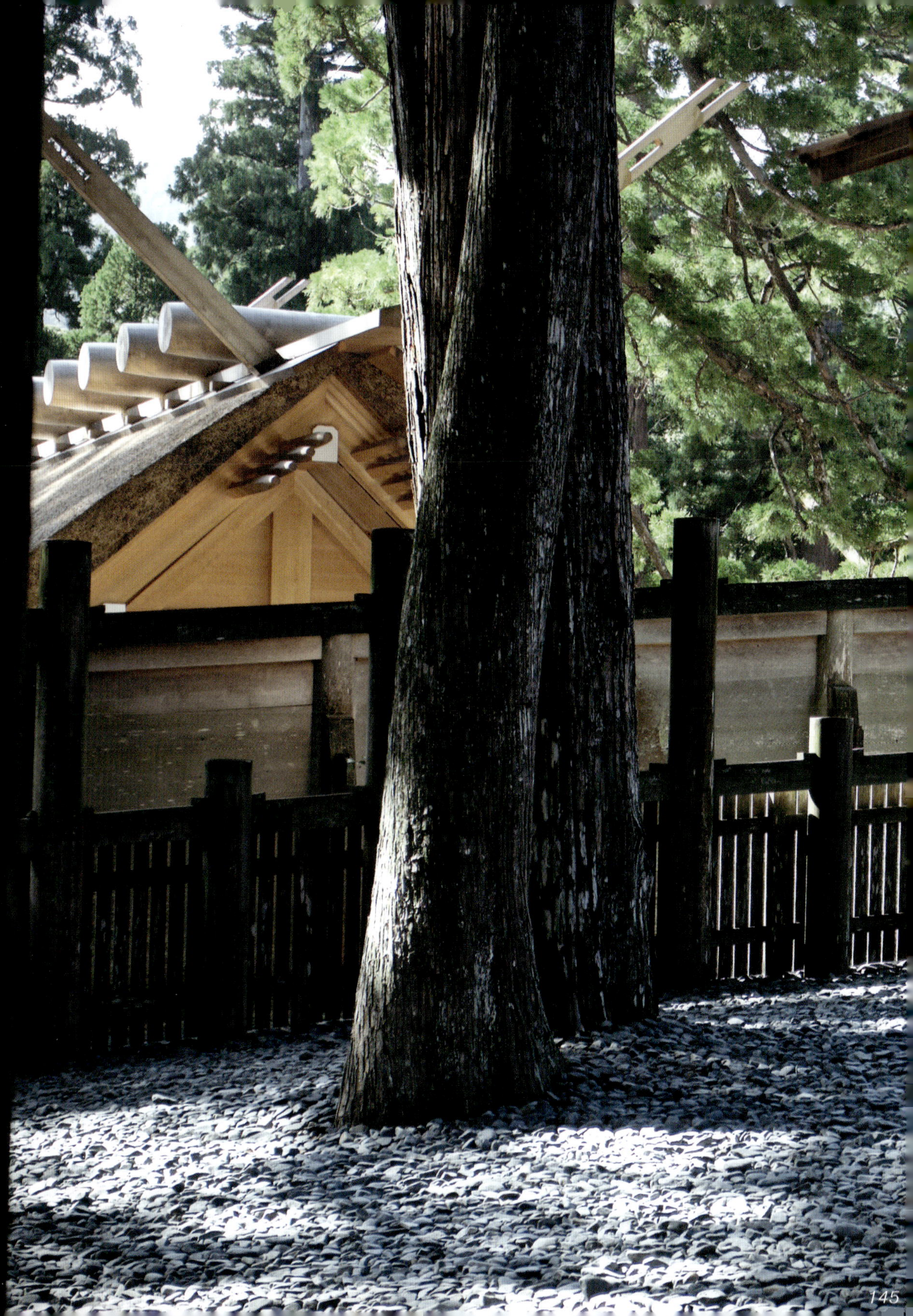

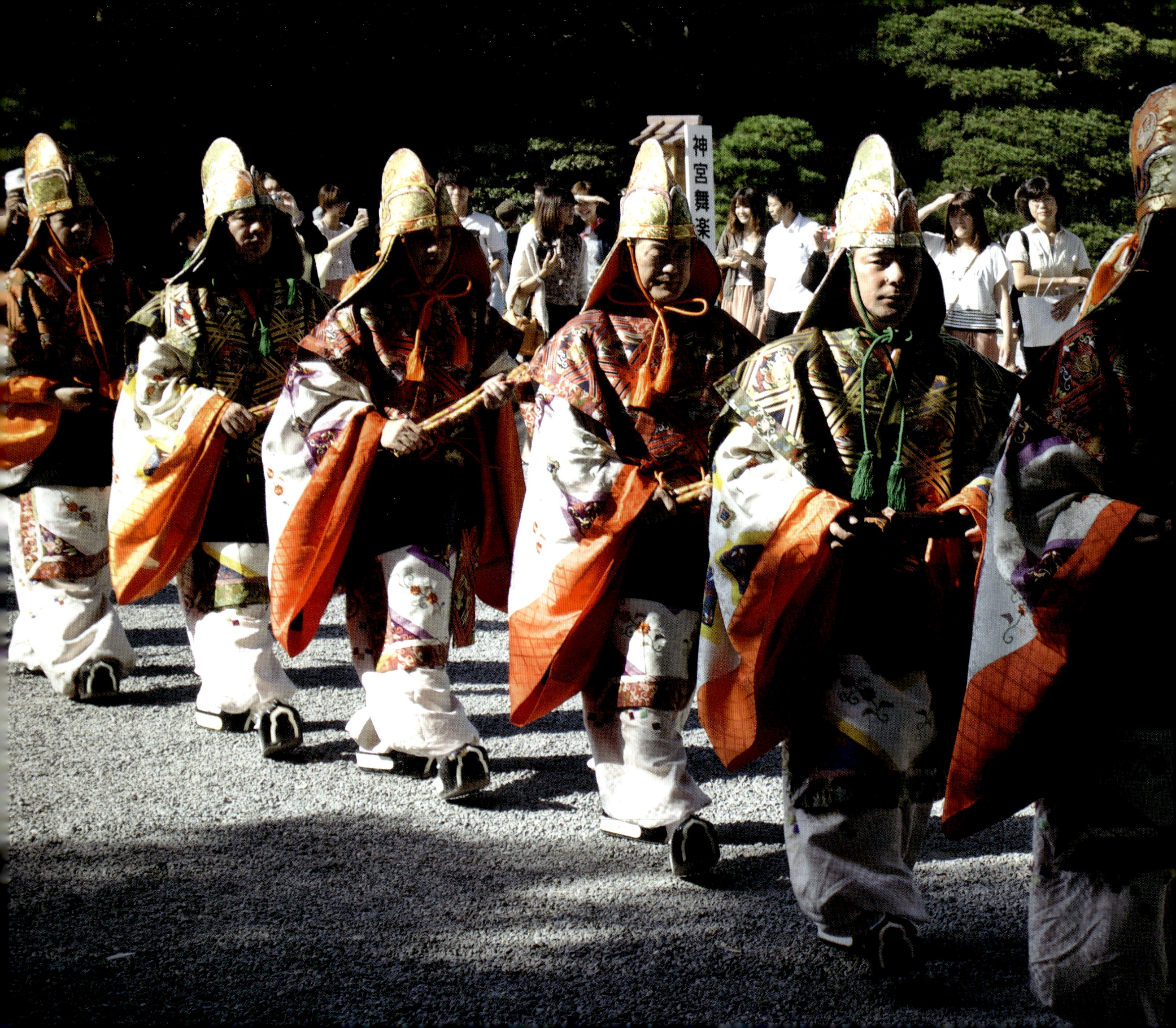
神宮舞楽

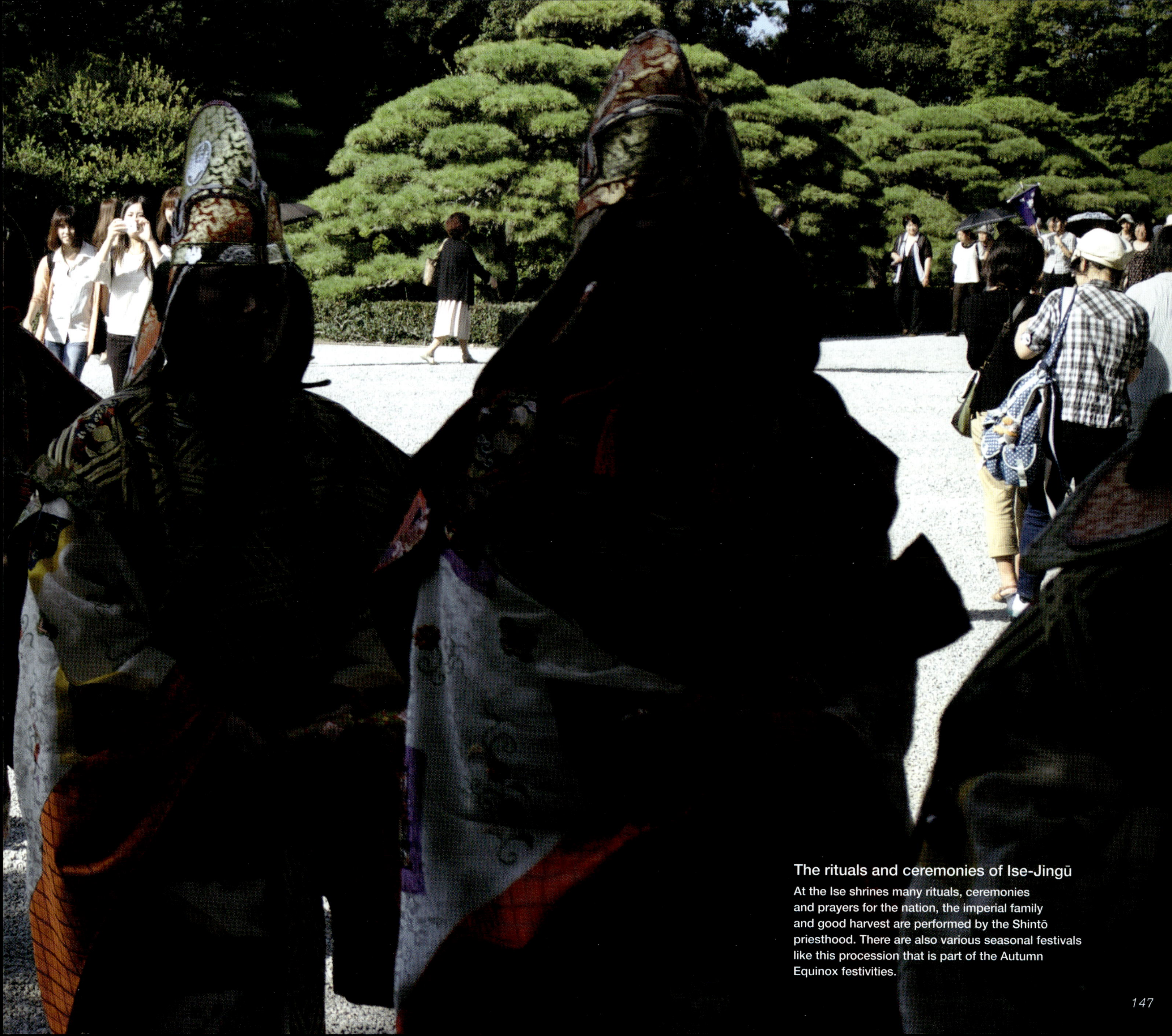

### The rituals and ceremonies of Ise-Jingū

At the Ise shrines many rituals, ceremonies and prayers for the nation, the imperial family and good harvest are performed by the Shintō priesthood. There are also various seasonal festivals like this procession that is part of the Autumn Equinox festivities.

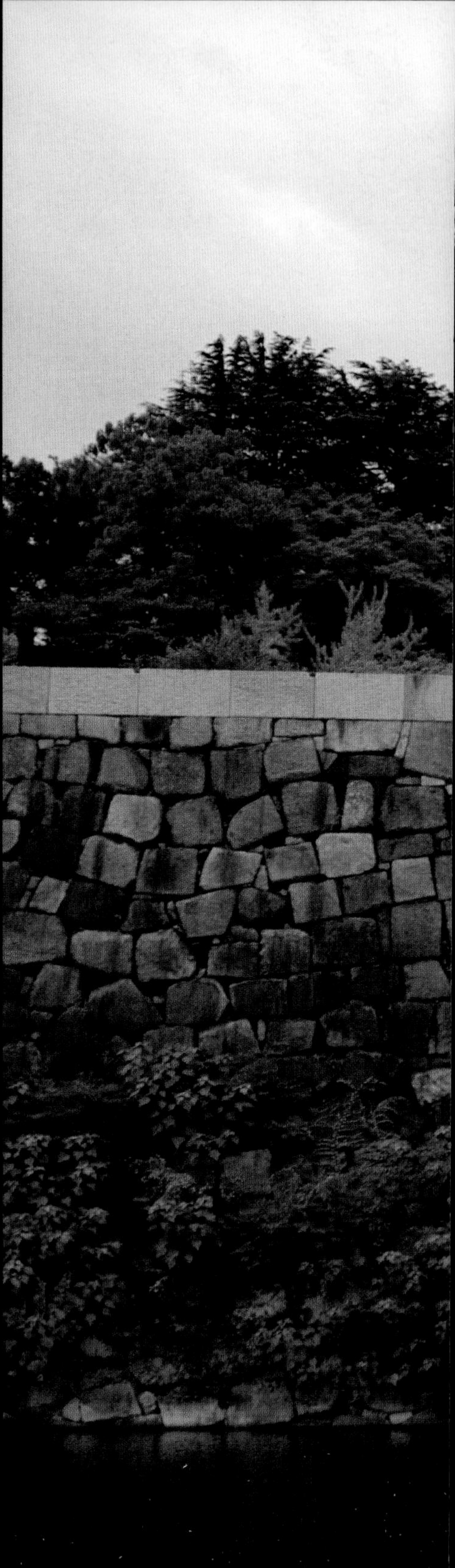

## Osaka Castle

The impressive Osaka Castle was completed in 1585 but despite massive layers of protection it did not survive the many wars. In the 1930's a perfect replica was built. Inside is an exhibition that explains the long and turbulent history of the castle in medieval Japan.

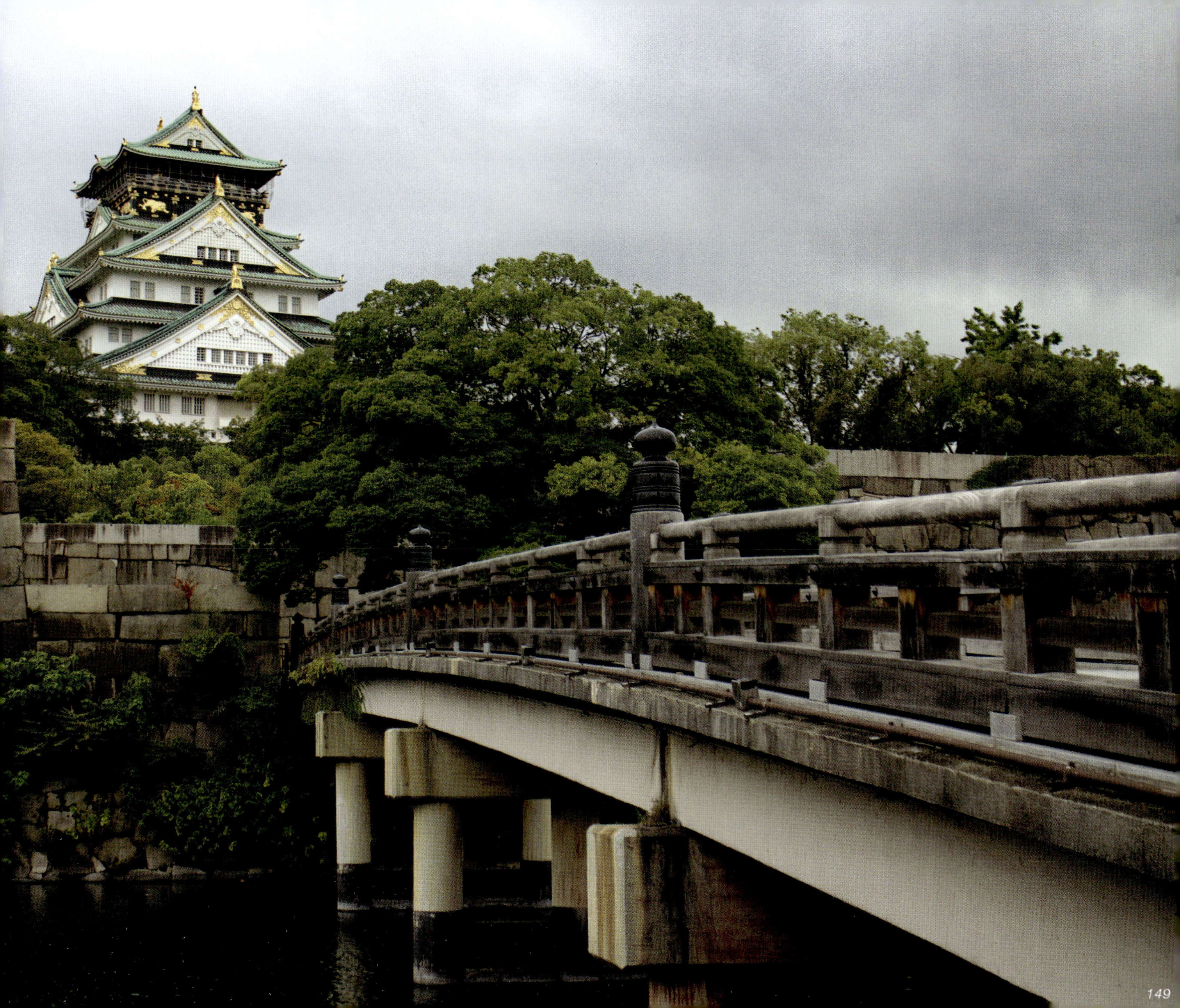

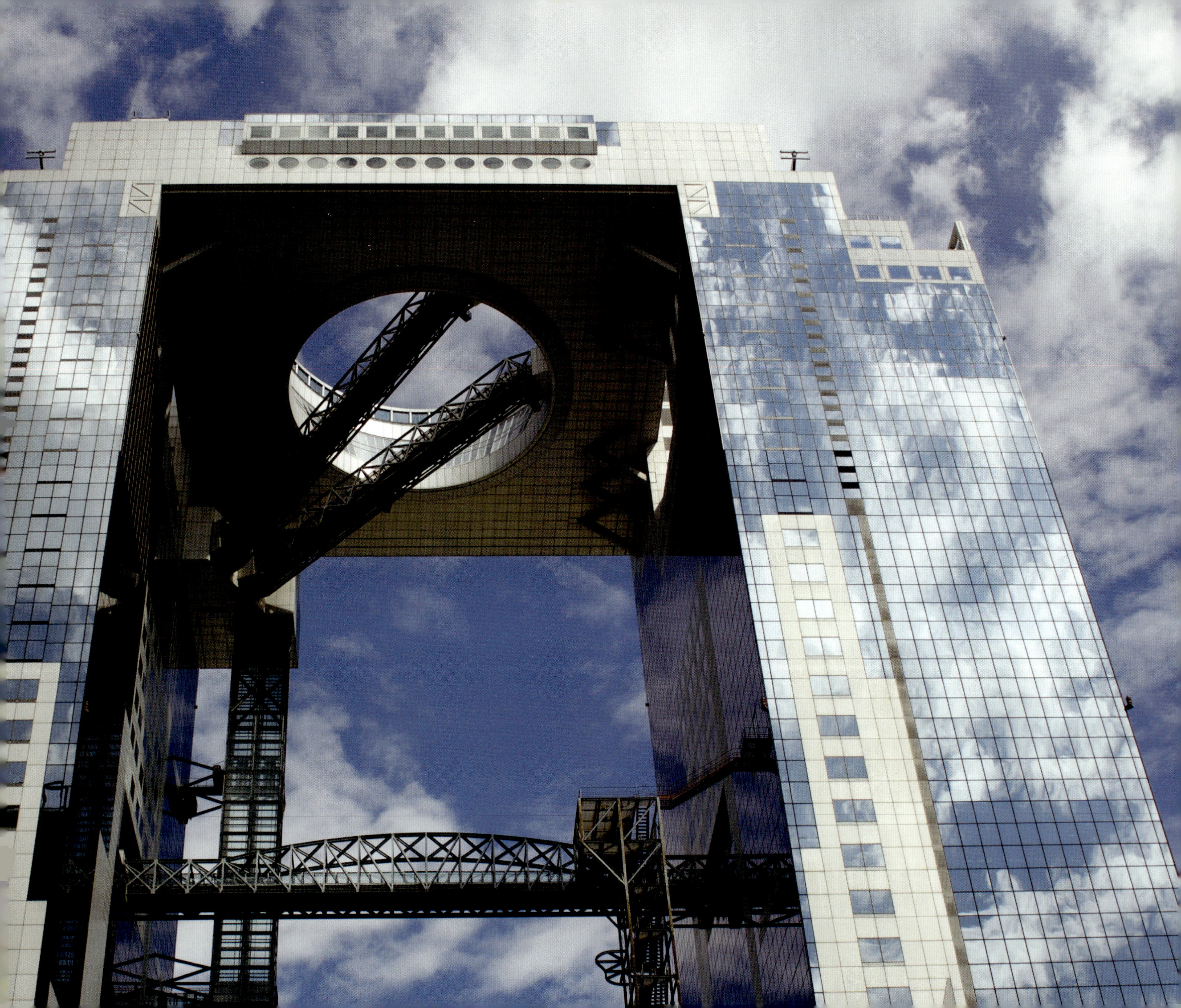

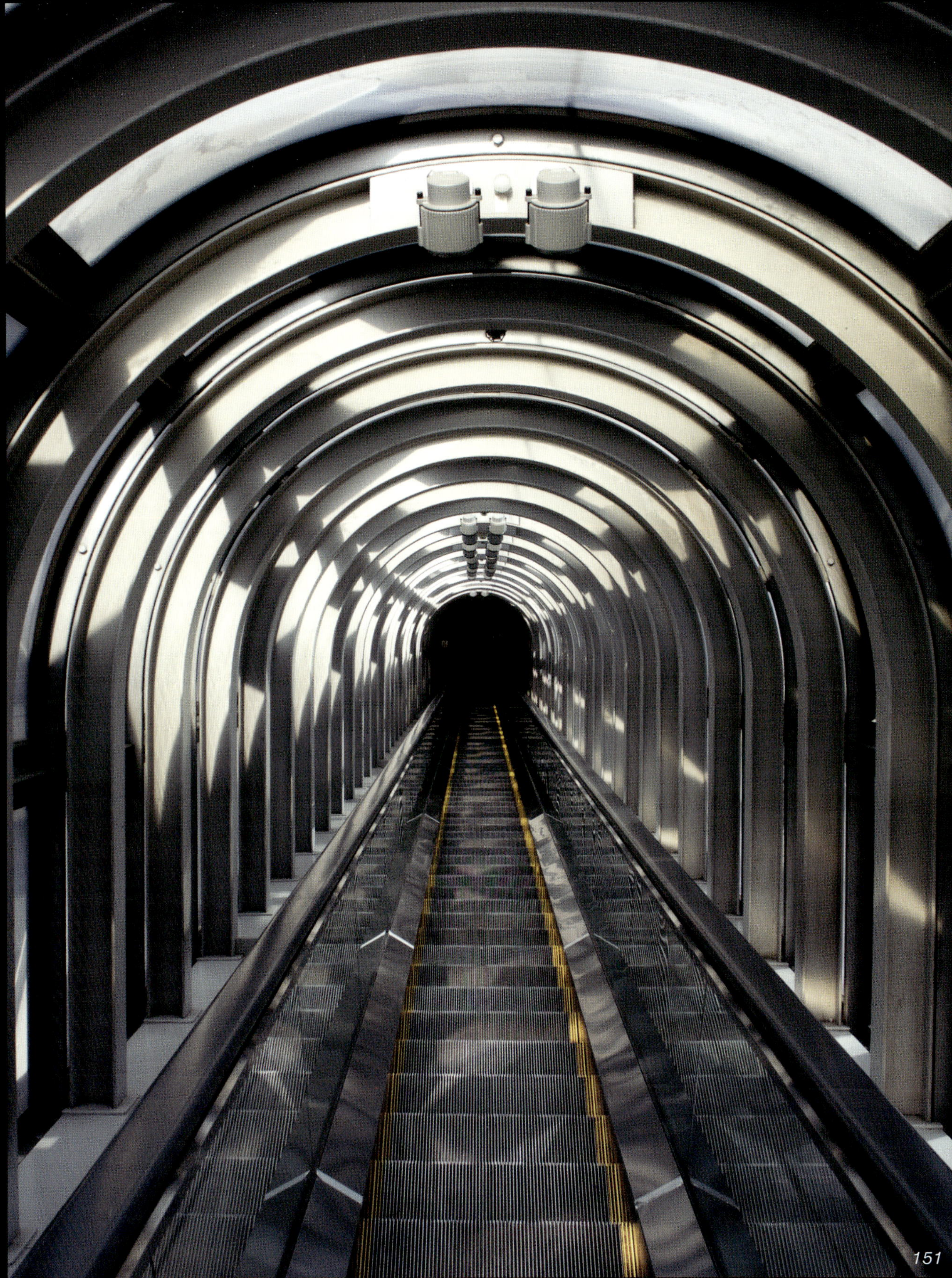

## The Umeda Sky Building

The Umeda Sky Building features in various architectural shortlists of most spectacular buildings. It is one of the landmarks in the north of Osaka and the magnificent floating garden observatory on the 39th floor has commanding views over the city and port.

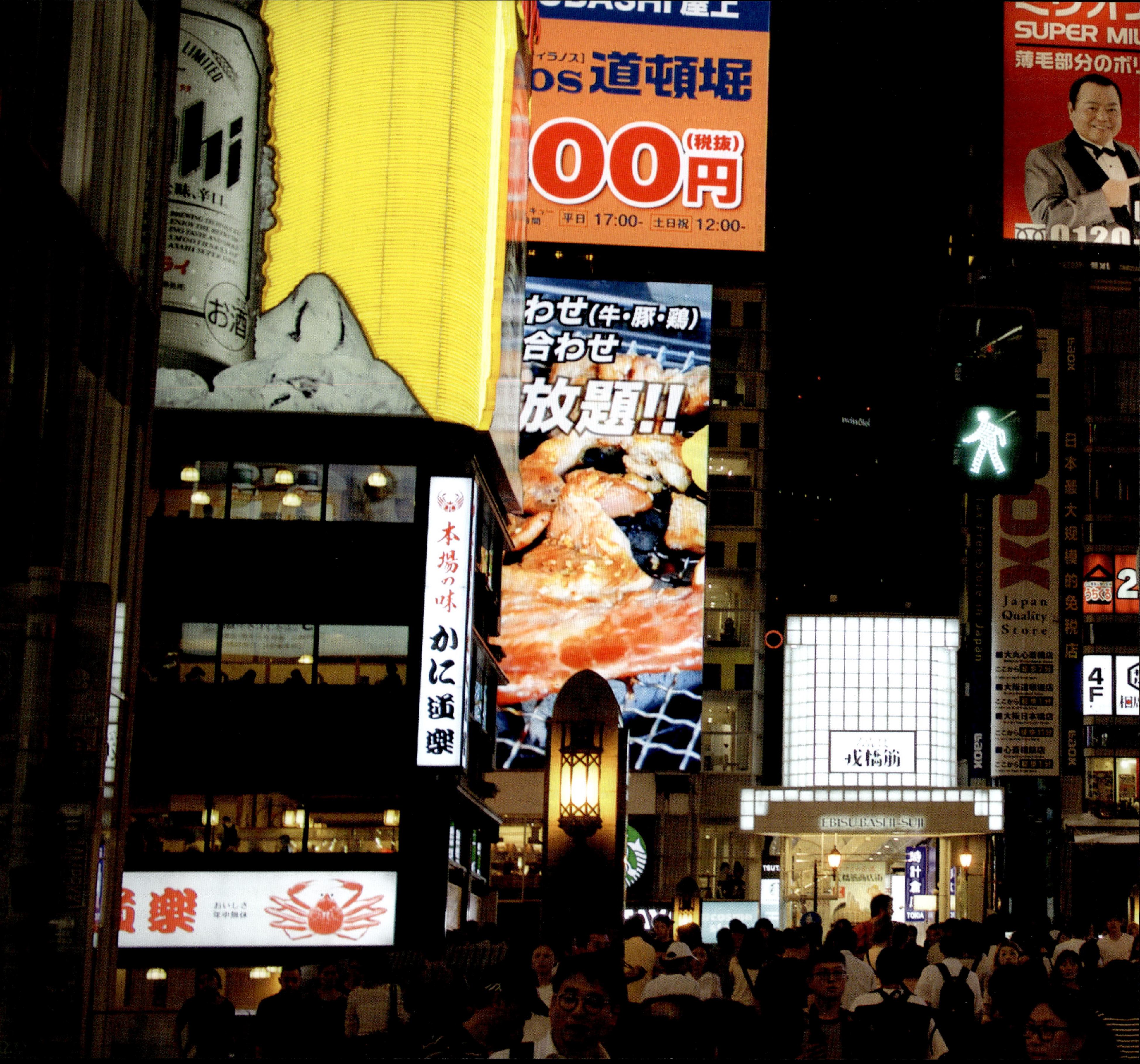

道頓堀
00円
(税抜)
平日 17:00- 土日祝 12:00-
SUPER MI
わせ(牛・豚・鶏)
合わせ
放題!!
本場の味
かに道楽
Japan
Quality
Store
日本最大規模的免税店
4F
EBISUBASHI-SUJI

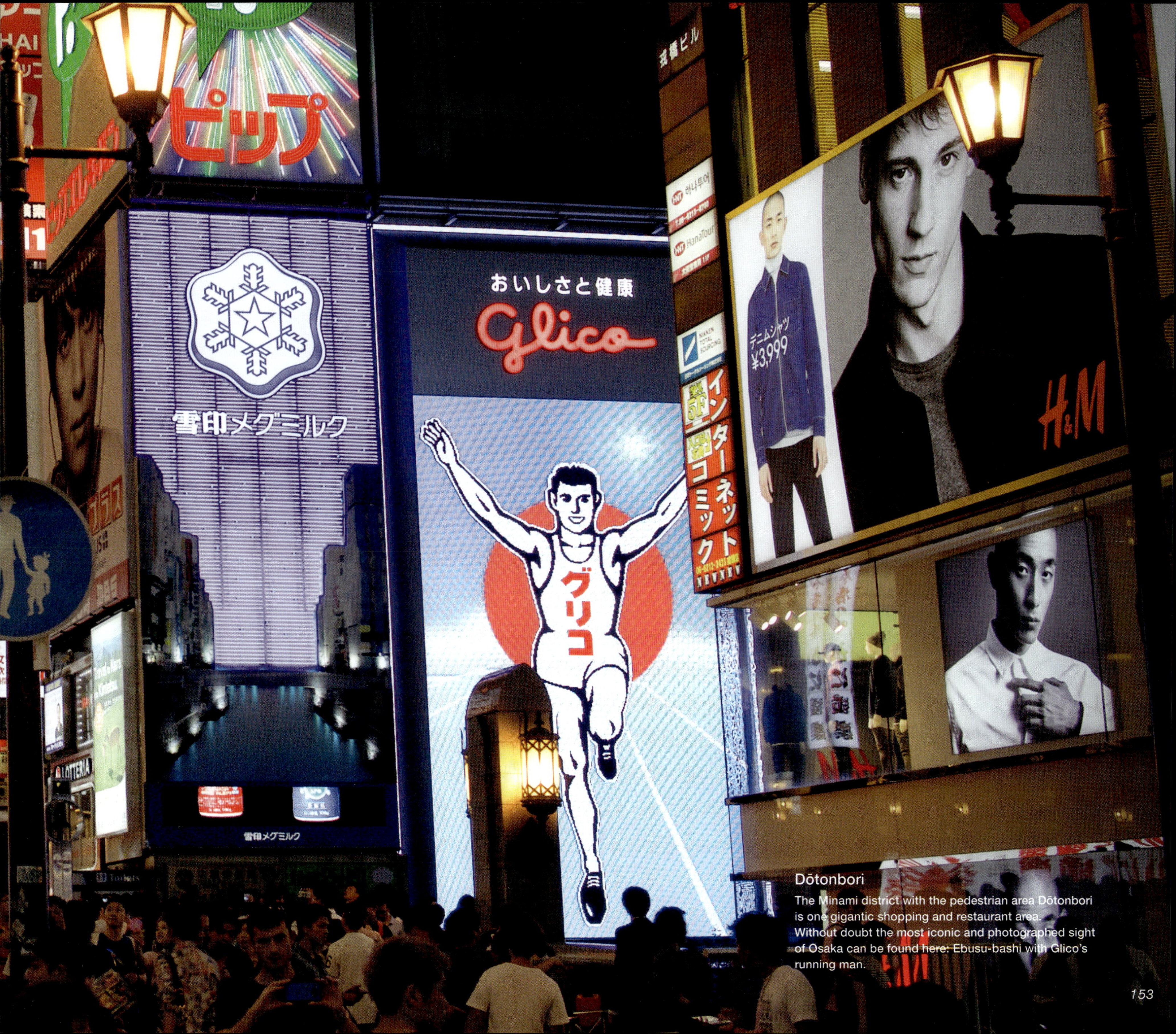


**Dōtonbori**

The Minami district with the pedestrian area Dōtonbori is one gigantic shopping and restaurant area. Without doubt the most iconic and photographed sight of Osaka can be found here: Ebusu-bashi with Glico's running man.

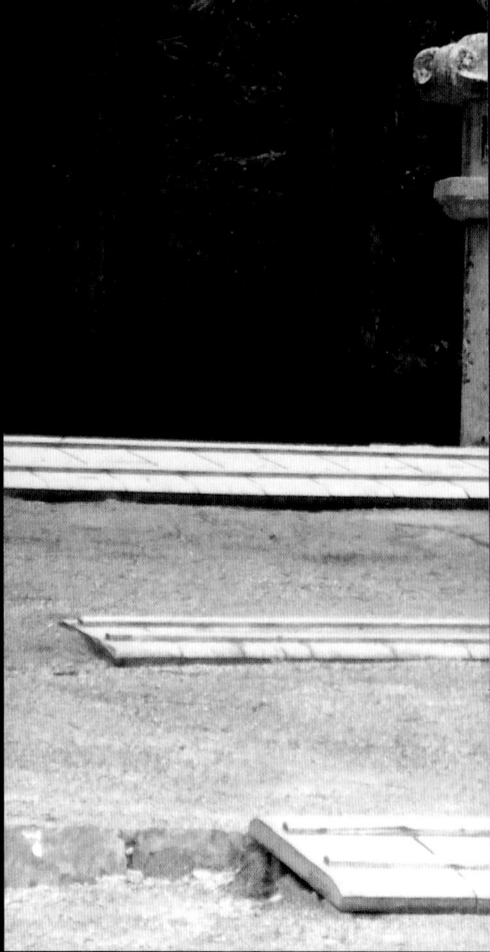

Buddhist monk at the entrance of the Saitō, the West Tower Pagoda. Originally completed by the successor of Kōbō Daishi in 886, the current pagoda is a replica from 1834.

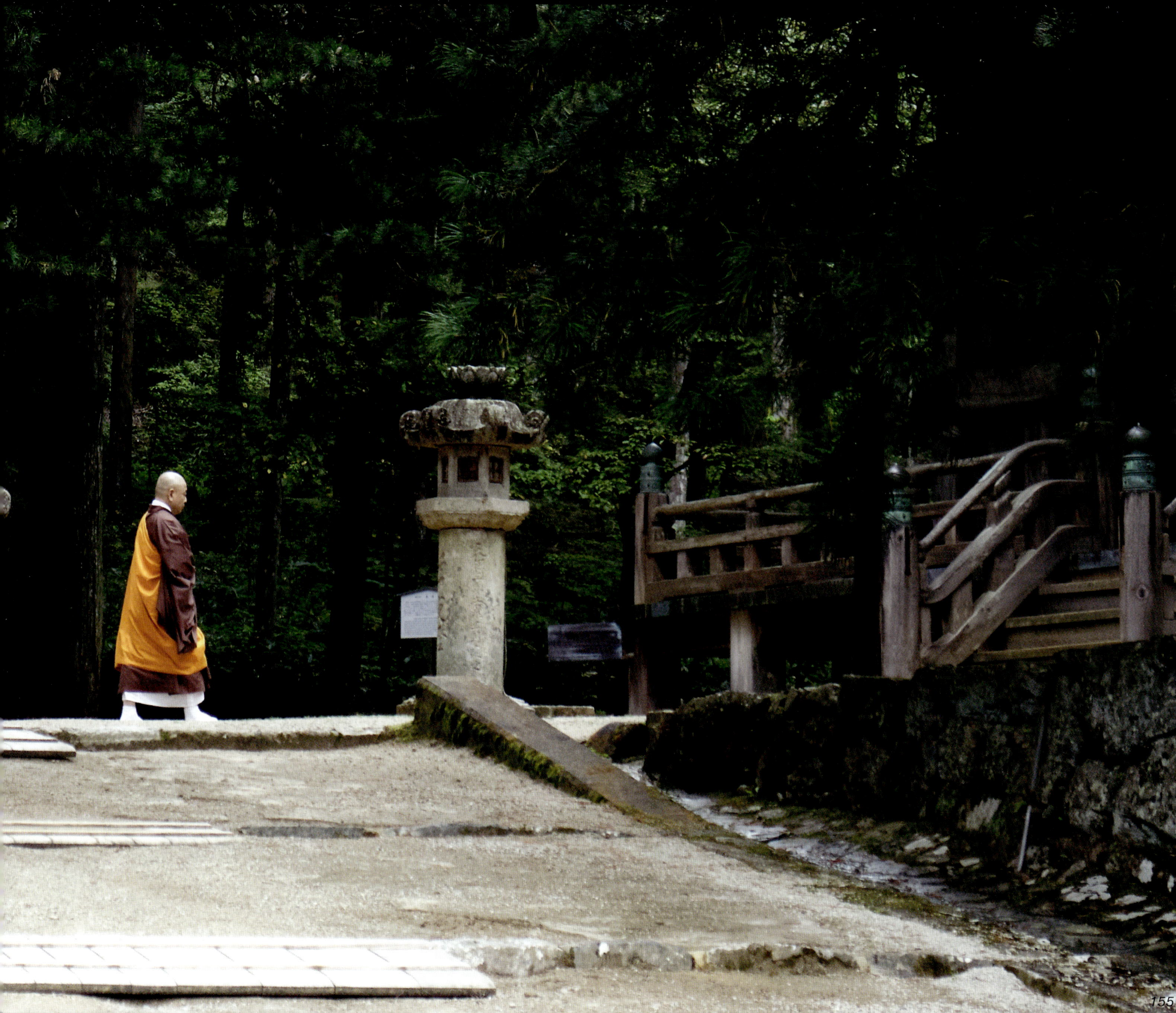

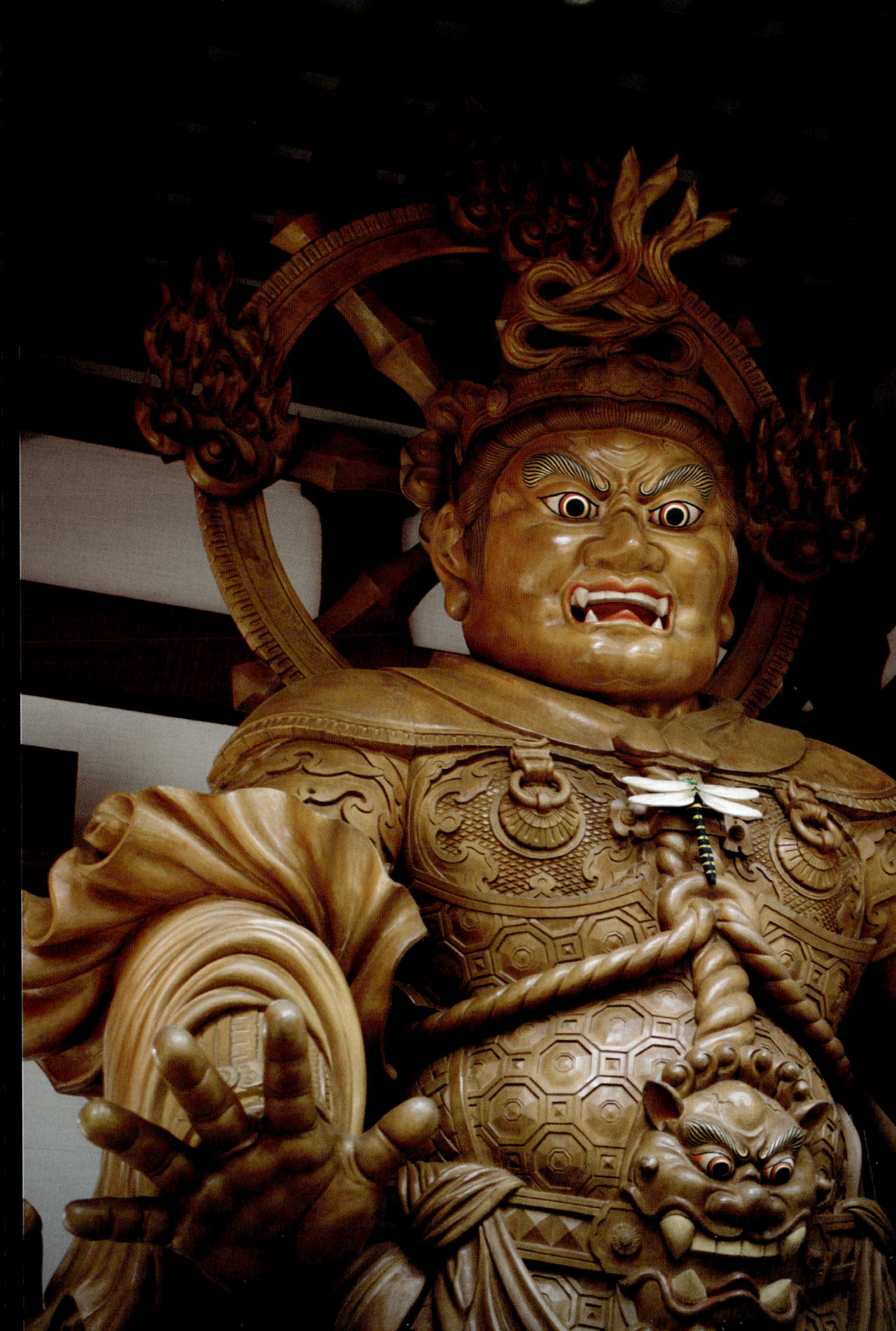

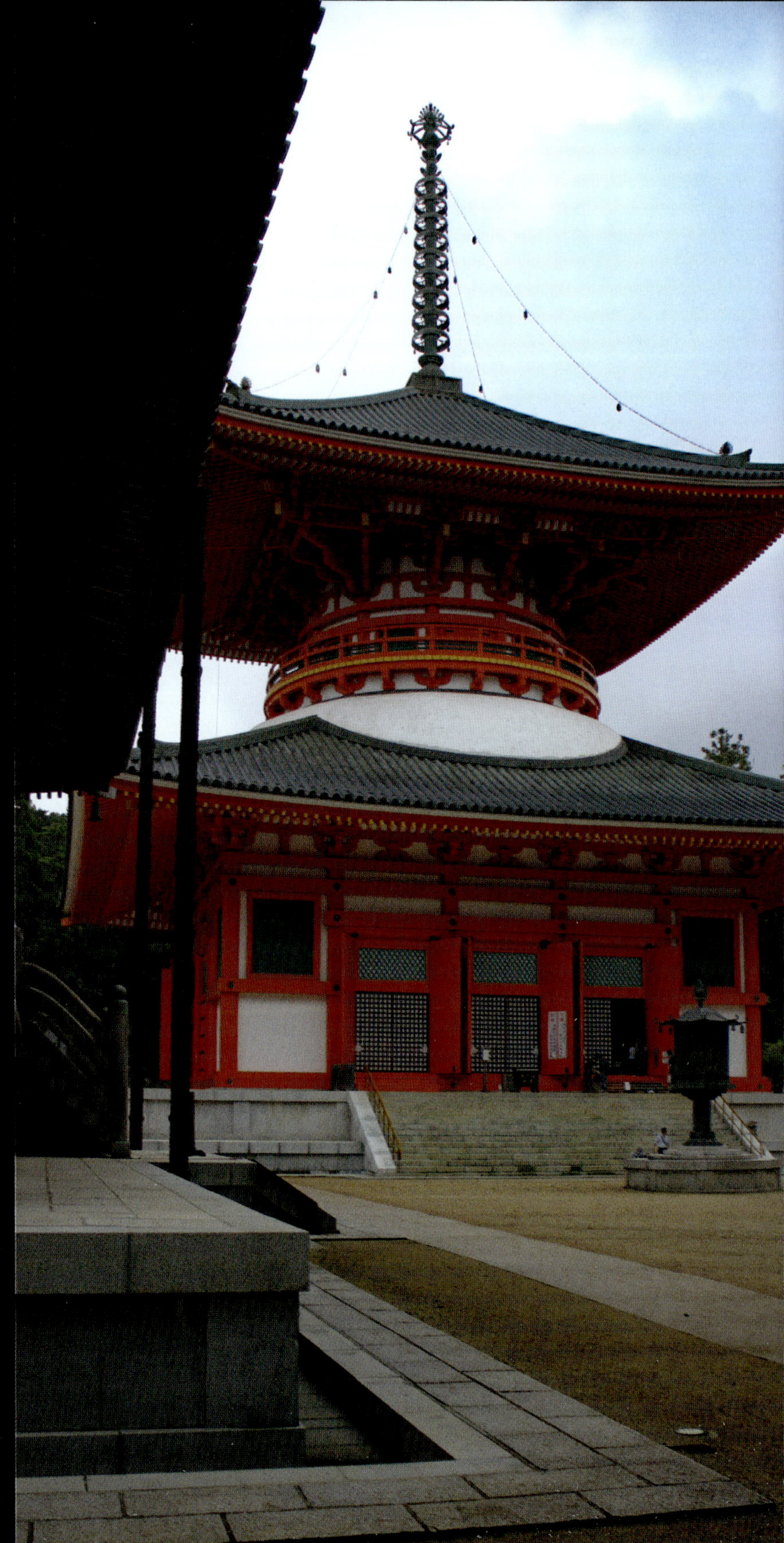

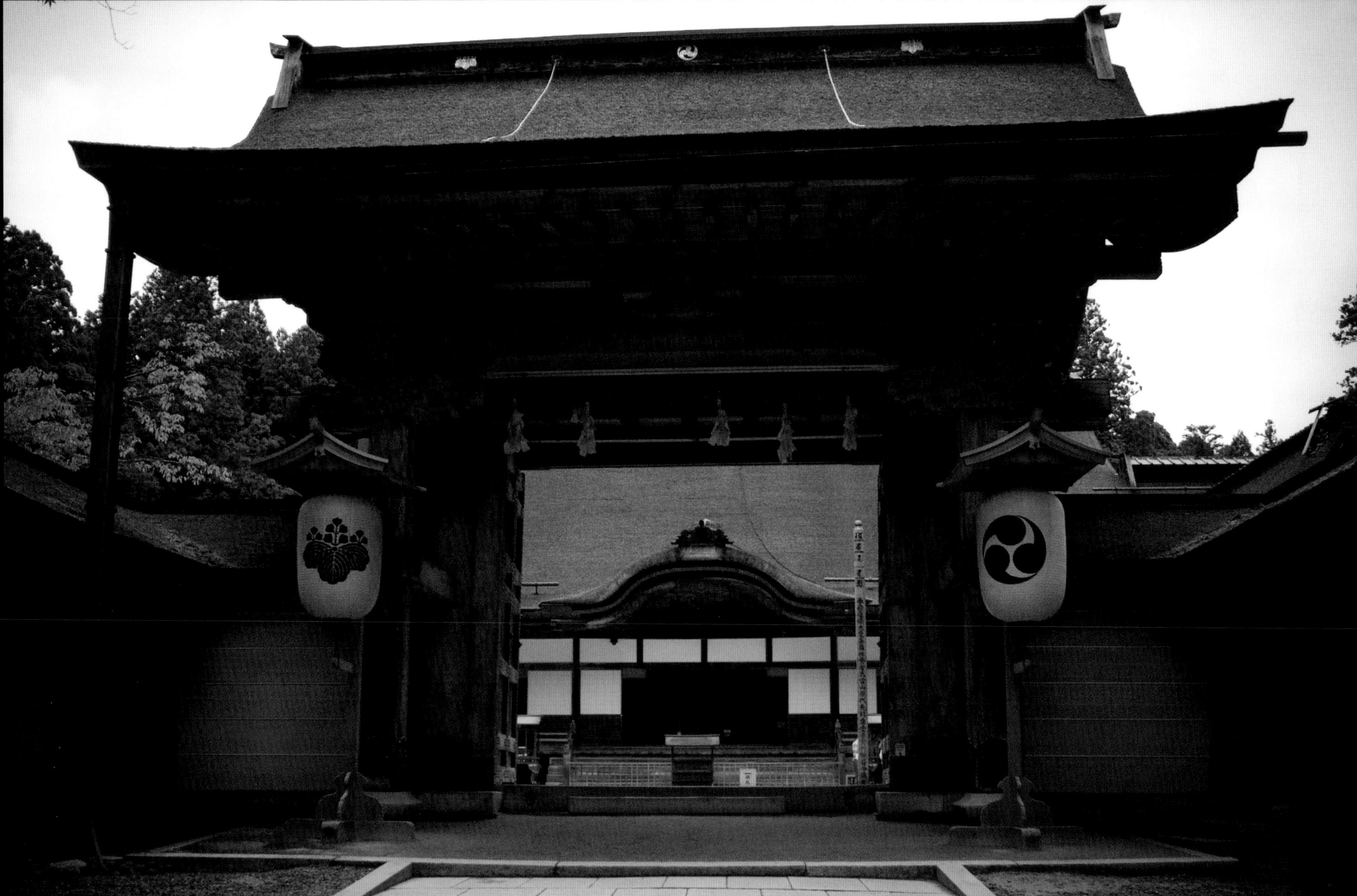

## Chū-mon

Statue of a Guardian King at Chū-mon.
This beautiful gate was completely refurbished for the 1,200th anniversary of the foundation of Kōya-san.

## Great Pagoda

The Daitō or Great Pagoda at the center of the Garan complex was planned by Kōbō Daishi and construction began in 816. Destroyed by fire several times the latest reconstruction dates from 1937.

## Kongōbu-ji

Central entrance of Kongōbu-ji. The Shingon School's headquarters are housed in this temple complex that dates from 1593.

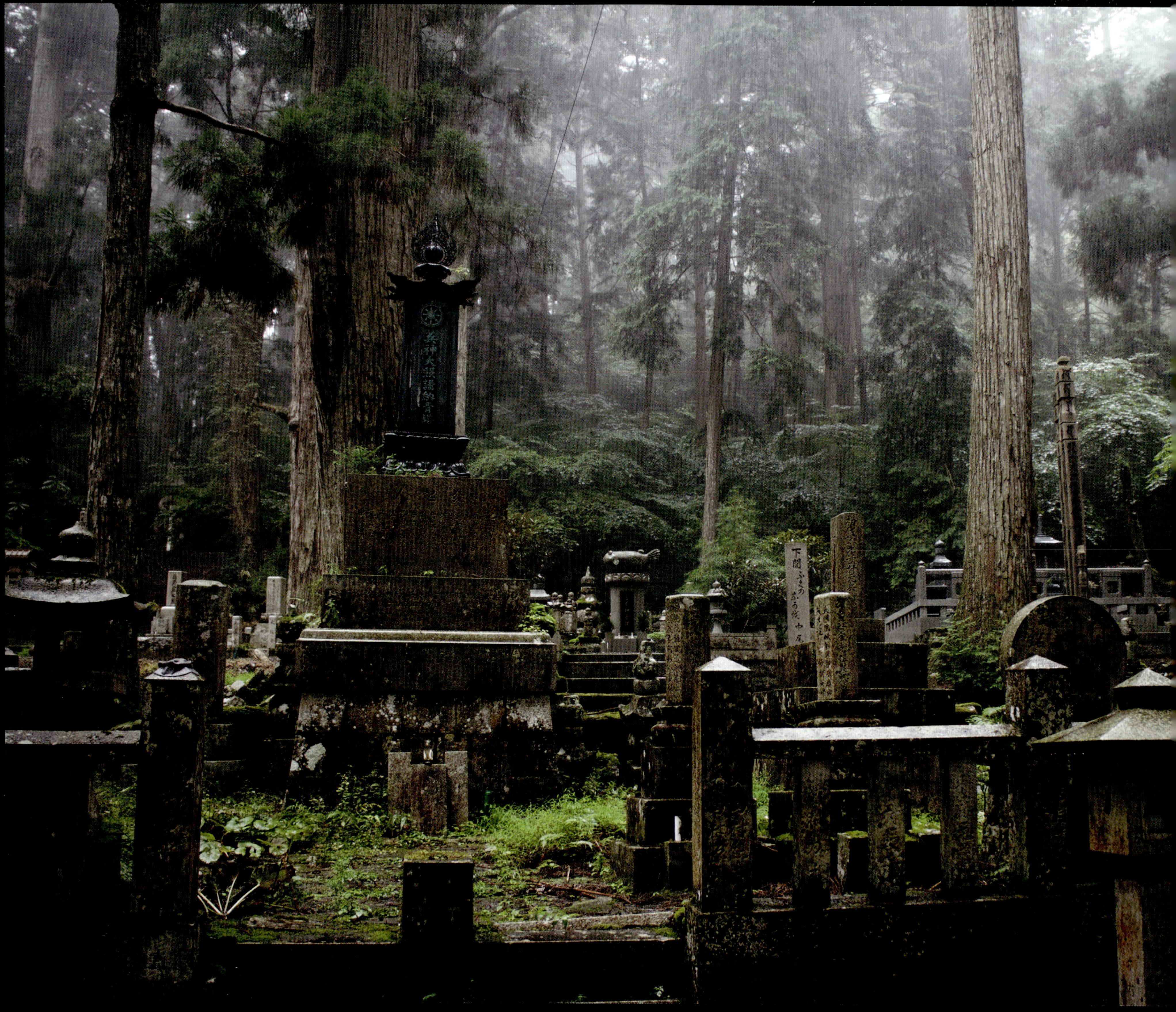

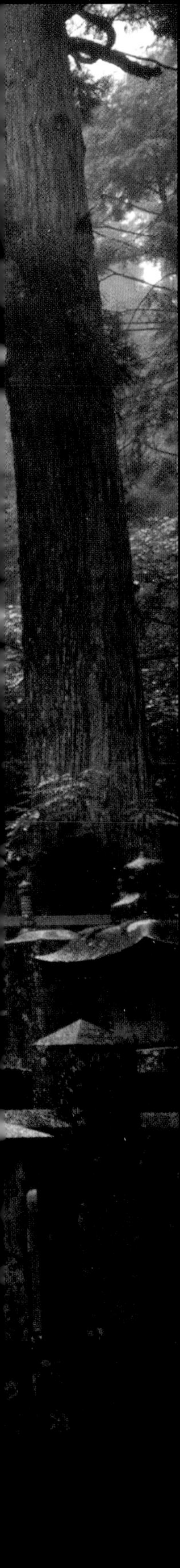

## Okunoin

Okunoin is the cemetery of Kōya-san located in a centuries old cedar forest. More than 200,000 gravestones in all sizes are placed along a 2-kilometer long path that leads to the mausoleum of Kōbō Daishi. The mossy graves, dark cedars and almost solemn silence give the long walk to the mausoleum a kind of mystical atmosphere, especially on a misty and rainy day.

### Mausoleum for Kōbō Daishi.

Kōbō Daishi passed away at the age of 62 on 21 March 835. According to the legend this is the place where he resides in a state of permanent meditation. Since his death meals are ritually offered twice a day.

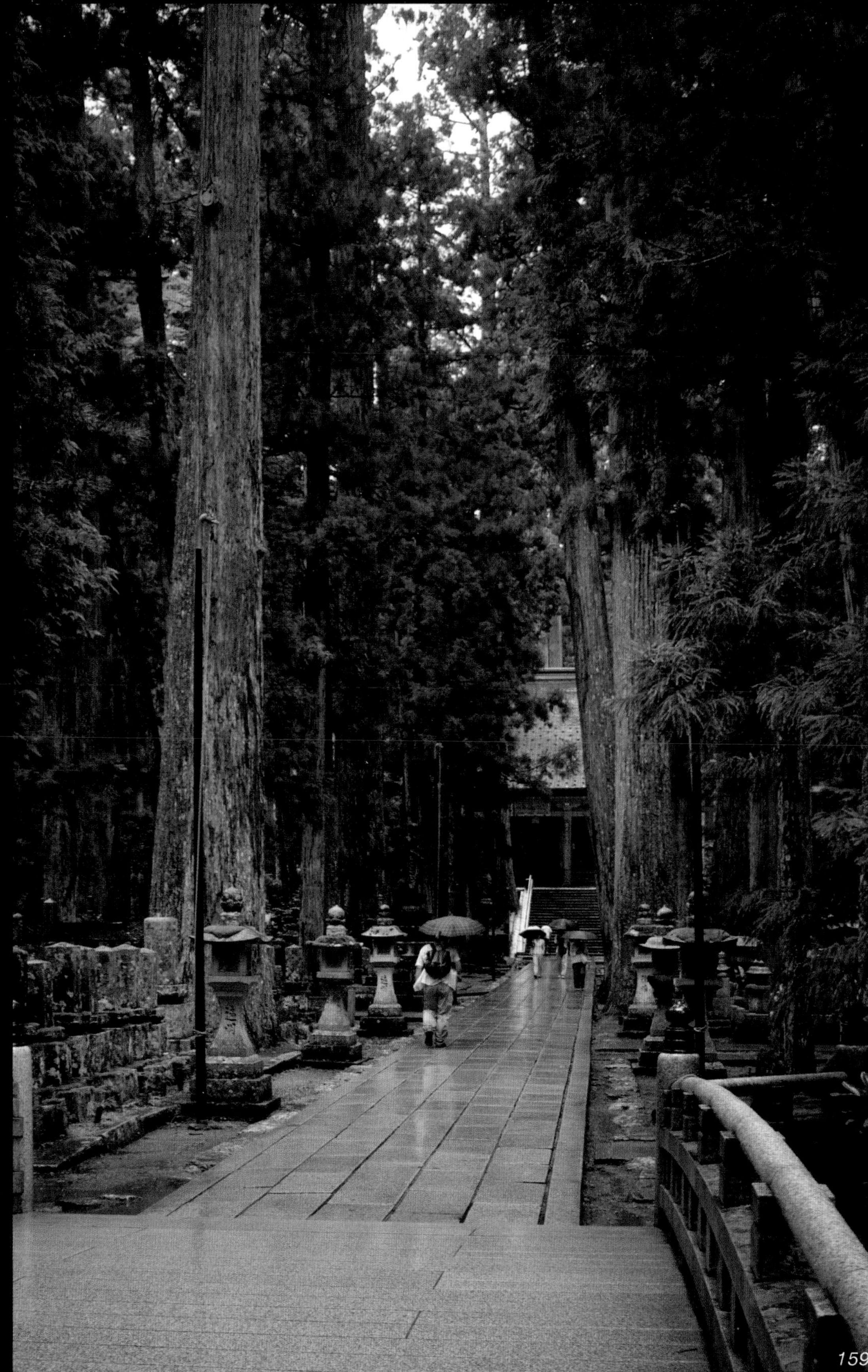

# Himeji

In 1993 Himeji castle, together with Hōryū-ji in Nara, became the first UNESCO World Heritage site in Japan. The elegantly built castle in Himeji sits on a bluff from where the Inland Sea can be seen in the far distance. Since the 14th century the castle premises were already in use because of its perfect strategic location. In 1601, when Ikeda Terumasa ruled the area, the 9-year lasting construction started. The castle miraculously survived war as well as heavy earthquakes and is one of the best-preserved feudal castles in the world.

It is a vast military stronghold with a central wooden tower covered by white plaster and fortified by massive walls and gates. Himeji castle's long history is filled with stories and legends about princesses, samurai, secret passageways... and fits all the clichés of what such feudal castle should look like.

Because of its dramatic beauty and epic dimensions the castle has been used in a large number of TV dramas, historical films and documentaries. Famous examples also known to the western visitors are Kurosawa's Akira masterpieces Kagemusha (1980) and Ran (1985), the TV series 'Shogun' from the eighties and the vintage James Bond movie You Only Live Twice.

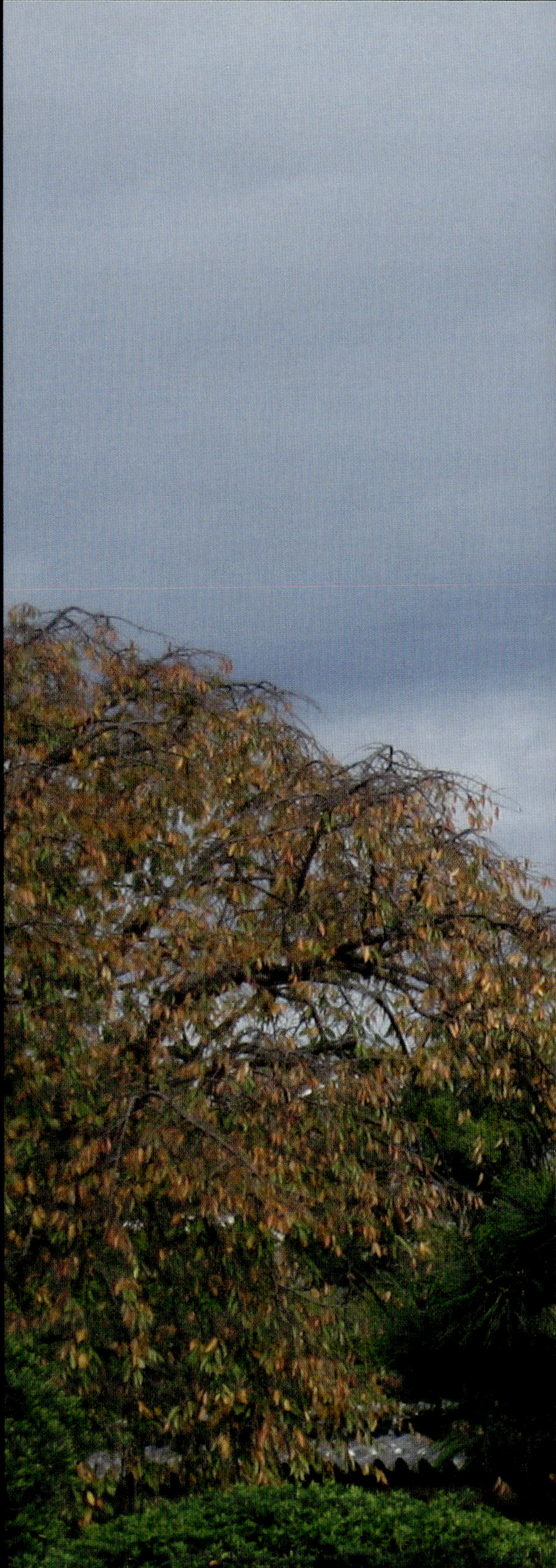

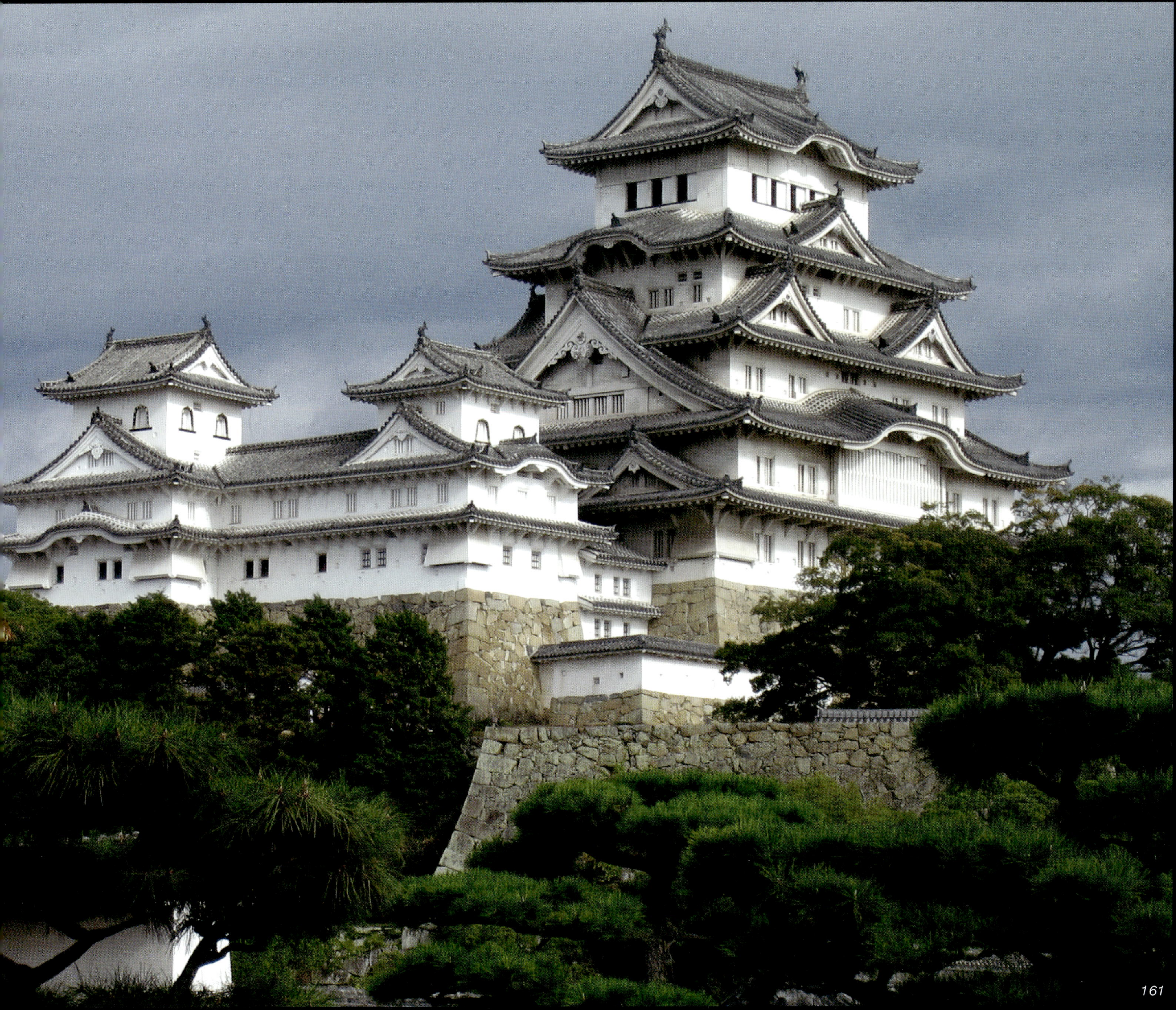

中国

# CHŪGOKU

Chūgoku is the most western end of Honshū. Traveling by public transport in this remote region takes time and therefore Chūgoku is less likely to be included as premier destination in a trip to Japan. However, travelers that are willing to explore the inland and coast by rental car or bicycle will be rewarded with abundant nature. Try to stay overnight at a traditional ryokan in one of the small villages where you will be greeted warmly by the owners. Most of these small inns receive few non-Japanese tourists and are keen to learn where you are from. I would strongly recommend to see at least Hiroshima and Miya-jima. Both places are conveniently located along the Sanyō Shinkansen line and can be reached from both the Ōsaka or Fukuoka direction.

# Hiroshima

When I arrived by Shinkansen in Hiroshima station late in the afternoon, the sun was shining an orange glow over the hills. Despite the intense warmth of that afternoon, witnessing in the Peace Memorial Museum the human tragedy and destructive impact of the A-bomb that detonated above Hiroshima on the morning of 6 august 1945 makes one shudder.

The apocalyptic catastrophe that hit the 350,000 inhabitants of Hiroshima caused the death of nearly 80,000 lives in a split second and many more in the months and years to come.

Yet the planning and decision of bombing Hiroshima and only a few days thereafter Nagasaki was not without warning or precedents. One of the stronger points of the museum is that it does not disregard the prelude to this dramatic day in the history of mankind. The reasoning behind the expansionism of the military government of Japan, the attack on Pearl Harbor and the role of Japan in the lasting war in the Pacific are explained as elements that may have contributed in the US decision to engage in nuclear warfare.

No matter how right or wrong the military strategy was, if there is one thing that the museum makes clear it is that the main victim was the civil population.

In the days immediately after the blast, Time Life's war photographer and correspondent Bernard Hoffman wrote on 3 September 1945 to the magazine's editor '...we were shocked and revolted by this new and terrible form of destruction. Compared to Hiroshima, Berlin, Hamburg, Cologne are practically untouched. What was formerly Japan's most modern, most westernized city, is now nothing more than a two-foot layer of twisted tin and rubble.'

Surely at that time no one would have expected that the old enemies USA and Japan would become strong allies and that Hiroshima would re-emerge again as the vibrant, dynamic and modern city it is was before World War II.

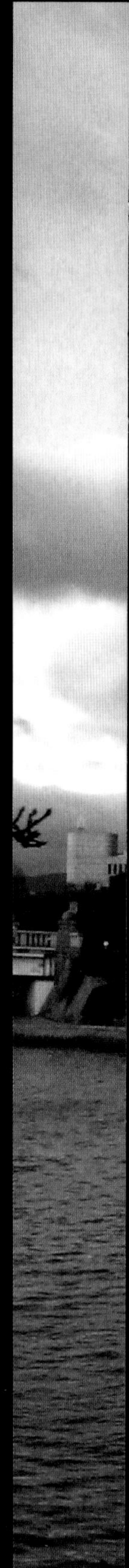

**A-Bomb Dome**

The A-Bomb Dome is the ruin of the former Hiroshima Prefectural Industrial Promotion Hall. It is the building closest to the center of the blast that remained standing.

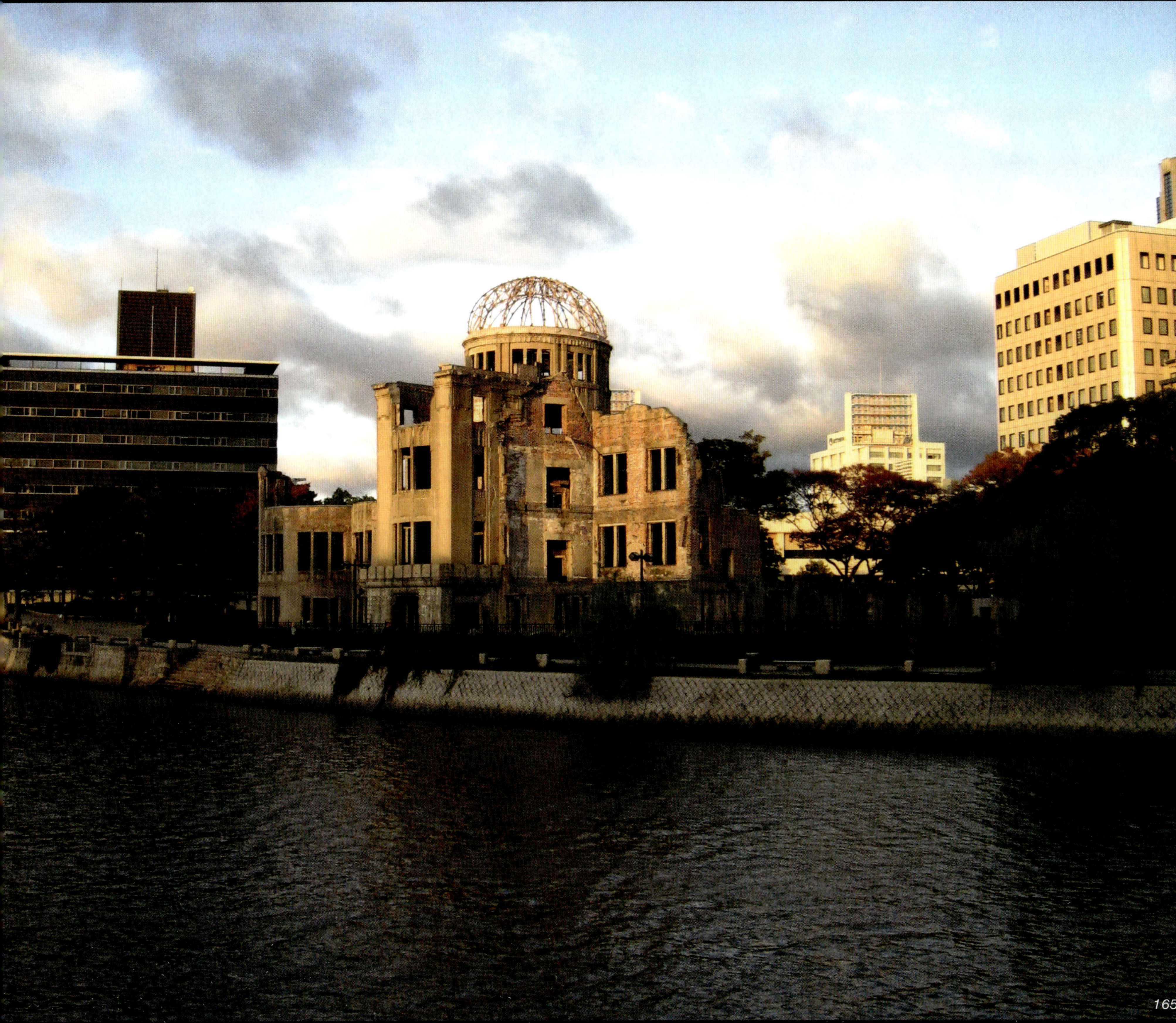

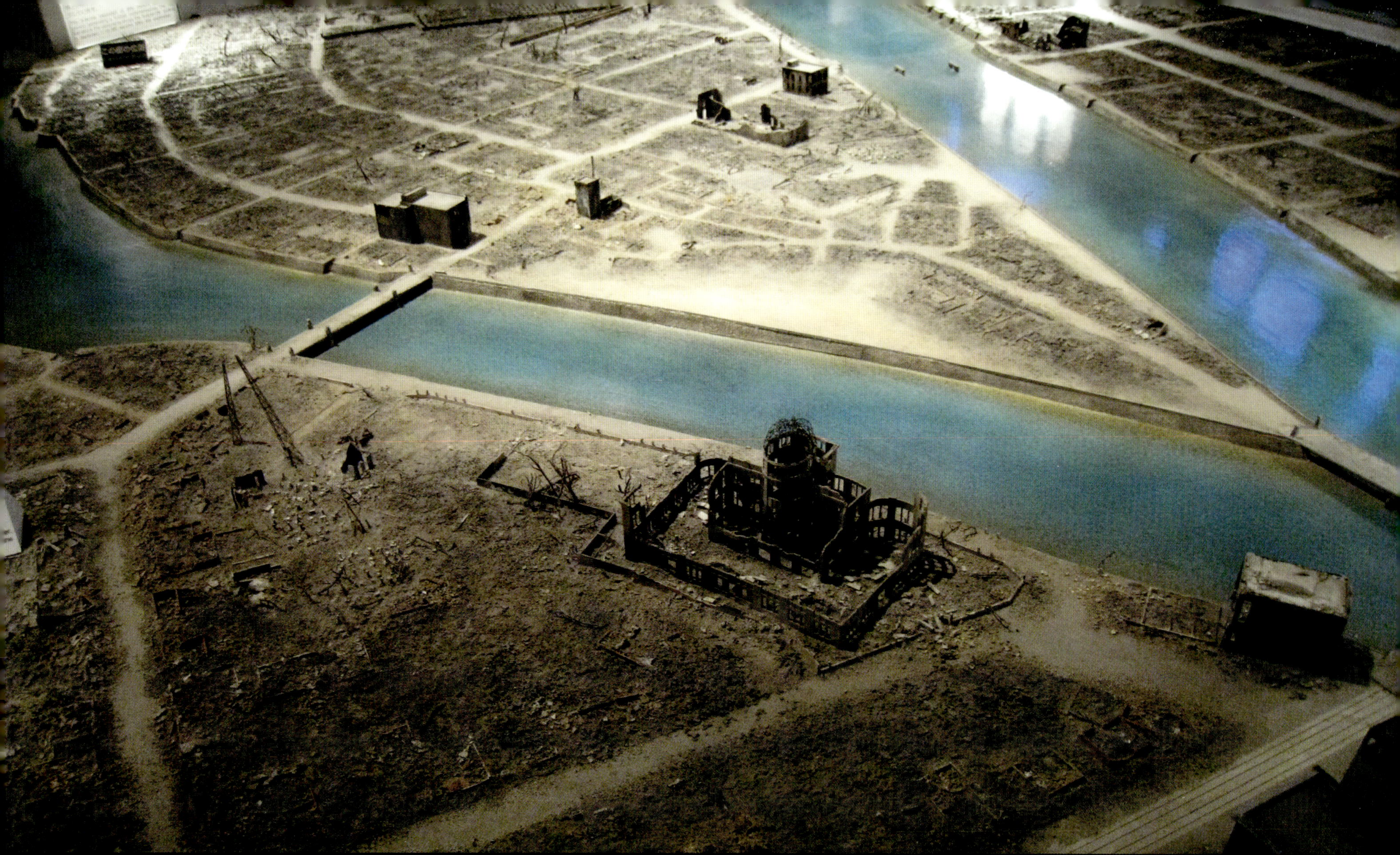

A 3D model of the city of Hiroshima immediately after the A-bomb was dropped can be seen in the Peace Memorial Museum.

### Memorial Cenotaph

The stone in the center of this arch shaped monument designed by Tange Kenzō holds a register with the names of all the persons who died from the bombing and reads 'Let all the souls here rest in peace, for we shall not repeat the evil.'

### Children's Peace Monument

The monument was unveiled on 5 May 1958 and symbolizes Sasaki Sadako holding an origami crane bird in her hands. Sadako was two and lived right in the city center when the A-bomb was dropped. She became ill as a result of the radiation. In line with a popular Japanese legend that one can make a wish after having folded 1,000 origami crane birds, Sadako, with the help of her classmates, made an attempt during her hospitalistion. She died at the age of 12 from leukemia.

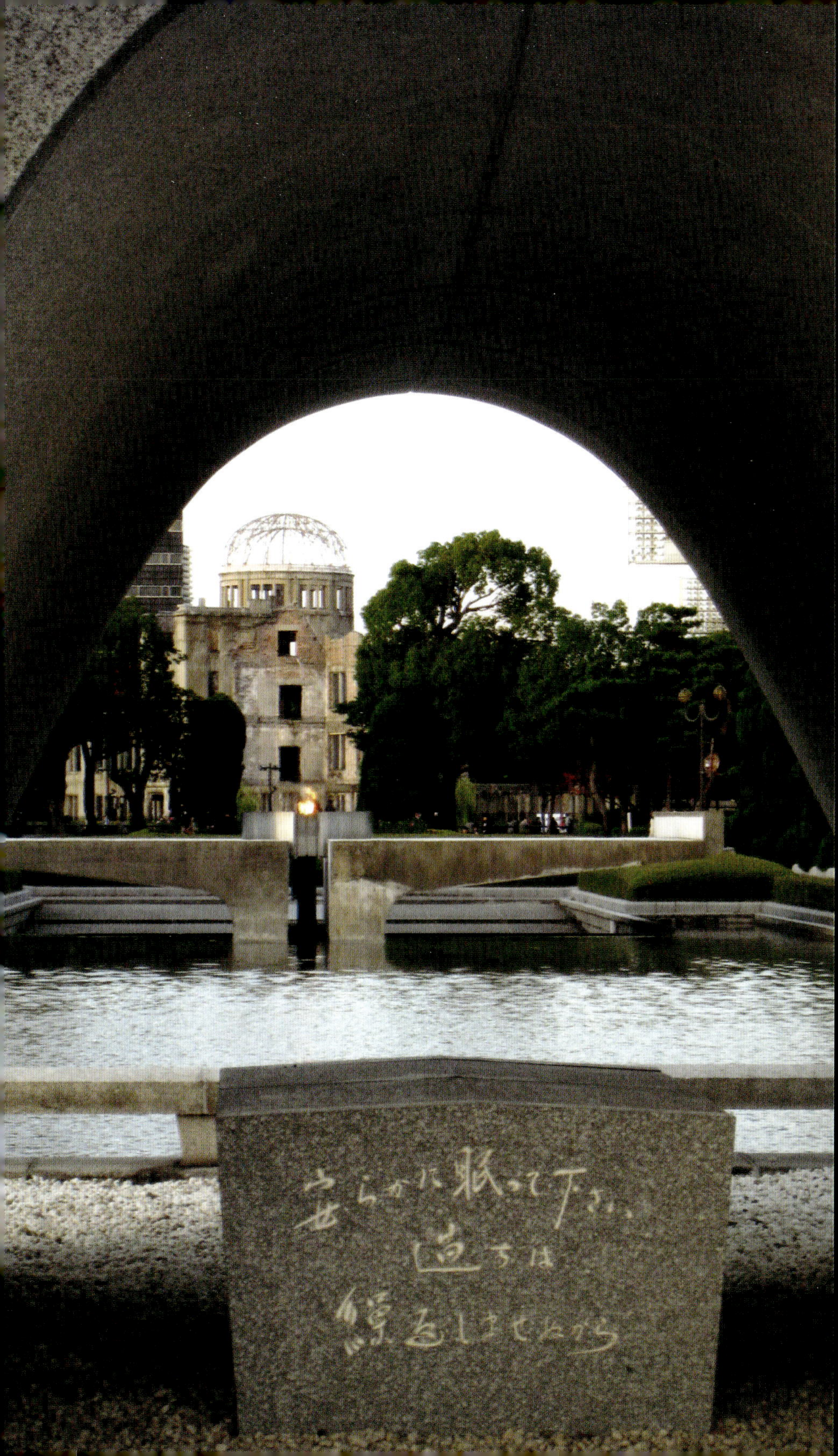
安らかに眠って下さい
過ちは
繰返しませぬから

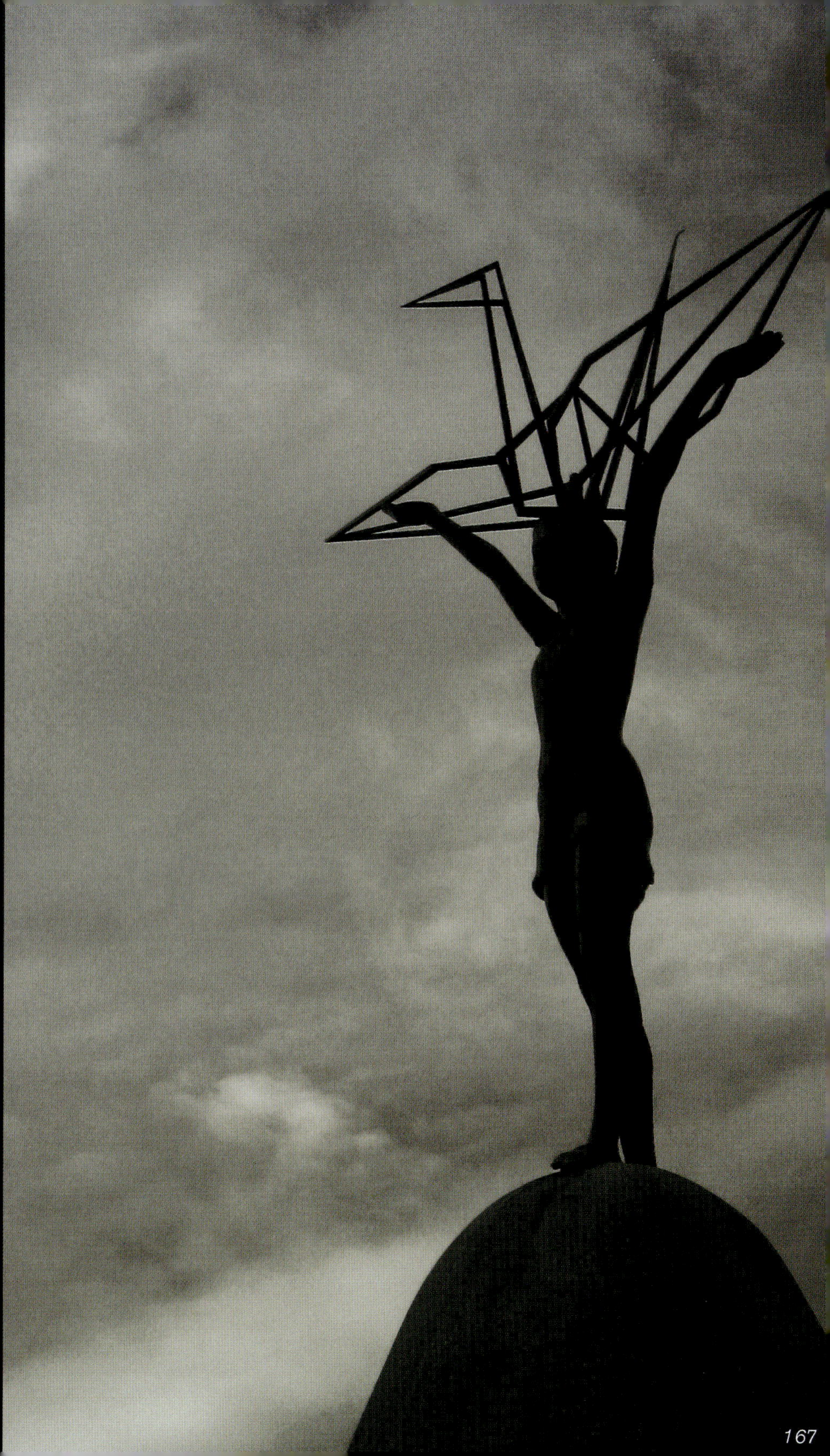

# Miyajima

The small island Miyajima at the Inland Sea is a UNESCO World Heritage site and one of Japan's most visited places. Apparently the UNESCO was not the only one very impressed with this site. Already in the early Edo period, the Confusianist, Gahō Hayashi, wrote that Itsukushima (Miyajima) together with Matsushima and Amanohashidate were the three most wonderful sights in Japan.

### Itsukushima-jinja

The top site of Miyajima is Itsukushima-jinja and the giant red torii standing in front of this Shintō shrine. Throughout the year various festivals are held at or near the shrine. If you are lucky enough to travel in the area around mid-August, do not miss the Hanabi Matsuri or fireworks festival held at the shrine, as it is one of the largest in Japan.

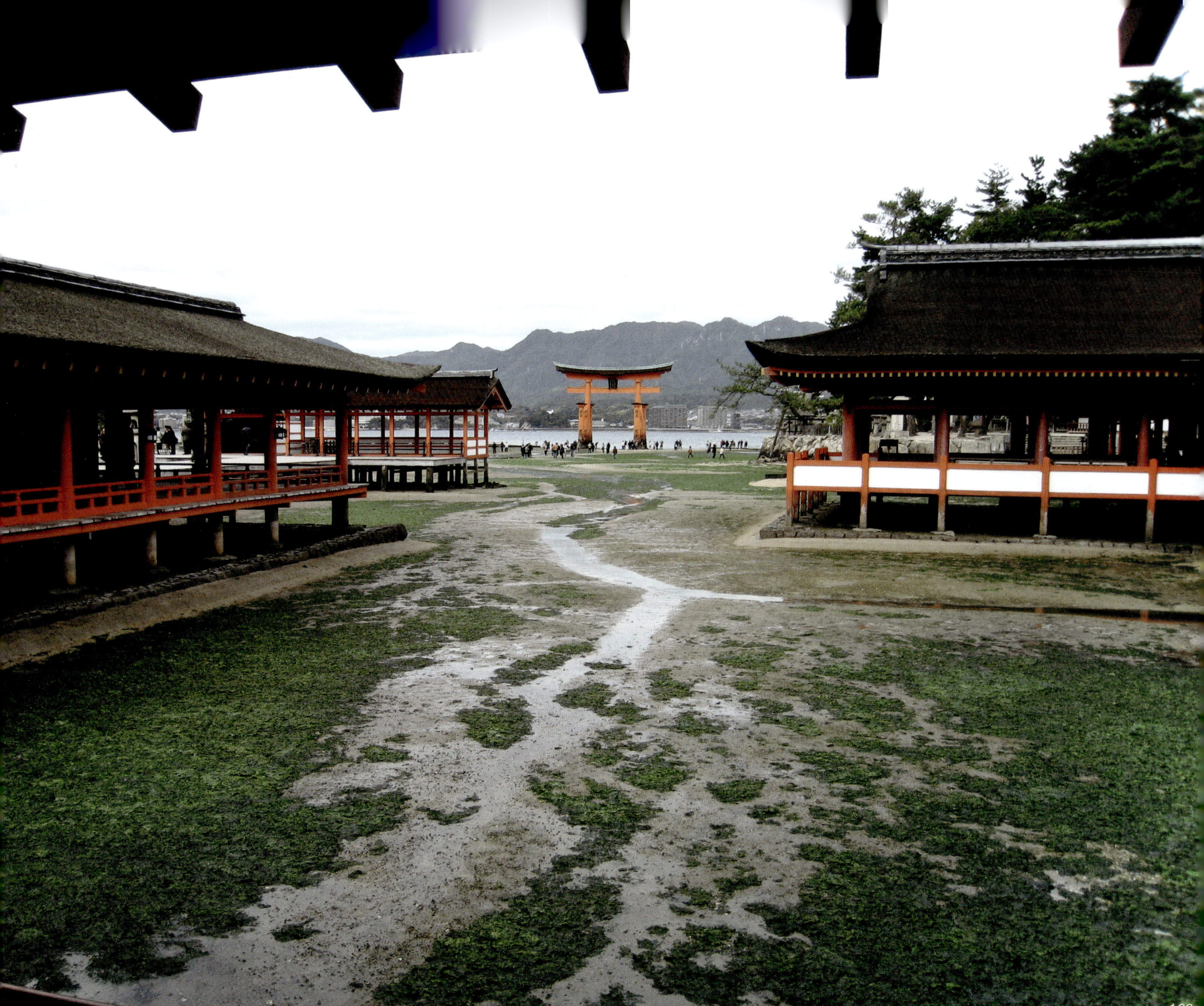

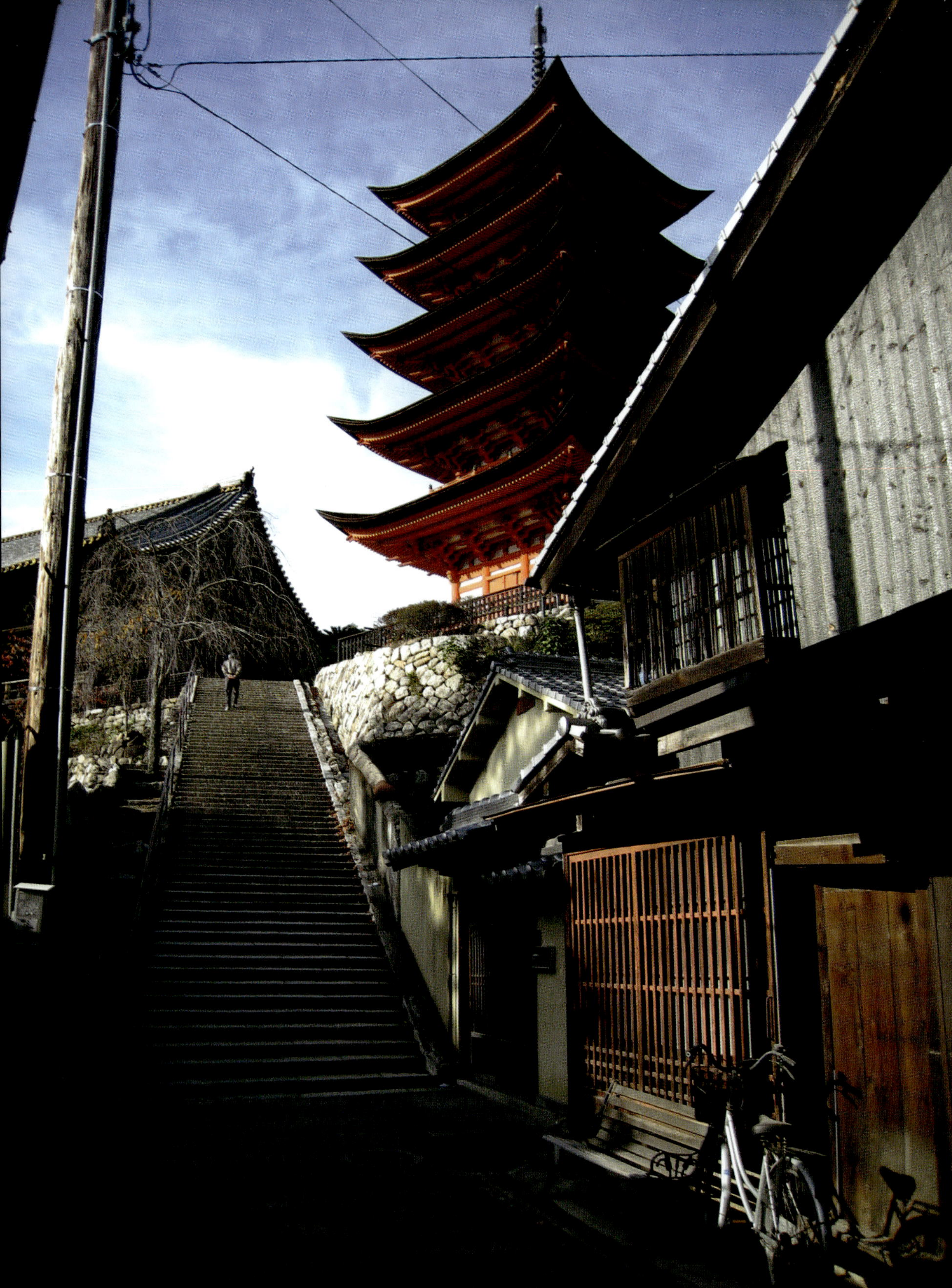

## Five-story pagoda

The small town on the island is rather touristic, but here and there it is possible to get away from the crowds. Do not miss this scenic sight of the five-story pagoda not far from the main shrine. The pagoda is 27-meter high and combines Chinese and Japanese styles.

## The Inland Sea

View of the Inland Sea, southwards from the summit of Mount Misen (535 m) on Miyajima. Clearly visible in the distance are Yashiro Island and the mountainous coast of Shikoku. Seeing this stunning panorama, I can only agree with Hirobumi Itō the first prime minister of Japan, who said that the true value of Miyajima as the most wonderful view of Japan 'is in the view from the top of Mount Misen'.

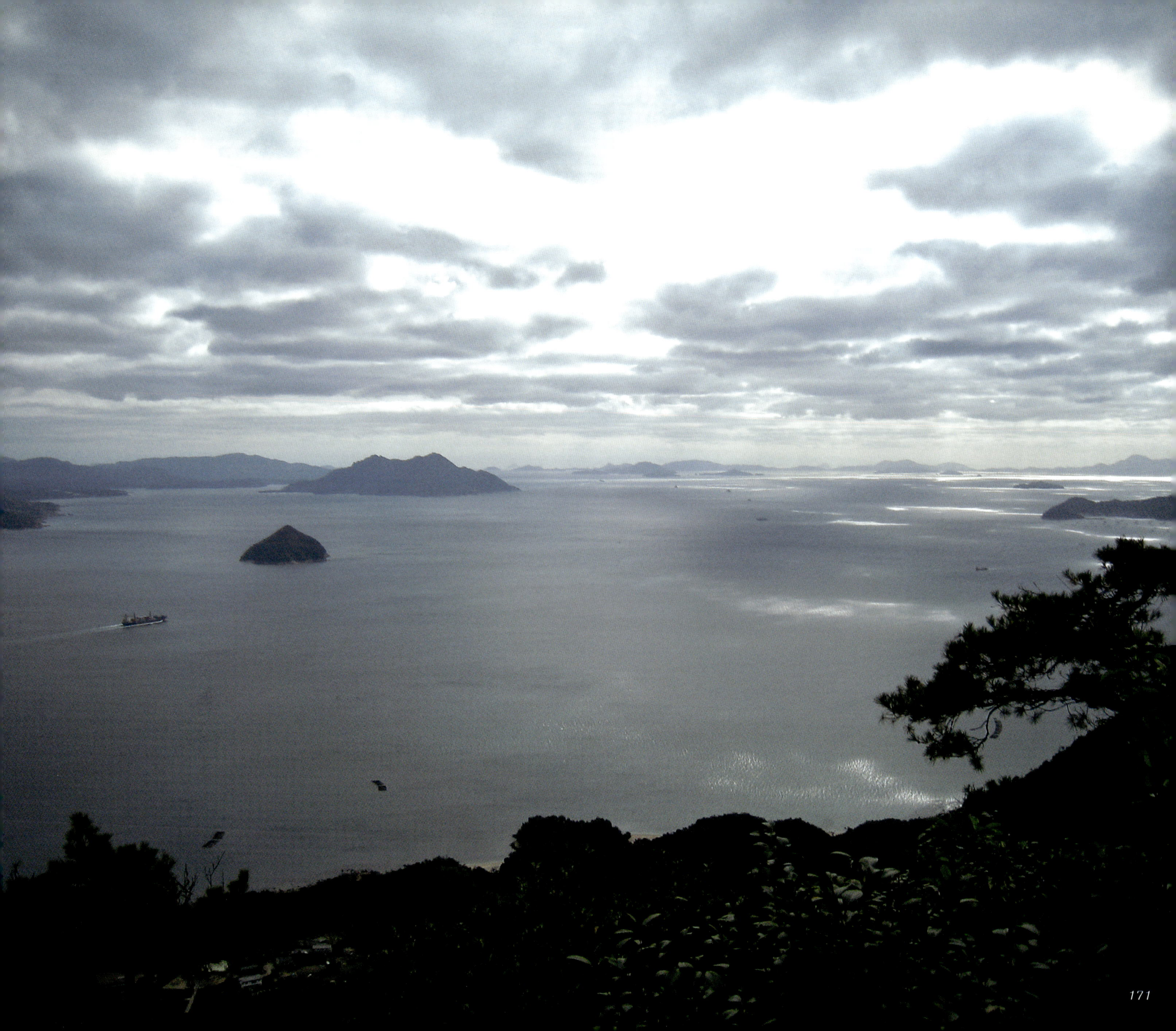

九州

Kyūshū is the third biggest island of Japan with an impressive coastline where the East China Sea flows into the Pacific Ocean. Kyūshū is known for some of Japan's best hot springs (especially the Beppu area), beautiful volcanic landscapes, the world's largest caldera, pristine beaches and inland vast areas of unspoiled nature.
If that is not enough add to that the big cities Fukuoka, Nagasaki, Kagoshima and Kumamoto with their longstanding history. These are very much worth a visit.

Since ancient times Kyūshū was an important maritime gateway to Asia and played a prominent role in Japan. According to the legends it was from here that the famous first emperor Jimmu, a descendant of the Sun goddess Amaterasu, moved to Honshū. Much later, Portuguese sailors, in search of new trade routes in the Pacific, were shipwrecked and reached the coast of Kyūshū in 1543. Soon to be followed in 1549 by the Jesuit priest Francis Xavier. Although foreigners were denied access to Japan during a large part of the Edo period, Dutch and Chinese merchants continued to trade from the port of Nagasaki.

In the mid 19th century the support of the Satsuma lords and samurai clans in Kyūshū were an important factor in the success of the Meiji restoration and the kick-off of modern Japan. Few years later into the Meiji rule, the legendary samurai Takamori Saigō could no longer agree with the government strategy. He led the revolt in Kyūshū in what became known as the Satsuma Rebellion of 1877. Outnumbered by the imperial army during the siege of Kumamoto castle Saigō's army was defeated and some months later he committed ritual suicide.

In today's Kyūshū the most important economic centers are Fukuoka and Nagasaki. This large port city recovered surprisingly well from the devastation after being hit on 9 August 1945 by the second A-bomb on Japan, just three days after Hiroshima.

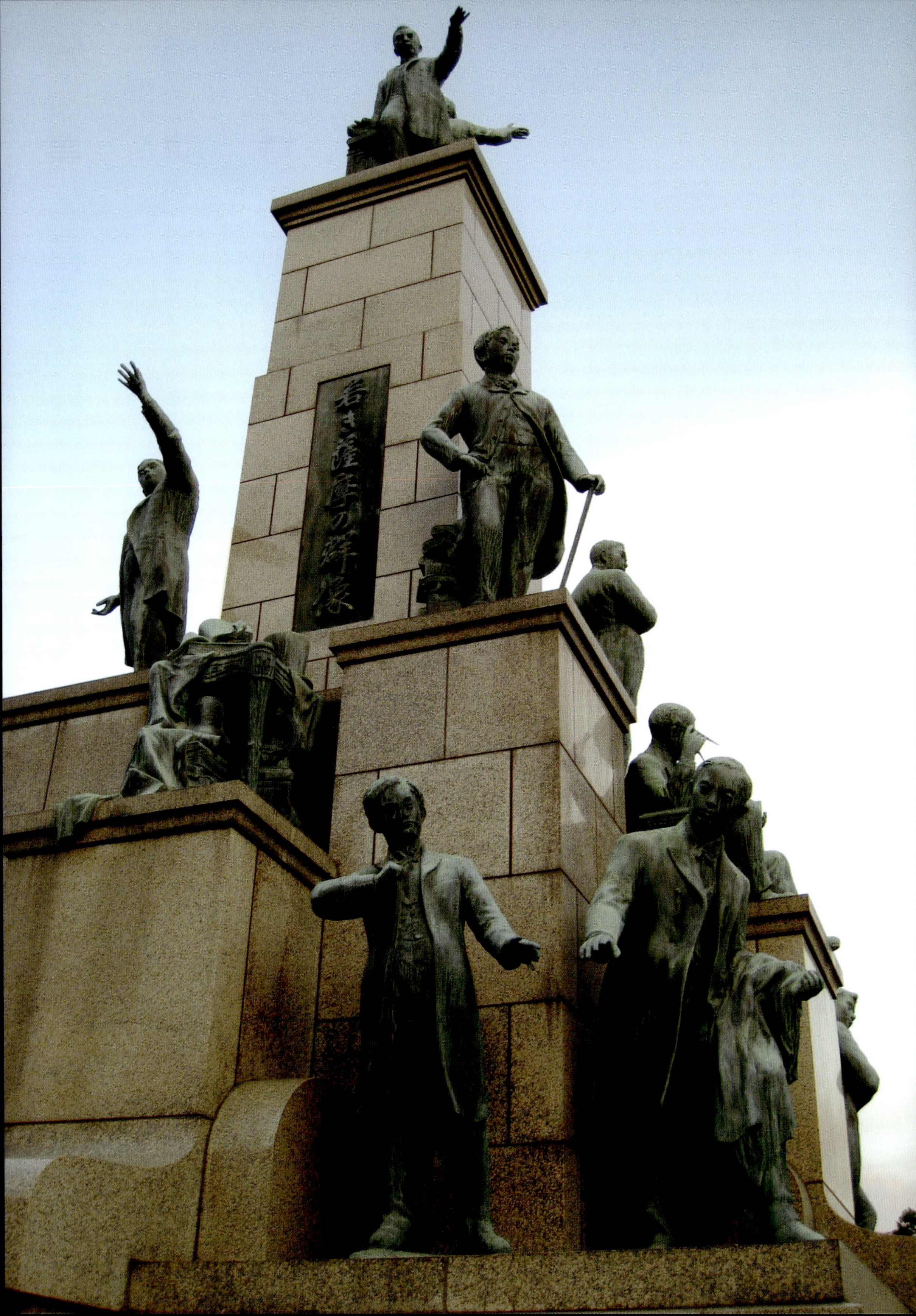


# Kagoshima

Kagoshima is situated at the most south-western tip of Kyūshū. It is sometimes compared with Napoli, its sister city in Italy, because of its splendid location at the idyllic bay of Kagoshima and the magnificent panorama of the Sakurajima volcano.

## Satsuma students

Right in the city center in front of the station is the statue for the Satsuma students. Satsuma, as the region used to be named, had a large form of autonomy and was always at the forefront of contacts with other cultures and nations.

In 1865, during the turbulent end of the Edo period when contact with the outside world was still forbidden, the Satsuma clan sent a team of its most brilliant students on a clandestine mission to study at university in the United Kingdom.
They would be among the first to learn in-depth modern western technology and languages and upon their return some would become Japan's ambassadors in western countries while others took up top functions in the Meiji government.

## The bay of Kagoshima

The Sakurajima volcano dominates the beautiful bay of Kagoshima. On the day this picture was taken, noticeably thick clouds of ash started gathering over the South and Showa crater. This increased activity of the volcano was the prelude to a rather severe eruption of the Showa crater in the days after.

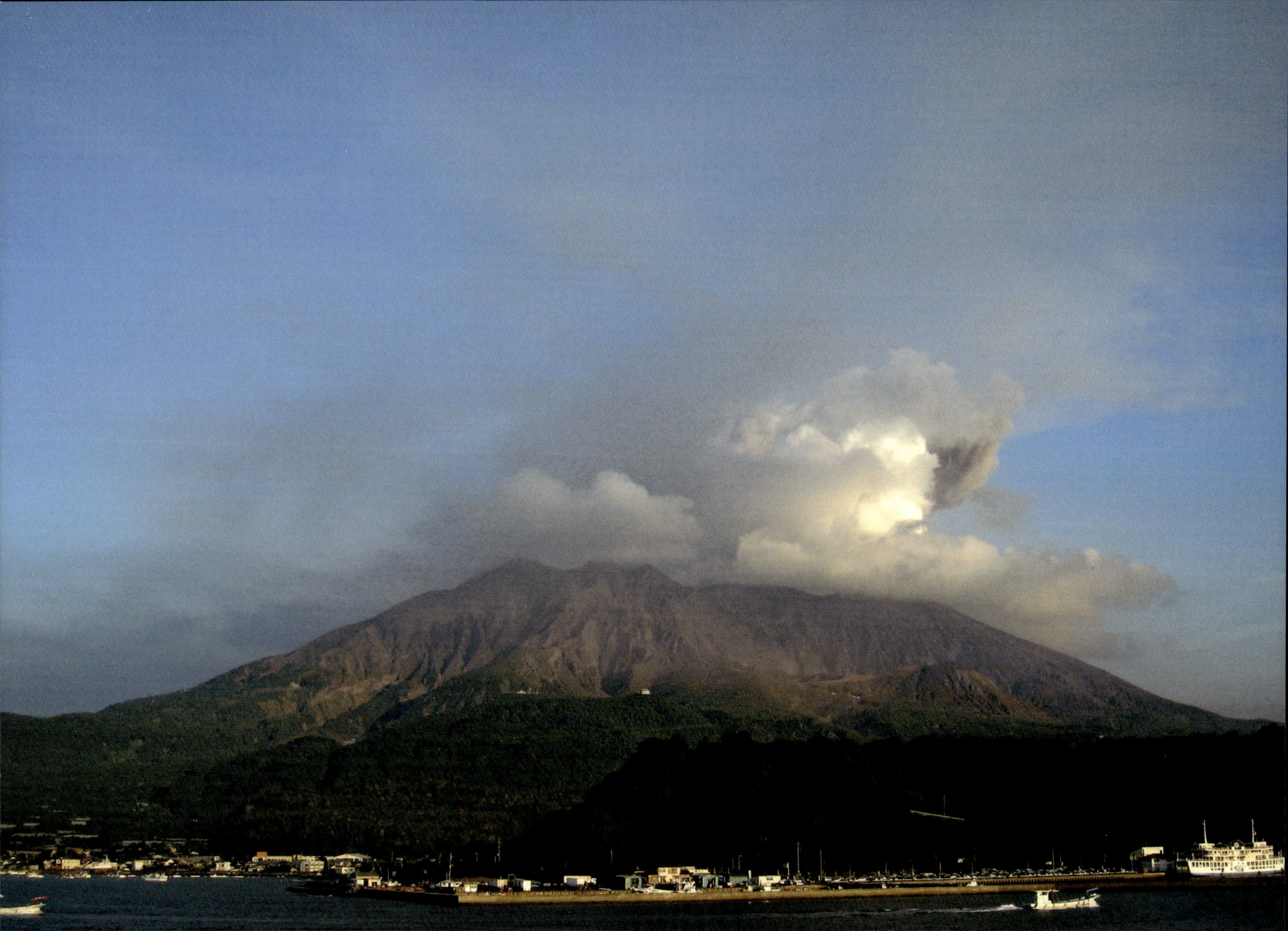

# Sakurajima and the Ring of Fire

The Japanese archipelago with its 7,000 islands is located on what is called 'the Pacific Ring of Fire'.
The Ring of Fire is actually a range of places with strong volcanic and seismic activity that stretches around the Pacific Ocean and encompasses New Zealand, Indonesia, The Philippines, Japan, the Bering Strait, Alaska and the entire Pacific coast of North and South America.

The dramatic beauty of volcanic landscapes in Japan attracts hikers, tourists and photographers not only from Japan but also from all over the world. Despite massive research and investments in early warning systems, unexpected eruptions can happen. In 2014 Mount Ontake, north of Nagoya, erupted without any advance warning signals in the days or hours before, killing dozens of hikers that were on the flank of the volcano.

Probably the best-known volcano in Japan is Mount Fuji, the country's epic symbol. Mount Fuji's last major eruption was in 1707 and the volcano has been relatively quiet since. A special division of Japan's Meteorological Agency monitors the mountain, together with more than 100 other volcanoes, on a 24-hour basis.

Another famous volcano that needs constant monitoring is Sakurajima in the Bay of Kagoshima. Sakurajima is considered as one of the most active volcanos in the world with continuous activity. Located only a short distance from the densely populated city Kagoshima, the volcano is considered very dangerous because of its highly explosive nature of its eruptions. Over the last 50 years the volcano has been very active at times spewing ashes 5 to 10 kilometer high.

Originally Sakurajima was an island. In 1914, after months of increased earthquake activity Sakurajima exploded in what is known as the Taishō eruption. The hot lava kept flowing for weeks connecting Sakurajima with the mainland in the southeast. Vintage photos show an eruption that must have looked apocalyptic in reality. Eyewitnesses described how in the morning of 12 January enormous explosions opened the western and eastern sides of the volcano, throwing a column of volcanic material more than 10 km in the air. Fortunately, most of the island's population and people from Kagoshima already fled. Nevertheless, later the same day a severe earthquake followed by a tsunami caused extensive damage to Kagoshima.

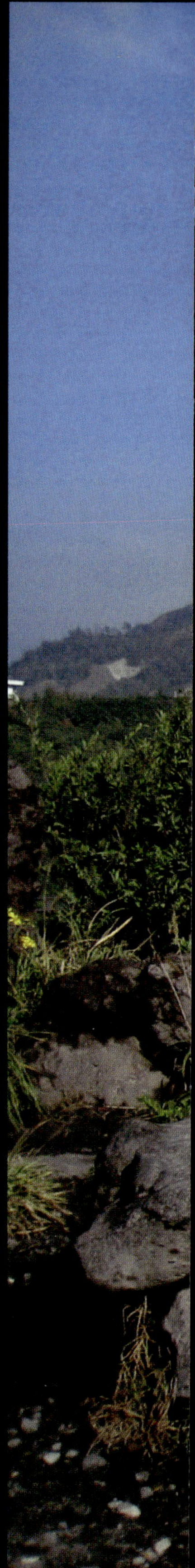

View from the Yunohira Observatory on Sakurajima. With 373 meter it is not only the highest but also the nearest point from where it is allowed to observe the volcano. In the background is the active north crater.

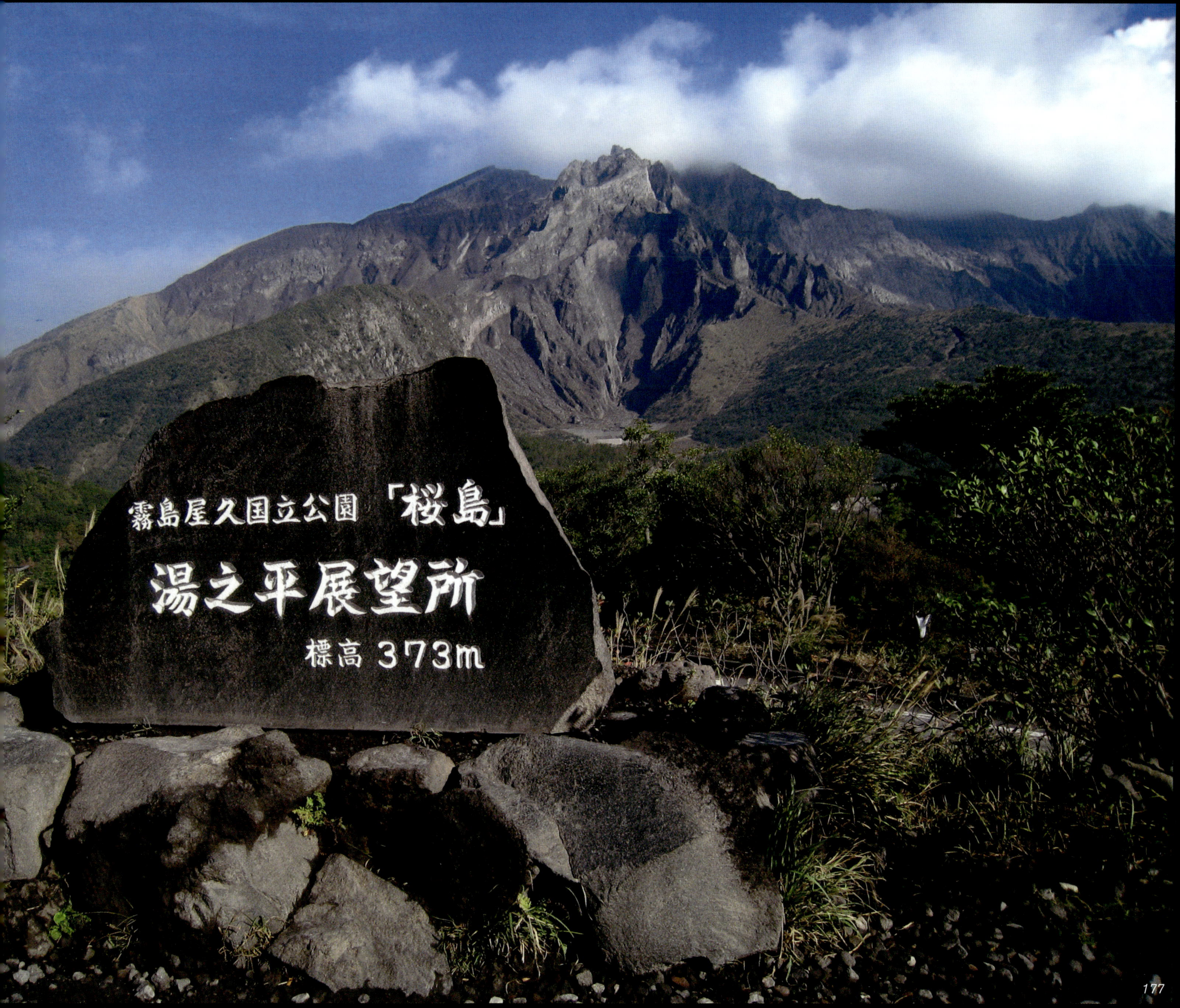
霧島屋久国立公園「桜島」
湯之平展望所
標高 373m

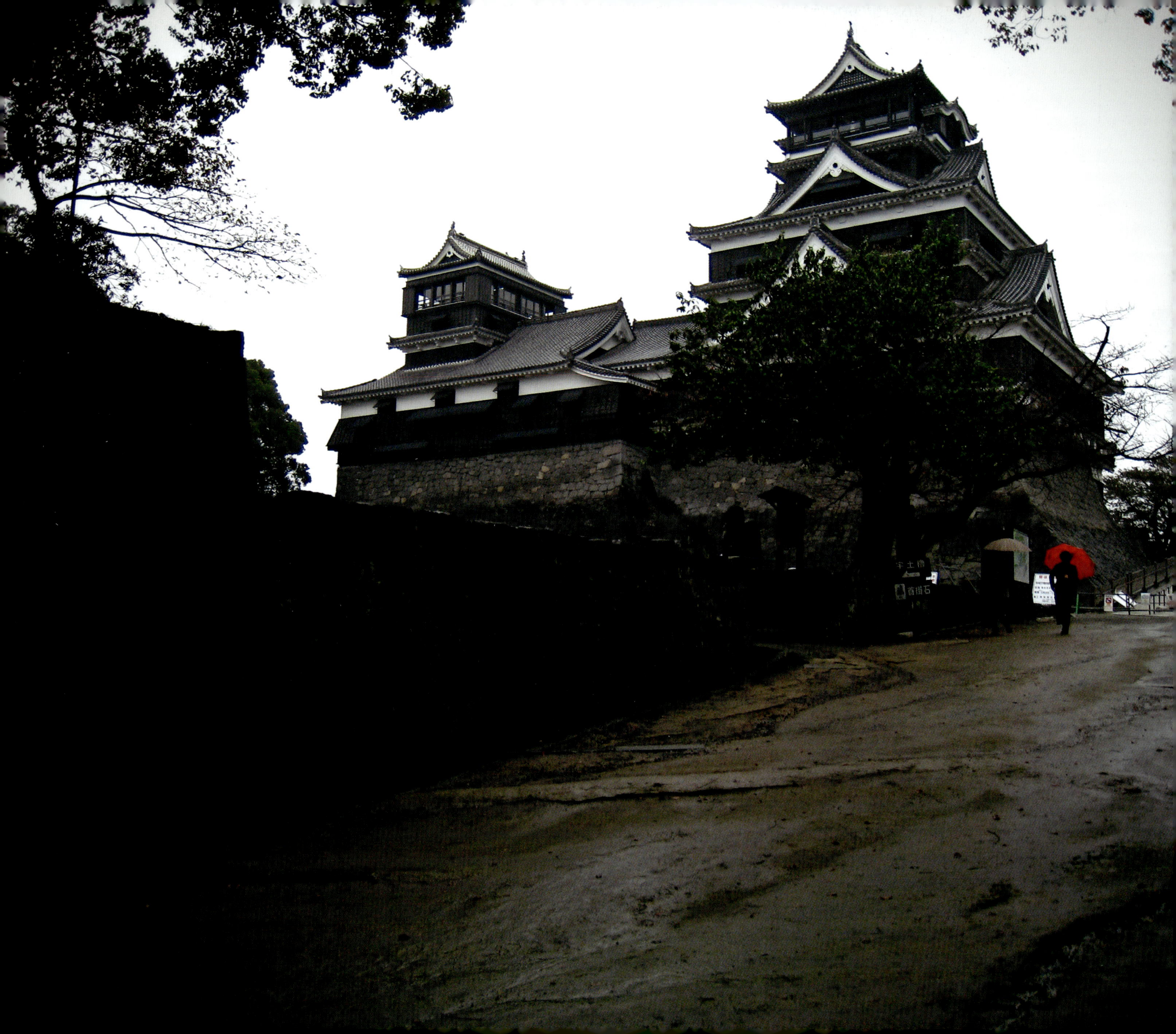
首掛石

## Kumamoto

The city center of Kumamoto is dominated by its heavily fortified castle, widely accepted to be one of the most monumental in Japan. It was built in the early 17th century by Katō Kiyomasa, who was an ally of Tokugawa Ieyasu in the battle of Sekigahara in 1600.

The castle was built on a hill and its steep massive walls stretching over kilometers around the main keeps made it almost impregnable. In 1877 the castle, occupied by troops of the imperial army, was besieged by Takamori Saigō's rebellion army for almost two months. Protected by the castle walls the siege failed but the central part of the castle was burned down and lay in rubble for years until it was rebuilt in 1960.

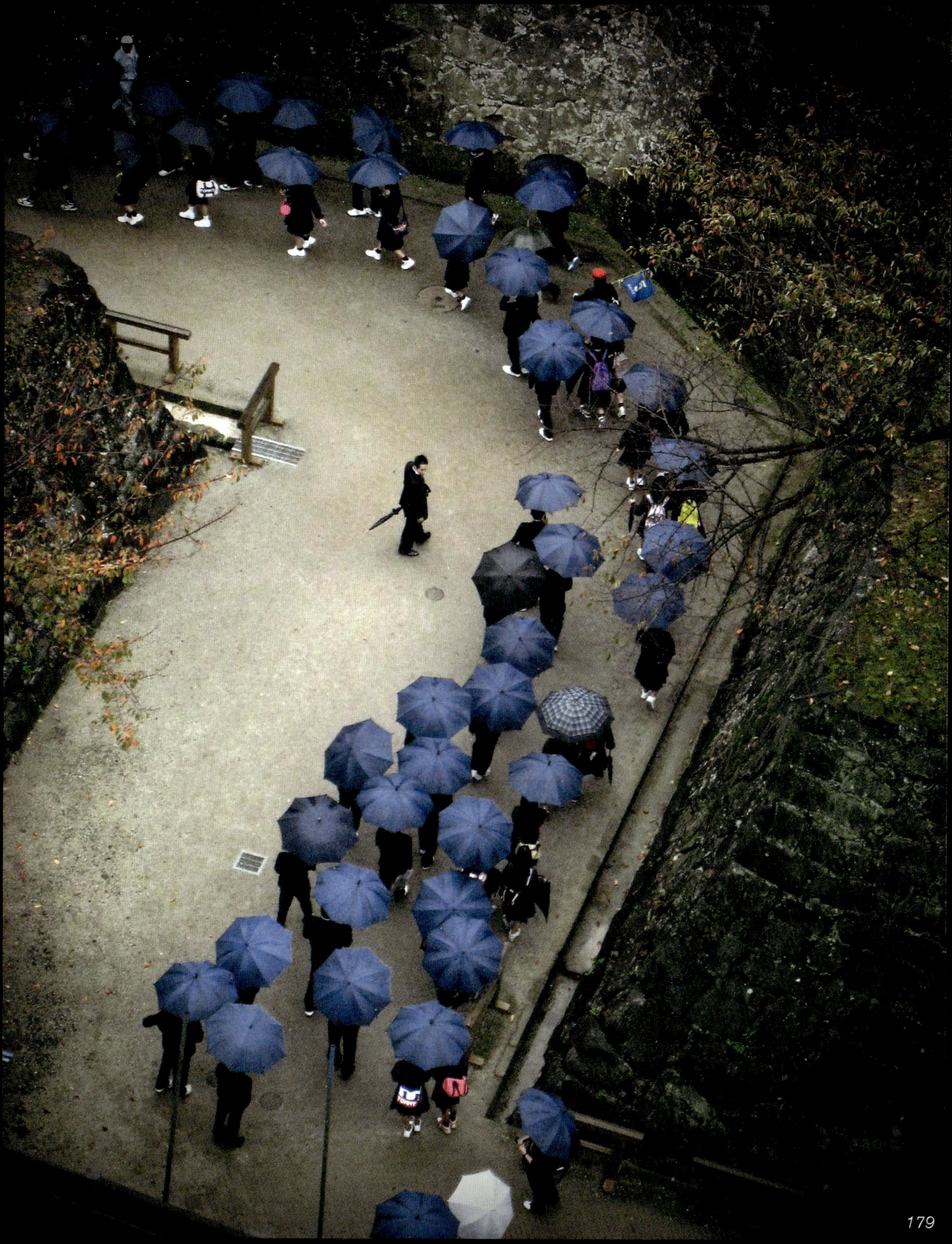

The castle's impressive yet elegantly built stone walls named musha-gaeshi, literally translated as 'warrior-repelling', withstood various earthquakes and artillery fire and managed to keep out invaders for over four centuries. Unfortunately, the deadly 7.3 magnitude earthquake of 16 April 2016 severely damaged the walls and central parts of the castle.

沖縄

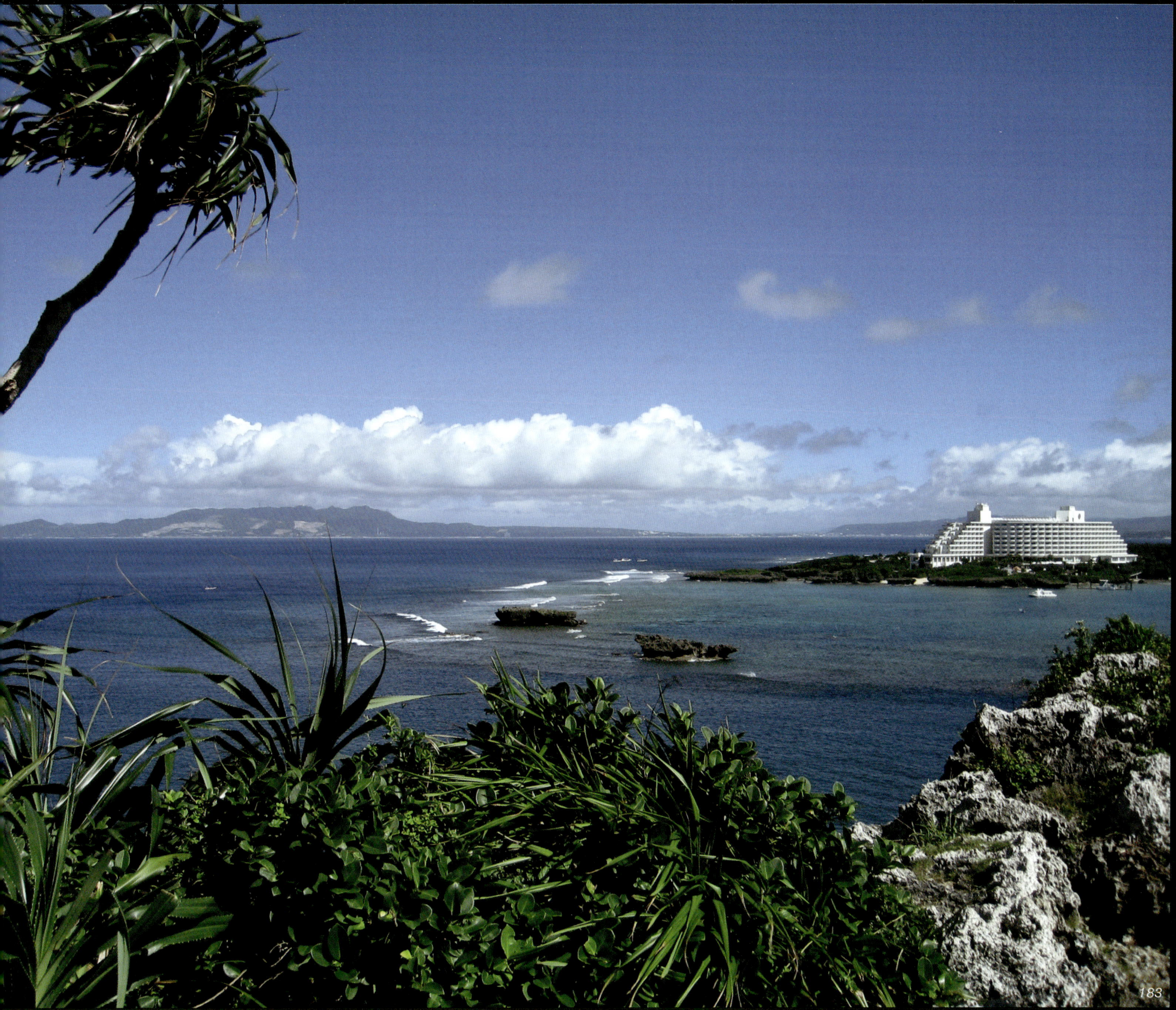

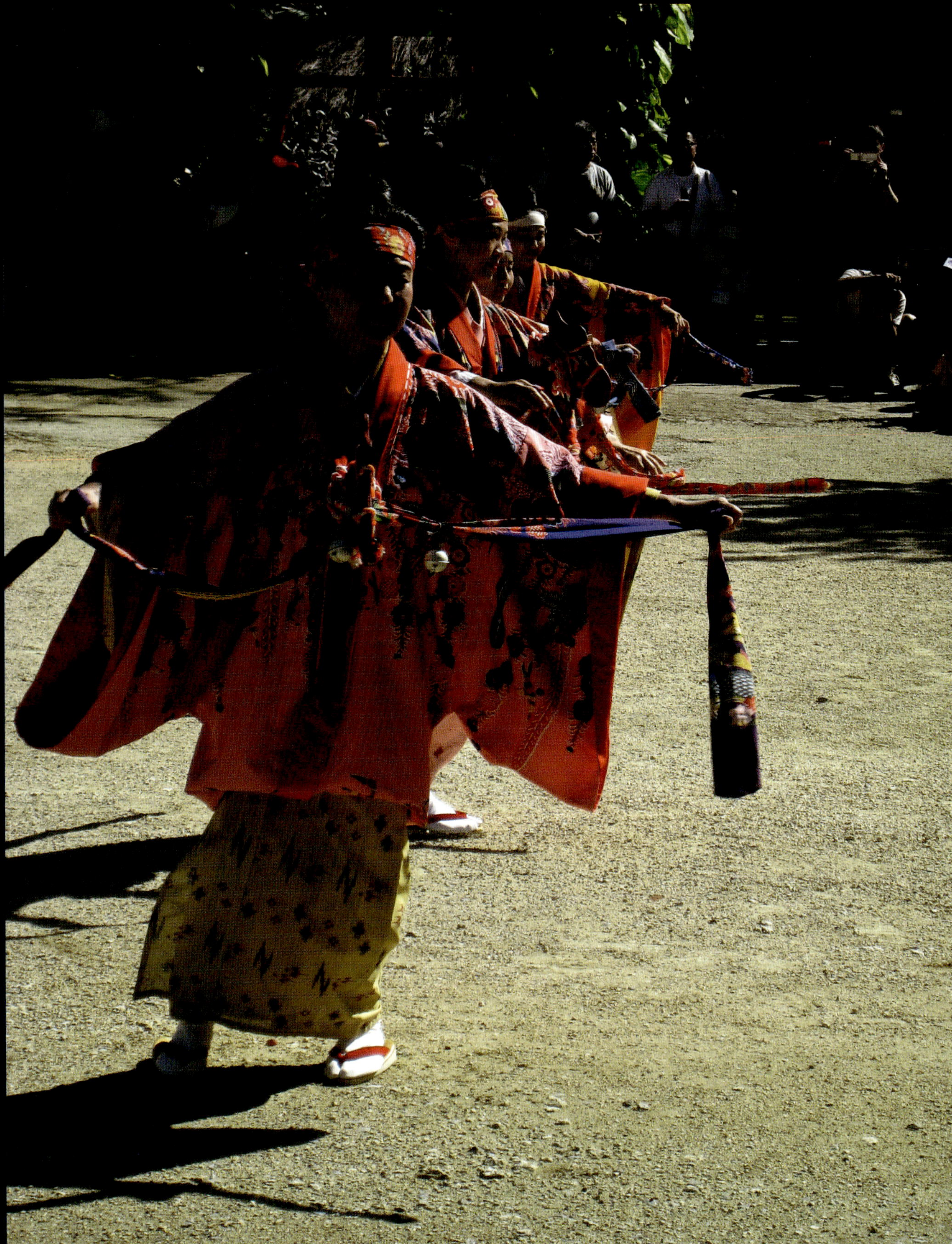

### Ryūkyū Dances

Okinawa is very proud of its unique cultural heritage of which music and dances are a vital part. Originally various dances were performed at the court for Chinese envoys and delegates from Satsuma. Today Eisa folk dance festivals are immensely popular and a modern witness of the musical traditions on the islands.

### Shuri Castle

This massive fortified castle overlooking Naha, the capital of Okinawa, has both strong Chinese and Japanese influences. For almost 500 years it was the royal court and diplomatic center of the kingdom. During World War II the Japanese army used it as their military headquarter in the south and subsequently it was almost completely destroyed during the Battle of Okinawa in 1945. Hardly noticeable is that the whole castle has been perfectly rebuilt based on ancient documents and pictures. In December of 2000 it was designated as a UNESCO World Heritage site.

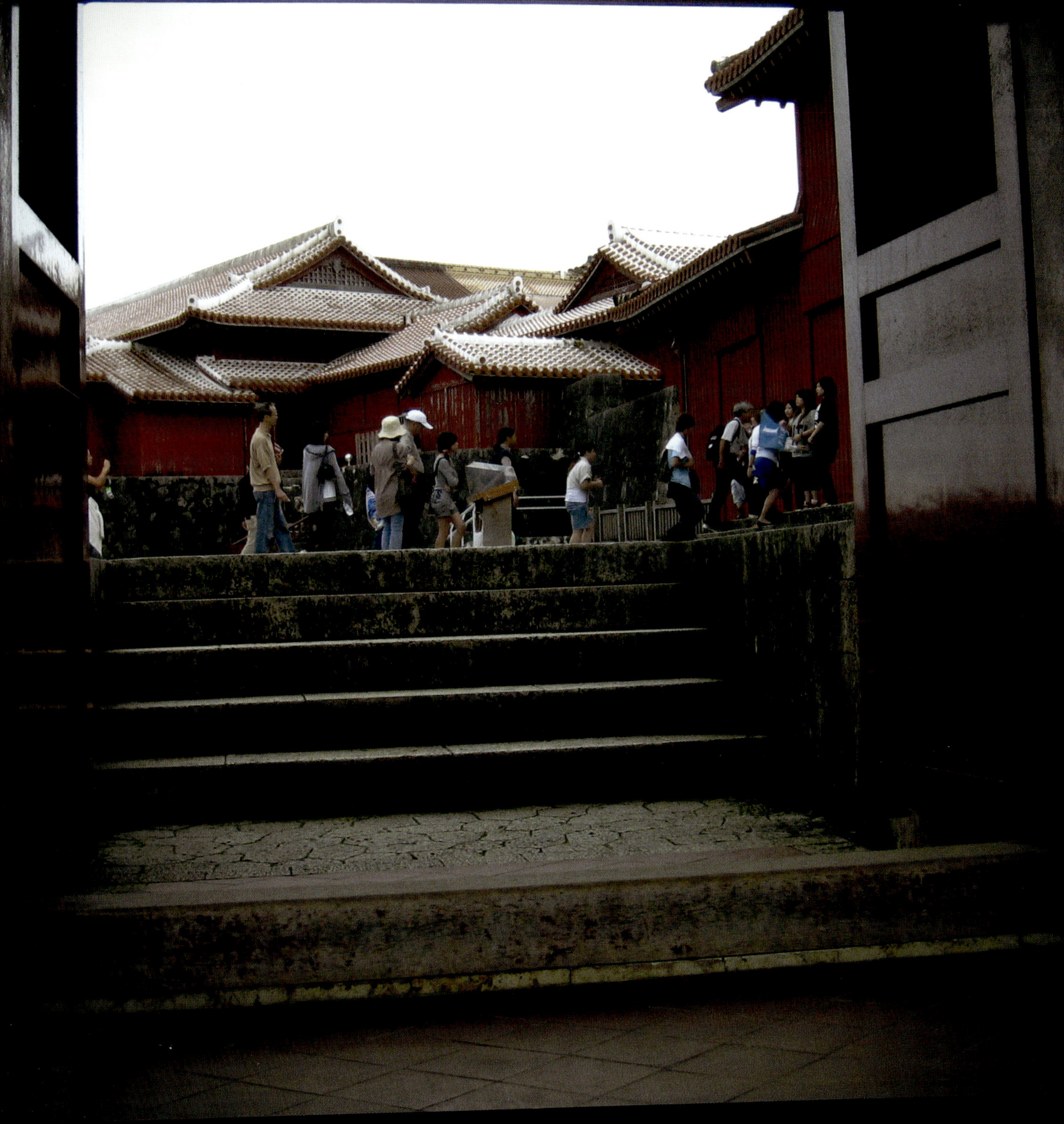

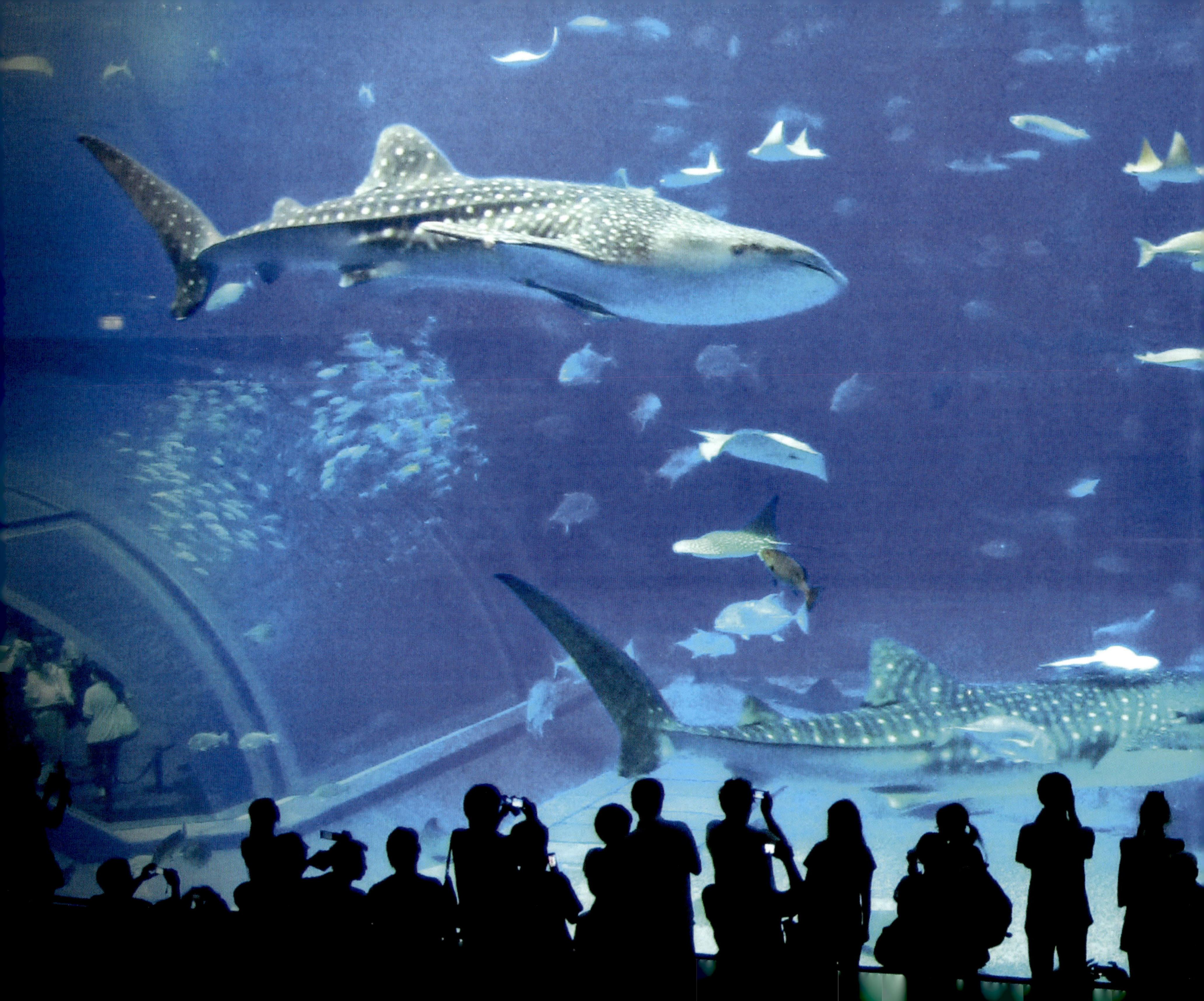

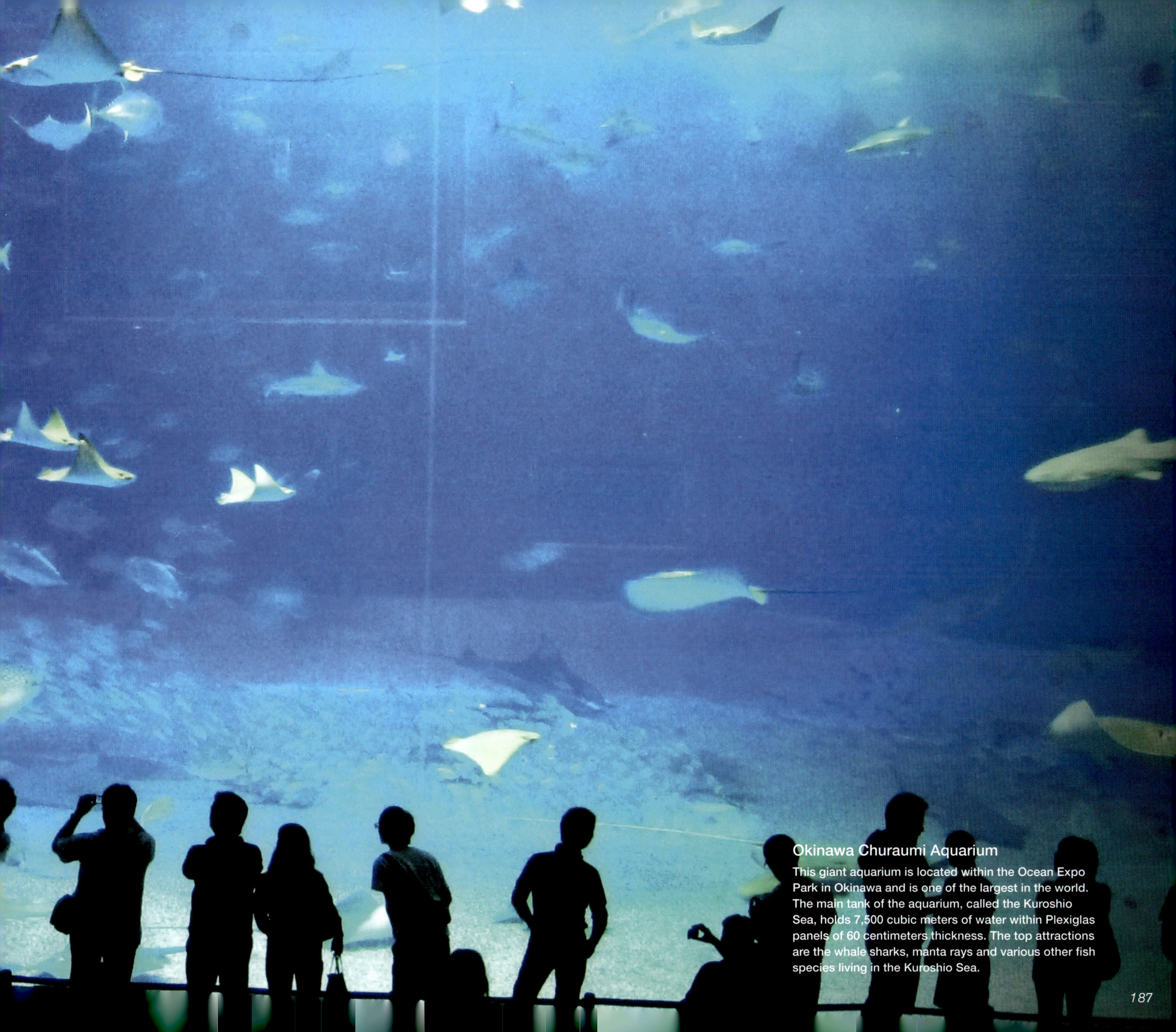

## Okinawa Churaumi Aquarium

This giant aquarium is located within the Ocean Expo Park in Okinawa and is one of the largest in the world. The main tank of the aquarium, called the Kuroshio Sea, holds 7,500 cubic meters of water within Plexiglas panels of 60 centimeters thickness. The top attractions are the whale sharks, manta rays and various other fish species living in the Kuroshio Sea.

# The Yaeyama Archipelago

To savor the true beauty of Japan's southern-most prefecture one should head another 500 kilometer southwest from Naha to the exotic Yaeyama Islands near the tropic of cancer.

Sandy beaches surrounded by Japan's largest coral reefs and unspoiled jungle forests make the islands a premier destination for snorkeling, diving and ecotourism.

Traditional villages where the pace of life is 'yukkuri' which means slowly or leisurely in Japanese reminded me of the old saying in France's Provence 'lentement le matin et pas trop vite le soir' that translates as 'take it easy in the morning and not to fast in the evening'.

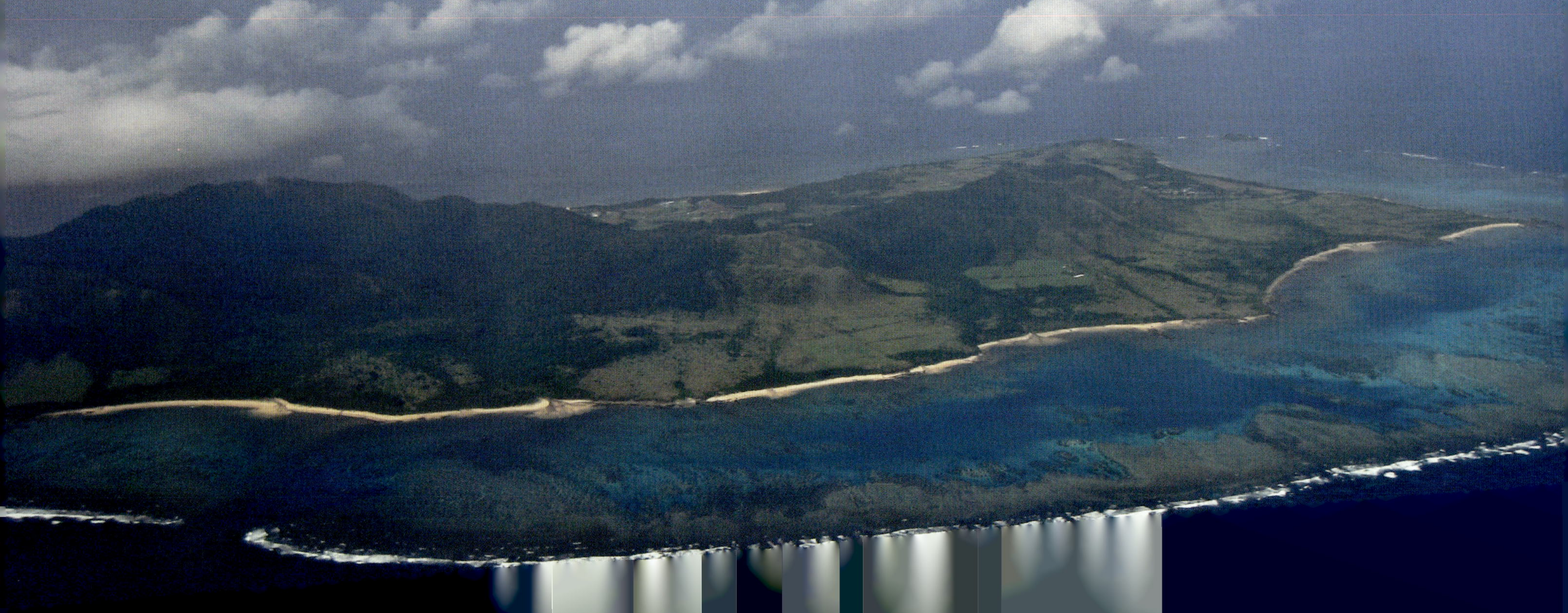

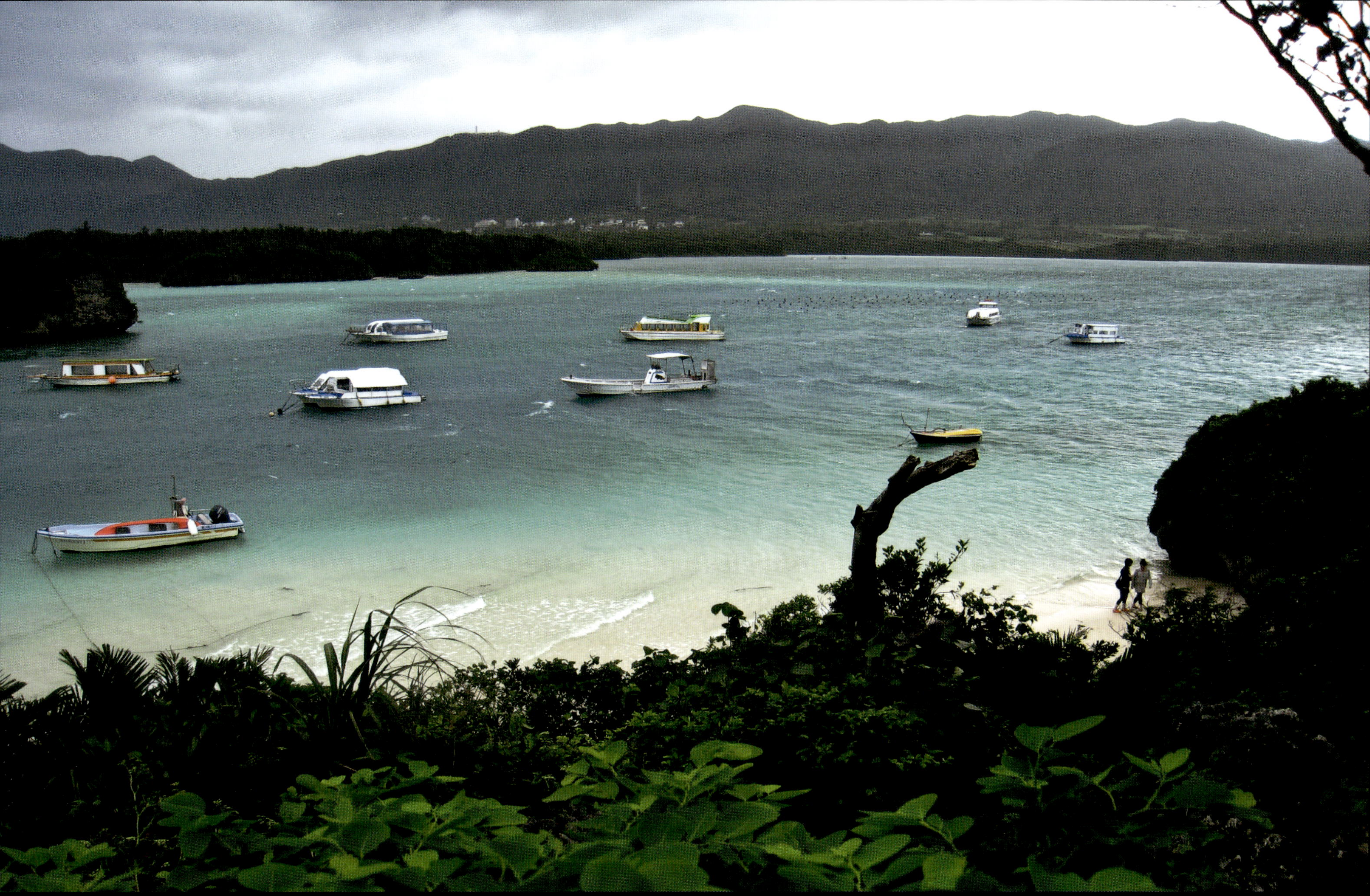

### Ishigaki island

Coral reefs and a beautiful ocean with colors ranging from azure to emerald green surround Ishigaki Island. The northern tip, Cape Hirakubo, where the East China Sea and the Pacific meet, is clearly visible. It is a popular place for sunset viewing.

### Kabira Bay

Kabira Bay on Ishigaki is especially renowned for its black pearl cultivation. Black pearls are extremely rare in nature and it was here that, for the first time in the world, cultivation of this mysterious black pearl started. Note the oyster banks in the center of the bay.

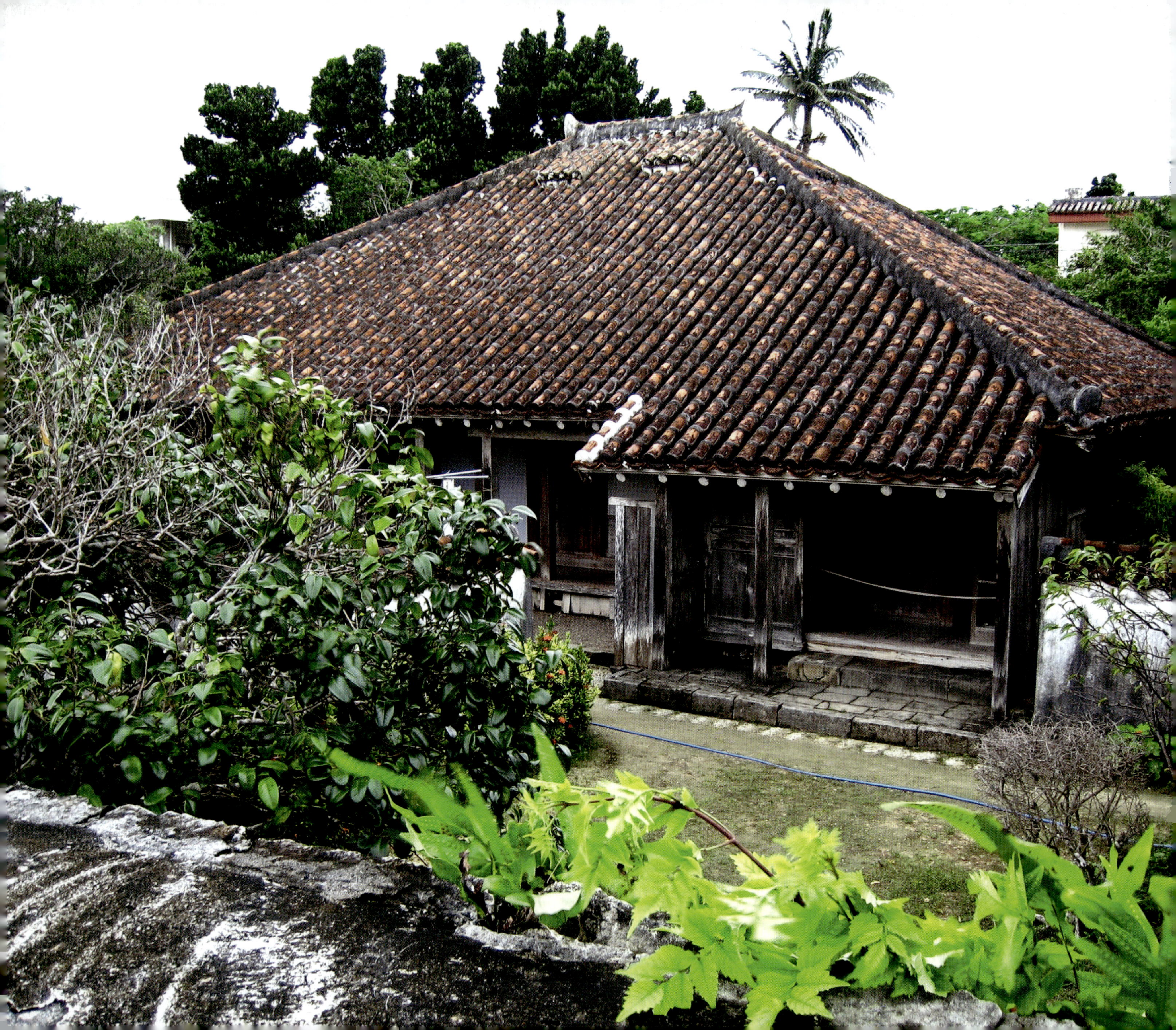

## Traditional house

The Miyara Dounchi House was built in 1819 by a government official of the Ryūkyū Kingdom in charge of the unification of Yaeyama. Typical are the traditional Okinawan red tile roofs and the walls in front of the houses protecting them against typhoons.

## Shisha

On all Ryūkyū islands a lot of shisha ('shiisaa' in Okinawan) can be seen. A shisha is a mythological figure with curly manes that is half dog half lion. As single statuettes, they often sit on the roof and when in pairs they are placed as guardians next to the entrance of buildings. The right one has its mouth open to scare off evil whereas the left one has its mouth closed or is smiling to keep the good spirits inside. This elaborate example can be seen at the Toujin grave memorial. This monument was erected for the many Chinese laborers that were put on transport to California, but died here after shipwrecking on the coast of Ishigaki.

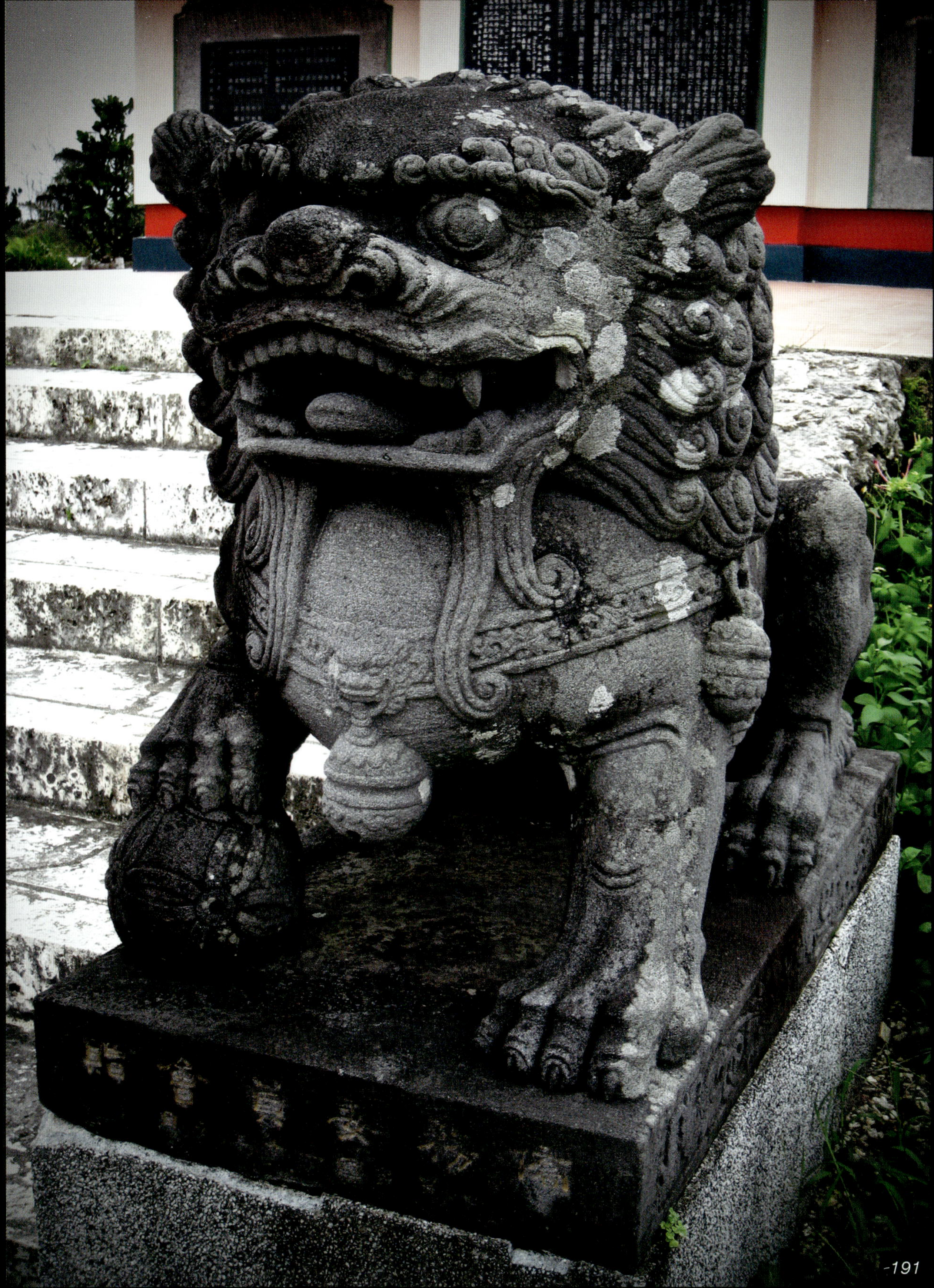

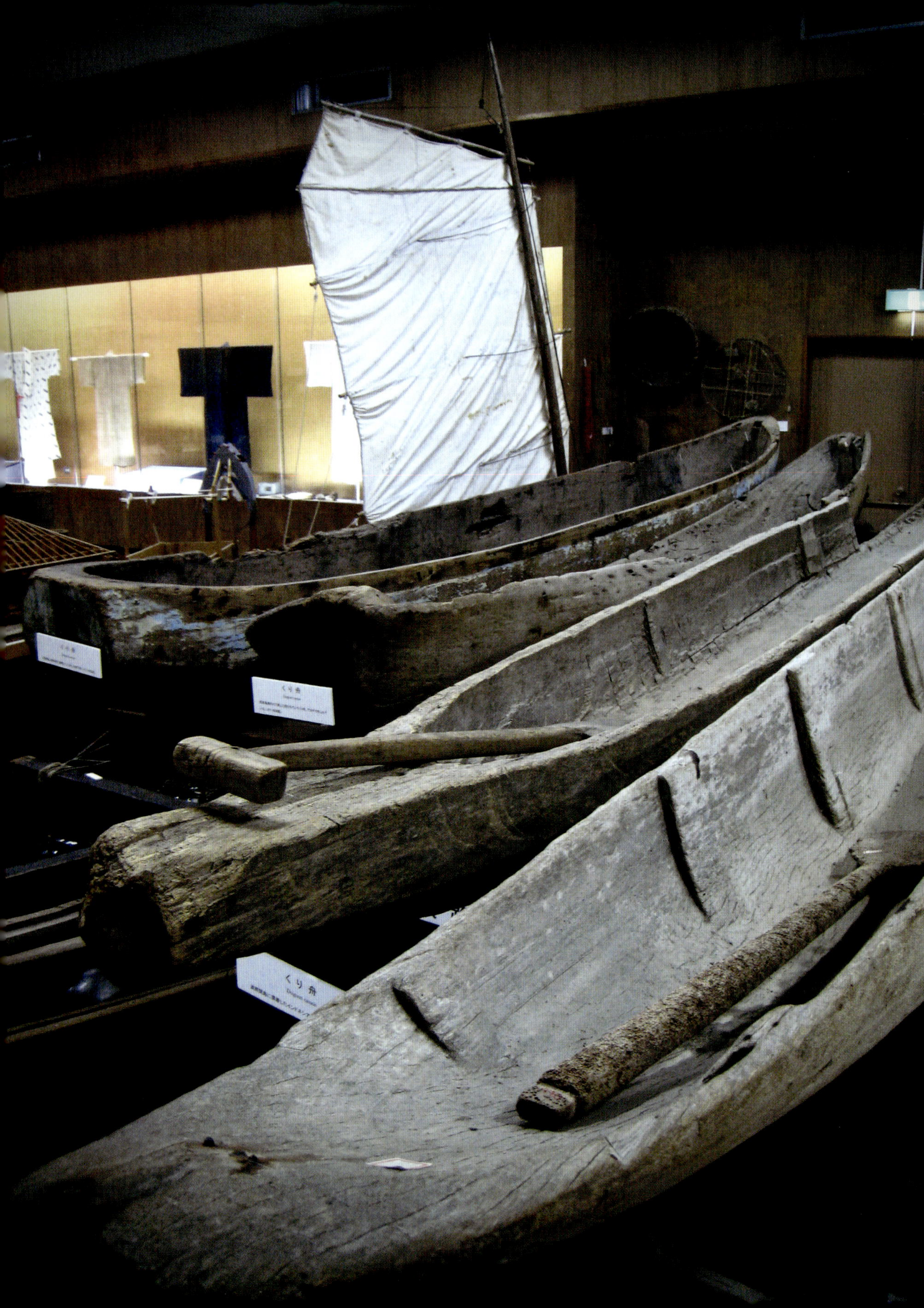


### Yaeyama Museum

Little is known about the first inhabitants of the Yaeyama Islands. Being much closer to Taiwan than to the other islands of the Okinawa archipelago evidence indicates that the pre-historic occupation of the Yaeyama Islands probably originated from present day Taiwan by Austronesian speaking populations. Ishigaki has a small but interesting museum with around 5,000 artifacts that explain the cultural and maritime history of these remote islands.

### Iriomote Island

Iriomote Island, almost 300 square kilometers large, is the second largest island of the whole Okinawa Archipelago. It is part of the huge Iriomote-Ishigaki National Park and deep inland a large area is preserved as untouchable primeval forest. It is the habitat of the Iriomote cat, the island's most famous inhabitant and prominently visible as a mascot on Iriomote's tour busses. This night animal is part of the leopard cat family, and was only discovered in 1965.

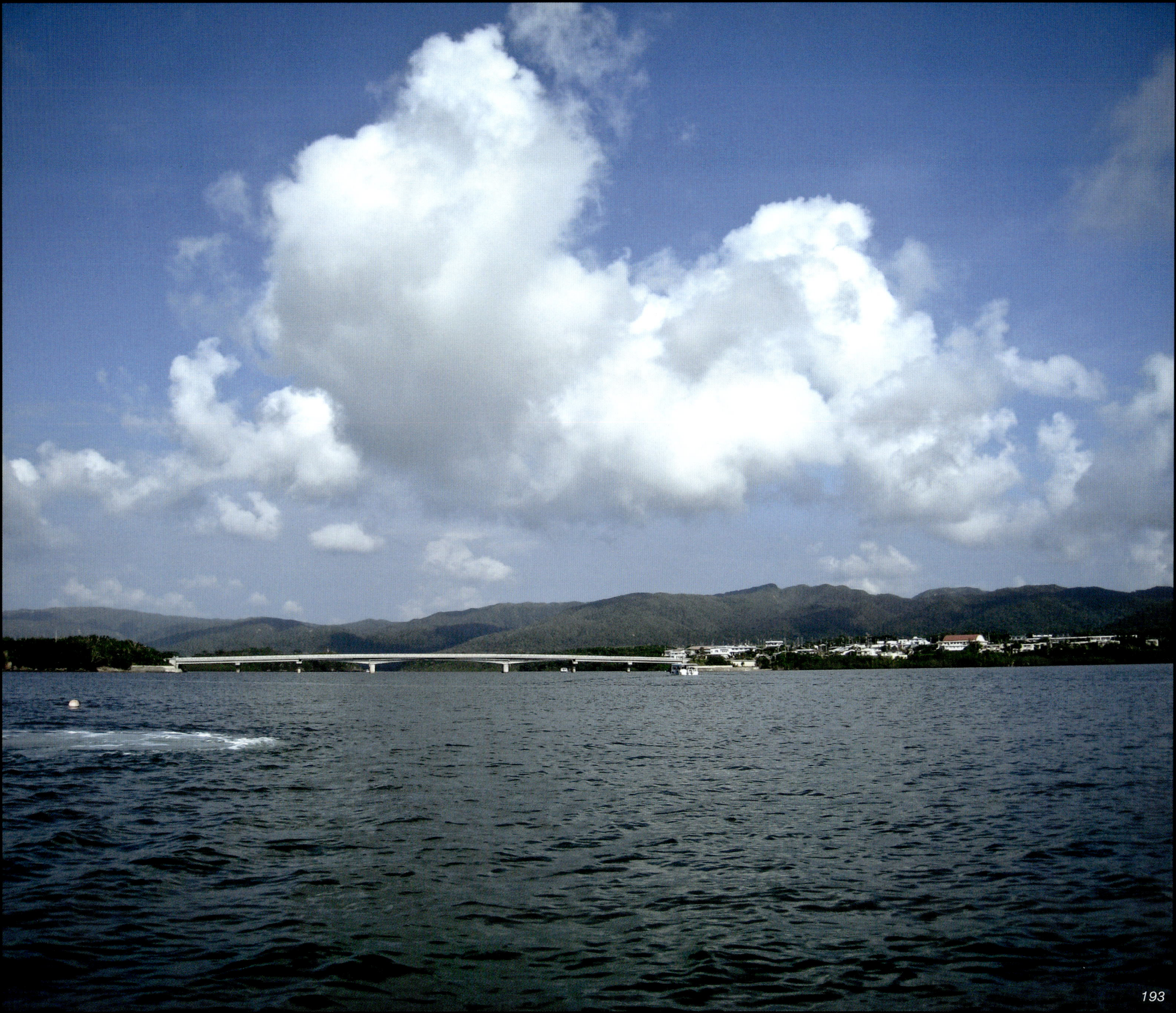

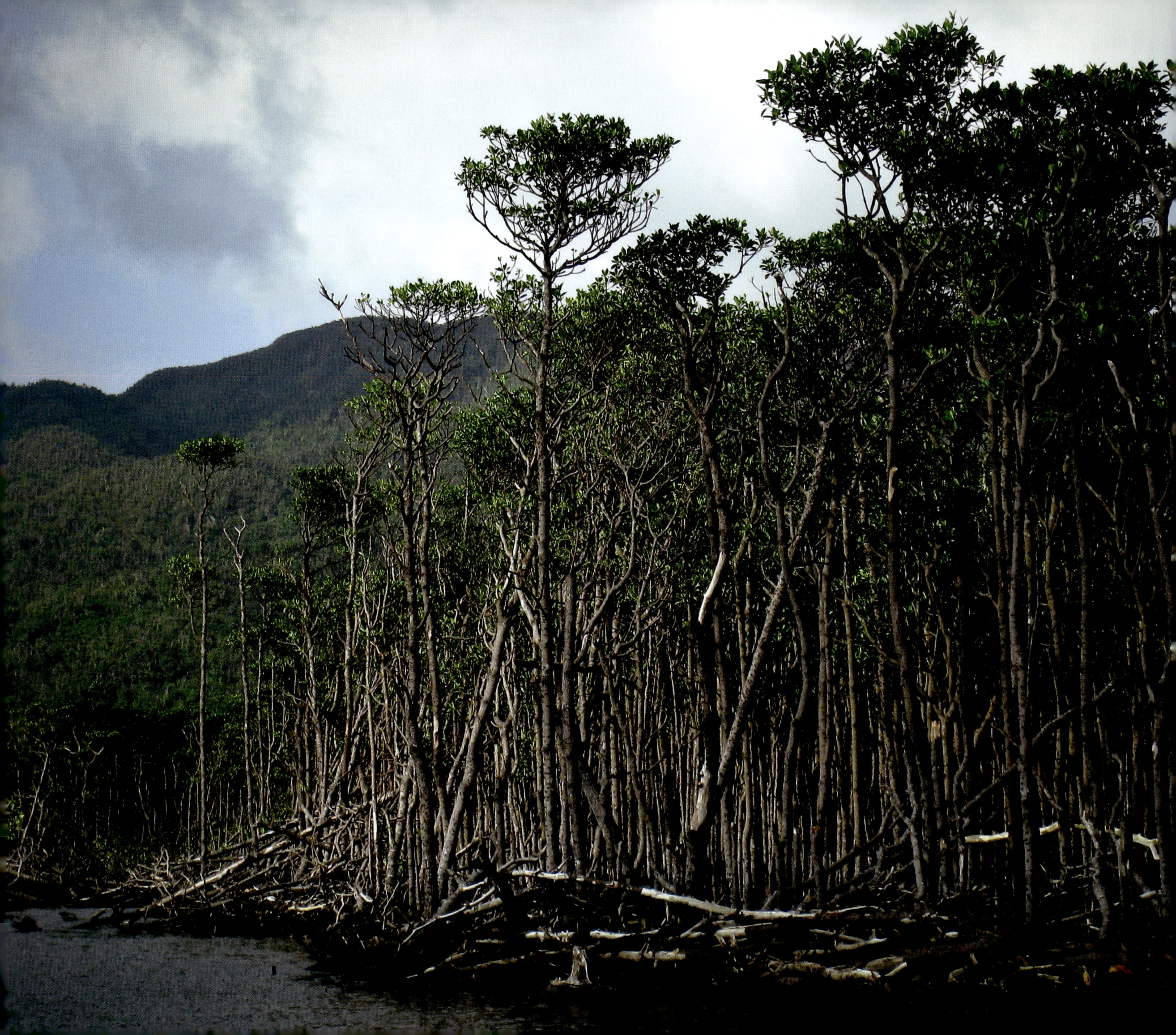

## Primeval forests

Along the brackish water of the main rivers on Iriomote Island various species of mangrove trees can be seen. The island is ideal for kayaking and admiring the plants and wildlife up close.

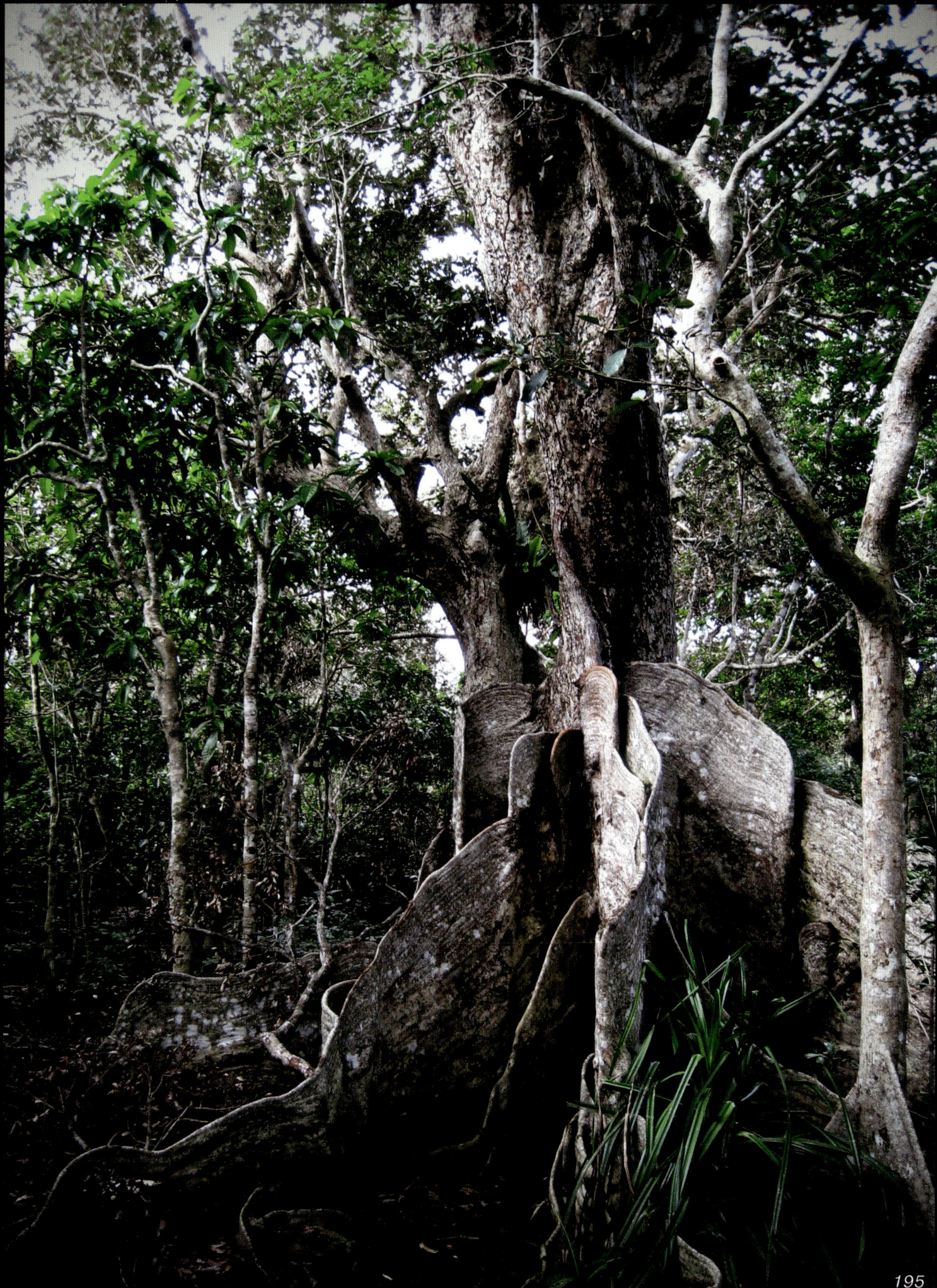

### Heritiera littorales

This Sakishima Sappanwood tree (Heritiera littorales) far upstream the Nakama River is estimated to be 400 years old. The hard timber of these trees was highly valued for making boats, while their roots served as rudders.

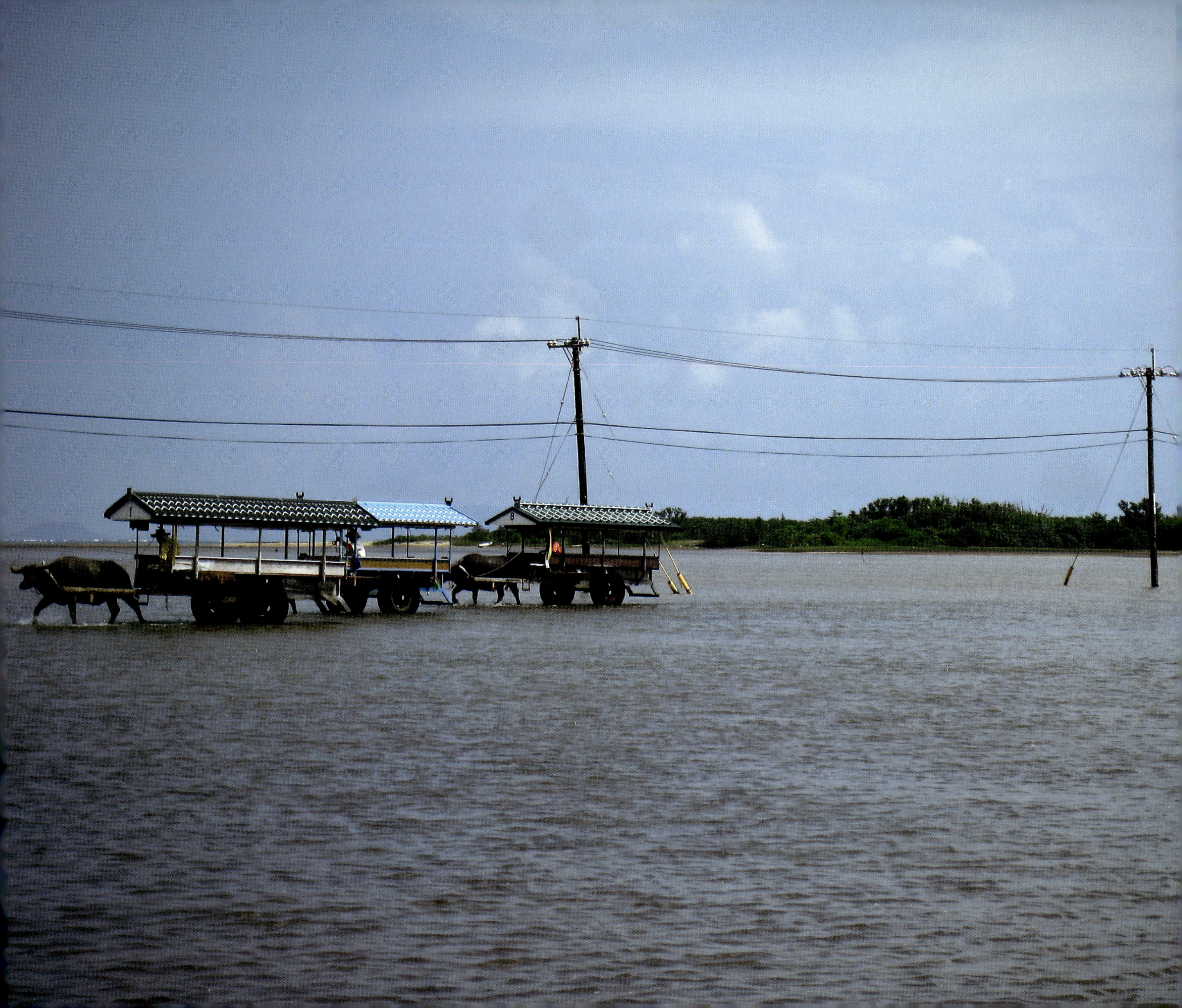

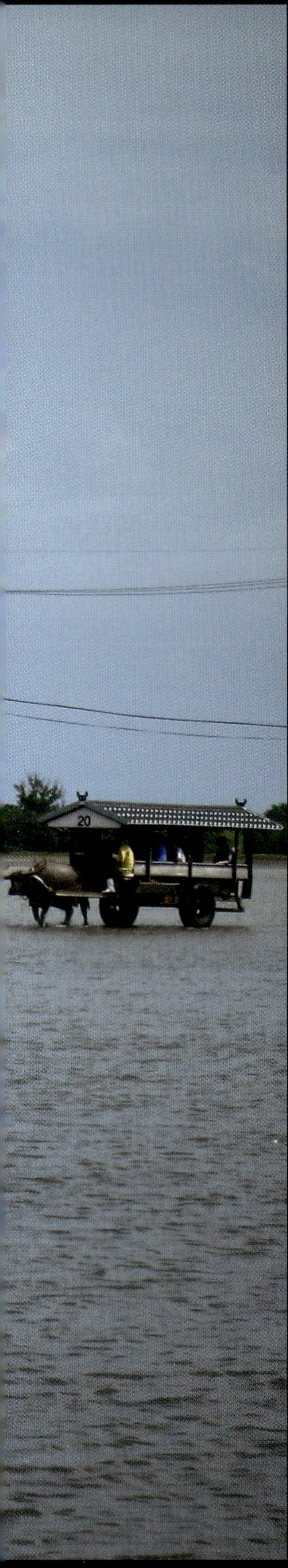

## Yubu-jima

The tiny island Yubu-jima is separated from Iriomote by a shallow strip of ocean. It is the smallest island in the Yaeyama Archipelago and can be reached by water buffalo taxi or by foot. The island showcases a nice collection of subtropical flowers such as Callistemon or bottle brush, originally from Australia.

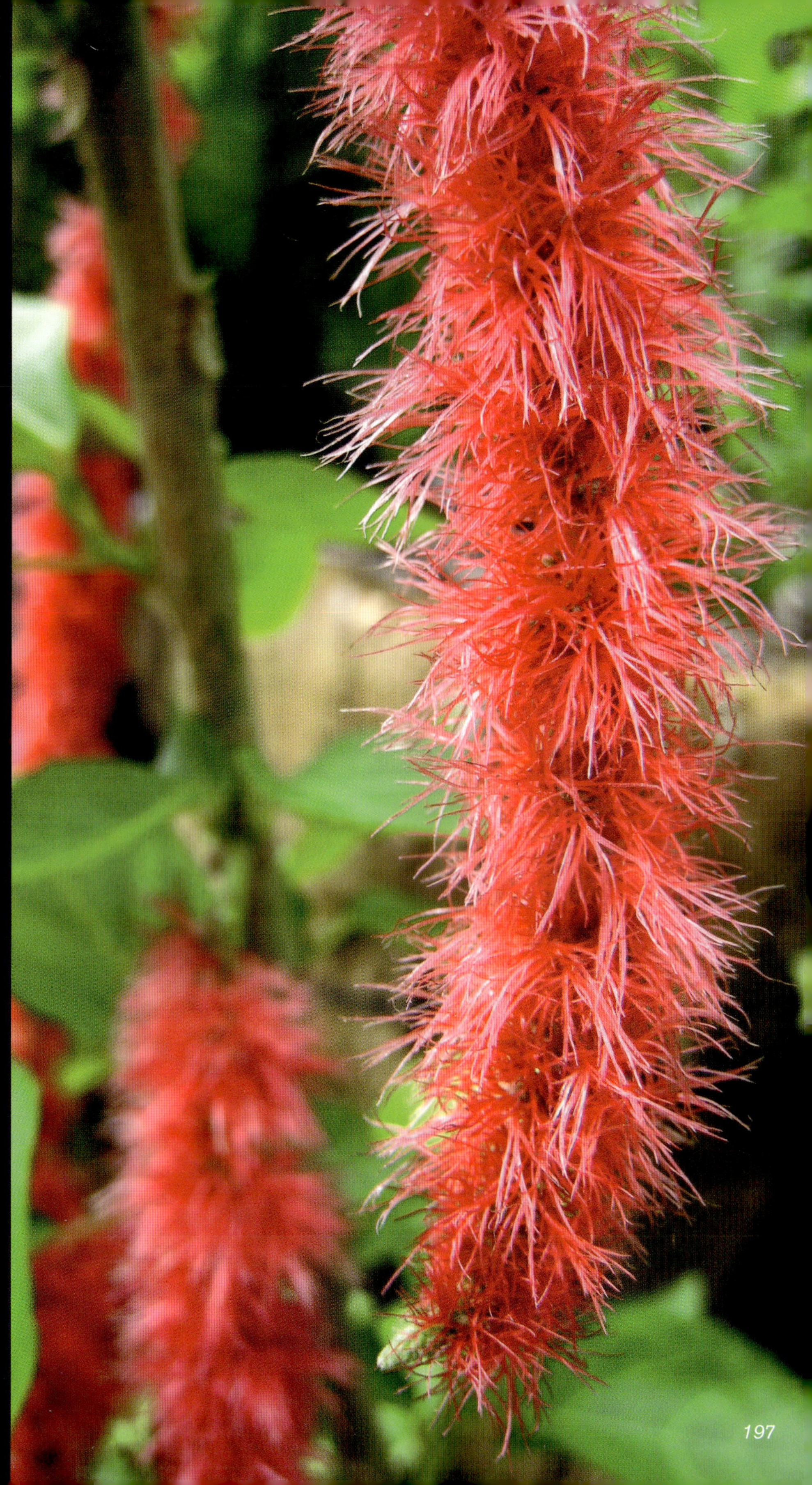

# SEASONS

Most regions in Japan have four distinct seasons. This is one of the factors that make Japan an attractive destination any time of the year. In line with the changes in weather and vegetation you can experience different activities, enjoy completely different cuisine or attend one of the many seasonal festivals.

The climates in Japan range from subarctic in the north to subtropical in the south. When in winter the southern islands in Okinawa still enjoy a modererate 20 degrees, the north of Hokkaidō may experience temperatures that drop to minus 20 degrees or even lower. Even on the same latitude there are vast differences in weather between the east and west coast.

The strong influence of Kuroshio, the warm current of the Pacific Ocean, keeps winters on the east coast mild while the Siberian cold fronts over the Sea of Japan bring snow and bitter frost over large parts of the north west coast and the Alps.

## Spring

In spring temperatures rise quickly all over Japan. The snow in the Alps melts and Mount Fuji's snow cap, visible from Tokyo in winter, fades fast. The famous cherry blossoms, known in Japan as 'sakura', are in full bloom starting from as early as mid March in Kyūshū until the end of April in Hokkaidō . It is a nice period to visit Japan as temperatures are still relatively mild and flowers are abundant. Cherry blossom festivals are held and many Japanese visit the giant snow walls along the Tateyama - Kurobe Alpine Route during this time of the year.

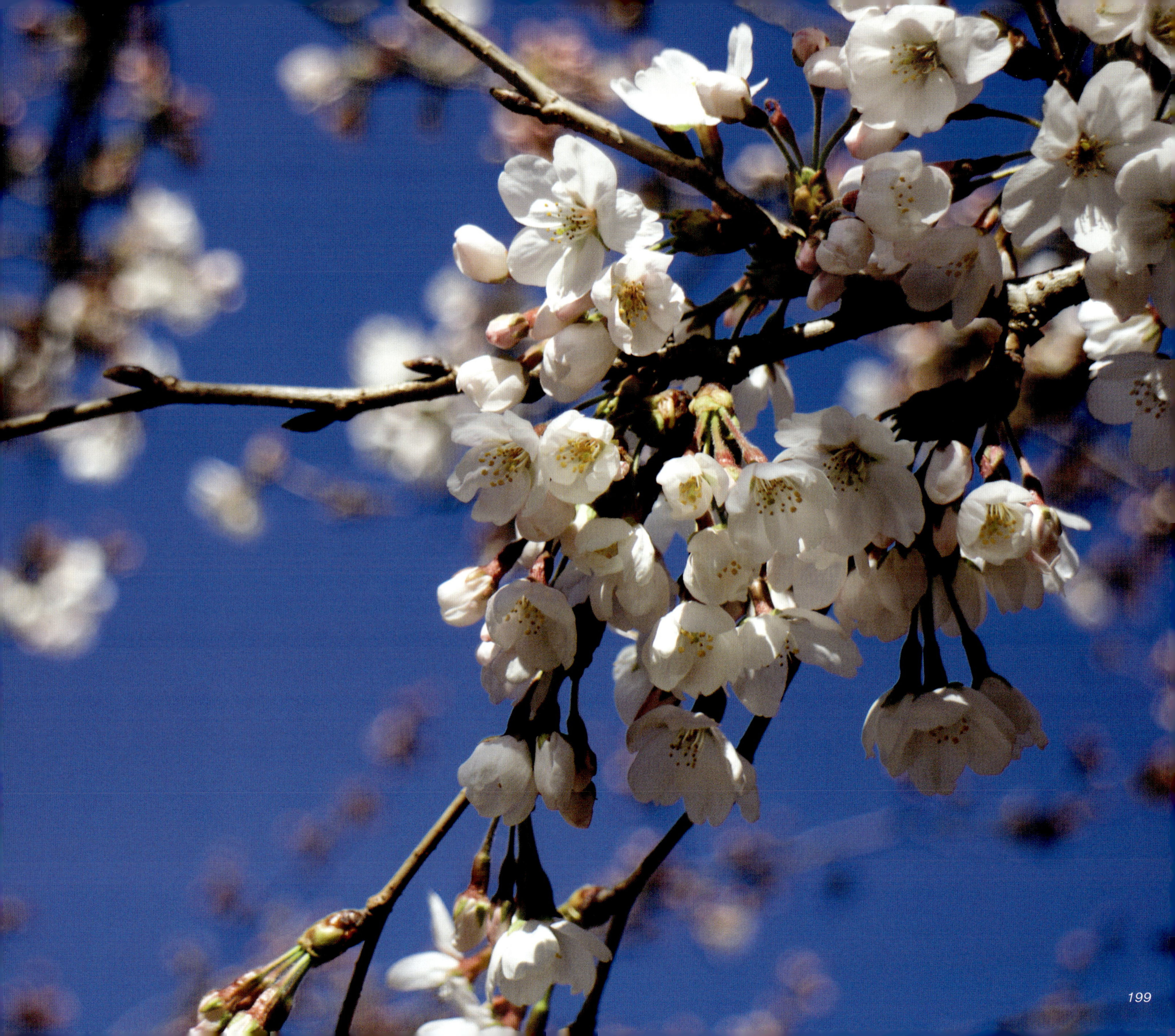

# Summer

Apart from Hokkaidō, summers are hot and very humid all over Japan. At the end of spring and beginning of summer the warm tropical air clashes with the retreating polar air. This period, from June to early July, is the rainy season called 'tsuyu'. From July onwards nice weather takes the overhand and (with the exception of Hokkaidō) average temperatures rise above 25 degrees in most areas of Japan. In the south the first tropical cyclones that kick of the typhoon season are formed.

Summer in Japan is a very lively season during which large festivals and fireworks are held all over the country.

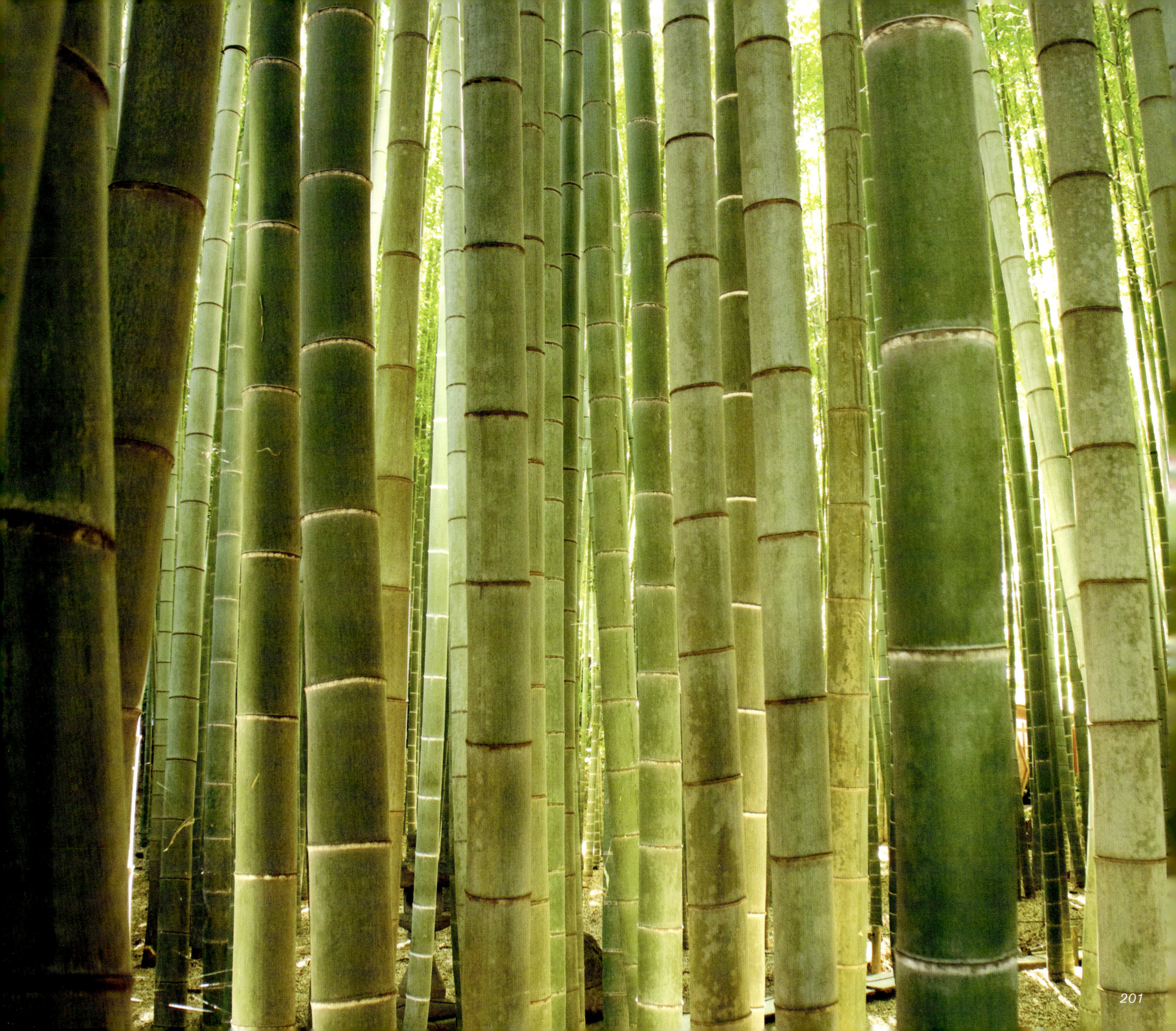

## Autumn

Especially in late autumn there are long, sunny and dry periods and temperatures are very comfortable. Colourful autumn leaves, known as 'kōyō' in Japanese draw just as many visitors, if not more, as the cherry blossoms do in spring. Starting in the north in late September and moving down south until mid November the autumn foliage with its almost flashy yellow, orange and red colors are stunning. Especially in the weekends lots of domestic tourists visit the national parks and epic places such as Nikkō and the temples and shrines of Kyoto.

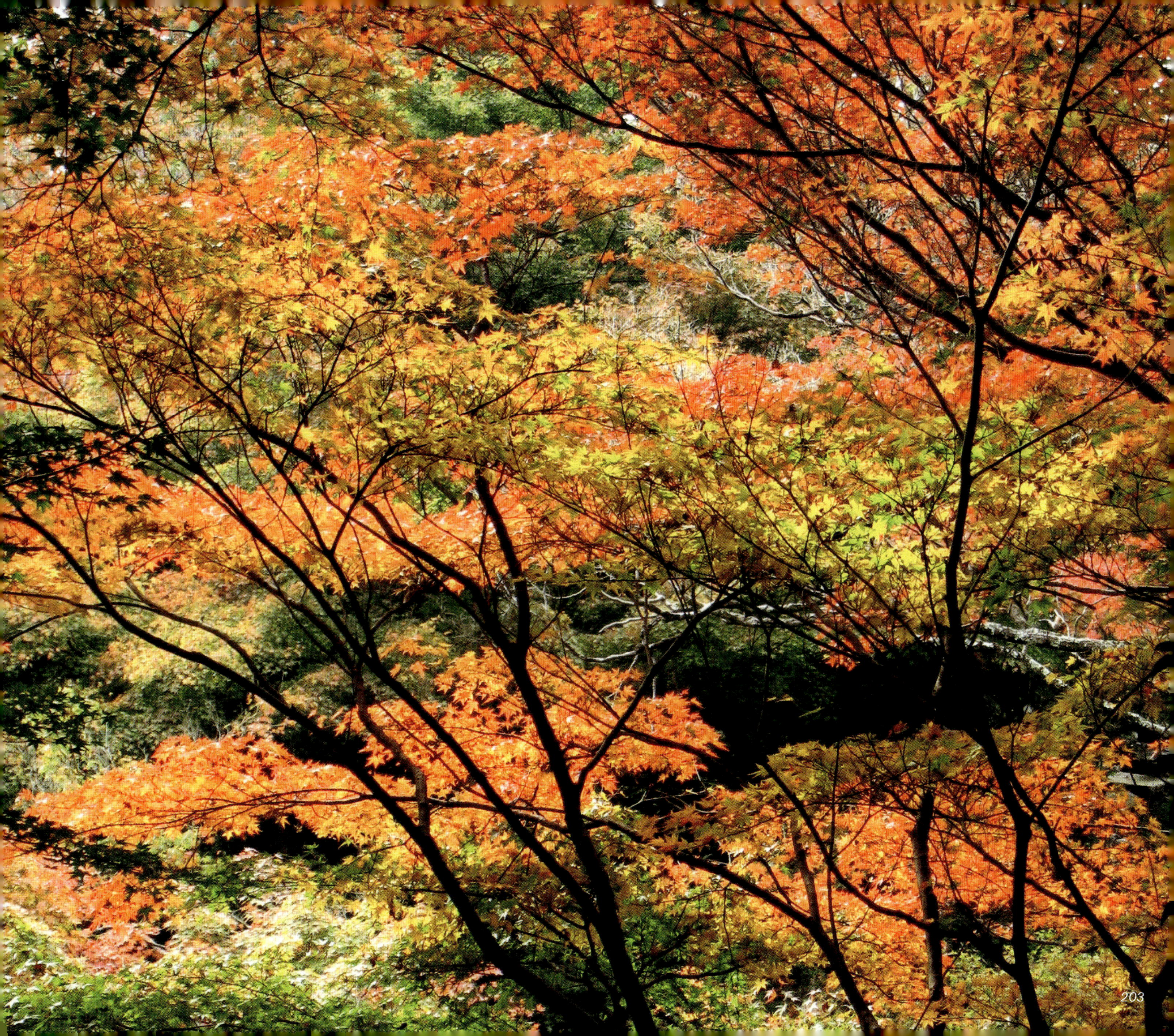

## Winter

Depending on what part of Japan you are traveling to, there will be a completely different experience of winter. Winter in Kyūshū and in the big cities on the east coast such as Tokyo and Osaka seldom brings frost and snow and there are long periods with sunny days. In contrast; in the Japanese Alps, along the northern coast of the Sea of Japan and in Hokkaidō , temperatures drop quickly with very high levels of snowfall for many months. These are perfect conditions for skiing, snowboarding and snow hiking. In the winter season various illumination events are held across the country and the Sapporo Snow Festival in Hokkaidō attracts about two million spectators.

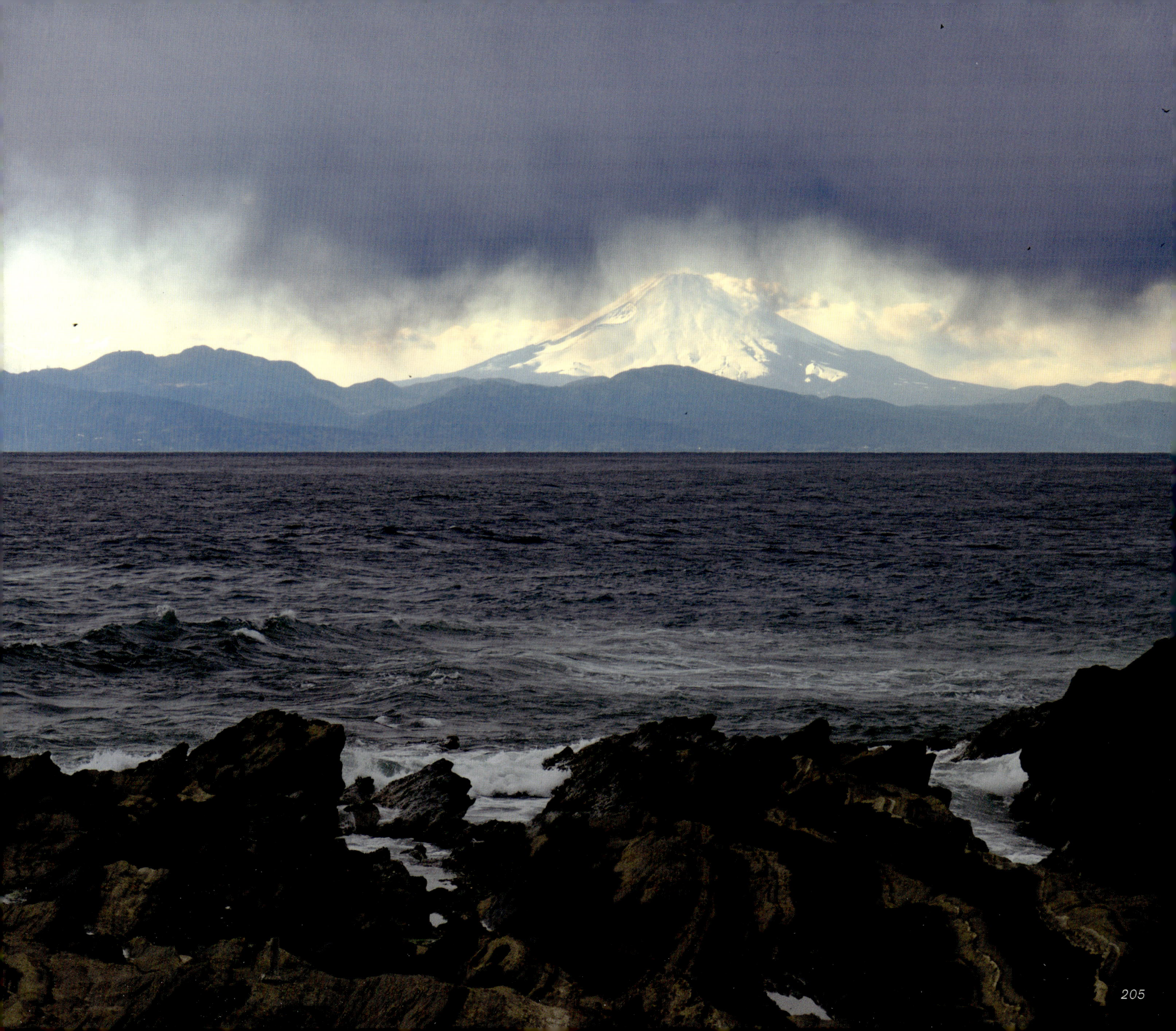

# TIMELINE

ca 14500 – ca 300 BC
**Jōmon culture**

The exact starting date of this era is under debate of scholars. It refers to the period in Japan's history when cord markings, named Jōmon in Japanese, were decorating the pottery.

ca 300 BC – ca 300 AD
**Yayoi culture**

Yayoi was the place in Tokyo where the first artefacts and pottery of this culture were found, hence the name of this era. It is believed that around this time rice cultivation started, although recent findings suggest this may have been much earlier.

ca 300 AD – ca 700
**Kofun culture**

Kofun, meaning 'old tomb' in Japanese, are earthen burial mounds initially built for people of the ruling class and later also for commoners. Early Shintō rituals were in place and various clans started to concentrate power in Yamato in the present day Nara Prefecture.

538 – 710
**The Yamato Confederacy**

Recent research suggests that early in this period a succession of Yamato Kings considerably strengthened their military rule and that there were increasing cultural and trade ties with the rest of East Asia.
Empress Suiko (554 - 628) and Prince regent Shōtoku (574 - 622) laid the foundations of an imperial state.
It was in this period that Prince Shōtoku signed a letter to the emperor of China as the ruler of 'the land of the rising sun'.
By the mid 6th century Buddhism was introduced in Japan and started to influence the Japanese culture.
This period ends with the establishment of the imperial capital at Heijō-kyō, present day Nara, in 710.

710 – 794
**Nara period**

Inspired by the T'ang dynasty of China the state administration became more and more structured and Buddhism became de facto a state religion. It is a period where the written language was developed and unprecedented cultural and artistic progress was made.

By the end of this period it was felt that the Buddhist institutions in Nara became far too dominant and

Emperor Kanmu decided to move the capital to Kyoto, then named Heian-kyō, capital of peace and tranquility, where it would remain for a millennium until 1868.

794 – 1192
**Heian period**

Gradually, art, literature and the writing system all developed a Japanese style, while the aristocracy and court flourished as described in the book Tale of Genji that dates from ca 1,000 AD.

The very powerful Fujiwara clan actually ruled in place of the Emperor until in the 12th century the rivaling military clans Minamoto and Taira succeeded in considerably strengthening their wealth and power.

In 1185, during the epic sea battle of Dan-no-ura the Minamoto brothers Yoritomo and Yoshitsune defeated the Taira clan. Soon thereafter the brothers fell in a conflict in which Yoshitsune was killed and Yoritomo seized the military power from the emperor.

1192 – 1333
**Kamakura period**

Appointed by the emperor, Minamoto no Yoritomo establishes the first shogunate in Kamakura in 1192. Before this period Buddhism was more confined to the aristocracy and intellectuals, but from now on the religion started spreading quickly and reached the commoners.

By the end of the 13th century an impoverished shogunate started to lose grip on the country and Mongol armadas made attempts to try to invade Japan. In 1281 – helped by a kamikaze or 'divine wind' – the Mongol fleet was devastated by a typhoon.

1333 – 1392
**Nanboku-chō period**

For a short, but very turbulent period following the collapse of the Kamakura shogunate and the failed Kenmu restoration, Japan was faced with a northern and southern rivaling court.

1392 - 1573
**Muromachi period**

During this period the imperial court as well as the shoguns lost their central authority in favor of feudal lords or daimyō. It was a period where clans fought for power and lower classes revolted because of the economic deterioration of the country.

By the end of the Muromachi period the first Europeans arrived and with them western innovations and Christianity were imported in Japan.

1573 - 1603
**Azuchi – Momoyama period**

In this critical period in Japan's history three lords: Nobunaga, Hideyoshi and Tokugawa managed to unify large parts of Japan under their control. Finally, the decisive Battle of Sekigahara in 1600 made an end to decades of turmoil and was at the basis of the unification of Japan. In this last major battle in feudal Japan Tokugawa Ieyasu emerged victorious and seized power. It is widely seen as the start of the Tokugawa shogunate that would rule the country for more than 250 years.

1603 - 1868
**Edo period**

The Tokugawa shogunate managed to keep the landlords under control and by doing so created the basis for a long period of stability and steady domestic development of the country. To avoid that foreign influences would threaten the shogunate, Japan became a closed country with very limited foreign trade and contacts in the mid 17th century. However, by 1850 the military and political power of the shogunate became weak and there was increasing pressure from other nations as well as from within Japan to open the country for trade.

In 1853 the US sent commodore Perry with his fleet of 'black ships' to Japan. Under this huge pressure the Tokugawa shogunate was left with no other option than to open the ports for trade. Western minded clans supported the emperor and in October 1867 shogun Tokugawa Yoshinobu formally applied to have the imperial power restored.

1868 – 1912
**Meiji period**

Emperor Meiji was only 16 when the restoration of the imperial rule was declared on January 3rd 1868. The old feudal structures were dismantled, causing some revolt and rebellion, the military power was restored and many western products, innovations and cultural aspects were introduced. It was a period of quick modernization that would help Japan enter the modernity of the early 20th century.

1912 – 1926
**Taishō**

1926 – 1989
**Shōwa**

1989 – now
**Heisei**

### Text and photography
Marc Popelier

### Japanese calligraphy
Ikeda Mikiyo

### The author wishes to thank
An Theunynck for her counsel and Jaak Van Damme for having shared his passion about Japan. Without their enthusiasm this project would not have started. Ikeda Mikiyo who wrote the beautiful Japanese calligraphy for each chapter. Frans Hoorelbeke for his wise words in the preface. The publishing team at Stichting Kunstboek, Nakamura Mio, Kaspar Chabot, Jeroen van der Donck, Yamamoto Hiroyuki and especially Nishida Saori for their valuable comments on the manuscript. Chie, Kentoman and Ai for being my guide on some of the daytrips near Tokyo. Chef Hashimoto from Sushi Hashimoto in Yokohama for his courtesy.
Takano Masashi and Vincent Schepens from All Nippon Airways, Eric Van Hoof from E&Y's Japan Business Services network, Frans Hoorelbeke from Daikin, Paul Ryckaseys from Imagine Travel, Jan Lambrechts from Ichiban Consult, Geert Joosten from Gevaco Advocaten and Sara Davidson from the Hasselt Japanese Garden for their kind business support.
Nakamura Naoko, my anchor in Japan ever since we met in 2002 and the best friend I could hope for. The very first copy of this book is for her.

### Notes:
Photos on pages 82 – 85 © Shutterstock

Macrons are used where the vowel should be prolonged in pronunciation. The macron is omitted from names, places such as Tokyo and historical words as shogun that are used in modern English without macron.

### Final editing
Katrien Van Moerbeke

### Art direction
Jaak Van Damme

### Layout
www.groupvandamme.eu

### Published by
Stichting Kunstboek bvba
Legeweg 165
B-8020 Oostkamp (BE)
+32 50 46 19 10
info@stichtingkunstboek.com
www.stichtingkunstboek.com

Printed in the EU
2nd print run, May 2017

ISBN 978-90-5856-561-7
D/2016/6407/20
NUR: 517/612





This book was published with the support of